THE NEW NATURAL

A SURVEY OF BRITISH N⟨

GARDEN BIRDS

THE NEW NATURALIST LIBRARY

GARDEN BIRDS

MIKE TOMS

THIS BOOK IS DEDICATED
TO CHRIS MEAD AND DAVID GLUE,
WHOSE KNOWLEDGE OF GARDEN BIRDS
AND PASSION FOR THEIR STUDY, IS MUCH MISSED.

This edition published in 2019 by William Collins,
An imprint of HarperCollins Publishers

HarperCollins Publishers
1 London Bridge Street
London SE1 9GF

WilliamCollinsBooks.com

First published 2019

© Mike Toms, 2019

Photographs © Individual copyright holders

A CIP catalogue record for this book is available
from the British Library.

Set in FF Nexus, designed and produced by
Tom Cabot/ketchup

Printed in China by RR Donnelley APS

Hardback
ISBN 978-0-00-816474-4

Paperback
ISBN 978-0-00-816475-1

Contents

Editors' Preface

G IVEN THE EXPLOSION OF INTEREST in garden birds, their habits and feeding since the 1960s, this is an addition to the New Naturalist Library that was crying out to be written. Many, perhaps most of us, are familiar with a range of garden birds on a day-to-day basis. That range may be large or small, but familiarity engenders an interest in how the birds are faring and an enthusiasm for taking part in censuses and surveys: ideal seeding ground for what are now called citizen science projects. Against this background, the Editorial Board was fortunate to be able to call on an author tailor-made for the task in Mike Toms. Mike will be familiar to NN readers as the author of the very popular and very readable text on owls (NN 125, 2014). He has spent most of his working life with the British Trust for Ornithology. Over and above his personal fascination with owls, he has been involved in the organisation and analyses of the various BTO Garden Bird studies and, thus, is the ideal author for this authoritative text.

The text opens with an analysis of the role of gardens in the ecology and general prosperity of our commoner land bird populations and an assessment of the diversity that we have created. Interestingly, though we think of gardens as ubiquitous, the land area that they occupy, at just over 400,000 ha, is only slightly larger than the county of Suffolk, and less than 10 per cent of British land area with some form of statutory protection. That said, the potential for interest and fascination that they offer, far outweighs those statistics. In the second chapter, Mike Toms explores the phenomenal growth of garden bird feeding since the end of the Second World War and the equally amazing diversity of foodstuffs now available, particularly seeds. Long gone are the days of throwing out a handful of scraps from the table to satisfy our feathered friends!

Subsequent chapters cover the provision of nesting opportunities, nest boxes and other aspects of the breeding season (Chapter 3), and the aptly-named 'Opportunities and Risks' (Chapter 4) outlines the disease health hazards (sometimes devastating) that birds face at feeding stations. Enthusiastic gatherings squabbling at feeders become vulnerable to lurking sharp-eyed predators like Sparrowhawks *Accipiter nisus*. Chapter 5, 'Behaviour', emphasises the opportunities (and privileges) on offer in gardens, to watch birds interacting at close quarters, and demonstrates how simply watching can develop into (equally enjoyable) studying, far more easily than in the general open countryside. Equally absorbing and fascinating are the varied aspects of garden bird watching in Chapter 6, 'Birds, Gardens and People', which, among other things, emphasises the many benefits, including to physical and mental health, that people can derive from the interactions.

The last chapter is an extremely useful compendium of succinct accounts of the most regularly observed garden birds, with, in each case, tabulated biological data (clutch size, incubation period, breeding attempts per annum, etc.) followed by an account of the particular relevance of the species to our gardens. It lists, without fear or favour, 'the good, the bad and the ugly' of garden birds and items of fascination too numerous to note, other than to offer examples. Few outside the southeast of England would have considered the Ring-necked Parakeet *Psittacula krameri* as a garden bird, but these raucous and colourful aliens (although now with a self-sustaining feral population) can be a domineering force disrupting the feeding and nesting of other species. The Magpie *Pica pica*, not a popular garden bird, has its evil reputation as a predator of nests and nestlings accurately assessed, and moderated. Perhaps strangest of all, the Red Kite *Milvus milvus* – which most of us would consider an unlikely garden bird – is now numerous enough near its centres of reintroduction to visit garden feeding stations routinely, and some populations are showing signs of dietary imbalance, the natural food of carcasses, road kills etc. being substantially better for them than the household waste scraps usually on offer in gardens.

Much else of equal fascination awaits – now please do read on and enjoy *Garden Birds* to the full.

Author's Foreword and Acknowledgements

PRIVATE GARDENS PROVIDE OPPORTUNITIES FOR engagement with the natural world, delivering connection with a broad range of different plants and animals. Birds are one of the most obvious and accessible components of the community of species using our gardens, visiting bird tables and hanging feeders, and occupying the nest boxes that we erect for them. Familiar species, like Robin, House Sparrow and Blackbird, provide a common currency, the basis to conversations had between neighbours, relatives and friends. That we choose to engage with garden birds, and talk about their visits and behaviour, underlines the central place that they play in our lives. For those who never venture into the wider countryside, garden birds can provide a window onto the natural world, helping to restore lost connections and contributing to health and well-being. But what about the birds themselves; what role do gardens play in their ecology and behaviour? What do we really know about the risks and benefits that shape how and why birds use gardens and the resources present within them?

Over the past two decades, I have been fortunate enough to have worked on garden birds, and with those who chose to watch them in their gardens. Through 'citizen science' projects, most notably the weekly BTO Garden BirdWatch scheme, I have been able to study the different ways in which wild birds use our gardens. I have been able to examine garden use in relation to the wider landscape, exploring both the seasonality of garden use and the longer-term patterns that have followed changes in how we manage the countryside. Thanks to the efforts and support of the volunteers participating in citizen science schemes, I have been able to explore some of the questions surrounding garden use and the role that gardens and their resources play in the lives of visiting birds, addressing the benefits of food provision, the risks of disease transmission and the threats posed by predatory species.

Such research underlines that the ecological processes operating within the garden environment are similar to those operating elsewhere, providing us with opportunities to learn about the wider world and to recognise the role that gardens play within the broader suite of habitats that make up our countryside. Gardens and the wider built environment pose some particular challenges for wild birds; they also offer unique opportunities. The process of urbanisation means that more land will be occupied by urban landscapes and we need to understand the implications of this if we are to deliver built environments that can also work for birds and other wildlife, rather than just for ourselves. Much of the work outlined in this book, carried out by researchers around the globe, delivers the scientific evidence and understanding that we will need as we seek to inform decision-makers and support conservation practitioners. I am fortunate enough to have played a small part in this work, and I hope that reading about it excites you as much as it excites those of us carrying out the research and citizen science.

This book would not have been possible without the help, support and generosity of many people. In particular I would like to thank those with whom I have been fortunate enough to have worked on garden birds: Margaret Askew, Andrew Cannon, Dan Chamberlain, David Glue, Tim Harrison, Donna Hobbs, Becky Lawson, Dave Leech, Amy Lewis, Chris Mead, Kate Plummer, Jacky and Alic Prior, Kate Risely, Clare Simm, Gavin Siriwardena and Paul Stancliffe. I am most grateful to Myles Archibald, Hazel Eriksson, Julia Koppitz and the staff at William Collins; to Jim Flegg and the New Naturalist Editorial Board, and to Tom Cabot for his work on design and layout. Once again, I have been extremely fortunate to have my words graced by cover artwork produced by Robert Gillmor. The photographs that grace this book and bring the text to life were very generously and kindly provided by Mark Grantham, John Harding, Jill Pakenham, Hazel Rothwell, Tom Streeter and Moss Taylor, to all of whom I am very grateful. Thanks are also due to the staff of the BTO, its volunteers and those who have supported the work on garden birds through projects like Garden BirdWatch. The BTO, its staff and volunteers are truly inspirational and I am very grateful to have found such a wonderful place of employment. Finally, I would like to thank Annabel Hill for her love and support, and for helping to make this book possible.

Mike Toms
November 2018

CHAPTER 1

Gardens and Birds

PRIVATE GARDENS ARE A FEATURE of most of the dwellings found within the UK. A study by Davies *et al.* (2009), using data from a number of different datasets, put the proportion of households with an associated garden at 87 per cent. The researchers then used this information, alongside figures for mean garden size and the number of households, to calculate the total area of gardens within the UK. The resulting figure, some 432,964 ha, represents an area larger than the county of Suffolk but still an order of magnitude less than the 4.7 million ha of UK land that is under statutory protection.

While such figures underline that gardens only make up a relatively small part of the UK land area, they are *the* habitat within which many of us engage with birds and other forms of wildlife. This gives them special importance, not

FIG 1. Private gardens vary considerably in their size, composition and use, presenting a series of different opportunities for birds. (Mike Toms)

least because gardens provide the best opportunities to empower UK citizens with the conservation and research understanding needed to support sustainable planning, lifestyle and land management decisions. Birds are of particular importance in this context because they are one of the most visible, accessible and appreciated components of the wider natural world. If we can understand how they use gardens, and how this use is perceived by the people who have access to those gardens, then we can begin to provide the evidence and messaging needed to support public engagement with the natural world more widely.

We also need to recognise that gardens come in many different forms; at the simplest level they have tended to be split into those that are urban, suburban or rural in nature, but there is substantial variation within these broad categories. Many gardens fall within urbanised landscapes, so we also need to understand the relationships that exist between gardens and their surroundings. We know, for example, that city-centre gardens are just one form of urban green space and that birds, being mobile, will move between a city's many different patches of such space. But how important is the spatial arrangement of these different patches or the temporal pattern of feeding resources available within

FIG 2. The Robin is perhaps the most familiar of our 'garden birds' but in reality it is a species of woodland edge habitats. (John Harding)

them? Many of the same questions can be asked of those birds using rural gardens, perhaps bordered by arable farmland or woodland plantations. This underlines that gardens should not be viewed in isolation but rather as a part of a wider landscape over which birds may range. In some cases these ranging movements may take birds not just beyond the boundaries of the gardens and often urbanised landscapes within which they sit, but also beyond the borders of countries or even continents.

It is for this reason that this book on garden birds starts by looking at the nature of the garden habitat and the garden's place within a wider landscape context. Inevitably, this will require us to look at urban ecology and the processes that shape the urban environment, and to look into a future where the ongoing process of urbanisation sees an ever-growing number of us living within towns and cities. We will also use this chapter as an opportunity to ask 'what is a garden bird?' and to examine the nature of garden bird communities. Are they, for example, just those species that happen to be generally common and widespread across the wider landscape, or is there something special about garden bird species and the communities that they form.

THE URBAN ENVIRONMENT

One of the most shocking statistics relating to the human population is that showing the proportion of the global population now living within urbanised landscapes (see Figure 3); this figure, which passed 50 per cent in 2008, is projected to reach 66 per cent by 2050 (United Nations, 2014). This increase brings with it an associated increase in the amount of land under urban cover. Urbanisation is an ongoing process and considered to be one of the greatest threats facing species and their ecosystems. It is of particular concern because some of the most intensive urban development is projected to occur within key global biodiversity hotspots (Elmqvist et al., 2013). The growth in the numbers of households globally, and within biodiversity hotspot regions in particular, has been more rapid than aggregated human population growth, reflecting that average household size continues to fall. This is relevant because the reduction in average household size is thought to have added 233 million additional households to biodiversity hotspot countries alone between 2000 and 2015 (Liu et al., 2003). It seems all the more important than ever to understand the implications of urbanisation for biodiversity; to some extent this urgency has been recognised by the research community, with increasing numbers of studies helping to unravel how birds and other forms of wildlife make use of the

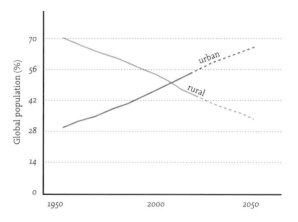

FIG 3. The proportion of the human population living within urbanised landscapes passed 50% in 2008 and is predicted to reach 66% by 2050. Redrawn from United Nations data.

urban environment and revealing what urban expansion means for their wider populations. Urbanisation also has implications for the ways in which the human population interacts with the wider natural world, of which it is a part, so we also need to learn about these relationships and what they mean for both birds and people; this is something that we will explore in Chapter 6.

The process of urbanisation involves the conversion of natural or semi-natural landscapes – the latter including farmed land – into ones that are characterised by high densities of artificial structures and impervious surfaces. Urbanised landscapes contain fragmented and highly disturbed habitats, are occupied by high densities of people and show an elevated availability of certain resources. Associated with the process of urbanisation is the modification of ecological processes, particularly those linked with nutrient cycling and water flow. The density of bird species within such landscapes is best explained by anthropogenic features and is often negatively associated with the amount of urban cover. This underlines the importance of urban green space, especially gardens and (for some species) urban parks and woodland. Although many bird species decline in abundance once an area has become urbanised, some are able to take advantage of the new opportunities that have been created. Because different species respond to urbanisation in different ways, we typically see a dramatic shift in the structure of avian communities living within urban landscapes and the habitats, like gardens and urban parks, found within them.

Alongside the structural changes seen, which may alter nesting opportunities or the availability of food resources, urbanisation also results in increased levels of disturbance, noise, night-time light and pollution, all of which may impact birds and other wildlife. While some of these impacts may be generally negative across species, there may be instances where such effects are not felt equally. Noise pollution can impact on some species more than others, for example, perhaps because of the frequencies at which such noise tends to occur; bird species whose songs are pitched towards lower frequencies may be affected more than those whose high-pitched songs can still be heard above the background noise. Other species may show a behavioural response, perhaps moving the time at which they sing or even altering the characteristics of the song itself. It has been found, for example, that Robin *Erithacus rubecula* populations breeding in noisy parts of urban Sheffield sing at night, with the levels of daytime noise experienced by these individuals a better predictor of their nocturnal singing behaviour than levels of night-time light pollution, the latter previously considered to have been the driver for nocturnal song in this species (Fuller *et al.*, 2007a).

Not all of the changes that occur during urbanisation are necessarily negative; the provision of food at garden feeding stations (Chapter 2) is regarded as being generally beneficial, buffering the temporal variation in food availability that is typical of natural landscapes and thought to limit populations. The availability of anthropogenic food, either at garden feeding stations or present as food scraps, is thought to be one of the main factors driving the structure of urban bird communities, something to which we will return shortly. A number of studies have found that urbanisation stabilises both the richness and composition of bird communities, perhaps because there is greater predictability of, and less variation within, the climate and resource availability of more urbanised landscapes (Suhonen *et al.*, 2009; Leveau & Leveau, 2012).

As we'll also discover later in this chapter, some species are better able to cope with or respond to the impacts and opportunities of the built environment than others, and there are particular traits within bird families or species groups which may lead to them being more likely to adapt to the urban environment (Blair, 1996). This raises the question of just what is a garden bird.

WHAT IS A GARDEN BIRD?

Some people take the term 'garden bird' to mean a species that is common and widespread, adaptable and found just as commonly in other habitats. While this is certainly true of many garden birds, it is not true of every species found to use gardens on a regular basis. The phrase 'common or garden' – meaning something that is common and consequently of little value – may have also added to the sense that garden birds have little conservation value and are thus of little interest. This may be exacerbated by the sense that gardens themselves are an artificial habitat, highly modified and managed and thus greatly removed from more natural habitats and processes. However, it needs to be remembered that many of the habitats that we consider to form the countryside – such as farmland and woodland – are also often highly managed and very different to wholly natural landscapes untouched by human activities. Once we recognise this, then it becomes possible to accept garden birds less as a distinct type of bird and more as simply a subset of a wider population using a broad range of habitats.

Look at any book on UK garden birds and you will see species that are summer migrants (Swift *Apus apus*, House Martin *Delichon urbicum*, Spotted Flycatcher *Muscicapa striata*), winter visitors (Redwing *Turdus iliacus*, Waxwing *Bomybycilla garrulus*, Brambling *Fringilla montifringilla*, Fieldfare *Turdus pilaris*), insectivores (Goldcrest *Regulus regulus*, Wren *Troglodytes troglodytes*), omnivores (Carrion Crow *Corvus corone*), cavity nesters (Blue Tit *Cyanistes caeruleus*, Great Tit *Parus major*) or have low dispersive ability (House Sparrow *Passer domesticus*), all underlining the variety of ecological traits encountered within our garden bird community. Certain ecological traits may come to the fore if you look at particular components of the wider community; for example, an examination of the birds using garden feeding stations may suggest the dominance of granivorous and omnivorous species rather than insectivores, a reflection of the types of food being provided (Shochat *et al.*, 2010). A different pattern may be seen in winter from summer, when looking at some aspect of the breeding community, or indeed when looking at the same component (e.g. cavity-nesting) but in different geographical locations. We know, for example, that cavity-nesting species are well represented within the UK garden bird community, having adapted to nest boxes, but are far less common in that of Australia, where native cavity nesters rely on natural tree cavities rather than boxes (Shanahan *et al.*, 2014).

Globally, certain species are well represented within garden bird communities, including Rock Dove/Feral Pigeon *Columba livia*, House Sparrow and Starling *Sturnus vulgaris* (Aronson *et al.*, 2014). Also widely represented – at least within the wider urban environment – are introduced or 'invasive' species such as Mallard *Anas platyrhynchos*, Canada Goose *Branta canadensis*, Collared Dove *Streptopelia decaocto* and Ring-necked Parakeet *Psittacula krameri*, plus (in those places beyond their native range) House Sparrow, Starling and Rock Dove/Feral Pigeon. As a group, corvids appear to be well represented, as do pigeons and doves, leading some authors to suggest that urban bird communities globally are becoming more homogenous in their composition (either directly, in terms of particular species, or indirectly, through different species occupying similar ecological niches). This process is something that we will discuss in the next section.

FIG 4. Blackbird is best considered as an 'urban adopter', a species that is opportunistic in the way that it uses gardens and the resources that they offer. (John Harding)

The species of birds associated with the urban environment – of which gardens are a key component – can be divided into three main types. These are the 'urban exploiters', the 'urban adopters' and the 'urban relicts'. Exploiters are those species, like Feral Pigeon, that are typically abundant within urban areas and which depend upon the anthropogenic resources available within the built environment. Adopters also make use of the resources but are more opportunistic in how they do this, and many of our familiar garden birds can be regarded as being of this kind – think of the Blackbirds *Turdus merula* and Siskins *Spinus spinus* that move into gardens during the winter months. Urban relict species are those whose population has managed to hang on within a fragment of their former habitat that is now contained within a wider urbanised landscape; such species tend to be found outside of western Europe, where new cities have emerged quickly within formerly wildlife-rich habitats. Another term that may be encountered when discussing urban bird populations is 'urban avoiders', those species that are absent or very poorly represented within the urban bird community.

The Rock Dove/Feral Pigeon is one of the oldest and most cosmopolitan commensal species, whose huge global population reflects early domestication and the subsequent transportation and introduction to sites across the world. The very high Feral Pigeon densities encountered in many cities is, to a large degree, a consequence of supplementary feeding and discarded human food, and the presence of buildings and other structures with an abundance of suitable nest sites. In some cities, such as Singapore, these populations are derived from the rapid expansion of a genetically homogenous group of founder individuals (Tang *et al.*, 2018), underlining how a species can very rapidly colonise an urban area given favourable conditions. Similar patterns may be seen in introduced populations of House Sparrow, Starling and Collared Dove.

The notion that species found in a high proportion of the world's cities, such as Starling, are successful generalists and able to breed anywhere, does require some refinement. Work by Gwénaëlle Mennechez and Philippe Clergeau has, for example, revealed that while the abundance of breeding Starlings does appear to be similar throughout the urbanisation gradient, the degree of urbanisation still has a measurable negative impact on its breeding success. Working in western France, Mennechez and Clergeau (2006) found that the amount of food delivered to Starling nestlings in more urbanised areas was significantly lower than that delivered elsewhere along the urbanisation gradient, resulting in smaller nestling masses. These urban Starlings were found to produce fewer young, each of seemingly lower quality; while they were able to maintain breeding populations in these highly urban habitats, the species was not as successful as a simple measure of breeding abundance might suggest. This is something to which we will return in Chapter 3.

URBAN BIRD COMMUNITIES

Surprisingly perhaps, one in five of the world's 10,000 or so bird species is found in the highly urbanised landscapes of major cities, including 36 species that have been identified by the IUCN global Red List as threatened with extinction. (Aronson *et al.*, 2014). Globally, the species richness of urban bird communities ranges from 24 species to 368, with a global median of 112.5 species (Aronson *et al.*, 2014). As just noted, a number of studies, typically involving work carried out within a single city, have suggested that the process of urbanisation results in urban bird communities that are becoming increasingly similar over time, and dominated by a few key species. This process is known as homogenisation and is thought to come about because urbanisation not only extirpates native species from an area but also promotes the establishment of non-native species capable of adapting to the new conditions (Luck & Smallbone, 2010). Although these new conditions tend to be similar in cities across the world, they do not in themselves promote the same species winners; instead, it is our preference for certain species (transporting them to new settlements) that has resulted in the homogenisation seen at a global scale (McKinney, 2006).

In their review of the bird communities of 54 cities, spread over 36 countries and 6 continents, Aronson *et al.* (2014) found that cities tended to retain similar compositional patterns within their distinct biogeographic regions. While certain non-native species were shared across many of the cities studied, the urban communities had not yet become taxonomically homogenised at a global scale – they retained the characteristics of their local region pool. Four species were found in more than 80 per cent of the cities examined; these being the familiar Feral Pigeon, House Sparrow, Starling and Barn Swallow *Hirundo rustica*. With the exception of Australasia, the proportion of non-native species found within each urban community was similar (at 3 per cent), Australasia being somewhat higher because of the large number of non-native species introduced into New Zealand by settlers. Work within Europe (Jokimäki & Kaisanlahti-Jokimäki, 2003; Clergeau *et al.*, 2006) suggests that urbanisation here might bring about homogenisation by decreasing the abundance of ground-nesting species and those preferring bush-shrub habitats, but also noting that it is difficult to generalise because of the effects of latitude and diversity in the urban habitats studied.

What is interesting about species seemingly well adapted to the urban environment is that they tend to share a number of traits (Leveau, 2013). They tend to be omnivorous in their diet, largely sedentary in habits and able to utilise a range of artificial nesting sites (Máthé & Batáry, 2015). Table 1 highlights the broad ecological traits of the garden bird species considered in this book. As we have seen, omnivores and granivores (seed-eating species) tend to dominate the garden bird community, with insectivores often poorly represented. This suggests that invertebrate populations within gardens and the wider urban environment may not be sufficient to support populations of insect-eating birds. It also has implications for breeding success more widely, since most small birds feed their chicks on invertebrates. Work by Croci & Clergeau (2008) also suggests that 'urban adapter' species are those that are sedentary in habits and omnivorous, though with the additional traits of preferring forest environments, being widely distributed, and being high-nesters with large wingspans. Croci & Clergeau (2008) also note that 'urban avoider' species tend to be those that allocate more energy to their breeding attempts than 'urban adaptor' species, a trait that might make it difficult for them to adapt to new environments. Logically, given the absence of larger and older trees with natural cavities, you might predict cavity-nesting birds to be less common in urban environments. However, the presence of substantial numbers of nest boxes appears to help at least some of these species, most notably the tits, though those requiring large cavities often lose out.

TABLE 1. Common garden birds, their ecological traits and status. * Goldcrest and Long-tailed Tit are open-nesting species, whose nest is fully domed. Conservation status is derived from the

Species	Status	Diet
Pheasant	Resident	Omnivorous
Red Kite	Resident	Scavenger/Predator
Sparrowhawk	Resident	Small birds
Black-headed Gull	Resident/Winter visitor	Omnivorous
Feral Pigeon	Resident	Plant material/Scavenger
Stock Dove	Resident	Seeds/Plant material
Woodpigeon	Resident	Plant material/Seeds
Collared Dove	Resident	Seeds/Plant material
Tawny Owl	Resident	Small mammals
Swift	Summer migrant	Invertebrates
Green Woodpecker	Resident	Invertebrates
Great Spotted Woodpecker	Resident	Invertebrates/Seeds
Ring-necked Parakeet	Resident	Plant material/Seeds
Magpie	Resident	Omnivorous
Jay	Resident	Invertebrates/Seeds
Jackdaw	Resident	Invertebrates/Omnivorous
Rook	Resident	Invertebrates/Omnivorous
Carrion Crow	Resident	Omnivorous
Goldcrest	Resident	Invertebrates
Blue Tit	Resident	Invertebrates/Seeds
Great Tit	Resident	Invertebrates/Seeds
Coal Tit	Resident	Invertebrates/Seeds
House Martin	Summer migrant	Invertebrates
Long-tailed Tit	Resident	Invertebrates
Blackcap	Summer migrant/Winter visitor	Invertebrates/Fruits
Nuthatch	Resident	Invertebrates/Seeds
Treecreeper	Resident	Invertebrates
Wren	Resident	Invertebrates
Starling	Resident/Winter visitor	Invertebrates/Fruits
Blackbird	Resident/Winter visitor	Invertebrates/Fruits
Fieldfare	Winter visitor	Invertebrates/Fruits
Song Thrush	Resident	Invertebrates/Fruits
Redwing	Winter visitor	Invertebrates/Fruits
Mistle Thrush	Resident	Invertebrates/Fruits
Spotted Flycatcher	Summer migrant	Invertebrates
Robin	Resident	Invertebrates/Fruits
Dunnock	Resident	Invertebrates/Seeds
House Sparrow	Resident	Seeds/Plant material
Tree Sparrow	Resident	Seeds
Pied Wagtail	Resident	Invertebrates
Brambling	Winter visitor	Seeds/Invertebrates
Chaffinch	Resident/Winter visitor	Invertebrates/Seeds
Bullfinch	Resident	Seeds/Plant material
Greenfinch	Resident/Winter visitor	Seeds
Goldfinch	Resident/Partial migrant	Seeds
Siskin	Resident/Winter visitor	Seeds
Yellowhammer	Resident	Seeds/Invertebrates
Reed Bunting	Resident	Seeds/Invertebrates

Birds of Conservation Concern (BOCC) List, which classifies species as Red-, Amber- or Green-listed based on a number of criteria. Non-native species with feral populations are not assessed by BOCC.

Nest site	Conservation status	Breeding population
Ground-nesting	Not listed	2.2 million females
Open-nesting	Green-listed	1,600 pairs
Open-nesting	Green-listed	33,000 pairs
Ground-nesting	Green-listed	130,000 pairs
Open/Cavity-nesting	Not listed	540,000 pairs
Cavity/Open-nesting	Amber-listed	260,000 territories
Open/Tree-nesting	Green-listed	5.3 million pairs
Open/Tree-nesting	Green-listed	990,000 pairs
Cavity-nesting	Amber-listed	50,000 pairs
Cavity-nesting	Amber-listed	87,000 pairs
Cavity-nesting	Green-listed	52,000 pairs
Cavity-nesting	Green-listed	140,000 pairs
Cavity-nesting	Not listed	8,600 pairs
Open/Tree-nesting	Green-listed	550,000 pairs
Open/Tree-nesting	Green-listed	170,000 pairs
Cavity-nesting	Green-listed	1.3 million pairs
Open/Tree-nesting	Green-listed	990,000 pairs
Open/Tree-nesting	Green-listed	1 million territories
Open-nesting*	Green-listed	520,000 territories
Cavity-nesting	Green-listed	3.4 million territories
Cavity-nesting	Green-listed	2.5 million territories
Cavity-nesting	Green-listed	680,000 territories
Cavity-nesting	Amber-listed	510,000 pairs
Open-nesting*	Green-listed	330,000 territories
Open/Tree-nesting	Green-listed	1.1 million territories
Cavity-nesting	Green-listed	220,000 territories
Cavity-nesting	Green-listed	180,000 territories
Cavity-nesting	Green-listed	7.7 million territories
Cavity-nesting	Red-listed	1.8 million pairs
Open-nesting	Green-listed	4.9 million pairs
Open-nesting	Red-listed	1–5 pairs
Open-nesting	Red-listed	1.1 million pairs
Open-nesting	Red-listed	1–5 pairs
Open-nesting	Red-listed	160,000 territories
Open-nesting	Red-listed	33,000 territories
Cavity/Open-nesting	Green-listed	6 million territories
Open-nesting	Amber-listed	2.3 million territories
Cavity/Open-nesting	Red-listed	5.1 million pairs
Cavity-nesting	Red-listed	180,000 territories
Open/Cavity-nesting	Green-listed	460,000 pairs
Open-nesting	Green-listed	1–2 pairs
Open-nesting	Green-listed	5.8 million territories
Open-nesting	Amber-listed	190,000 territories
Open-nesting	Green-listed	1.7 million pairs
Open-nesting	Green-listed	1.2 million pairs
Open-nesting	Green-listed	410,000 pairs
Open-nesting	Red-listed	700,000 pairs
Ground-nesting	Amber-listed	230,000 pairs

That wild birds can take advantage of the opportunities afforded by human activities is evident from changes in urban-nesting gull populations within the UK, which have increased substantially over a short period of time; this increase has occurred despite the fact that coastal populations of the same species have been in decline. It is thought that much of this increase has been driven by the availability of food scraps on our urban streets and at landfill sites, coupled with the relatively predator-free nesting opportunities available (Ross-Smith *et al.*, 2014).

Interestingly, much of the ecological work looking at urban birds has tended to adopt a binary approach, separating species into urban and non-urban classes and then looking for differences in their ecological and/or physiological traits (e.g. Møller, 2009). Such work has underlined, for example, that insectivores, cavity nesters and migrants are under-represented within urban bird communities, while species showing high rates of feeding innovation, high annual fecundity and high adult survival rates are over-represented. However, such an approach – where species are lumped into one or the other of these two groupings – fails to account for important differences in how individual species may respond to urbanisation, or to differences in how a species may respond in different parts of its geographic range. When you consider these differences, then many of the identified traits characteristic of one or other community disappear (Evans *et al.*, 2011).

The nature of urban bird communities has been the subject of study and review for a number of years and several common patterns emerge. It appears, for example, that local factors are more important in determining the species richness of these communities than factors operating at a wider regional scale, and that urban communities respond positively to the availability of supplementary feeding and the structural complexity of local habitat, but negatively to the degree of human disturbance (Evans *et al.*, 2009a). While there is likely to be continuing debate around this topic (e.g. Møller, 2014), it does appear that, at the species level, generalists are better suited to the urban environment than specialists, as are those species that nest off the ground. Generalist species are known to be less susceptible to, and may even benefit from, environmental disturbance of the sort associated with urbanisation (McKinney & Lockwood, 1999), and they are also the species that appear to be coping best with a changing global climate (Davey *et al.*, 2012), something that may also be behind their apparent success in our towns, cities and gardens. Broader environmental tolerance is something that has been demonstrated in urban birds, most clearly through a study by Frances Bonier and colleagues, who compared the elevational and latitudinal distributions of 217 urban birds found in 73 of the world's largest cities with the distributions of 247 rural congeners. The results of this work showed that urban bird species had markedly broader environmental tolerance than rural congeners, suggesting that a broad environmental tolerance may predispose some species to thrive within urban habitats (Bonier *et al.*, 2007).

UK GARDEN BIRDS, THE SIZE OF THEIR POPULATIONS AND COMMUNITY STRUCTURE

The BTO/JNCC/RSPB Breeding Bird Survey (BBS) is the core scheme used to monitor the population trends of a broad range of breeding bird species across the UK. Some 3,000 participants visit randomly selected 1-km survey squares and record the bird species that they encounter there. The birds seen are recorded in a series of distance bands running out parallel to the line transects along which each observer walks. This approach, coupled with the collection of habitat information for each of the transect sections, allows researchers to calculate density estimates by habitat for each of the bird species commonly recorded.

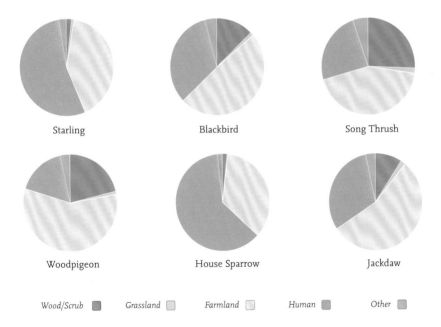

FIG 5. Data from the BTO/JNCC/RSPB Breeding Bird Survey underline the sizeable populations of certain species breeding in urbanised landscapes. Redrawn from data presented by Newson *et al.* (2005).

These can then be multiplied up by the area of each habitat type nationally to calculate population estimates based on habitat type, which in turn provide a sense of the bird populations associated with gardens and wider urbanised landscapes (Newson *et al.*, 2005).

This approach suggests that some of the national population estimates previously given for familiar species, like Blackbird, Starling, House Sparrow, Greenfinch *Chloris chloris*, Jackdaw *Crovus monedula* and Woodpigeon *Columba palumbus*, have been underestimated because the built environment and its gardens had not been properly taken into account. The BBS habitat-based approach indicates the importance of urban, suburban and rural human habitats for species like House Sparrow and Starling, which have 61.5 per cent and 53.9 per cent respectively of their breeding population found here. The survey has also enabled the production of figures suggesting that the habitats directly associated with human sites (urban, suburban and rural) could represent 27,919 km^2 (2,791,900 ha) or 10.9 per cent of UK land area. This can be further broken down as urban (2.2 per cent), suburban (5.1 per cent) and rural human sites (3.6 per cent). The figure of 10.9 per cent is somewhat higher than the 6 per cent figure that has been derived from the Corinne Land Cover map. Given the different assumptions involved, it seems likely that the true figure lies somewhere between the two approaches and possibly closer to the 6 per cent derived from satellite imagery. Using the figure of 432,964 ha, presented at the top of this chapter and calculated by Davies *et al.* (2009) for the area of UK gardens, and the two figures just mentioned (Newson *et al.* 2,791,900 ha, Land Cover map 1,454,970 ha) for the amount of built-upon land, suggests that gardens might represent between 16 per cent and 30 per cent of the land area present within UK cities, towns and villages, and 1.79 per cent of total land area.

Gardens and their associated houses are of particular importance to House Martin and Swift, two species that national monitoring schemes like the Breeding Bird Survey struggle to monitor. While these two summer visitors are clearly dependent upon buildings for the nesting opportunities that they provide, the nature of the surrounding gardens is much less important. Resident species, such as House Sparrow and Starling, also make use of domestic dwellings for their nesting opportunities but are more closely tied to the nature of the gardens within which these dwellings are located. The presence of shrubby cover is important for House Sparrow, while Starlings appear to favour properties where there is access to nearby areas of short vegetation – such as garden lawns or amenity grassland. Another summer migrant, the Spotted Flycatcher, also appears to be dependent on the nature of the gardens it occupies, seemingly preferring rural or larger suburban gardens with mature trees and an abundance of small flying insects.

A number of bird species use gardens at a particular time of the year, arriving to take advantage of feeding opportunities when conditions elsewhere become less favourable. This is something that we will examine in greater detail in Chapter 2 but it is worth noting here how the early winter arrival of migrant thrushes and finches boosts resident populations and sees birds taking windfall apples and the fruits of berry-producing shrubs. Joining these less obvious visitors (which look the same as year-round residents, such as Blackbird and Chaffinch *Fringilla coelebs*) are more obvious migrants, including Brambling, Redwing, Fieldfare and Waxwing. Such species tend to forage over large areas, responding to the availability of favoured foods, and so are able to take advantage of the seasonal resources present in many gardens.

COMMUNITY STRUCTURE AND GARDEN TYPES

As the figures produced by Newson *et al.* (2005) illustrate, the garden bird community contains a significant component of the wider breeding populations of a number of key species. In addition, Newson *et al.*'s work underlines that many garden species also occur alongside one another within other communities – such as the farmland bird community and the woodland bird community. There may be differences between these communities in terms of species interactions, such that one species does better than another in one habitat but not elsewhere. Such differences in community structure can also be seen from smaller and more focussed studies. Work on tit populations across different UK habitats reveals that Great Tits usually outnumber Blue Tits in woodland populations, often by 2:1 or more. In a suburban population studied by Cowie & Hinsley (1987), the situation was reversed, with Blue Tit outnumbering its larger relative by 3:1 or more. This suggests that Blue Tits might be better suited to the urban environment than Great Tits.

Gardens vary greatly in their size and structure, and consequently in their use by birds. Although we often categorise gardens into urban, suburban and rural, this is a rather simplistic approach and fails to adequately account for the variation that exists both within individual gardens and in the wider habitat framework within which they sit. Within the UK, as much as 7 per cent of land area may be located within towns and cities with a human population in excess of 10,000 people. Some 80 per cent of the UK population lives in these areas, with 40 per cent of the population living within London and our other major conurbations. In an attempt to document the extent and structure of the gardens associated with these conurbations, Alison Loram

FIG 6. Blue Tits typically outnumber Great Tits in the urban environment, by as much as 3:1, but are the less numerous species within traditional woodland habitats. (John Harding)

and colleagues at the University of Sheffield took a detailed look at the cities of Edinburgh, Belfast, Oxford, Cardiff and Leicester (Loram *et al.*, 2007). The researchers surveyed a sample of at least 500 properties from each of the five cities, revealing that 99 per cent had an associated garden. The size of the gardens – whose median areas varied across the different cities, from 96.4 m^2 (Belfast) to 213.0 m^2 (Edinburgh) – was closely related to the type of housing present; the general pattern revealing that garden size roughly doubles as you move from terrace housing, to semi-detached to detached. Relatively small gardens (<400 m^2) were much more numerous within the cities than larger gardens, contributing disproportionately to the total garden area present. This has important consequences for engaging householders in nature conservation through practices such as wildlife-friendly gardening (see Chapter 6), because a small garden might not seem particularly important in a wider context to a householder. I have often heard the phrase 'what difference can I make; my garden is only small' but it is important to remember that individual gardens do not exist in isolation; they are instead part of a wider ecological network.

Loram's work also revealed the spatial pattern of gardens within each of the cities, reflecting variation in the density of the human population and the associated densities of housing stock. The history of each city, together with the geography of its location, contributed to the pattern of housing seen; the notion of a simple gradient in garden size, from the leafy suburbs with their large gardens through to courtyard gardens in the urban centre, was disrupted by these and other factors. This also meant that there was no clear relationship between garden size and distance to the edge of the conurbation within any of the five cities studied. This is important when we look at urban bird populations in more general terms as, for example, examined through the work of Chamberlain *et al.* (2009a) and others.

At a wider spatial scale, it is possible to use data from the BTO/JNCC/RSPB Breeding Bird Survey to examine the densities of bird species across the broader landscape and, as was done by Tratalos *et al.* (2007), to look at the relationship between avian abundance, species richness and housing densities within urban areas. Tratalos *et al.* (2007) found that total species richness – and that of 27 urban-indicator species – increased from low to moderate household densities, before then declining as you reached higher household densities. Avian abundance showed a rather different pattern, increasing across a wider range of household densities and then only declining at the highest household densities. The researchers were also able to look at the patterns in abundance seen within individual species, highlighting some interesting differences between them. Importantly, however, most of the species showed a hump-shaped relationship with household density, declining at the highest densities. A somewhat worrying finding, highlighted by the team, was that avian abundance almost invariably began to decline at a point below the density of housing required by the UK government for new developments.

A number of studies have highlighted that within cities it is the suburbs that support the greatest variety of bird species, something that is reflected in the hump-shaped distribution of the relationship between species richness and housing density mentioned above. A widely accepted hypothesis for the shape of this relationship is that the observed pattern is due to the increased habitat heterogeneity present at intermediate levels of urbanisation – i.e. that the suburbs are more diverse than either the more urbanised town centres or the farmland habitats that so often surround our towns and cities. However, it may also be the case that there is a higher availability of food resources in our suburbs than elsewhere (see Chapter 2) and that this, rather than habitat heterogeneity, shapes species richness.

Where a garden is located along the rural to urban gradient may influence the community of garden birds associated with it. This is something that we have been able to examine by using data from the BTO's Garden BirdWatch project

FIG 7. Analysis of BTO Garden BirdWatch data revealed that while most bird species were associated with larger gardens, Starling was one of four species found to be more likely to occur in smaller gardens. (Jill Pakenham)

(Chamberlain *et al.*, 2004a). Looking at nearly 13,000 garden sites contributing weekly data on garden birds between 1995 and 2002, we examined the extent to which the occurrence of individual garden bird species at a site was determined by features within the garden itself or by the nature of the surrounding landscape. Garden size was taken into account because we found that, in most cases, species were more likely to occur in large gardens (and larger gardens were more likely to occur in rural habitats and to have high tree and hedge cover). Exceptions to this were House Sparrow, Collared Dove, Black-headed Gull *Chroicocephalus ridibundus* and Starling, all of which were more likely to occur in small gardens.

Once we had controlled for the effects of garden size and the provision of food at garden feeding stations, we found that the likelihood of many species occurring in gardens was dependent on the nature of the surrounding local habitat rather than on features within the garden itself. We found that 12 of the 40 species examined were most likely to occur where the habitat outside the garden was rural in nature – these included open-nesting passerines associated with woodland or woodland edge (Wren, Robin, Blackbird, Blackcap *Sylvia atricapilla* and Chaffinch), hole-nesting (Great Spotted Woodpecker *Dendrocopos major*, Blue Tit and Coal Tit *Periparus ater*) or farmland (Pied Wagtail *Motacilla alba*, Rook *Corvus frugilegus*, Greenfinch, Goldfinch *Carduelis carduelis* and Yellowhammer *Emberiza citrinella*). Just seven species showed a probability of occurrence that was highest in gardens located within urban habitats, these being House Sparrow, Feral Pigeon, Starling, Magpie *Pica pica*, Black-headed Gull, Woodpigeon and Collared Dove.

The features within a garden may sometimes be more important than those in the surrounding landscape, as work carried out in Hobart, Tasmania, demonstrates. Daniels and Kirkpatrick (2006) examined how garden and wider landscape features influenced the abundance and species richness of bird species in 214 suburban gardens and found that the percentage cover of shrubs had a very important influence on the garden birds present, with the presence of shrubby vegetation favouring small native woodland birds and the New Holland Honeyeater *Phylidonyris novaehollandiae* in particular. The same study also underlined the importance of native vegetation for the nectar- and fruit-eating bird species native to Tasmania, but did note that such species also made use of non-native plants. In contrast, introduced bird species – such as Blackbird, House Sparrow and Goldfinch – only used non-native vegetation.

A piece of UK work looking more broadly across a single urban area – the city of Bristol – identified three different bird communities: one composed of species associated with broadleaf woodland and/or inland waterbodies, one associated with high-density housing and residential gardens, and one intermediate to these two and associated with low-density housing and variable amounts of woodland (Baker *et al.*, 2010). More detailed examination of these three communities suggests that the diversity of bird species present within urban areas may be dependent on the availability of blocks of natural and semi-natural habitat, with areas dominated solely by residential gardens supporting fewer species. However, despite the lower species diversity of residential gardens, these areas may support particularly high densities of those species that are present. This is something that is reinforced by other work (e.g. McKinney & Lockwood, 1999).

The spatial arrangement and pattern of gardens and other forms of urban green space also has consequences for the extent to which birds use different patches. Connectivity of suitable habitat patches may be less of a problem for birds than it is for less mobile species, but it has still been shown to be of importance. Esteban Fernández-Juricic, for example, highlighted the importance of wooded streets as potential corridors for birds living in urban Madrid (Fernández-Juricic, 2000), while work in North America has revealed that even the movement of urban-adapted species is influenced by the structure and composition of urban habitats (Evans *et al.*, 2017).

FIG 8. The presence of green cover within urban areas is of particular importance to urban birds, shaping both their distribution and their ability to move between different parts of the built environment. (Mike Toms)

While there has been relatively little work examining how features within and around gardens influence the bird species present, rather more work has been done on other components of urban green space (Jokimäki, 1999). Some of the findings from these studies may provide an indication of how similar features may influence garden bird communities. Work on areas of public green space within London has, for example, underlined the importance of patch size, the presence of waterbodies and the provision of areas of scrubby cover and weedy patches (Chamberlain *et al.*, 2004b). Importantly, some of this work has also underlined the importance of gardens in promoting the species richness of the bird communities using other types of urban green space, such as parks (Chamberlain *et al.*, 2004b). Interactions between gardens, urban green space and the wider built environment may be complex, with the non-biotic components of a city (such as building height and architectural style) also a potential influence on the nature of the bird communities present. Work in Paris, for example, has demonstrated that building height can influence the abundance of particular avian guilds, such that the abundance of omnivorous species was found by Vincent Pellissier to be influenced by the interaction between building heterogeneity and the proportion of low and medium-height buildings present (Pellissier *et al.*, 2012). The findings of this work have implications for urban planning.

Although our work examining the BTO Garden BirdWatch dataset (see Chapter 6) underlines the greater importance of features outside of a garden in determining its use, there do appear to be some garden characteristics that shape the extent to which a garden is visited by particular bird species. Several finch species appear to favour those gardens (and garden feeding stations) that are associated with the presence of tall and mature trees (either within the garden or nearby). Greenfinches, Chaffinches and Goldfinches appear to prefer to fly into tall trees before dropping down to garden feeding stations to feed. Similarly, the presence of thick shrubby cover near to feeding stations appears to increase their use by House Sparrows. The presence of berry-producing shrubs and trees will influence whether or not a garden is visited by wintering thrushes or Waxwings, while the presence of a pond appears to be a particularly attractive feature during the summer months for many different garden bird species.

HOW THE URBAN ENVIRONMENT IMPACTS ON BIRDS AND THEIR POPULATIONS

Over recent years there has been an increasing push to understand the finer-scale effects of the urban environment – of which gardens are a significant component – on the ecology, health, behaviour and physiology of birds. Such effects have been studied both at the level of the individual bird and at the level of the population or community. As we shall see in this section, some of these effects can have significant consequences, determining which species thrive in our town and city gardens and which struggle.

Three of the most striking ways in which urban habitats and gardens differ from more natural landscapes are in the availability, predictability and novelty of key resources, most notably food (provided at garden feeding stations) and nesting opportunities (provided through nest boxes). As we will discover in Chapter 2, the presence of food at garden feeding stations can lead to the creation of a more predictable environment (both through time, and spatially across the city or town). This can have profound consequences for urban birds, as work on Northern Cardinal *Cardinalis cardinalis* populations in Ohio has demonstrated. Rodewald & Arcese (2017) found that female cardinals, breeding in urban habitats within their study area, were more similar in their contribution to the next generation than was the case for those breeding in rural habitats, where a pattern of winners and losers was more evident. Importantly, this difference occurred despite comparable variation in body condition across the habitats studied. The urban cardinal population, then, is more homogenous in terms of its breeding performance than the rural population.

Living within an urban environment is thought to impact on the health of the organisms found there and we know, for example, that urban pollution elevates the levels of oxidative stress (see Chapter 4) seen in humans and birds (Isaksson, 2010). Researchers have measured the levels of oxidative stress in urban populations of study species and compared these with individuals living in other, more natural habitats. Other researchers have looked instead at the levels of particular hormones, again using these to tease out possible health effects. More recently, attention has turned to telomeres; these are the nucleoprotein structures found at the end of chromosomes. Telomeres are thought to promote genome stability and there is good evidence to associate the length of a telomere with lifespan, mortality rate and disease risk. This suggests that telomeres may prove a useful 'biomarker' for phenotypic quality and ageing. If the pressures of urban living modify an individual's oxidative balance, then this may result in the shortening of telomere length and indicate a health effect.

FIG 9. Being raised in an urban environment significantly reduces telomere length in Great Tits. Telomeres are the nucleoprotein structures found at the end of chromosomes and thought to promote genome stability. They have been linked to health and longevity. (Jill Pakenham)

Through an experiment in which nestling Great Tits were cross-fostered, Salmón *et al.* (2016) found that being raised in an urban environment significantly reduced telomere length compared to that of nestlings raised in a rural environment. However, this finding could not be replicated by a similar study in France (Biard *et al.*, 2017). A larger study, this time of Blackbirds, also found that urban-dwelling individuals had shorter telomeres than those living elsewhere, adding evidence to this growing area of research interest (Ibáñez-Álamo *et al.*, 2018). While Clotilde Biard's study failed to find differences in telomere length between urban and rural populations of Great Tits in France, the work did reveal differences in chick growth (rural chicks were larger and heavier) and in plumage colouration (the yellow carotenoid-based plumage was more colourful in rural chicks – see also Chapter 2), suggestive of developmental constraints within the urban populations. Measures of 'damage' in relation to the impacts of urbanisation have been shown to vary between species with, for example, Salmón *et al.* (2017) determining that sparrow species show greater overall damage than that seen in tits.

There is the suspicion then, that gardens and the wider urban habitat are sub-optimal for many bird species (though not all). If this is the case, then we might expect to see the presence of three features that have been found to be characteristic of sub-optimal habitats elsewhere. These are:

i)   a greater proportion of young breeders and more floating individuals;
ii) less stable populations, whose numbers fluctuate from year to year; and
iii) low breeding density.

The idea that populations living within sub-optimal habitats are more likely to fluctuate from year to year is linked to the notion of 'source-sink' dynamics, where populations living within high-quality habitats produce a surplus of young each year, but competition for breeding territories in these high-quality habitats is high, resulting in many young and less dominant individuals moving away to occupy territories in less optimal habitats. This also explains the first characteristic that we mentioned – the greater proportion of young birds in sub-optimal habitats. We certainly see this in suburban tit populations (Cowie & Hinsley, 1987; Junker-Bornholdt & Schmidt, 1999) but it isn't always the case. Work on farmland Blackbird populations has revealed the presence of greater numbers of young males in this habitat (Hatchwell *et al.*, 1996a), and David Snow – in his classic treatise on urban Blackbirds – speculated that urban populations act as a source population for a rural sink (Snow, 1958). Snow had demonstrated that his urban Blackbirds were generating a significant surplus of youngsters each year, some 1.7 yearlings per pair when only 0.7 yearlings per pair were needed to maintain a stable population.

Urban living may also lead to greater exposure to humans, perhaps resulting in increased tolerance of their presence and reduced levels of 'fear'. Work on urban Great Tits has highlighted that they are less neophobic and show shorter flight initiation distances (see Chapter 6) than their rural counterparts (Møller *et al.*, 2015; Charmantier *et al.*, 2017). They also appear to have a more proactive coping strategy when dealing with stressful situations (Senar *et al.*, 2017a).

DISEASE AND THE URBAN ENVIRONMENT

Chapter 4 explores the diseases affecting garden birds in detail, but it is important to give a brief overview here of how disease risks differ between urban and rural environments. Comparisons between the diseases of urban and rural populations of birds have yielded mixed results when it comes to seeking general patterns of occurrence and prevalence. Some studies, such as the work of Grégoire *et al.* (2002), Fokidis *et al.* (2008) and Evans *et al.* (2009a), have found reduced parasite loads in urban populations of garden bird species, including Blackbird. Others, such as Giraudeau *et al.* (2014) have found higher levels of disease in more urban

FIG 10. Garden feeding stations have been implicated in the transmission of disease between different species of garden bird, but the presence of supplementary food also has positive benefits for birds like this Brambling. (Jill Pakenham)

areas. Giraudeau's work revealed that the severity of coccidian infection in House Finch *Haemorhous mexicanus* and the prevalence of pox virus were both inversely related to the proportion of undisturbed habitat within the Phoenix metropolitan area. Patterns of disease infection along urban to rural gradients, and across the different habitats within the urban environment, may differ between diseases, in part a reflection of variation in how different diseases are transmitted. In the case of parasites, transmission may require an intermediate host that is absent from the urban environment (Sitko & Zaleśny, 2014), but for other diseases – including those transmitted between individuals through contaminated food – transmission rates may increase in gardens and other urban sites because of the high densities of birds attracted to garden feeding stations (Lawson *et al.*, 2018). The provision of food at garden feeding stations may also influence disease dynamics (Galbraith *et al.*, 2017a).

ARE GARDENS IMPORTANT?

As the figures presented within this chapter demonstrate, gardens and the wider built environment support significant proportions of the breeding populations of certain bird species. In addition, gardens and their associated resources may be important for particular birds at other times of the year or during periods when the availability of key resources within the wider environment is at a seasonal low. This underlines that gardens are important, and not just for species flagged as being of conservation concern. How we manage our gardens and the resources they contain has consequences for bird populations and, as we shall see later in this book, may also help to drive evolutionary change. It is important to remember that garden bird populations do not exist in isolation, since birds are well able to move between different habitats or regions. While gardens may not be as suitable as certain other habitats for breeding, they may be better in other ways, at least for some species.

We are, however, far from fully understanding the role that gardens play in a wider context, particularly in relation to source-sink dynamics, and it is certainly too early to be able to quantify the true value (or cost) of garden living for bird populations here in the UK, in Europe or North America, let alone elsewhere in the world. The mobility of birds makes it difficult to follow individuals throughout their full life cycle; in turn, this prevents us from being able to determine why particular individuals use gardens and the consequences or benefits of this use on future events in their lives. For a young Great Tit, raised in a piece of mature deciduous woodland bordering a city's suburbs, the presence

FIG 11. Gardens across the globe vary greatly in their structure and in the plants they contain, something that can reflect both cultural differences and local conditions. (Mike Toms)

of suitable food in garden bird feeders may enable it to survive its first winter when it would otherwise have died. While this fortunate individual may fail to secure a prime woodland breeding territory the following year, and instead end up making a failed breeding attempt in a garden setting, it may still have the opportunity to occupy a woodland territory in a subsequent year. In the end, this individual's lifetime reproductive success may still be better for having used a garden and its resources, than would have been the case had it only ever lived within a woodland site.

CONCLUDING REMARKS

Before we leave this chapter and turn to look in more detail at particular aspects of the garden environment, it is worth reminding ourselves that the gardens present here in the UK, and across much of western Europe and North America, are often very different from those in other parts of the world. Thinking about gardens in a more global context forces you to move away from the predominantly recreational basis to gardens located within western Europe and North America. Many home gardens elsewhere are very different and provide families with space to engage in food production for subsistence or small-scale marketing. Such gardens may also play an important social or cultural role, perhaps acting as spaces within which knowledge related to agricultural practices can be shared. The management of these spaces creates structures and microclimates that are typically very different from the surrounding countryside; in this respect they can be considered alongside the more familiar urban and suburban gardens of western Europe, even though they look and act very differently (Guarino & Hoogendijk, 2004). It is known, for example, that 'home gardens' support high levels of inter- and intra-specific plant diversity, making them important in a global context, but far less is known about the role that they play for wider biodiversity and, in the context of this book, wild birds (Galluzzi *et al.*, 2010). For the most part, however, we will just consider the gardens of western Europe, North America and Australasia in this book, something that also reflects where the greater amount of research has been carried out. The pattern of research worldwide isn't just linked to particular geographic areas, since it has also been demonstrated that there is a positive and significant association between the degree of urbanisation of a species and how frequently it has been the subject of scientific study (Ibáñez-Álamo *et al.*, 2017).

This chapter has highlighted the fact that gardens come in many different forms and that this has consequences for the communities of birds associated with them. The birds present in our gardens are the species that have, for the most part, adapted to the process of urbanisation to take advantage of the resources and other opportunities that gardens and the wider built environment provide. While some of these species populations are resident within the built environment, others make use of our gardens on a seasonal basis. Most UK gardens are located within highly urbanised landscapes; with urban land cover globally predicted to triple between 2000 and 2030 (United Nations, 2014), we can expect to see future changes in our garden bird communities. Such changes are part of an ongoing process that has altered the distribution of bird species, changed the composition of avian communities, brought about local extinctions and altered behaviour. It is these features and processes that we will examine of the following chapters, starting with feeding opportunities (Chapter 2), then moving on to an examination of breeding behaviour (Chapter 3), disease risk (Chapter 4) and behaviour (Chapter 5).

Foods and Feeding

F EEDING WILD BIRDS IS UNDOUBTEDLY a popular pastime here in the UK and a great many of us put out mixed seed, sunflower hearts and fat- or suet-based products for our garden birds. The addition of such food to the environment represents a substantial supplementation of the resources available to wild birds, yet we still lack a clear understanding of its effects. In a wider research context, we know that food supplementation can increase survival rates (Brittingham & Temple, 1988a), change community and population structure (Galbraith *et al.*, 2017b), alter behaviour (Saggese *et al.*, 2011; Plummer *et al.*, 2015) and impact on wider biodiversity (Orros *et al.*, 2015a). It has also been linked to disease transmission in birds (Lawson *et al.*, 2018) and to health and well-being benefits in people.

Through this chapter we will explore how and why supplementary food is provided to garden birds, how provision varies across countries, cities and cultures, and the consequences that such provision has for the birds that visit our gardens to partake of this significant resource. Understanding why people feed wild birds and the extent to which they appreciate its costs and benefits will be central to our exploration, as will a review of the scale of food provisioning, which is where we will start this chapter.

THE PROVISION OF FOOD FOR WILD BIRDS

It has been estimated that between one-quarter and two-thirds of households across major parts of Europe, North America, Australia and New Zealand provide food for wild birds (Thomas, 2000; Ishigame & Baxter, 2007; United States Fish &

FIG 12. Suet-based foods, such as fat balls, have become very popular with UK householders, their use targeted at small garden birds like tits and Starlings. (John Harding)

Wildlife Service, 2011; Davies *et al.*, 2012). Within the UK, and using figures from the English Housing Survey and other studies, Davies *et al.* (2009) reported that 48 per cent of households, and 51 per cent of households with a garden, participated in feeding wild birds. Perhaps more interestingly, the study also reported that 28 per cent of households, and 23 per cent of households with a garden, specifically used bird feeders. An earlier and often quoted study by Cowie & Hinsley (1988a) put the figure at 75 per cent, but was based on a small sample of households (in Cardiff) and did not properly account for those questionnaires that were not returned. Work in Reading, Berkshire, using a face-to-face questionnaire approach outside supermarkets, came up with a figure of 55.3 per cent for the proportion feeding wild birds, of which 65 per cent reported that they fed all year round (Orros & Fellowes, 2015b). Marketing work by the RSPB, using two separate telephone surveys of randomly selected groups of 1,000 people and carried out in summer and winter 2004, indicated that 56 to 61 per cent per cent of people over the age of 16 had fed their garden birds during the past year (RSPB, unpublished).

A rough calculation by Zoe Davies and colleagues, based on the population sizes of birds known to use seed feeders, suggests that there is at least one bird feeder for every nine potentially feeder-using birds. This does not allow for the fact that many households provide food in more than one feeder, or that many bird feeders are sitting empty at any one point in time. RSPB data, again from their marketing survey, suggest that on a typical summer's day one in every seven gardens has at least one empty bird feeder. Even so, it does underline the potential scale of food provisioning taking place within the UK – something Davies *et al.* (2009) have suggested could equate to a standing crop of 2,580 tonnes of bird food. Figures from the Pet Food Manufacturers Association put UK bird food sales at *c*. 150,000 tonnes annually, representative of an annual consumer spend in excess of £200 million. O'Leary & Jones (2006) suggest that in excess of 500,000 tonnes of food is provided annually across the UK and US combined, while United Nation's figures from 2005 put the global bird food industry's value at \$5–6 billion, with growth of *c*. 4 per cent annually since the 1980s (Lin, 2005).

Thanks to the periodic National Survey of Fishing, Hunting, and Wildlife-Associated Recreation, we know that expenditure on wild bird foods within the United States has doubled over a 20-year period, exceeding \$4 billion per year by 2011 (United States Fish & Wildlife Service, 1991; 2011). We lack a comparable survey within the UK, and securing commercially sensitive sales information from the wild bird care sector is problematic, but it is thought that the current

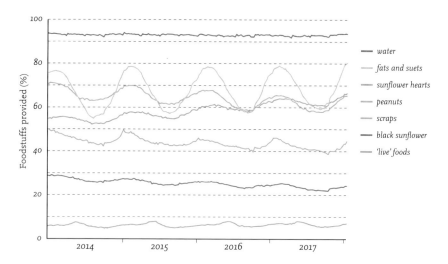

FIG 13. The proportion of BTO Garden BirdWatch participants presenting different foodstuffs at their garden feeding stations each week across four of the project years (2014–17). Note the increase in fat and suet provision during the winter months. 'Live' foods include dried mealworms. Data reproduced with permission from BTO.

annual UK spend on wild bird care products (food, feeders and nest boxes) is between £220 million and £500 million (Fuller *et al.*, 2012).

Information from the weekly submissions made by BTO Garden BirdWatchers provides a measure of the change seen in different types of bird food (see Figure 13) but these data come from a subset of the national population (see Chapter 6) and do not reveal the actual quantities provided. Having said this, as part of BTO's work on microevolution in Blackcaps (see later in this chapter), we were able to estimate that the total volume of sunflower hearts and fat products provided by BTO Garden BirdWatchers during the winter months more than doubled from 6.35 tonnes to 17.26 tonnes over the course of a 12-year period (Plummer *et al.*, 2015).

WHY DO PEOPLE FEED WILD BIRDS?

While bird feeding is clearly influenced by external factors, such as socioeconomic status and having access to a garden, it is also shaped by intrinsic and motivational factors. At its heart, bird feeding may be seen as a humane act, an act of kindness reflecting a wish to help a fellow creature. However, this act may be further shaped by other motivations, such as guilt or a wish to learn. Despite the obvious commercial advantages to be gained by understanding motivations for feeding wild birds, there has been relatively little work in this area and many of our assumptions about why people provide supplementary food for wild birds remain untested (Jones & Reynolds, 2008). Understanding motivations requires a considered and rigorously scientific approach; it is all too easy to inadvertently bias a response from a study subject by asking a question in the wrong way.

The work that has been done suggests that people feed wild birds for a range of different reasons driven by underlying environmental, cultural and philosophical perceptions (Davies *et al.*, 2012). Many people derive pleasure from feeding wild birds and in many instances the provision of food is simply a reflection of this. Others feed because they are concerned about wild birds (and other creatures) and wish to nurture and support them. Some provide food because of the experiential knowledge that is gained, while others seek to counter the guilt that they feel over wider human impacts on the environment.

Examination of a random sample of 1,000 participants in BTO's weekly Garden BirdWatch scheme (Schreiber, 2010) found that 'pleasure', 'contributing to the survival of wild birds' and 'studying behaviour' were the top three justifications given by respondents for feeding. 'Responding to environmental degradation' and 'teaching children' were also given as reasons for feeding.

FIG 14. Peanuts were one of the first foods provided specifically for wild birds visiting UK gardens. Originally presented loose or in net bags, peanuts are now typically provided in mesh feeders, though their use has fallen with the arrival of new high-energy seeds. (Jill Pakenham)

Of course, participants in a citizen science scheme like Garden BirdWatch are unlikely to be representative of the wider UK public; they have sufficient interest in garden birds to have become involved in a rigorous monitoring scheme and will have been exposed to articles delivering information and messages on the practices associated with feeding wild birds. At this point it is just worth noting that the provision of supplementary food is sometimes practised for other reasons; conservation practitioners use supplementary food to enhance the survival and reproductive success of endangered species, while others use it to reduce predation pressure by provisioning predators; some use it to bring animals to sites where they can be observed or even hunted.

The provision of food at garden feeding stations, and indeed the wider participation in wildlife-friendly gardening, may also be a response to peer pressures or the development of a shared social ideal, or to the opportunities provided by having the time and/or financial resources required. The 'luxury effect' noted by Hope *et al.* (2003), Kinzig *et al.* (2005) and others, where wealthier neighbourhoods support greater levels of vegetation cover and have a greater richness of vertebrate taxa, may also apply to the provision of food for wild birds. We'll return to this as we move through the next two sections.

As well as seeking to understand the motivations for feeding, it is also important to understand any concerns that those feeding wild birds may have about the practice. While some individuals may only see feeding as being beneficial – for their own interest or for the welfare of the birds themselves – others may continue to feed even if they have concerns about particular aspects of the practice. The sample of BTO Garden BirdWatch participants just mentioned were also asked whether they had any concerns about feeding and, if so, what these might be. Just under half of the respondents noted that they did have concerns; those highlighted being the risk of disease transmission, the risk of attracting predators, and the risk of attracting unwanted species to the garden.

THE VARIATION IN FOOD PROVISION

Across northern Europe and North America the feeding of wild birds appears to have once been a winter practice, suggesting that food was provided in recognition of the challenging winter conditions being faced by birds. To some extent feeding remains a winter practice; as data from BTO Garden BirdWatch reveal, the proportion of its participants providing supplementary food shows a strong seasonal pattern with increasing provision during the winter months. Up until the 1980s, the prevailing view was that feeding wild birds during the breeding season would lead to adult birds feeding their young on unsuitable foods and perhaps lead to nestlings choking on 'indigestible foodstuffs such as peanuts'. Despite this, a pronounced move towards feeding year-round was made during the 1980s, when the advice provided by both the RSPB and BTO switched from winter only to feeding throughout the year.

The switch in BTO's position was evidence-based and derived from work carried out by Patrick Thompson, who organised a special spring extension to the BTO's Garden Bird Feeding Survey (Thompson, 1987). The study sought to compare the numbers of feeding birds in the spring with those seen in winter and to determine which species made use of garden feeding stations during this period. Some 181 participants took part in the winter component, with 113 contributing to the spring extension. While fewer species were recorded in the spring component than in the winter, the same species were present in the top 12 in both studies; for some species the level of feeding in spring was as high as, or higher, than that seen in autumn or winter. In House Sparrow, for example, feeding activity peaked in late spring. Other species, e.g. Robin, Blue Tit and Great Tit, used provided food extensively through into the first month of the spring survey, but after this their use of this resource dropped markedly. This drop in use was thought to reflect a shift towards natural prey, which generally become more abundant in spring. That seed-eating species, like Dunnock *Prunella modularis* and Greenfinch, did not move away from provided food quite so quickly perhaps underlines a lack of seed availability more widely until later into the year.

The second component of Thompson's study looked at the breeding season use of supplementary food (peanuts) by Blue Tits and Great Tits across 13 gardens at Ashridge Park, Hertfordshire. This population had been studied by the BTO's Chris Mead since 1977. Chris was a key figure in the development of several projects studying garden birds. The garden-nesting Blue Tits bred significantly earlier than those breeding in nearby woodland and laid larger clutches. There was no difference in the timing of laying between the two Great Tit populations but the garden-breeding birds laid significantly smaller clutches than their woodland counterparts, and there was no significant difference in the fledging success of

FIG 15. While the food available at garden feeding stations appears to be important to young Blue Tits once they have left the nest, it is only rarely provided to nestlings by adult birds. (John Harding)

either species between the two habitats. The feeding habits of the adult tits were also carefully monitored. While Great Tits were very rarely seen to feed their young on peanuts (less than 7 per cent of visits), the Blue Tits were never seen to do this. Importantly, no young tits were reported to have died from ingesting nuts.

Elsewhere, both Cowie & Hinsley (1987) and Perrins (1979) have noted a lower fledging success in tits using gardens compared to woodland habitats, with much of this down to chick starvation, despite the fact that supplementary foods are available in this habitat. This underlines the reluctance of adult tits to feed their young on supplementary food. Collectively, the evidence from Thompson's study and the wider literature convinced BTO to change its advice on year-round feeding, recognising that the extra food may provide a 'valuable food source to adult birds'. The advice to switch to year-round feeding in Germany was made even more strongly by Peter Berthold and Gabriele Mohr, both respected researchers, whose book *Vögel füttern, aber richtig* – loosely translated as 'feeding birds, but right' – made a scientifically based case for year-round feeding. Although initially criticised in some scientific circles, the book was well received by birdwatchers, shifting 50,000 copies within two years of first publication. Figures from the UK, taken from the RSPB's marketing study, suggest that winter and summer feeding levels are now fairly similar, at least in terms of the proportion of people providing food (53 per cent summer and 59 per cent winter).

DIFFERENCES BETWEEN INDIVIDUALS

The suspicion that some people are more likely to put out food for birds than others has proved difficult to test, in a large part because of the methodological difficulties in securing a random and representative sample of respondents when carrying out questionnaire-based studies. The scale at which the data are collected can also cause problems for their interpretation. Fuller *et al.* (2012), for example, found that three different measures of socioeconomic status – household income, the age of householders and the number of individuals comprising the household – were poor predictors of bird feeding behaviour at the national level; however, all three were found to be strongly related to both the presence of bird feeding and the spatial density of bird feeding stations when they just looked at the city of Sheffield. It appeared that by aggregating data at a wider scale, the researchers had averaged away important fine-scale differences. The Sheffield data revealed that bird feeding and the spatial density of bird feeders increased as household income increased but showed an interesting 'humped' relationship with the age and number of householders.

Provisioning may also vary between individuals in terms of how often they put out food, the types of foods they provide and where the food is presented. Roughly a quarter of those interviewed by the RSPB put out food daily, with half putting out food at least once a week, and food was presented roughly equally across bird feeders (33 per cent), bird tables (27 per cent) and on the ground (30 per cent). Davies *et al.* (2012) found that just 29 per cent of the households they studied provided food at least once a week. The work in Reading, mentioned earlier in this chapter, had a more detailed second component; this looked at a subset of people feeding birds within the city, charting what they provided over a two-year period. As well as the finding that a significantly higher proportion of the individuals feeding year round provisioned daily, compared to those who only fed the birds during autumn and winter, the Reading work also collected valuable information on the amount of food being given. This revealed that each day the median amount provided per garden was 127 g, though ranging from 18 g to 3,573 g. Knowing what food was being provisioned, and in what quantities, enabled Orros and Fellowes to calculate a daily energy value of 628 kcal provisioned per garden per day. In addition to variation in the quantities of food

FIG 16. Various members of the crow family, including Carrion Crow, have taken advantage of the feeding opportunities available at garden feeding stations. Work in North America has highlighted how the nature of these opportunities may vary regionally. (John Harding)

provided, there was also variation in the types of food provided, with 91 per cent of individuals provisioning one to three types of food. Mixed seed was the most commonly provisioned food, by both mass and kcal; interestingly, 43 per cent of individuals still provisioned household scraps.

Work in the US has also examined the question of who feeds wild birds, revealing that older people are more likely to provide supplementary food than young people (Lepczyk *et al.*, 2012), and are more likely to be women and to have achieved higher educational qualifications than those not participating (Lepczyk *et al.*, 2004a). Mark Goddard, working on why people in Leeds garden for wildlife, also found that the frequency of bird feeding increased with age (Goddard *et al.*, 2013). The RSPB marketing study, which is probably the study that is most representative of the wider UK population, found that interviewees 35 years of age or older were more likely to feed their birds than those under 35 (RSPB, unpublished). Of course, the characteristics of those provisioning wild birds may sometimes confound attempts to examine the relationships between food provision and other features – for example, housing density (something we touched on in the previous chapter).

REGIONAL DIFFERENCES

Cultural differences in attitudes to birds may explain many of the regional differences in the types and quantities of supplementary food provided for garden birds. The biggest markets for wild bird food and feeding products are based in Europe and North America but even within these regions there are differences between countries and peoples. Within Europe, for example, the feeding of wild birds is common in Germany, Poland, Finland, Switzerland, the UK and the Netherlands, but not in France, Spain or indeed other Mediterranean countries. That cultural differences might be behind the patterns seen within Europe could be suggested by the differing attitudes towards the hunting of small wild birds, still a common practice in the south of Europe but not in the north. Could the differences within Europe also relate to geography and the harsher winter weather encountered further north within the continent?

As Lepczyk *et al.* (2012) found, some of these regional differences in provisioning practices within North America do indeed relate to climatic conditions. Through a series of parallel studies Christopher Lepczyk and colleagues found that householders in Michigan and Arizona had differing attitudes towards the provision of supplementary food for birds; while 66 per cent of respondents in Michigan provided food, just 43 per cent of

FIG 17. Granivorous (seed-eating) species, like Yellowhammer, dominate at UK garden feeding stations, while insect-eating species tend to be less common. (Jill Pakenham)

those in Arizona did so. The authors put this down to the fact that Michigan is a region that experiences severe winter weather, during which birds face harsher environmental conditions, while Arizona has a more favourable winter climate. In addition, Lepczyk found that Michigan residents were more likely to provide high-quality supplementary foods (such as thistle and sunflower seeds) than those living in Arizona. One further pattern of interest can be seen in in Lepczyk's study: relatively fewer urban residents engaged in the provision of high-quality food than was the case for non-urban residents; they were, instead, more likely to provide food of a lower quality.

Similar findings were reported from Poland, where Tryjanowski *et al.* (2015) found that urban and rural areas differed in the availability of food, offered intentionally or unintentionally to wild birds during the winter months. Both intentional and unintentional food provision was greater within urban areas than it was in rural locations. While the number of bird feeders and feeding stations differed significantly between the two habitats, the proportion of feeders containing food was similar. Tryjanowkski found differences between the two habitats in the availability of several foodstuffs, with seed feeders and waste food significantly more common in the urban area and animal fat more common at rural sites.

There also clear regional differences in the types of food being provided for wild birds at garden feeding stations in different countries. While the main foods provided at garden feeding stations in the UK and elsewhere in Europe are seed-based, in North American backyards we see the additional use of sugar solution feeders for hummingbirds, and in Australia we see many more high-protein foods provided (such as meat and cheese), reflecting the differing range of species more commonly encountered in Australian backyards.

A BRIEF HISTORY OF FOODS AND FEEDERS

Quite where our willingness to feed wild birds originated is unclear but it is likely that food scraps have been provided to wild birds over hundreds of generations. Perhaps the earliest written evidence of material encouraging the feeding of wild birds is that provided in ancient Hindu writings from the Vedic period (c. 1500–500 BCE). This material describes the practice of *Bhuta Yajna*, which was one of the five great sacrifices used to develop the spiritual growth of a man. *Bhuta Yajna* involved the placing of food offerings known as *bali* on the ground; these being intended for 'animals, birds, insects, wandering outcastes and beings of the invisible worlds'.

Wild bird feeding in the form that we know it today receives very little mention in historical documents and it is not until the 1800s that we see references encouraging or supporting the practice. Allen (1967) refers to the *ornithotrophe*, a device developed by John Freeman Milward Dovaston – a minor romantic poet and regular contributor of articles to Loudon's *Magazine of Natural History*. The device was essentially a modified trough, fitted with rows of perches and filled with household and farmyard scraps. A man with an obvious talent for self-promotion, Dovaston promoted the device and its success in attracting birds through letters to the magazine penned under the pseudonym of Von Osdat. Reference to the device also made an appearance in notes to the preface of the first volume of Bewick's *A History of British Birds*. Bird tables were certainly in use by the 1850s, and promotion of feeding of urban birds is mentioned as early as 1875, through a piece that appeared in the 16 February edition of the *Edinburgh Evening News*. This article noted that a society for feeding birds in winter had established 22 feeding stations across the town, recognising their important role in controlling insect pests.

As Darryl Jones notes (Jones, 2018), perhaps one of the most important events in the development of bird feeding within the UK was the 1908 publication in English of a German book on how to attract and protect wild birds. Written by Martin Hieseman, the book was based on the work of Baron Hans Freiherr von

FIG 18. The use of coconut shells, filled with fat or suet, is still popular with both garden birds and those who feed them. (Mike Toms)

Berlepsch, a nobleman who had spent a considerable amount of time conducting ornithological experiments on his large estate. Included within the publication were several 'appliances' that had been developed to provide wild birds with food. Of these, the 'food bell' and 'food house' would be recognisable today; a somewhat more outlandish appliance – though you can see where the Baron was coming from – was the 'food tree'. This was a small spruce or fir tree over which a mixture of meat, bread, poppy flour, millet, oats, elderberries and seeds, bound together with beef or mutton fat, was poured. A smaller version of this appliance – the 'food stick' – presumably was aimed at those with less opportunity to produce small conifers quite so readily.

Over the ensuing decades more publications followed, some of which proved instrumental in shifting us towards today's pattern of year-round feeding. The growing interest in feeding wild birds was certainly being recognised as a characteristic of the UK population; a 1910 article in *Punch* magazine identified bird feeding as a national pastime and included a number of adverts for feeding devices. A major development in bird feeding occurred when Droll Yankees' 1960 A-6F tubular bird feeder was produced. This device supported the delivery of seed, particularly sunflower seed, keeping it dry and secure. More recent changes have largely sought to modify the successful Droll Yankees' design, for example by looking at the shape and positioning of the feeding ports and their associated perches.

THE TYPES OF FOODS PROVIDED

It wasn't just the development of feeding devices that proved to be important. In the US, the Kellogg Seed Company, which had been selling birdseed since the end of the First World War, brought a seed mix – the 'Audubon Society Mixture' – to market, a mix that had been developed in association with the Audubon Society following a series of experiments to determine which foods were preferred by wild birds. Five years later, 'Swoop' Wild Bird Food appeared in the UK and soon after that came new forms of sunflower seed and the tiny black seeds of Niger *Guizotia abyssinica*. While the main markets for wild birdseed are in Europe and North America, the key production areas lie elsewhere, in eastern Europe (particularly important for sunflower seed), China, India and Myanmar.

The foods provided at garden feeding stations differ in their composition, both in terms of macronutrients like carbohydrate, fat and protein, and micronutrients like calcium, carotenoids and vitamin E. All are important for birds, though in differing amounts and some may be more important at particular times of the year than at others. Protein, for example, plays an important role in female birds as they prepare for the demanding production of a clutch of eggs. When you look at the foods most commonly provided at garden feeding stations here in the UK, you soon discover that they typically have a higher fat content relative to that of protein: black sunflower seeds (fat 44.4 per cent : protein 18.0 per cent), peanuts (44.5 per cent : 28.7 per cent) and peanut cake (70.5 per cent : 17.1 per cent) (Jones, 2018). In addition to their carbohydrate, protein and fat content, foods like peanuts and sunflower seeds may be important sources of micronutrients, such as vitamin E. As will become clear later in this chapter, these micronutrients are not just important for the adult bird; they are also important for eggs and their developing embryos.

Sunflower seeds and sunflower hearts
The sunflower seeds used for bird feeding have a relatively high edible oil content, something that results from several decades of work using selective breeding. The plant itself originates in North America and was initially cultivated by Native Americans, the seed probably arriving in Europe through Spain.

FIG 19. Sunflower hearts, with their high edible oil content, are very popular with garden birds like Goldfinch. The popularity of these seeds has as much to do with Russian agronomists as it does with American entrepreneurs. (John Harding)

Russian agronomists took a great deal of interest in sunflower seeds and began a programme of work selecting for those that were high in oil, successfully delivering an increase in edible oil content from 20 per cent to almost 50 per cent. These high edible oil lines from Russia were reintroduced into North America after the Second World War, rekindling interest in the crop. It is from here that sunflower seeds appear to have entered the bird food market, although eastern Europe and Russia – which account for just under half of the worldwide production – are now the most important source for sunflowers entering the UK market. Worldwide production is about 40 million tonnes.

Sunflower seeds and their oil have a range of market uses, with the black-husked oilseed type a staple for bird food; this was introduced into the UK in the 1970s. Sunflower hearts were first introduced to the UK market during the early 2000s, their use proving popular with both wild birds and with the people putting out food. Unlike black sunflower seeds, hearts are already de-husked so leave less mess under bird feeders that then needs to be cleaned up. The lack of a husk also reduces handling times for feeding birds, which makes the hearts energetically more attractive that the traditional black sunflower seeds. At 6,100 kcal per kg, the calorie content of sunflower hearts is better than that of peanuts (5,700 kcal per kg); because the hearts have been de-husked, by weight they are also significantly higher in kcal than black sunflower seeds (5,000 kcal per kg).

Peanuts

Peanuts, also known as monkey nuts or groundnuts, are the edible seeds of *Arachis hypogaea*, a cultivated leguminous plant originating from a genus that developed in southwest Brazil and northeast Paraguay, where the most ancient species in the genus still grow. Available evidence suggests that *Arachis hypogaea* itself emerged within the hunter/cultivator communities present in Peru and/or Argentina. Peanut shells dated to 1800–1500 BCE have been excavated from sites near Casma and Bermejo in Peru and in the High Andes of northwest Argentina. There is also evidence of early presence in China, suggesting that mariners from China visited the South American region and returned home with peanuts. Evidence from shipwreck remains off the South American coast adds further support to this hypothesis.

In recent history, and up until the 1960s, peanut production was dominated by countries within the sub-Saharan region of Africa, but this changed rapidly following low yields, change in domestic policies and a reduction in market pull (Pazderka & Emmott, 2010). Over the same period (see Table 2), China became

TABLE 2. Peanut production and exportation at a global scale, 2001–07. Data from Pazderka & Emmot (2010).

Peanut production		Peanut exportation	
Country	*Volume (million tonnes)*	*County*	*Volume (million tonnes)*
China	13,936,443	China	700,391
India	6,869,829	Argentina	272,869
Nigeria	3,280,514	US	191,650
US	1,821,787	India	188,064
Indonesia	1,381,771	Netherlands	116,776
Myanmar	890,929	Vietnam	62,514
Sudan	782,286	Nicaragua	55,237
Senegal	526,637	Brazil	31,140
Vietnam	442,929	South Africa	25,832
Ghana	426,664	Gambia	19,000

the dominant producer of peanuts, securing 37 per cent of the producer market share by the mid-2000s and benefitting from internal agricultural reforms and the development of its market economy. Production within some countries (e.g. India and Indonesia) is more targeted towards internal markets than export and there has also been an interesting development in the market for value-added prepared peanuts, which is why the Netherlands features so prominently in the export table.

Peanuts can vary in their quality, both between regions and in relation to local climatic factors. There is, for example, a general acceptance that those produced in China are of better quality than those originating in India because of the higher oil content that they contain. With more than 100 countries cultivating peanuts, of many different varieties, it is easy to see how the wild bird food peanut market now has global reach. As we will discover in Chapter 4, peanuts are not without their problems; the presence of aflatoxin is a major threat to the market and to peanuts destined for wild bird food. In some years and areas, whole crops can be lost because of the presence of aflatoxin – which is toxic to both humans and birds – and this is why, for example, US producers can spend in excess of $27 million annually in order to ensure that their peanuts meet the agreed standards for aflatoxin control.

Peanuts were once a staple at UK garden feeding stations, initially presented in mesh bags, and to some extent still are for many of those who feed wild birds. However, the development of new seed mixes and the popularity of sunflower seeds and hearts with both birds and bird feeders have reduced their prominence. It is not unusual for those providing food to comment that the peanuts in their feeders often go largely untouched, except for visiting Great Spotted Woodpeckers and occasional Nuthatches *Sitta europaea*.

Seed mixes

A wide range of seed mixes is now available for use in feeding wild birds and these can vary greatly in their composition. In addition to seed-only mixes, some also include fat- or suet-based material or have invertebrate protein or fruit added to them. Watch a Greenfinch feeding at a feeder containing a seed mix and you'll soon discover that the bird will typically select certain seeds and drop others. This pattern of selection reflects the fact the different seeds and grains vary in both their nutritional content and in the time required to process them. A feeding bird is seemingly able to balance these two components and make an appropriate selection.

Recognising the different nutritional content of different types of seed, and wishing to secure an advantage in what is a highly competitive market, a

TABLE 3. The Birdcare Standards Association sets the following compulsory standards for seed mixes carrying the Birdcare Standards Association logo.

Seed mixes must comprise the following minimum and maximum percentages:				
Group 1	Group 2	Group 3	Group 4	Group 5
Minimum 20% (combined total): Black Sunflower; Sunflower Hearts; Peanut Granules; Niger; Suet Pellets; High Protein Soft foods (minimum 16%); & crumbles	Maximum 80% (combined total): Canary; Millet – red/ white/yellow/ panicum/jap/ hulled; Split/ cut Maize; Dari (also known as milo & sorghum); Pinhead Oatmeal; Small Striped Sunflower; Safflower; Hempseed	Maximum 20% (combined total): Medium Striped Sunflower; White Sunflower; Red Rape; Linseed; Mawseed; Gold of Pleasure; Sesame; Lettuce; Grass seeds; Buckwheat (hulled & whole); Dried fruits; Dried crustacean (i.e. *Gammarus*); Dried insects (i.e. Waterfly); Elderberries; Juniper Berries; Mountain Ash Berries; Rosehip; Dried Crickets; Whole Oats	Maximum 60% (combined total): Wheat; Naked Oats; Groats; Flaked Naked Oats; Flaked Wheat; Flaked Maize; Jumbo Oats	Maximum 5% (combined total): Grit (coral & oystershell); Black Rape/ Mustard

The following ingredients are not permitted in mixtures displaying the BSA logo:		
Whole Peanuts Biscuit Extruded Dried Pellets (e.g. dried biscuit) Seasoned/spiced or salted ingredients Large Striped Sunflower	Lentils Whole Pulses Vetch Whole Maize Flaked Barley	Dried Rice Split Peas Barley

number of wild bird care companies have signed up to the Birdcare Standards Association, an industry body that is governed by a set of guidelines. The guidelines for wild birdseed (see Table 3) effectively identify certain foodstuffs as being largely unsuitable. These, which include buckwheat and whole oats, sometimes feature prominently in cheaper seed mixes, where they effectively provide a bulking agent, which is little used by the birds. When looking for a seed mix, you often find that you get what you pay for, the better-quality mixes commanding a premium. However, you also need to consider the species that will be feeding on the mix; if, for example, the main recipients will be House Sparrows, then a mix with larger seeds and grains is likely to be better used than one which is made mostly of smaller seeds which the sparrows find difficult and time-consuming to process.

Niger

The small seeds of Niger were originally used to produce a cooking oil by peoples living within eastern Africa, and cultivation probably first occurred in the Ethiopian highlands. The seed was renamed 'Nyjer' in the US, in part to clarify its pronunciation and avoid unfortunate associations with a similar-looking slang word, being registered as a trademark of Wild Bird Feeding Industry, a now well-established US company, in 1998. It is sometimes referred to, incorrectly, as 'thistle' seed. As a flower, Niger had certainly been introduced to British gardens by 1806, and the species has been known in the wild since 1876. There is a suggestion from national botanical surveys that its occurrence in the wild is increasing, perhaps because of its use in bird food. As a commercial crop, Niger is mainly grown in India, Ethiopia and – to a lesser extent – Myanmar, underlining the global scale of production that ends up on UK garden centre shelves.

Use as a supplementary food for wild birds came rather later, the seed starting as something of a niche 'conditioning' product used by cage bird enthusiasts. It was known to be popular with American Goldfinch *Spinus tristis* and Pine Siskin *Spinus pinus* in the US in the 1960s, and it was the association with Goldfinches here in the UK that helped its popularity to increase. The seed's small size leads to it being favoured by fine-billed species like Goldfinch and Siskin, with larger-billed species finding it too delicate to bother with. The small size also requires the use of a special 'nyjer feeder', whose small feeding ports prevent the seed from flowing out of the feeder and onto the ground – which is what happens if you inadvertently put the seed into a standard feeder. Initially, it seems that the provision of Niger seed at garden feeding stations encouraged the arrival of Goldfinches, with some participants in the BTO Garden BirdWatch scheme commenting on how they had never had visiting Goldfinches until they started provisioning the seed. Others, however, failed to attract them to Niger, even where it was provided alongside other foods at garden feeding stations. One of the interesting patterns of Niger use by Goldfinches appears to be the move away to sunflower hearts over recent years; this may be linked to the decline in

FIG 20. With their fine bill, Siskins are one of the species to have taken to Niger seeds, though they seem to prefer sunflower hearts if these are available and there is little competition from larger species like Greenfinch. (John Harding)

UK Greenfinch populations following the emergence of finch trichomonosis (see Chapter 4) and the release of Goldfinches from competition with this larger and more dominant species. Niger seed may still be an important food for Siskin and Lesser Redpoll *Acanthis cabaret*, the latter species now being seen more commonly at UK garden feeding stations.

Fat and suet products

Although highly variable in terms of their content, a high-quality fat product may have in excess of 8,500 kcal per kg, something that makes these products particularly attractive for use during the winter months. Fat- and suet-based products come in a diversity of forms, probably the most familiar of which are 'fat balls' and square or rectangular blocks. Fat balls almost always used to be sold within plastic mesh netting, something that was occasionally responsible for the death of a feeding bird, either caught by its foot or by its barbed tongue. Although a substantial number of netted fat balls are still sold (and purchased) within the UK market, there has been a welcome move towards un-netted fat balls.

Suet may also be presented in a pelletised form, something that is popular with Starlings, or in or around objects such as plastic sticks or coconut shells – popular with Blue Tits and Great Tits. Suet products often contain additional material, perhaps added to increase the range of species that will take it, to broaden its nutritional composition or to secure a marketing advantage. These include seeds, nuts, berries and insect protein (typically mealworms). Suet products may also contain ash in variable quantities, added in order to bind the material together and to reduce the chances of the product breaking down. Again, the Bird Care Standards Association has a set of rules relating to this type of product, though these are geared more towards the source of the fat, rather than the composition of the product or content of additional material. The standards are as follows:

i)   suet should be derived from animals that have received ante- and post-mortem examination by veterinary officers and found to be fit for human consumption;

ii) all suet should be processed at a fully licensed and approved EU or US abattoir, and

iii) any suet products that are blended with peanuts, either in whole or granular form, must use peanuts that contain a nil detectable aflatoxin level.

Live foods

The term 'live foods' refers to the provision of insects, typically mealworms and wax worms, which are bred specifically for this and the wider pet food market. These may be provided alive or, more commonly, in a desiccated form. Mealworms are not worms but larvae of darkling beetles belonging to the genus *Tenebrio*. Within the UK it is the larvae of the Yellow Mealworm *Tenebrio molitor* that are most commonly used as food for wild and aviary birds, captive reptiles and amphibians. The smaller sized larvae of the Dark Mealworm *Tenebrio obscura* are sometimes used. As their name suggests, mealworms have a long association with human beings, occurring as pests of grain and other cereal products. Mealworms are fairly easy to rear, both at home and commercially, and a number of companies are now involved in the large-scale farming of these beetles, producing insect protein not just for wild birds and the pets already mentioned but also as a contribution to cat and dog food products and, looking to the future, human foods (Grau *et al.*, 2017).

FIG 21. Mealworms are often very popular with Starlings, Robins and Blackbirds, with individual birds quickly learning to exploit them where they are offered. (John Harding)

Wild birds seem to prefer live mealworms, presumably because they attract attention by their movements, but probably because they are far closer in their composition to wild caught food. Mealworms have a high protein (13–22 per cent) and fat (9–20 per cent) content and are also a source of polyunsaturated fatty acids, essential amino acids and zinc. Perhaps surprisingly, they have a significantly higher nutritional value than either beef or chicken.

Other foods
Bread appears to be a popular food with householders, perhaps because it provides an opportunity for them to direct unwanted crusts or stale slices towards other creatures perceived to be in need of sustenance. Its nutritional value is, in the context of garden birds, unclear. Bread was by far the commonest food provided by householders who responded to a questionnaire survey carried out in Cardiff in the 1980s (Cowie & Hinsley, 1988a), with *c.* 90 per cent of respondents provisioning bread in both winter and summer. Galbraith *et al.* (2014) found bread to be the most commonly provisioned food in their study, estimating that the equivalent of more than five million loaves was put out by New Zealand residents annually.

FIG 22. A small number of UK householders put out meat scraps or even whole carcasses for visiting Red Kites. (Jill Pakenham)

Apart from the small number of householders nationally who provide meat for visiting Red Kites *Milvus milvus*, only a small proportion of the kitchen scraps fed to wild birds here in the UK include meat. The situation is very different in Australia where the provision of meat is fairly typical. This reflects clear differences between the main groups of birds visiting garden feeding stations here in the UK (seed-eating species) and in Australia (omnivorous species, such as Laughing Kookabura *Dacelo novaeguineae*, Australian Magpie *Gymnorhina tibicen* and Grey Butcherbird *Cracticus torquatus*). As we'll see later in this chapter, the provision of meat has potential implications for wild bird health.

In parts of North America, sugar solution is used to attract and feed hummingbirds. Typically made from one-part cane sugar to four-parts water, the solution is seen as a supplementary food rather than a replacement for the sugars that these tiny birds would normally secure from flowers. While those hummingbirds tested appear to be more strongly influenced by the position of a food source rather than its colour, many feeders are red in colour because this is perceived as increasing their attractiveness to hummingbirds. Once a food source has been identified, colour may act as an important discriminator stimulus and it may be that individuals learn to associate this colour with these new nectaring opportunities (Miller & Miller, 1971). The increasing use of hummingbird feeders has been linked to the changes in the range of Anna's Hummingbird *Calypte anna*, a species that now overwinters and presumably breeds at more northerly latitudes than it did a few decades ago. Examination of Project FeederWatch data (see Chapter 6 for more on this project) demonstrates that more participants in the large-scale study now offer sugar solution in hummingbird feeders than once did, though it is unclear whether the increase in feeder provision has driven the range expansion of this hummingbird species, or the range expansion has led to more people putting out hummingbird feeders (Greig *et al.*, 2017).

THE NATURAL FOODS AVAILABLE WITHIN GARDENS

Invertebrates

Many of the birds making use of garden feeding stations also feed on invertebrates; for some garden birds, such as Wren, it is the insects and spiders found within the garden that are the food of choice. Because species like Wren usually ignore the food provided at bird tables and in hanging feeders, their presence in the garden can be easily overlooked. We don't know a great deal about how the features present within gardens and across the wider urban environment shape the community of invertebrates that is found there. While there are some obvious relationships, others are masked by the complexity of the many microhabitats present and the influence of components within the wider landscape. Work carried out as part of the Biodiversity in Urban Gardens project (BUGS) underlines the difficulties in seeking to identify relationships between invertebrate abundance and particular features (Smith *et al.*, 2006a).

The plant species growing within gardens will have a shaping influence on many of the invertebrate species present, not least because the plants provide many of the feeding opportunities that such invertebrates require. A typical garden flora will almost certainly comprise a mixture of native and non-native species, and the latter may prove unsuitable for insects because of their chemical composition or structural characteristics. Things may not be as bad as you might assume, however, since the chemistry of individual plant species tends to be fairly similar within a family and many of the non-native plants introduced into UK gardens belong to families that also contain a native component. The BUGS project revealed that of the 1,166 plant species recorded in 61 Sheffield gardens, 70 per cent were non-native; however, at the family level, just 36 per cent of the families were alien in origin (Smith *et al.*, 2006b).

FIG 23. While some hoverfly species avoid being predated by mimicking less palatable species, other garden-visiting flies may be taken by Spotted Flycatchers and other bird species. (Mike Toms)

Despite this, there is evidence from work carried out in the suburban landscapes of southeastern Pennsylvania, US, that native planting can be better for both invertebrates and the birds that feed on them (Burghardt *et al.*, 2008). Karin Burghardt and colleagues looked at a number of avian and lepidopteran community measures across paired suburban properties, one property in each pair being planted with entirely native plants and the other with a conventional suburban mix of natives and non-natives. The native-planted properties were found to support significantly more caterpillars and range of caterpillar species and had a significantly greater abundance, species richness and diversity of birds; they also had more breeding pairs of native bird species.

The structure of plants can be an issue where the cultivars presented in garden centres and plant catalogues are divergent from native forms. For example, the 'double cultivars' of certain flower forms, which prove popular with gardeners because of their extended flowering season and novel appearance, are less suitable for nectar-feeding insects and they also set less seed. If flower selection and form reduces opportunities for invertebrates within the garden,

FIG 24. The larvae of craneflies and other soil-dwelling invertebrates taken from garden lawns are important for Starlings and other species. (Jill Pakenham)

then it will also reduce opportunities for insect-eating birds. One consequence of this can be seen in the generally lower productivity of tit species within the urban environment. Great Tits and Blue Tits feed their young on small caterpillars and appear to struggle to find enough of these in many urban and suburban gardens (Cowie & Hinsley, 1987).

It is also important to recognise the widespread use of insecticides and related compounds in gardens, since these have the potential to both reduce prey availability and to enter the food chain, where problems may then occur. More widely within the built environment there is the risk from pollution, such as with heavy metals (see Chapter 4), which can also impact on the availability of invertebrates and alter the composition of the prey communities available to foraging birds (Eeva *et al.*, 2005).

Fruits, seeds and nectar

Garden plants can also provide food for visiting birds more directly, through their fruits and seeds; in fact, many plants rely on birds to act as dispersal agents for their seeds, offering a nutritious fleshy fruit to attract the bird to take the seed. For example, the natural foods taken by garden-wintering Blackcaps include the berries of *Cotoneaster*, Honeysuckle *Lonicera*, Holly *Ilex aquifolium*, Mistletoe *Viscum album* and Sea-buckthorn *Hippophae rhamnoides*. Blackcaps have also been reported feeding on the seeds of Daisy Bush *Brachyglottis greyi* (Hardy, 1978). The different fruits and seeds become available at different times of the year, though predominantly from October through to January, and this can alter the shape of the bird community visiting gardens. The movement into gardens of wintering Redwing, Fieldfare and Waxwing may reflect the availability of favoured berries in gardens and their scarcity elsewhere. It has been noted, for example, that the timing of hedgerow cutting within the UK's arable landscapes may remove large quantities of the berry standing crop from the wider landscape, leaving gardens as an important resource (Croxton & Sparks, 2004).

Some of these berries are favoured over others and in some cases a long fruiting season, such as in Holly, can suggest that the berry isn't particularly favoured by visiting birds, only being eaten once other options are no longer available. In addition to the differences seen between different plant species, the nutritional characteristics of individual fruits may also vary with season. In many berries, the water content of the pulp decreases as the season progresses, while the average lipid content increases. Berry colour may be used as a signal, alerting berry-eating birds to the reward on offer, and there is evidence that birds may select fruits of a particular colour because of their nutritional value. Some bird species appear to select fruits with a high anthocyanin content; anthocyanin is an antioxidant and berries rich in this pigment tend to be black in colour or ultraviolet reflecting. Work on Blackcaps indicates that individuals actively select for anthocyanins in their diet and that they use fruit colour as an honest signal of anthocyanin rewards when foraging (Schaefer *et al.*, 2007).

The consequences of the variation seen in fruits leads to species-specific preferences within the bird species that feed upon them. A series of studies by David and Barbara Snow has highlighted some of these preferences. Mistle Thrush, for example, was found to favour sloes over haws, while the preference was reversed in both Redwing and Fieldfare. Song Thrush *Turdus philomelos* showed a clear preference for Yew *Taxus baccata*, Elder *Sambucus nigra* and Guelder Rose *Viburnum opulus*, and the apparent avoidance of rosehips, while Blackbird was found to be fairly catholic in its tastes (Snow & Snow, 1988). Blackcaps make use of smaller berries in gardens, such as those of *Cotoneaster*

FIG 25. Berry-producing garden shrubs can be very popular with Mistle Thrushes and other visiting thrushes, together with Blackcaps and Waxwings. (John Harding)

conspicua (Fitzpatrick, 1996a), reflecting their almost entirely frugivorous diet (when fruit is available) within the Mediterranean wintering area (Jordano & Herrera, 1981), although it is interesting to note the importance of supplementary foods presented at garden feeding stations highlighted by Plummer *et al.* (2015) and explored later in this chapter.

The presence of non-native berry-producing shrubs in gardens, while potentially a valuable food resource for visiting birds, brings with it a possible conservation issue. Since birds are the main dispersal agent for the seeds held within berries, they are a potential route by which non-native species may become more widely established within the wider countryside (Greenberg & Walter, 2010).

It is not just the berries that birds seek; some, such as Greenfinch, are after the seeds themselves. This can prompt plants to incorporate toxic compounds into the seed coat or its lining. Although it is the absence within the wider countryside of the seeds of larger shrubs and trees that can drive birds to garden feeding stations (see later in this chapter), it is important to note that some of our garden birds specialise in the seeds of smaller plants. The Goldfinch, for

TABLE 4. Suitable plants for providing berries and seeds for garden birds. Adapted from Toms *et al.*, (2008).

Suitable berry-producing plants for birds	Suitable seed-producing plants for birds
Bird Cherry *Prunus padus*	Alder *Alnus glutinosa*
Blackberry *Rubus fruticosus* agg.	Beech *Fagus sylvaticus*
Blackthorn *Prunus spinosa*	Dandelion *Taraxacum* spp.
Crabapple *Malus sylvestris*	Devil's Bit Scabious *Succisa pratensis*
Dog Rose *Rosa canina*	Field Scabious *Knautia arvensis*
Elder *Sambucus nigra*	Greater Knapweed *Centaurea scabiosa*
Guelder Rose *Viburnum opulus*	Hazel *Corylus avellana*
Hawthorn *Crataegus monogyna*	Hornbeam *Carpinus betulus*
Holly *Ilex aquifolium*	Lavender *Lavandula* spp.
Honeysuckle *Lonicera periclymenum*	Lemon Balm *Melissa officinalis*
Ivy *Hedera helix*	Silver Birch *Betula pendula*
Mezereon *Daphne mezereon*	Sunflower *Helianthus annuus*
Midland Hawthorn *Crataegus laevigata*	Teasel *Dipsacus fullonum*
Mistletoe *Viscum album*	Thistles *Carduus* spp./*Cirsium* spp.
Perfoliate Honeysuckle *Lonicera caprifolium*	
Oregon Grape *Mahonia aquifolium*	
Chinese Photinia *Photinia davidiana*	
Rowan *Sorbus aucuparia*	
Sea-buckthorn *Hippophae rhamnoides*	
Wayfaring Tree *Viburnum lantana*	
Whitebeam *Sorbus aria*	
Wild Cherry *Prunus avium*	
Wild Privet *Ligustrum vulgare*	
Wild Service Tree *Sorbus torminalis*	
Yew *Taxus baccata*	

example, specialises in seeds of the Compositae family, particularly the thistles and dandelions and it is this habit that probably first brought them into gardens to feed on ornamental thistles, teasel, lavender and cornflower (Glue, 1996). Maddock (1988) reports how, from the winter of 1983/84, a few Goldfinches would visit a suburban Oxfordshire garden to feed on lavender and dry teasel heads. Their interest was maintained by brushing the teasel heads with Niger. Over the following winter, up to two dozen Goldfinches again visited the teasel head before turning to a mix of Niger, canary seed and millet provided at a garden feeding station. Important berry- and seed-producing plants for birds are shown in Table 4.

On occasion, garden birds have been reported stealing nectar from flowering plants, the latter typically exotic species whose flowers show features used to attract birds as pollinators (Búrquez, 1989; Proctor *et al.*, 1996). Reports from within the UK have included Blue Tit – feeding from Crown Imperial *Fritillaria imperialis* (Thompson *et al.*, 1996); Blackcap – feeding from *Mahonia* (Harrup, 1998); and Blackcap feeding from *Kniphofia*. In addition, the behaviour is widely recognised in a number of the warbler species migrating through the Mediterranean region (Cecere *et al.*, 2011). Nectar feeding has also been recorded for a number of European plants (see the review by Ford, 1985), including those in the genera *Rhamnus, Ferula, Acer, Crataegus, Ribes* and *Salix*.

Nectar feeding is thought to be a widespread behaviour in UK Blue Tits, with the species recorded feeding from a variety of flowers across 33 counties within the UK (Fitzpatrick, 1994). There has also been a small amount of more detailed work, examining the contribution that nectar taken from Flowering Currant *Ribes sanguineum* makes to Blue Tit spring diet (Fitzpatrick, 1994). This revealed that although the nectar was not the preferred food – it was used most when peanuts were unavailable because of competition from other birds – it was a highly profitable food source, contributing up to 50 per cent of the average daily metabolic rates of the Blue Tits studied. The use of nectar sources by suburban populations of predominantly nectar-feeding birds has been examined in Australia, with a view to understanding the contribution that native and exotic shrubs make towards the available nectar resource (French *et al.*, 2005).

FOOD SELECTION BY GARDEN BIRDS

The contribution that food provisioned at garden feeding stations makes to the energetic and nutritional requirements of garden birds varies between seasons and between species. It also varies between the different types of food provided, with some higher in fat or protein content than others, and with differences in the amount of time required to 'handle' and process the food. It is difficult to study the feeding preferences of birds out in the field, particularly in a garden setting where individual birds can find alternative feeding opportunities nearby. A small amount of work has been done here in the UK with, for example, Greenwood & Clarke (1991) examining the selection of black-striped sunflower seeds and peanuts – peanuts were the preferred food taken.

One of the biggest studies to have been carried out was that undertaken by Geis (1980) in the United States. The study, carried out between November 1977 and July 1979, made use of a network of volunteers, observing and recording feeding preferences at specially designed feeding stations, capturing details of 179,000 feeding visits. Geis adopted a standard approach, whereby the food types

FIG 26. Large-billed species like House Sparrow are more likely to take larger seeds from a seed mix, the smallest seeds being difficult for them to handle. (John Harding)

being tested were compared against two 'standard' foods commonly provided by householders: black-striped sunflower seed and white proso millet. The results of the work underlined a general pattern of preferences across the bird species visiting and also highlighted the individual preferences of particular species. American Goldfinch, for example, favoured hulled sunflower seeds over Niger, with Niger favoured over oil-type sunflower seeds, black-striped sunflower seeds and white proso millet. In contrast, House Sparrows favoured white proso millet but would feed on almost anything, with the exception of flax and rape seed. Selection of Niger by fine-billed finches is something that has been documented in other studies (Horn *et al.*, 2014).

The abilities of wild birds to select foodstuffs based on their nutritional characteristics is, as we have just seen in relation to fruits and berries, evident from observational studies; it is also evident from experimental work, though this is more limited. Work on Common Myna *Acridotheres tristis* has, for example, revealed that urban populations display a strong preference for food with a high protein content, favouring this over foods with high lipid and high carbohydrate contents in field-based trials (Machovsky-Capuska *et al.*, 2016). This work suggested that these urban Common Mynas were protein limited, something reinforced by the way in which the birds competed for access to this food.

Two reportedly individually identifiable Blue Tits, visiting a bird feeder in a suburban Belfast garden during winter, were estimated to have obtained 25.36 per cent and 44.47 per cent of their daily energy requirements from peanuts (Fitzpatrick, 1995); comparable figures from the same study for two Great Tits were 16.41 per cent and 22.2 per cent. Although this study doesn't adequately deal with questions over how the birds could be recognised as individuals from their plumage characteristics, the work has been used to suggest that these suburban individuals were obtaining a significant component of their daily energy requirement from the food supplied. Better-documented studies, this time on provisioned Black-capped Chickadees *Poecile atricapillus* in Alaska, found that individuals were obtaining up to 29 per cent of their daily energy requirements from the food supplied (Brittingham & Temple, 1992a; Karasov *et al.*, 1992).

Selection for particular food items might also be shaped by how that food is presented. Garden bird species that would feed within trees and shrubs when foraging in the wider countryside – such as the tits – were some of the first to take advantage of seeds and peanuts presented in hanging feeders and mesh

FIG 27. Like Robin and Wren, the Dunnock prefers to feed on the ground but it will venture onto bird tables and, occasionally, onto hanging feeders. (John Harding)

cages. The strong feet of these species enable them to grip hold of small perches or mesh, something that ground-feeding species like Robin, Dunnock and Blackbird would find too challenging. These latter species would be more likely to feed from a bird table or to take food from the ground. Changes in feeder design, most notably in the shape and size of feeder perches, can exert a big influence on which birds are then able to feed. The move from a straight perch to an 'o' shaped perch seems to have aided Robins to feed from hanging feeders. The advice to those feeding garden birds is to feed a range of foods in a number of different ways, providing opportunities for the different species and their favoured means and locations for taking food.

HOW AND WHEN BIRDS USE GARDEN FEEDERS

As we will see in the following section, the use of garden feeding stations is influenced by food availability over wider areas, from that available in the nearby countryside to that available many hundreds of miles away in other countries. Before we turn to look at the use of gardens in this wider context, we will start by looking at how the location of feeding opportunities within a garden can influence its use. The foraging behaviour of small birds is influenced by the conflicting demands of needing to feed but also to avoid predators; during the breeding season, the need to maintain a territory and attract a mate can, for many individuals, also be added to these demands (Lima & Dill, 1990). These considerations are likely to influence key decisions about where and when to feed, and we know, for example, that the pattern of arrivals and departures throughout the day at garden feeding stations is shaped by the balance of risk between starvation and predation.

Juvenile Blue Tits and Great Tits are known to be subordinate to older individuals and have been shown to make greater use of bird feeders located further from cover (and with a higher risk of Sparrowhawk *Accipiter nisus* predation) than adult birds. Hinsley *et al.* (1995) reported that 40 per cent of the tits they trapped at a feeder located close to cover were adults, with this figure dropping to 17 per cent at a feeder located further away. Another garden-based study found a similar pattern, this time looking at a number of garden bird species (Cowie & Simons, 1991). Cowie and Simons found that total food consumption declined with distance from cover in their experimental study using feeders positioned at different distances from vegetation. The House Sparrows in their study only used the feeder closest to cover, with Blue Tit only slightly more willing to feed further out into the garden. Only Greenfinch seemed comfortable feeding on the more exposed feeders; this species tended to arrive to feed in sizeable flocks and it seems likely that this flocking behaviour increased the chances that a potential predator would be spotted early enough for the birds to make their escape. Interestingly, the proportion of time that individual birds spent manipulating food items decreased in favour of increased vigilance when birds were feeding further from cover, again underlining the need to balance the energetic and nutritional returns against the risk of predation. Krebs (1980), looking at handling times in Great Tits, found that food-deprived individuals demonstrated shorter food-handling times than satiated individuals, presumably because they spent less time scanning for predators in order to take on board as much food as possible. A study by Suhonen (1993) has also demonstrated that foraging site selection in tits – this time mixed flocks of Crested Tit *Lophophanes cristatus* and Willow Tit *Poecile montana* – is influenced by a combination of the dominance relationships present and the perceived risk of predation by Pygmy Owls *Glaucidium passerinum*.

Most small birds will rush to the available cover if a predator is detected nearby; at some point they must then make a decision to leave the safety that the

FIG 28. The small size of the Coal Tit, and its low ranking within the garden bird dominance hierarchy, may be one reason why this species often takes a seed from a garden feeding station to eat it in a nearby bush or shrub. It may also cache seed for use at a later date. (John Harding)

cover provides in order to resume feeding. Several pieces of work demonstrate that this return to feeding is influenced by the age and status of the individuals involved. De Laet (1985), Hegner (1985) and Hogstad (1988) found that dominant Great Tits, Blue Tits and Willow Tits (respectively) typically would not leave the available cover until subordinate individuals had first done so. Some individuals will make use of the available cover more directly, for example by carrying food items from feeders into nearby cover for consumption. Research has demonstrated that the chances of a bird doing this increase as the distance to cover decreases, the size of the food item increases or if the individual is less dominant than other individuals that are also using the feeding stations. In the UK, Coal Tits will often remove food from feeding stations to consume elsewhere, presumably because they are some way down the pecking order.

The balance of energetic demands, predation risk and competition from other individuals also shapes the time at which birds feed over the course of a day. We are all familiar with the dawn peak in feeding activity seen in garden birds here in the UK. However, this is not the only peak in activity seen at garden feeding stations, since many observers have reported a second peak towards late morning and a third just before dusk. Fitzpatrick (1997) examined these temporal patterns in feeder use by studying the birds visiting feeders in a Belfast garden. Her work, carried out during the winter months, revealed the patterns of activity at garden feeders for House Sparrow, Blue Tit and Great Tit. Although there were some differences between the three species, the broad patterns underlined the three peaks reported elsewhere.

The use of garden feeders may also be influenced by which other species are present, perhaps mediated through dominance hierarchies (see Chapter 6), or because of individual behaviour. The use of camera traps and PIT tags (which allow the automated identification of individual birds) has enabled researchers to look at some of the factors that may modify the ways in which feeding stations are accessed. Galbraith *et al.* (2017b), for example, have been able to establish if individual birds are consistent in their use of supplementary food over time or whether use might vary seasonally. Working in New Zealand, the researchers found that although House Sparrows were numerous at monitored feeding stations, individuals were highly variable in their feeder use. In contrast, feeding station use by visiting Spotted Doves *Streptopelia chinensis* tended to be based around a core group of individuals who were highly consistent in their behaviour. Work carried out in the UK (Crates *et al.*, 2016; Jack, 2016) has also reported variation between both species and individuals in their use of feeding stations.

THE USE OF GARDEN FEEDING STATIONS AND GARDEN TYPE

The extent to which garden feeding stations are used is shaped first and foremost by where the garden is located; put up a peanut feeder in a garden in the Scottish Highlands and you might just attract Crested Tit; place the same feeder in a garden in suburban Surrey and you won't, but you might attract Ring-necked Parakeet. In addition to geography, the nature of the surrounding habitat will play its part. A rural garden in the east of England, surrounded by farmland, might receive visiting Yellowhammer and Reed Bunting *Emberiza schoeniclus* late in the winter when farmland seed supplies are very low, while one located next to a conifer plantation will be visited by Siskin and Coal Tit. We might therefore expect some general patterns to arise, indicating the likely garden bird community in gardens of different types and located within different landscapes. This is something that we have been able to examine by using data from BTO

FIG 29. Black-headed Gulls are occasional visitors to garden feeding stations, rarely seen in summer when they have their characteristic chocolate brown heads, but sometimes forced to turn to gardens during periods of poor winter weather. (John Harding)

Garden BirdWatch (see Chapter 6 for more on this project). This work looked at the probability of occurrence in Garden BirdWatch gardens for 40 species (Chamberlain *et al.*, 2004a). There were 26 species that showed a significant association with the habitat character outside of the garden and in most cases the probability of occurrence was higher in gardens located within rural habitats. For several species the probability of occurrence was very low in all but the most rural habitats (Pied Wagtail, Rook, Siskin – winter only – and Yellowhammer). Interestingly, there were some species that were more likely to occur in gardens located within more urbanised habitats, including: Black-headed Gull (medium and large gardens), Feral Pigeon, Magpie (large gardens), Starling and House Sparrow. Several species showed obvious peaks in their occurrence at intermediate scores, suggesting an association with suburban gardens; these included Coal Tit, Long-tailed Tit *Aegithalos caudatus*, Nuthatch, Treecreeper *Certhia familiaris*, Jay *Garrulus glandarius*, Magpie (medium gardens) and Bullfinch *Pyrrhula pyrrhula*.

THE USE OF GARDEN FEEDERS IN RELATION TO WIDER AVAILABILITY OF FOOD

As we have just touched on, the use of garden feeders by seed-eating birds is likely to be influenced by the availability of favoured seeds within the wider environment. This is likely to be particularly relevant in relation to tree seeds, since many tree species produce very large numbers of seeds in some years but not others – a process known as masting. In mast years, the very large volume of seeds produced is thought to saturate seed predators with an over-abundance of food, leaving some seeds to germinate untouched. Since the seed crop produced the following year is typically very much smaller, the populations of seed predators are prevented from growing sharply, leaving the balance in favour of the trees when they next come to produce a bumper crop. A number of studies have shown that the population size and breeding performance of various bird species is linked to these masting events. But can such masting events influence the extent to which seed-eating birds make use of garden feeding stations?

This is something that has been investigated by using the garden bird datasets collected by the BTO through the Garden Bird Feeding Survey (for Beech *Fagus sylvatica*) and Garden BirdWatch (for Sitka Spruce *Picea sitchensis*). Chamberlain *et al.* (2007a) found that the probability of occurrence at garden feeding stations for seven beechmast-eating species (Great Spotted Woodpecker, Woodpigeon, Great Tit, Coal Tit, Nuthatch, Jay and Chaffinch) was significantly

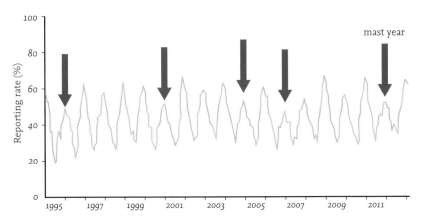

FIG 30. Coal Tits make greater use of garden feeding stations in those winters when the Sitka Spruce seed crop is poor. Data reproduced from BTO Garden BirdWatch with permission.

lower in those years when a masting event occurred. A similar pattern was found for Siskin and Coal Tit in relation to Sitka Spruce, a species known to produce mast crops at intervals of three to five years (McKenzie *et al.*, 2007). The seed and cone crops produced by these trees are synchronised, within a species, over very large areas, which is why such patterns can be seen very clearly in the BTO datasets. As we will see in the final chapter of this book, Sitka Spruce has been of particular importance to Coal Tit and Siskin populations within the UK, with its small seeds (relative to those of other conifers) proving particularly valuable. The availability of conifer seed to small birds may also be shaped by weather conditions, since it is known that conifer cones open to release their seed on dry days but remain firmly closed when it is wet (Harris, 1969). This may explain the apparent increase in bird-feeder use witnessed in my own garden on damp days during late winter, when Siskin numbers generally peak within gardens.

There is also evidence of a movement into (largely) rural gardens during the late winter period, with farmland buntings and finches showing their annual peak in garden use at this time according to data from BTO Garden BirdWatch (see Figure 31). The late winter period is known to be a difficult time for seed-eating birds using farmland habitats, the loss of overwinter stubbles leaving a 'hungry gap' in food availability (Siriwardena *et al.*, 2008), something that may prompt the birds to aggregate in patches of habitat where seeds can still be found (Gillings *et al.*, 2008) or to move out of farmland and into other habitats (Gillings & Beaven,

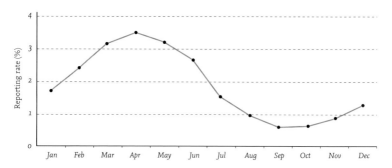

FIG 31. The use of garden feeding stations by Yellowhammers peaks during the second half of the winter, a period during which farmland seed supplies are at their lowest. Data reproduced from BTO Garden BirdWatch with permission.

2004). Examination of data from the Winter Farmland Bird Survey (Gillings & Beaven, 2004), alongside that from BTO Garden BirdWatch for the same weeks, is suggestive of a movement out of farmland and into gardens for Goldfinch and potentially other species (Figure 32). Further supporting evidence comes from the long-running Garden Bird Feeding Survey. This shows an increase in the use of gardens by Reed Bunting and Yellowhammer during the period of greatest agricultural intensification (Chamberlain *et al.*, 2003; 2005); although not supported by formal statistical tests, it could reflect increased use of garden foods because of a decline in seed availability within wider farming landscapes.

Work carried out in France supports the value of rural gardens for farmland birds during the winter months. Using data from the French Garden Birdwatch scheme, Pierret & Jiguet (2018) looked at garden use by farmland bird species along a gradient denoting agricultural intensification. Garden feeders located within intensively cultivated landscapes were found to attract more birds, with this relationship strongest for truly farmland species. The pattern became more pronounced as the winter progressed, suggesting that as farmland seed supplies become depleted, so farmland birds increasingly turn to gardens.

One scarce farmland bird for which a number of rural gardens may be of particular importance within the UK is the Cirl Bunting *Emberiza cirlus*, whose small Devonshire population makes regular use of garden feeding stations in the south of the county during the winter months. Of course, to fully understand the role that gardens play in the ecology of bird communities breeding within farmland, we need to be able to track their individual movements, something that is becoming increasingly possible through the use of emerging technologies,

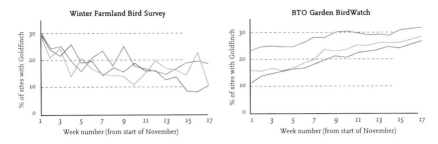

FIG 32. Data from two BTO surveys suggest a movement into gardens by Goldfinches as the winter progresses, something that could be studied in greater detail through the use of ringing or tagging technologies. Data reproduced from BTO with permission.

such as PIT tags. The pull of garden feeding stations has wider implications for those involved in survey work, particularly during the winter months. Ask any volunteer who has participated in bird atlasing during the winter months, and found themselves in an area of open country, and they will tell you how it is the rural gardens and their feeding stations that are the place to look for small birds. This effect has been studied experimentally through work carried out in Maine, US, where researchers were testing a bird survey technique widely used in the breeding season and involving an observer making a series of stops along a linear and driven route. At each stop the observer would carry out a 'point count' noting the bird species recorded during a fixed time interval before moving on to the next stop. By examining the densities of birds recorded at stops with and without a feeding station, the researchers found that for five species densities were higher at stops with feeding stations. As well as this, presence of the food appeared to influence the birds' habitat selection, pulling them into edge habitats.

IS THE PROVISION OF SUPPLEMENTARY FOOD FOR WILD BIRDS A GOOD THING?

Little work has been done to examine differences in the potential costs or benefits of different types of food – at its simplest, high-quality or low-quality foods. We are not yet in a position to be able to determine whether it is better to encourage people to feed wild birds, regardless of the type of food that they provide, because it fosters a sense of connection with the natural world, or discourage the provision of feeding altogether if we cannot provide foods that are entirely suitable for the species that we are trying to help. We provide supplementary food and garden for wildlife more generally because we see these activities as being beneficial for wildlife. However, while these resource subsidies and habitat modifications may provide opportunities for birds and other wildlife within our increasingly urbanised landscapes, they may also fundamentally alter ecological processes and community structure (Shochat, 2004). Understanding these potential impacts requires new research.

Later in this chapter we will look in more detail at some of the costs and benefits for birds of feeding on food provided at garden feeding stations (or experimentally in other habitats). One study, however, is worth mentioning here since it nicely summarises some of these costs and benefits. The study in question was carried out over three years and examined how bird feeding impacts bird health – something that involved looking at body condition, stress, antioxidant levels, nutritional condition, immune function and levels of disease – for wild bird communities in two forested sites, one where food was provisioned and one where it wasn't (Wilcoxen et al., 2015). Wilcoxen's study revealed some clear and beneficial effects; birds at the fed site had significantly larger fat stores, greater antioxidant capacity and reduced stress. In addition, fed birds also showed better body condition and better nutritional condition, though not in every year. However, fed birds were more likely to be suffering from disease. Ten months after the feeding experiment had ended, the researchers repeated the sampling carried out at the two sites; this time the differences had gone, adding further supporting evidence that the differences had been due to the provision of food. Feeding does, it seems, deliver some health benefits, but these come with a certain level of cost.

DOES PROVIDING FOOD ENCOURAGE DEPENDENCY?

One of the most common criticisms of the practice of providing food for wild birds is that it causes dependency, prompting questions as to what happens to birds if feeding stops, and are individuals that use feeders regularly able to then recognise natural foods or have the skills needed to exploit them? Little work has been done on the question of dependency, in part a reflection of the often quoted work done by Brittingham & Temple (1992b) – see below – and in part a reflection of knowledge gained on how small birds track different feeding opportunities.

Brittingham and Temple recognised that two different types of dependency may occur. Over the short term, birds visiting a feeder may come to expect that

FIG 33. The question of whether wild birds become dependent on garden feeding stations has been largely answered by scientific studies; these indicate that small birds are aware of other feeding opportunities and will quickly turn to these if food is no longer available at a given site. (John Harding)

particular location to provide food; if the feeder is left empty or is removed, then the bird may suffer. Over the longer term, those individuals that are heavy users of feeders may lose the ability to recognise naturally occurring food items, lose the skills to handle them and suffer from reduced survival rates. Working on two resident populations of Black-capped Chickadee, Brittingham and Temple tested whether the population that had utilised feeders in the past experienced lower survival rates than a population that had never been exposed to them during a winter when feeders were not available to either population. The researchers found no difference between the average monthly survival rates of the two populations and concluded that there was no evidence for dependency in this species.

The question of whether the sudden cessation of food provision can have a negative effect on individual birds has not been tested but is not thought to be a particular issue. The thinking that supports this view comes from the work on chickadees, which demonstrates that individual birds track a number of food patches at the same time, sampling these no matter how abundant food is at any one patch (Brittingham & Temple, 1992b). For a chickadee living in the northern part of North America – and being one of the smallest bird species to remain so far north during the winter months – tracking a range of food patches has clear survival benefits; if conditions change and one patch is no longer available, individuals already know where other patches are located. The sudden loss of a feeding opportunity might be more of an issue for other species, but one would expect the urban environment and its gardens to provide multiple feeding opportunities within a short distance of each other. This is something that has been examined, to a small degree, through the work of Patrick Thompson, who looked at the effect of interrupting regular food provision in gardens on the numbers and behaviour of House Sparrows and Greenfinches (Thompson, 1989). Thompson's work revealed that the daily pattern of feeding station use was unaffected by the number of neighbouring gardens providing food. However, the numbers of individuals using the experimental garden feeding station was dependent on food provision in neighbouring gardens. When the number of neighbouring gardens providing food was reduced, there was an increase in activity within the experimental garden, where feeding had continued.

THE VALUE OF GARDEN FEEDING STATIONS FOR WILD BIRDS

Many of the individuals providing food for birds at their garden feeding stations during the winter months do so because they believe that it will help the birds through a difficult period of the year. The provision of food might improve the survival rates of fed individuals, but to what degree. Work on Black-capped Chickadees in North America has revealed that supplementary feeding can make a significant difference to overwinter survival. The fed chickadees studied by Brittingham & Temple (1988a) were significantly heavier than unfed birds and, while this difference in weight was very small (equivalent to just 1 per cent of body weight and representing two hours of foraging time), it made a big difference to their longer-term survival rates. Fed individuals had a 70 per cent survival rate through to the end of the winter and beyond, compared with just 30 per cent in unfed birds. Work on Willow Tits and Crested Tits, carried out in coniferous woodland near Gothenburg in Sweden by Jansson et al. (1981), also found that the provision of additional food resource improved winter survival significantly. In this case, the three researchers noted that the provisioned food helped to reduce predation risk by allowing individuals to spend more time in far more protected places than they would frequent under natural food conditions.

FOOD PROVISION AND MEASURES OF REPRODUCTIVE SUCCESS

Various studies have demonstrated that increasing the availability of food resources through the provision of supplementary food can advance the onset of breeding, prolong the period over which breeding takes place and increase both the number of young raised per breeding attempt and the number of breeding attempts made. Work on Florida Scrub-jays *Aphelocoma coerulescens* (Fleischer *et al.*, 2003; Schoech *et al.*, 2004) has, for example, revealed that populations with access to supplementary food can start breeding up to 17 days earlier than populations without such access. Similar findings have been revealed for Australian Magpie (Rollinson & Jones, 2002).

The timing of breeding

The work on Florida Scrub-jays reveals both the differences that supplementary food provision can make to the timing of breeding and some of the mechanisms behind it. Suburban scrub-jay populations have access to supplemented food in the form of peanuts, cracked corn, birdseed, bread and pet food, with up to 30 per cent of their diet made up of such items (Fleischer *et al.*, 2003). This food forms a predictable resource, which is in contrast to the unpredictable nature of resources experienced by wildland populations. Predictability appears to be important and probably explains why Fleischer *et al.* (2003) found their suburban scrub-jay populations to be consistent in the timing of their breeding across years, while wildland populations varied. Having a predictable food source in the form of supplemented food may well explain why suburban scrub-jay populations spend less time foraging and more time perching than wildland birds – scrub-jays use a sentinel system, with perching birds alerting other individuals to the presence of potential predators. Suburban scrub-jays also handled more food items per hour, suggesting that their foraging was more efficient. Interestingly, while food consumption rates were not found to vary between the two habitats, those individuals that were the most efficient foragers were also the earliest breeders.

So what does the work on scrub-jays tell us about the effects of supplementary feeding on the timing of breeding? If, as the work of Fleischer *et al.* (2003) suggests, foraging efficiency increases through access to garden feeding stations, the predictability of this significant food resource may provide the birds with a suitable cue for the appropriate timing of breeding. Of course, the supplementary food might influence the timing of breeding in other ways, perhaps by altering female body condition or behaviour. These two possibilities are known as the 'anticipation hypothesis', where females use food availability as a cue for the onset of breeding, and the 'constraint hypothesis' – where food availability constrains the female's ability to produce eggs.

Earlier work by the same research group (Schoech & Bowman, 2001) revealed few differences in female body condition prior to breeding between suburban and wildland populations, suggesting instead that the rate of food intake or time spent foraging – both of which are shaped by food predictability – were more important. Later work on Florida Scrub-jays has attempted to look in greater detail at some of the underlying mechanisms, focussing on protein in the food taken by the birds and also monitoring the levels of key reproductive hormones. Protein is thought to be of particular importance, with evidence suggesting that wildland scrub-jay populations are protein limited – they have lower levels of plasma protein than suburban birds (Schoech & Bowman, 2003). Wildland scrub-jays feed on acorns, the tannic acids in which have been shown to reduce the ability to assimilate proteins. Schoech & Bowman provided their study populations with supplementary food of two different types; one was high in fat and high in protein ('HFHP'), and one was high in fat but low in protein ('HFLP'). Scrub-jays in both treatment groups bred earlier than those in an unfed control group, but birds in the HFLP group bred later than those in the HFHP group.

The researchers then looked at testosterone levels in male scrub-jays, estradiol levels in females, and corticosterone levels in both sexes. The HFHP males had higher testosterone levels than either the HFLP or control group males, but no difference was found in estradiol levels in the females. Estradiol mediates maturation of the ovarian follicles and also appears to stimulate nest building and solicitation behaviour, so the researchers had hypothesised that there would be differences in this key hormone between groups. That the high-protein diet influenced a key male hormone rather than a key female hormone could suggest that male scrub-jays play a larger role in determining when reproduction commences than the females. The corticosterone findings were particularly interesting because they revealed that the levels of this 'stress'-related hormone were lower in suburban populations of the scrub-jays than in either the HFHP, HFHP or control group – though HFHP birds had lower corticosterone levels than HFLP or control group birds. This suggests that the predictability of food resources may influence corticosterone levels and that corticosterone may play a role in the timing of reproduction. This work highlights the complex pathways by which something as apparently simple as the provision of additional food resources may have on the timing of breeding in birds.

Work on species found breeding in UK gardens has generally identified a similar pattern, with the provision of supplementary food leading to earlier

FIG 34. The presence of supplementary food at garden feeding stations can advance the timing of breeding in species like Blue Tit, something that has been proved experimentally here in the UK. (Jill Pakenham)

laying in Blue Tits in Northern Ireland (Robb *et al.*, 2008a). Robb's Blue Tits laid an average of 2.5 days earlier than unfed birds. However, Plummer *et al.* (2013), working on Blue Tits, found that laying dates did not differ significantly between their fed and unfed groups. It is worth just noting that most of these studies have been carried out in woodland habitats rather than in gardens, something that reflects the very great difficulty in running controlled experiments within an urban setting (see Chapter 6). Elsewhere, the laying dates of Willow Tit and Crested Tit were advanced by 2–5 and 5–8 days respectively when provided with sunflower seed and a tallow-based mix containing soy protein, wheat germ, sunflower seed, vitamins and minerals (Brömssen & Jansson, 1980). In a review of 59 studies, Robb *et al.* (2008b) found that 58 per cent reported significantly earlier laying dates in supplemented populations. Some studies, but not others, suggest that supplementary food may shorten incubation periods (Nilsson & Smith, 1988; Nager *et al.*, 1997, Harrison *et al.*, 2010). The Harrison *et al.* (2010) study revealed that supplemented Great Tits reduced their incubation period in each of the three study years, while Blue Tits did so in two of the three years.

Clutch size, egg and offspring quality and fledging success

The formation of an egg is not only costly in terms of energy but also in terms of nutrients, such as protein. If females are limited by resources as they go into the egg laying period, then it follows that the provision of suitable resources may lead to an increase in clutch size. However, the evidence for this is mixed, with some authors finding an effect (e.g. Soler & Soler, 1996) but not others (Brömssen & Jansson, 1980; Svensson & Nilsson, 1995). In one case, the provision of supplementary food appeared to reduce clutch size significantly in Blue Tits and Great Tits breeding in a Worcestershire woodland (Harrison *et al.*, 2010). The Harrison study revealed an interesting mix of results; in addition to the significant reduction in clutch size and the shortened incubation periods noted above, food supplementation from several weeks pre-laying through to hatching appeared to reduce hatching success in Blue Tits, but not Great Tits. Robb *et al.*'s review, mentioned earlier, found that in 44 studies that dealt with food supplementation and both laying dates and clutch size, 12 reported increases in both and 16 reported increases in clutch size alone (Robb *et al.*, 2008b).

The provision of supplementary food, just prior to and during egg laying, has been shown to result in increased deposition of carotenoids within the yolk of an egg, leading to increased hatching success (Møller *et al.*, 2008) and, subsequently, higher rates of adult survival (McGraw *et al.*, 2005). Chicks hatched from eggs with high levels of antioxidants have been shown to have lower rates of mortality in the days following hatching (Royle *et al.*, 2011), so micronutrients stored by the female bird and derived from supplementary food, could deliver benefits to the resulting chicks. However, the findings of various studies show some differences. Supplementary feeding during the winter months – this time with fat – has been shown to affect investment

FIG 35. Supplementary food has been shown to influence the number and quality of offspring produced by birds like Great Tit. (Mike Toms)

in egg production, resulting in a smaller relative yolk mass in larger eggs and reduced yolk carotenoid concentration in early breeding Blue Tits (Plummer *et al.*, 2013); these negative effects were absent in Blue Tits fed with fat plus vitamin E (see below). Egg size increases were reported in 38 per cent of the studies examined by Robb *et al.* (2008b). Returning to Florida Scrub-jays, Jim Reynolds (Reynolds *et al.*, 2003) found that females fed with a high-fat high-protein diet produced heavier third eggs, containing more water and more protein than the eggs of unsupplemented individuals.

Of course, one of the key figures when discussing breeding success is the number of chicks that fledge from the nest; while this is obviously influenced by some of the factors we have just discussed – such as the number of eggs – it is worth looking at whether supplementary feeding influences this figure. Working on a Blue Tit population in Northern Ireland, Gillian Robb and colleagues found that supplementary feeding significantly affected the numbers of chicks that fledged, such that individuals for which peanuts had been provided during the winter months fledged almost one extra chick per nest compared to those without access to the food (Robb *et al.*, 2008a). Although Brömsson & Jansson (1980) did not find any effects of food supplementation on clutch size or the number of fledglings in Willow Tit or Crested Tit, they did find that Crested Tit nestlings were significantly heavier within the fed study site and that there was a tendency to produce second clutches more often in the experimental area.

One area where concern has been raised about the practice of feeding garden birds during the breeding season is in relation to nestling health and well-being. It has been suggested that garden birds might feed their nestlings on artificial foods provided at garden feeding stations in preference to the natural, predominantly invertebrate-based, foods that they actually need. This suggests that garden birds are either lazy or unable to identify foods as being unsuitable for their nestlings. However, given what we know about food selection behaviour in wild birds, and which has been presented elsewhere in this chapter, both of these suggestions seem unlikely. Cowie & Hinsley (1988a; 1988b) examined nestling diet in a population of suburban Blue Tits and Great Tits, using nest cameras to identify the food provided by parent birds and how this was delivered. The cameras revealed that, on average, 15 per cent of the nestling diet of each of the two species was made up of artificial foods, notably bread, fat and peanuts. The amount provided varied between pairs, ranging from 6 per cent to 34 per cent in Great Tit and from 6 to 28 per cent in Blue Tit. Despite this, the researchers failed to find any relationship between the amount of artificial food provided and measures of nestling health. That adult garden birds are able to make appropriate decisions about the food they provide to their chicks

FIG 36. Adult birds appear to be able to identify appropriate foods for their nestlings and fledglings, with most species feeding their young on invertebrate prey while they are still in the nest, and making use of bird table fare as the young develop towards independence. (John Harding)

can be seen from observations that if additional insect food is made available to nesting tits, or if their brood size is artificially reduced by removing some of the nestlings, the parent birds respond by dropping artificial foodstuffs from their diet and increasing the numbers of invertebrates provisioned.

Supplementary food, such as that presented to birds within the garden environment, may have consequences for other measures of breeding success, and indeed for other aspects of the breeding cycle. Studies have revealed that nesting adults, provided with additional food, will often reduce foraging effort, something that can provide time for other activities – such as predator vigilance (Arcese & Smith, 1988). It can also have some rather surprising effects. Conservationists, working to secure a future for the Kakapo *Strigops habroptilus* through supplementary feeding of the worryingly small female population, discovered to their horror that the quality of food being provided led to a male-biased sex ratio in the resulting chicks. It is thought that this came about because the female is the heterogametic sex – it has two different sex chromosomes – and can in some instances determine the sex ratio of offspring at the point of fertilisation. A change to the food quality being provided saw a more balanced sex ratio restored (Robertson *et al.*, 2006).

Diet and nutrition have also been linked to important traits associated with reproduction, including mate selection. Mate selection is often based around traits that indicate the quality of a potential mate. Such traits, which include plumage colouration and song complexity, are often nutritionally or energetically costly to maintain.

THE HEALTH EFFECTS OF PROVIDING FOOD

Until recently, very little work had been done on the nutritional composition of the foods being provided at garden feeding stations; even now we are only just beginning to explore the health and other impacts of such provisioning. We know that the proteins and lipids found in naturally occurring foods play an important role in the control of reproduction, underlining that we need to establish how supplemented foods differ from what birds would be eating normally and what, if any, effects such differences have on the health and behaviour of individual birds. We also know that the provision of supplementary food can support birds as they replace lost feathers, something tested experimentally by Grubb & Cimprich (1990).

FIG 37. Although the black bib of male House Sparrows has an important function, signalling status, it is not as sensitive to nutritional conditions as one might expect. (John Harding)

A poor diet can have implications for the health of a wild bird, perhaps increasing susceptibility to disease or resulting in poor-quality plumage or other abnormalities. In geese and birds of prey, nutritional imbalance has been suggested as the primary cause of 'angel wing' disorder, while the effects of malnutrition on plumage characteristics have been seen in Brown-headed Cowbirds *Molothrus ater* (McGraw *et al.*, 2002). Interestingly, McGraw's work, which looked at both Brown-headed Cowbird and House Sparrow, found that important signalling plumage – the melanin-based black bib of male House Sparrows and the brown hood of the cowbirds – was not affected by nutritional stress. That such melanin-based ornaments are less sensitive to nutritional conditions during moult suggests these may signal hormonal status and/or competitive ability rather than represent an accurate signal of health.

The provision of meat at garden feeding stations, which is widely practised in Australia but not the UK, could have implications for the health of those birds feeding upon it. It has been demonstrated that birds like Australian Magpie, taking meat from garden feeding stations, have elevated levels of plasma cholesterol and fatty acids (Ishigame *et al.*, 2006). A secondary concern with meat is that it has an unbalanced calcium to phosphorous ratio – calcium absorption can be hindered by high phosphorus levels – which can lead to a range of skeletal or physiological problems.

The reliance on foods provided at garden feeding stations may lead to a dietary imbalance, directly affecting an individual bird, and/or impairing its reproductive potential during a subsequent breeding season. Where events in one season influence an individual's performance in a later season, this is known as a 'carry-over effect'. Such effects have received increasing attention over the last few years, particularly in relation to supplementary feeding. Another potential effect of food provision at garden feeding stations is that it may alter population structure, perhaps by enabling low quality individuals to recruit into the breeding population. The phenotypic quality of individuals is strongly influenced by oxidative stress, with this oxidative stress reflecting the imbalance between the harmful reactive oxygen species (known as ROSs) produced as by-products of metabolism and the body's antioxidant defence system (Selman *et al.*, 2012).

Carry-over effects are often talked about in terms of energetics, with macronutrients – such as fats – thought to be of particular importance. However, small birds, such as those visiting garden feeding stations in the UK, lack the capacity to store large amounts of fat, meaning they have to rely on daily food intake to meet the energetic demands imposed by reproduction. Because of this, it might be that micronutrients – such as antioxidants – are more important; these may be stored in the liver and any subcutaneous fat to deliver reserves that

FIG 38. Adult Great Spotted Woodpeckers bring their chicks to garden feeding stations soon after they have left the nest. Presumably knowledge of a reliable food source will help the young woodpeckers as they become independent. (Jill Pakenham)

can be utilised during a subsequent breeding season or at other times when they are needed (Metzger & Bairlein, 2011).

Work by Kate Plummer and colleagues has sought to establish the extent to which supplementary feeding produces the individual- and population-level effects we have just described (Plummer *et al.*, 2018). Plummer used different woodland populations of Blue Tits to compare the effects of providing fat, and fat plus vitamin E (an antioxidant), with a control population of unfed birds. Feeding was only carried out during the winter months, ending at least a month before the tits began egg laying. Provisioning with fat *and* vitamin E improved the survival, recruitment and breeding condition of birds that had been in significantly poorer condition prior to feeding; provisioning with fat only was found to have a detrimental impact on breeding birds. Because birds that had been supplied with fat and vitamin E were found to have lower levels of carotenoids in their breast feathers – lower levels of carotenoids being indicative of lower quality individuals – Plummer was able to conclude that supplementing with vitamin E and fat in winter had altered the survival and recruitment prospects of these lower quality individuals. It appears, therefore, that the provision of supplementary foods during the winter months can alter both the structure of the breeding population and the condition of individual breeding birds. Such effects can also have consequences beyond the breeding season where, for example, food provision alters levels of oxidative damage; in Plummer's study, individuals with higher blood plasma concentrations of malondialdehyde (indicative of oxidative damage) produced offspring that were structurally smaller and suffered from reduced fledging success.

The importance of antioxidants, like vitamin E, can also be seen from Plummer's work on yolk mass, mentioned earlier. While Plummer *et al.* (2013) found that winter provisioning with fat subsequently impaired an individual's ability to acquire, assimilate and/or mobilise key resources for yolk formation, this was not the case where vitamin E was also included in the food presented. A high-fat diet, such as that potentially obtained from the food provided at garden feeding stations, may well increase the requirement for antioxidants in order to combat the greater levels of oxidative damage associated with a diet rich in fats.

FOOD PROVISION, POPULATION SIZE AND COMMUNITY STRUCTURE

Plummer's work shows that the effects of food provision can potentially pass from one generation to the next, and alter the composition of breeding populations in subsequent seasons, but what about its impact at a wider community level? Work carried out in the Netherlands has revealed how the provision of supplementary food can lead to an increase in local population size, and how the scale of the effect can change in relation to the availability of wider food resources (van Balen, 1980). Research by van Balen monitored two populations of Great Tits, breeding in similar woodlands just 7 km apart; before introducing a regime of winter feeding, the two populations were similar and had been fluctuating more or less in parallel over several years. Following the introduction of feeding, the number of breeding pairs in the fed woodland increased to become 40 per cent higher than that in the unfed woodland. Not only this, but the scale of the difference varied according to the size of the beechmast crop; in poor beechmast years, the fed population was almost double that of the unfed population the following breeding season; following years with a good mast crop, there was little difference between the numbers of Great Tits breeding in the two woods. A similar finding was noted by Källander (1981), working in Sweden, whose first year of study (1969–70) coincided with a particularly severe winter. Despite this, Great Tits in a wood provisioned with sunflower seeds increased in number, while those in an unfed wood declined. The following year, in which there was a good crop of beechmast, saw populations in both woods increase.

If the provision of food at garden feeding stations leads to an increase in the numbers of birds locally, then we might expect to see a relationship between feeder density and bird numbers across individual towns and cities. There is some evidence of this from the work carried out in Sheffield (Fuller *et al.*, 2008; 2012), with the density of three of the seven urban-adapted species studied shown to be positively related to the density of bird feeders. House Sparrow showed the strongest pattern, with 57 per cent of the variation in House Sparrow densities explained by the density of bird feeders; the other two species were Blackbird and Starling. Interestingly, given the frequency with which Blue Tits and Great Tits are seen at garden feeding stations, it was surprising that they did not show such a relationship, yet Blackbird did.

Some of the strongest evidence for community-level effects comes from work carried out in New Zealand, where most of the native bird species able to persist within urban areas are either predominantly insectivorous (e.g. Grey Warbler *Gerygone igata*), frugivorous (e.g. New Zealand Pigeon *Hemiphaga novaeseelandiae*) or nectarivorous (e.g. Tūī *Prosthemadera novaeseelandiae*). In contrast, many of the introduced species are either granivorous (e.g. House Sparrow and Spotted Dove) or adaptable enough to take bird table fare. Much of the food provided at garden feeding stations in New Zealand would appear to favour the introduced species, something confirmed by Galbraith *et al.* (2015) through a feeding experiment. The introduction of feeding altered the community structure, with significant increases seen in the abundance of House Sparrow and Spotted Dove, and to a lesser degree in Starling and Song Thrush. The introduction of feeding was also shown to have a negative effect on the abundance of the native Grey Warbler. Once the feeding experiment ended, virtually all of the observed changes in community structure disappeared. Observational work on these birds (Galbraith *et al.*, 2017b) revealed that House Sparrow and Spotted Dove dominated the feeding stations.

Supplementary feeding in the Sydney area, Australia, together with the establishment of both native and non-native fruiting shrubs in gardens, is thought to have been a significant factor in the major changes seen over the

FIG 39. The presence of garden feeding stations is thought to have aided the successful colonisation of the UK by Collared Doves. (John Harding)

past 100 years in the diversity and abundance of parrots (Burgin & Saunders, 2007). The provision of food at garden feeding stations is thought to have aided colonisation and range expansion of the Collared Dove within the UK. Within North America, the northwards range expansions of House Finch, Tufted Titmouse *Baeolophus bicolor* and Northern Cardinal have also been attributed to the food available at garden feeding stations during the winter months.

INFLUENCE OF SUPPLEMENTARY FOOD ON NEST PREDATION

We have already seen how the provision of supplementary food can alter the timing of breeding and community structure. A special case of the latter relates to the ways in which the provision of supplementary foods can influence relationships between predators and their prey. This is of particular relevance when discussing urban and suburban gardens because anthropogenic foods have become a defining characteristic of urbanised landscapes (Warren *et al.*, 2006). The nature of interactions between breeding birds and their predators may be especially influenced by the provision of such supplementary foods because

FIG 40. There is little evidence that the presence of bird feeders and their use by Grey Squirrels leads to increased levels of nest predation in the local area, but such an effect has been seen for other predators. (John Harding)

both songbirds and their generalist predators readily exploit these resources, something that can lead to them occupying the same urban sites. BTO work, in the form of a meta-analysis led by Dan Chamberlain, failed to reveal any strong underlying pattern to the effects of urbanisation – and the associated anthropogenic food sources – on the relationship between predators and levels of nest predation (Chamberlain *et al.*, 2009a), but there have been some useful field experiments on the subject.

Supplementary food may reduce levels of nest predation by providing an alternative food supply for would-be nest predators; alternatively, it may increase levels of nest predation by attracting predators or elevating their population densities. Jennifer Malpass and her colleagues investigated how the presence of bird feeders affected predator abundance and nest survival of American Robin *Turdus migratorius* and Northern Cardinal across seven neighbourhoods in Ohio, US (Malpass *et al.*, 2017). Malpass found that the relative abundance of both Brown-headed Cowbird and American Crow *Corvus brachyrhynchos* – known nest predators of the two study species – was positively associated with the number of bird feeders present within a neighbourhood. No similar relationship was found for the other nest predators studied, which included Grey Squirrel *Sciurus carolinensis*, Blue Jay *Cyanocitta cristata* and Common Grackle *Quiscalus quiscula*. While the relative abundance of American Crow and Brown-headed Cowbird was greater in areas with bird feeders, there was no consistent relationship between the numbers of bird feeders and predation of the songbird nests.

DISEASE AND FOOD PROVISION

The presence of supplementary food at garden feeding stations may contribute positively to bird populations by increasing the availability of food during those periods when natural food supplies are in short supply. However, as will be explored in Chapter 4, the provision of food at bird tables and in hanging feeders may also facilitate the spread of disease. The relationships between food provision and disease occurrence can be more complex than they first appear. It is not simply that garden feeding stations attract large numbers of birds, and through this lead to increased opportunities for disease transmission; in some instances the presence of the food can act to ameliorate the impacts of disease. This is something that has been studied in North America, in relation to the outbreak of the bacterial disease mycoplasmal conjunctivitis in North American House Finches (Fischer & Miller, 2015).

Mycoplasmal conjunctivitis impairs vision, making it difficult for affected individuals to find and locate food. If such individuals have access to abundant and predictable food resources, this may afford them with the time and energy needed to recover. Interestingly, there is also some limited evidence that individuals infected at feeding stations may develop less severe symptoms than those infected elsewhere, something that may lead to a faster recovery. Fischer & Miller (2015) used information from the FHWAR (Fishing, Hunting and Wildlife-associated Recreation) census to examine how food provision influenced House Finch populations before and after the emergence of mycoplasmal conjunctivitis. The two researchers found that the availability of bird food appeared to have a positive effect on House Finch populations, with House Finch density prior to the disease outbreak strongly related to the density of US citizens providing food for birds. After the disease arrived, reducing House Finch numbers substantially, the relationship between feeder density and finch numbers remained.

A comparison was then made between pre- and post-disease emergence populations, the researchers seeking to determine whether finch populations declined more strongly where feeder densities were high – which is what you might expect if high densities of feeders lead to high rates of disease transmission and, through this, to a correspondingly greater level of population decline. The results of the study revealed a positive relationship between changes in finch densities and changes in feeder densities between the two periods, indicating that higher densities of feeders actually resulted in lower rates of population decline. This adds weight to the work of Dhondt *et al.* (2007), suggesting that food provision might act as a 'crutch' for sick birds and improve their chances of survival and recovery. Other factors also need to be considered, not least that House Finches may spread mycoplasmal conjunctivitis to other species, including House Sparrow and American Goldfinch.

FOOD PROVISION AND BEHAVIOUR

As we have already discovered, food resources are central to many different aspects of a bird's life, so it is little wonder then that the provision of food can alter behaviour. The area where we might expect to see clear evidence for changes in behaviour is in relation to territory, since territory provides a means of partitioning and defending resources, including food. Black-capped Chickadees

FIG 41. When supplementary food is available, both Blue Tits and Great Tits are less likely to join the mobile foraging flocks that are a feature of the early winter in woodland habitats in the UK. (Jill Pakenham)

show a degree of territoriality during the winter months, defending small foraging patches from intruders. However, as Wilson (2001) discovered, such territoriality breaks down when a significant food source is added to a foraging patch, the resident flock (typically the resident mated pair and six to ten first winter birds) unable to defend the new resource against the large numbers of other chickadees wanting to make use of it.

A feature of the tit species that are familiar to garden feeding stations here in the UK is their willingness to form mixed-species flocks during the autumn and winter months, a behaviour that also occurs in other tit species elsewhere in the world. This behaviour is thought to improve an individual's chances of finding food during those periods when food is scarce and encounter rates low. You might, therefore, expect to see the provision of supplementary food exert an influence on the tendency to form or join mixed-species flocks. This is exactly what Thomas Grubb found, working on tits in deciduous woodland in Oxfordshire (Grubb, 1987). Grubb was interested in whether mixed-species flocking was driven by predation risk, by food availability or by both. His results suggested that food was the primary driver; Blue Tits and Great Tits without access to supplementary food flocked with other species while foraging more often than was the case when supplementary food was available. Interestingly, Long-tailed Tits – which ignored the artificial food – foraged in mixed-species flocks regardless of whether or not provisioned food was available. Work in Japan on Varied Tit *Sittiparus varius* underlines the behavioural flexibility in whether or not individuals join mixed-species flocks (Kubuta & Nakamura, 2000), revealing that individuals participate in mixed-species flocks to obtain the short-term benefits of increased foraging efficiency but, independent of food provision, they also obtain long-term benefits from the stability of their pair bonds and strong site fidelity.

The studies just mentioned are relevant to the discussion of how the winter provision of food at garden feeding stations may alter the behaviour of the birds that visit. However, garden feeding may also change behaviour during the breeding season, something that may be of particular importance. As we shall see in our examination of the breeding ecology of garden birds (Chapter 3), the dawn chorus provides both a means to demonstrate ownership of a breeding territory and a mechanism to advertise your status as a mate. Research suggests that singing at dusk and, particularly, dawn may provide an honest signal of the energetic status of the singing male. If this is the case, then we might expect the availability of food in garden feeders to shape the performance of those males with access to it. Experimental work on Blackbirds supports this, with Cuthill & MacDonald (1990) finding that food-supplemented males sang significantly

FIG 42. Male Blackbirds with access to supplementary food sing for longer than those without access to such food, suggesting that the food provided at garden feeding stations might help local birds in defence of their territories and mate attraction. (Mike Toms)

more than unsupplemented males. This difference was largely the result of supplemented males initiating song earlier and having higher peak rates of song delivery. Could this mean that male Blackbirds with access to a reliable food source at garden feeding stations are more likely to attract a mate than those nesting in other habitats where perhaps food is more limiting? A similar piece of work, this time on Great Tits, casts some uncertainty on whether the relationship is as simple as it appears from the work done on Blackbirds. Katja Saggese and her collaborators provided male Great Tits with a continuous food supply over two weeks and then compared their singing activity with a group of unfed males (Saggese *et al.*, 2011). In contrast to Cuthill & MacDonald's findings, the food supplemented males started their dawn singing later than the control males, an effect that still continued two weeks after the provision of food had ended. The researchers were unsure of the reasons for what they had observed, but they felt that it could have been due to the presence of predators, attracted to the feeding stations, or something about the quality of the food itself.

FOOD PROVISION AND MOVEMENTS

Birds tend to reduce the size of the area over which they forage when provisioned with supplementary food, something that can lead to a reduction in the size of breeding territory and even a change in mating system in the case of Dunnock (Davies & Lundberg, 1984). As we will see in a moment in relation to Blackcaps, the provision of food in gardens can have a significant impact on movement and wintering behaviour.

Although not garden-related, the scale of feeding impacts can be seen from work on the White Stork *Ciconia ciconia*, a species that was wholly migratory in Europe but which has established resident populations across parts of Iberia largely in response to the year-round food available at landfill sites (Gilbert *et al.*, 2016). Landfills and food discarded by people have also played a role in the expansion of urban-breeding Lesser Black-backed Gulls *Larus fuscus* here in the UK (Coulson & Coulson, 2008), a species that now winters here in large numbers, when it formerly wintered in southern Europe and north and west Africa.

FOOD PROVISION AND THE EVOLUTION OF NEW BEHAVIOUR – WINTERING BLACKCAPS

The Blackcap is a common summer visitor to much of Britain, wintering in southern Europe and south into North Africa. Although there are occasional records, the Blackcap was rarely encountered in Britain during the winter months 60 years ago (Stafford, 1956). However, since the 1950s we have seen a rapid and substantial increase in wintering records, as information from both the *Garden Bird Feeding Survey* and *Bird Atlas 2007–11* show (Balmer *et al.*, 2013). Data from BTO-led bird atlases show that the Blackcap's wintering range in the UK has expanded by 77 per cent over the last 30 years. The increase in wintering numbers has come about because Blackcaps breeding in southern Germany and Austria have increasingly migrated in a northwesterly direction to Britain for the winter, rather than in a southwesterly direction to traditional wintering areas located in southern Spain (Helbig *et al.*, 1994). This new migration strategy has been shown to be genetically encoded (Berthold *et al.*, 1992), and is maintained via reproductive isolation and assortative mating, linked to fitness benefits on the breeding grounds (Bearhop *et al.*, 2005).

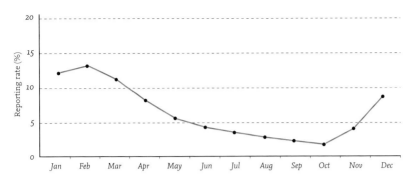

FIG 43. The use of gardens by Blackcaps peaks during the winter months. Data reproduced from BTO Garden BirdWatch with permission.

Early observations of increasing numbers of wintering Blackcaps coincided with the introduction of commercial bird foods (Callahan, 2014), suggesting that supplementary feeding at garden feeding stations might be applying a selection pressure for the evolution of this new migratory route. Interestingly, while the Blackcaps wintering in southern Spain are predominantly frugivorous in their dietary choices, those wintering in Britain are known to use a wide variety of supplementary food types (Tellería *et al.*, 2013; Plummer *et al.*, 2015). The availability of supplementary food is unlikely to be the sole driver of evolutionary change, however, and it is likely that a changing climate has also had some influence over the adoption of this new migration route and new wintering area. Winter conditions in Britain, and more widely across the Northern Hemisphere, are becoming milder, something that has enabled a number of species to shift their wintering range northwards (IPCC, 2013).

Unravelling these different drivers requires access to long-term datasets on food provision, Blackcap occurrence and climatic factors. Fortunately, BTO researchers have been able to use data from BTO's weekly Garden BirdWatch survey to explore the question of whether food provision has played a part in the evolution of a new migratory strategy in this central European Blackcap population (Plummer *et al.*, 2015). Earlier work using the BTO Garden BirdWatch dataset has revealed that Blackcaps are strongly associated with suburban gardens during the winter months (Chamberlain *et al.*, 2004a) which makes this dataset ideal for examining the interactions between food provision and Blackcap wintering behaviour. Examination of the foods provided in Garden BirdWatch gardens and their use by wintering Blackcaps revealed a strong preference by the birds for sunflower hearts and fat-based products. By calculating an annual measure of the proportion of winter weeks in which these foodstuffs were provided at each of 3,806 sites – each of which had a minimum of at least 16 weekly submissions in a minimum of at least nine winters – it has been possible to explore the relationship between Blackcap occurrence and food provision and how this has changed over time.

Wintering Blackcaps showed regional variation in their use of Garden BirdWatch gardens, with greater occupancy of sites in the south and west (see Figure 43), where wintering conditions are milder. Occupancy rates were influenced by both the provision of supplementary food and winter temperature. Birds were recorded more often in gardens that provided food more frequently, and showed a preference for sites that had a warmer local climate during the winter months. One of the most interesting findings was that Blackcap occurrence has become more strongly associated with the provision of fat products and sunflower hearts over time, suggesting that the birds are adapting their feeding habits to exploit human-provisioned foods. This supports the theory of Berthold & Terrill (1988) that the Blackcap's new migration strategy is likely to have evolved in response to increased supplementary feeding activities in gardens in Britain.

The results of the Plummer study also reveal that gardens are used less during milder winters, which – together with the relationship found with local climate – supports the hypothesis that an improving winter climate is likely to have enabled the Blackcap to increase its wintering range into Britain. In addition, the growing use of provisioned food adds further support to the work of Rolshausen et al. (2009), who have found that Blackcaps wintering in Britain have relatively narrower and longer beaks than those wintering in Spain. Such differences suggest that these British migrants have adapted to a more generalist diet than their Spanish counterparts, adding phenotypical divergence to the genetic divergence already documented between these two populations (Berthold et al., 1992). Rolshausen et al. also found differences in wing morphology, bill colour and plumage colour between the two populations.

WATER AND GARDEN BIRDS

Garden birds require water, both to drink and in many cases for bathing – though see Chapter 5. This water may be present in the form of a pond, puddle or bird bath and all can be well used by visiting birds. Figures from national studies suggest that 10 per cent of UK dwellings have a pond associated with them, though not all of these will be suitable for birds. Some may be netted to protect precious fish, while others may be steep-sided and inaccessible. Those with a shallow end or with branches that dip into the water are likely to be used most often, the birds able to perch within or close to the water when drinking or bathing. Just

FIG 44. Water is important for garden birds and the presence of a pond or other water source can prove very attractive to visiting birds. (Jill Pakenham)

over half of the respondents to a questionnaire survey carried out by Cowie & Hinsley (1988a) in suburban Cardiff reported providing water for visiting birds. The provision of water can influence the community of birds using a garden, with seed-eating species seemingly preferring sites at which they can both feed and drink. Water may also shape behaviour – for example, by providing some garden Blackbirds with the opportunity to develop the habit of catching and eating small newts and the tadpoles of Common Frog *Rana temporaria* – and play a role in disease transmission. Despite this, its importance has received little research interest and there is the potential here for much new information to be gained.

GARDEN BIRD FOOD AND OTHER WILDLIFE

The food available at garden feeding stations isn't just used by garden birds; it may be taken by other creatures or, in some instances, germinate and lead to the establishment of non-native flora. Many of the other beneficiaries of garden feeding are mammals, with mice, voles, rats and squirrels the most commonly reported feeders here in the UK. While some of these creatures are tolerated, or even encouraged, some are viewed as a pest. Common Rat *Rattus norvegicus* and

FIG 45. Some garden feeding station visitors are less welcome than others. (John Harding)

Grey Squirrel are the two most commonly seen as a negative consequence of garden feeding. The presence of Grey Squirrels at a garden feeding station may prevent birds from taking food, something determined experimentally by Hugh Hanmer and colleagues at the University of Reading (Hanmer *et al.*, 2018).

Efforts to deter squirrels from garden feeding stations tend to be based around either the physical adaptation of feeding devices or treatment of the food itself. Two other options – providing squirrels with their own feeder some distance from the feeding stations, and lethal control – are not widely practised. Treatment of peanuts and other foods with capsaicin – the pungent component that is responsible for the sensation one gets when eating chilli peppers – has proved a useful deterrent in trials carried out in the US (Curtis *et al.*, 2000). Treatment of sunflower seeds significantly reduced both the amount of seed taken by Grey Squirrels and the amount of time that they spent feeding, but did not affect the amount of seed taken by feeding birds. Capsaicin binds to pain receptors in mammals and has a number of other effects that result in many mammals finding the substance repellent. Although at least some bird species can taste capsaicin, it does not appear to be harmful or repellent to them. There is, however, one other finding worth mentioning here, which is that Grey Squirrels can learn to open treated sunflower seeds, avoiding the treated husk to feed on the heart (Fitzgerald *et al.*, 1995). Fortunately, a company in the US has developed a way to treat both the husk and the heart within.

A perhaps unforeseen consequence for wider biodiversity on the provision of food at garden feeding stations is that the presence of increased numbers of insectivorous or omnivorous birds can lead to increased levels of predation of garden-dwelling invertebrates. Investigating the possible effects of wild bird feeding on the size and survivorship of Pea Aphid *Acyrthosiphon psium* colonies in suburban gardens, Melanie Orros and Mark Fellowes found that the presence of bird feeders had a significant impact. Both the size and survivorship of aphid colonies was significantly reduced in gardens where a feeding station was present (Orros & Fellowes, 2012). The same researchers have also found that supplementary feeding of garden birds indirectly affects ground beetle populations (Orros *et al.*, 2015a), and work in the US suggests a similar impact on arthropods overwintering on bark (Martinson & Flaspohler, 2003).

CONCLUDING REMARKS

A key take-home message about bird feeding is that there is still a lot for us to learn; it is no longer appropriate to merely follow the simplistic view that feeding garden birds is largely beneficial, and that any deleterious aspects are outweighed by the benefits gained. Some authors have even suggested that bird feeders are ecological traps, perhaps tempting birds to initiate breeding attempts earlier in the year than is beneficial and leading to a mismatch between the food demands of the resulting chicks and the availability of the peak invertebrate resources on which they depend. The scrub-jays breeding in suburban habitats with access to supplementary food may well breed earlier but they can find themselves out of synch with the natural food items that they need for their growing nestlings, something that could potentially lead to decreased rather than increased breeding success (Schoech & Bowman, 2001).

The provision of supplementary foods, many of which would not be taken by these species within the wider environment, has complex effects on individual birds and their broader populations. The extent to which food provision is considered to be deleterious or beneficial will, in part, depend on whether you are examining its effects at the level of the individual bird or the wider population. Feeding can change the structure of populations, something that may have profound consequences for the size of broader populations, both of the species under study and, potentially, those of the other species with which it competes or interacts. The effects of supplementary food may also differ depending upon external factors, perhaps having the greatest impact when times are tough or in territories low in resources or occupied by inexperienced birds (Robb *et al.*, 2008a). This was certainly the case for Arcese & Smith (1988) working on a high-density population of Song Sparrow *Melospiza melodia*. Arcese & Smith found particularly large effects of supplementary feeding, presumably because the control birds – those without access to additional food – were under heavy competitive pressure, suppressing clutch size and other measures of breeding success. They found, for example, that fed birds laid 18 days earlier, on average, than control birds and were also more synchronous. One of the challenges to unravelling these effects is the difficulty in studying wild birds, of following individuals throughout their entire life cycle and in dealing with populations that may move between habitats and over significant distances.

CHAPTER 3

Nests, Nest Boxes and Breeding

Most readers will have encountered a bird nesting within their garden, perhaps a Blackbird nesting in a shrub or a Blue Tit occupying a nest box erected for the purpose. Many other nesting attempts will have gone unnoticed, the first indication of their occurrence revealed by the appearance of newly fledged youngsters on the garden lawn or at hanging feeders. But just how many birds nest in our gardens, and how do their nesting attempts and breeding success compare with those made by the same species in other habitats? This is something that we will explore through this chapter, which also includes a wider examination of territory, breeding behaviour and nesting opportunities. Courtship behaviour is covered more fully in Chapter 5.

HOW MANY BIRDS BREED IN GARDENS?

As we saw in Chapter 1, data from the BTO/JNCC/RSPB Breeding Bird Survey have been used to produce habitat-based population estimates for many UK species. The population estimates produced for those habitats associated with human sites – urban, suburban and rural habitation – suggest that sizeable proportions of the populations of several species breed alongside us, with many of these birds using the urban green space that is gardens (Newson *et al.*, 2005). That 33 per cent of our Blackbirds and 54 per cent of our Starlings breed alongside us means that how we manage urban green space, including gardens, can have a significant influence on a large component of their UK breeding populations.

FIG 46. Wrens are cavity nesters, but adaptable enough to take advantage of even the most unlikely cavities. (John Harding)

While these habitat-based population estimates are very valuable, they do not tell the whole story; the Breeding Bird Survey involves participants walking transects through randomly selected survey squares. While this approach works well within much of the wider countryside, it may not give a complete picture of the breeding bird populations to be found in urban areas. Since many urban birds will be breeding and feeding in private gardens, hidden from view by hedges, fences and buildings, it seems likely that Breeding Bird Survey observers will miss a proportion of the birds that they pass while carrying out their fieldwork. The method should allow the survey to pick up changes in urban populations over time, which is its purpose, but it might be less good at determining the size of these populations.

Similar criticisms can also be made of the approaches used to derive national population estimates from atlas data (e.g. Gibbons *et al.*, 1993). While atlas fieldwork covers all habitats, it again suffers from the difficulties of working within urban areas (see Chapter 6) and is likely to miss a sizeable proportion of the bird populations breeding there. Recognition of this problem can be seen when Gibbons *et al.* (1993) rejected their initial population estimate for House Sparrow in favour of one that had been derived largely from urban data presented by Dennis Summers-Smith (Summers-Smith, 1959). Summers-Smith's estimate took into account direct measures of House Sparrow density, made in urban and suburban sites within London, alongside those from rural areas. This suggests that finding other ways to secure information on the numbers of birds breeding within urban areas, and their associated green spaces and private gardens, could support the production of more robust estimates of national populations.

One approach, adopted by Bland et al. (2004), is to ask householders to survey their gardens for nesting birds and to report back on what they find. Richard Bland and John Tully, both retired teachers living in Bristol, worked with Jeremy Greenwood of the BTO on a garden-nesting survey, carried out in 2000. A questionnaire was sent to all 12,687 households participating in BTO Garden BirdWatch, with 6,035 useable responses returned. From these, and using additional information on the number and type of households present in the UK (taken from the 1991 housing census), it was possible to produce estimates for the garden populations of 17 familiar species. This approach makes a number of assumptions, most notably that survey respondents find all of the nests on their property and that those participating in the survey are representative of wider society. Neither of these assumptions is likely to be true, but it is unclear how big a difference this makes to the resulting estimates. Undercounting the number of nests will mean that the final estimate is lower than it should be; if Garden BirdWatch gardens are better for birds than non-Garden BirdWatch gardens, then it might mean that the final estimate is larger than it should be. Despite this, the estimates produced in the paper suggest that national population figures, derived from other methods, are too low for several species because we have not looked closely at gardens. The five species where the national estimates produced by Gibbons et al. (1993) are highly likely to have been significantly underestimated are Dunnock, Starling, Great Tit, Blue Tit and House Sparrow, with some evidence to suggest that Robin and Blackbird are also too low. The study also provides important information for Swift and House Martin.

While the different approaches used to derive population estimates for urban breeding birds have their individual limitations, it is useful to look across the range of figures produced to see if there are any general patterns (Table 5). Looking at the figures produced by Bland et al. (2004) suggests that domestic properties and their gardens may sustain densities of nesting birds approaching those seen in many woodland habitats, although the diversity of species present in gardens is considerably less than that seen in woodland. Of course, the figures presented in the table are for the most common and familiar species and do not tell us about the less common species that may also make use of gardens for breeding. We do know, however, that where a garden is located and which habitats

TABLE 5. Estimates of numbers of pairs of birds nesting in gardens in Great Britain derived from the BTO Garden Nesting Survey (Bland *et al.*, 2004), compared to those derived from the national Bird Atlas (Gibbons *et al.*, 1993), the latter split into figures calculated for all habitats other than farmland and woodland, and all habitats.

Species	Bland et al. (2004) Gardens	Gibbons et al. (1993) All habitats except Woodland and Farmland	All habitats
Woodpigeon	482,000	586,000	2,100,000
Collared Dove	487,000	43,000	200,000
Swift	395,000	—	80,000
Swallow	772,000	146,000	570,000
House Martin	1,165,000	—	375,000
Wren	981,000	1,641,000	7,100,000
Robin	1,343,000	755,000	4,200,000
Dunnock	907,000	295,000	2,000,000
Spotted Flycatcher	148,000	11,000	120,000
Blackbird	3,259,000	1,040,000	4,400,000
Song Thrush	527,000	176,000	990,000
Great Tit	2,388,000	204,000	1,600,000
Blue Tit	6,748,000	629,000	3,300,000
Coal Tit	256,000	64,000	610,000
Starling	2,231,000	327,000	1,100,000
House Sparrow	5,098,000	200,000	3,600,000
Tree Sparrow	286,000	3,000	110,000
Chaffinch	709,000	1,153,000	5,400,000
Greenfinch	579,000	114,000	530,000
Goldfinch	97,000	35,000	220,000

surround it will also shape the species using it for nesting. A quiet corner in a rural garden, perhaps with long grass or a tangle of nettles and bramble, might support nesting Red-legged Partridge *Alectoris rufa* or Blackcap, while the flat-roof of a Georgian town house might have a nesting Lesser Black-backed Gull.

Now that we have a sense of the numbers of breeding birds present within gardens and the wider urban area, we need to turn to the question of their importance. To some extent we have already touched on this by highlighting the numerical importance of the sizeable breeding populations to be found in gardens. However, such populations are only important for the wider population if they are productive and contribute young birds to the next generation. If the failure rates of nests built in gardens are high, or if the numbers of chicks produced is low, then garden nesting may be a very poor option for a bird. If this proves to be the case, then, as some authors have suggested, gardens may be an 'ecological trap' (Robb *et al.*, 2008b). This is what we will turn to look at now.

IS NESTING IN A GARDEN A GOOD OPTION?

There have been various studies looking at the breeding ecology of birds within gardens and the wider urban environment. Some of these have only looked at this habitat; some have looked at different types of urban habitat (e.g. urban versus suburban); and others have looked at how urban breeding compares with that seen in more natural habitats. One of the key measures to examine when seeking to determine whether nesting in a garden is a good option or not is productivity, the number of chicks fledged from the nesting attempt. This is a commonly reported measure but doesn't tell the whole story because it is the number of those fledglings who go on to recruit into the breeding population, and breed themselves, that actually determines future population size. If productivity is good but subsequent survival poor, then you may find a population is no better off than one in which productivity is poor but subsequent survival good. The difficulty in tracking individual birds through from the egg to when they breed explains why the number of young fledged is so commonly used as the measure of productivity. Since it can also be difficult to follow the sometimes multiple breeding attempts made by a pair across the breeding period, productivity tends to be reported as 'productivity per nesting attempt' rather than as 'productivity per season'.

Perhaps a good place to start is with the familiar Blue Tit and Great Tit, since these are the species that most readers are likely to have encountered breeding within their garden. They are also species for which a good deal of information on breeding biology has been collected, both in a variety of woodland habitats and, to a lesser extent, from within gardens and the wider environment. Cowie & Hinsley's study, carried out in two suburban areas within Cardiff, underlines that the breeding success of these two species is much lower in suburban gardens than it is in natural woodland habitats (Cowie & Hinsley, 1987). In addition to producing smaller clutches, suburban tits only managed to rear, on average, half as many young as their counterparts living in mixed deciduous woodland typically do. A particular characteristic of these suburban nesting attempts is

FIG 47. Gardens support a wide range of breeding birds, including species like Red-legged Partridge. (Jill Pakenham)

the mortality of nestlings due to starvation, suggestive of a shortage of favoured invertebrate food during the chick-rearing phase. Other UK work with an urban component has been carried out by Roger Riddington and Andy Gosler, working at Oxford University's Wytham Wood study site and in the surrounding area. Wytham is a mixed deciduous woodland, of the type that is most productive for nesting tits. Riddington & Gosler (1995) compared the breeding success of the Wytham Wood population with those pairs nesting in smaller woods and local gardens. Clutches initiated in Wytham were larger and started earlier, with larger broods, more fledged young and heavier fledglings, all underlining that the mixed deciduous woodland was the better breeding habitat; unfortunately, Riddington and Gosler did not separate out the garden nesting birds from the other habitat types lumped within their 'marginal habitat' category. Examination of nestling diet, through analysis of faecal sacs collected during nest monitoring visits, revealed that the woodland chicks received a better-quality diet, dominated by caterpillars; chick diet in the marginal habitats was dominated by adult flies, beetles and spiders.

The loss of nestlings is something that has also been reported from work carried out on garden-nesting and urban-nesting thrushes. Murray (2004) found that the daily failure rates of nestling Song Thrushes were significantly higher in gardens and parks than they were in nearby woodland sites. It is important to understand whether such nesting failure is the result of low food availability or increased predation risk. Evidence for a shortage of suitable invertebrate prey within gardens comes from a detailed study of House Sparrow populations living in and around the city of Leicester (Peach *et al.*, 2008). This study, led by Kate Vincent, found an average of just 2.02 chicks fledging per nesting attempt, with a quarter of nesting attempts failing to fledge any young at all. High levels of chick mortality were important in driving this poor performance, with 72 per cent of the chick mortality occurring within the first four days after hatching and most likely the result of starvation. Chick survival and chick body mass at 10–12 days old were both strongly related to the quality of chick diet, with chicks receiving a greater proportion of plant material faring worse than those receiving more invertebrates. An examination of the insects being provisioned to the chicks revealed the presence of craneflies, weevils, spiders, ants and aphids, but few of the grasshoppers and moth caterpillars seen in many other studies.

FIG 48. Grasshoppers feature in House Sparrow diet in many wider countryside studies but are largely absent from urban diets. (Mike Toms)

It has been shown that the body condition of House Sparrow chicks is a good predictor of future survival prospects during the period immediately after they have left the nest. Many of the chicks in the Leicester study were small and of low body weight, suggesting their future survival chances were poor. Interestingly, Liker *et al.* (2008) found that the body size and condition of adult House Sparrows was lower in an urban environment than a rural one, and that this difference was maintained even when captive individuals from the two populations were fed on identical diets. Liker *et al.* postulated that this was indicative of carry-over effects from a poor nestling diet. If this is the case, then we might predict that the poor condition, small-sized nestlings fledging from those Leicester nest boxes would go on to become poor condition, small-sized adults. It is unclear whether smaller size and poor body condition is common across urban bird populations but it has also been noted in urban tit populations in Germany (Junker-Bornholdt & Schmidt, 1999).

That the body condition of the chicks in the Leicestershire study was strongly and negatively related to local NO_2 concentrations, might suggest that pollution levels in this area were impacting the House Sparrows by reducing the availability of favoured prey. If this didn't result in starvation while they were in the nest, then it might still reduce their chances upon fledging. Peach *et al.* (2008) carried out some modelling work to see whether the productivity of this House Sparrow population was sufficient to sustain it longer term. In two of the three study years, the average annual production of young per pair was lower than the predicted threshold required to maintain a stable breeding population.

With all of these different studies, looking at different species in different ways, it can be difficult to tease out common patterns and to draw general conclusions. Attempts have been made to do this by using a technique known as meta-analysis; meta-analysis uses a statistical approach to combine the results from multiple studies. We used this approach to look at a suite of studies that had reported on various measures of breeding success from urban and non-urban sites, selecting only those studies that had made a comparison between paired sites – one urban and one non-urban (Chamberlain *et al.*, 2009a). Our meta-analysis revealed that, across the species studied, urban populations started breeding earlier in the year than non-urban populations but they were less productive, with all the different measures of productivity found to be higher in non-urban sites. Only the rate of nest failure was found not to differ between the two different habitat types.

These differences are of particular interest because relatively early breeding in natural or semi-natural habitats often leads to higher productivity; so why do we not see this in urban habitats? It could be that the supplementary food being provided in gardens supports early nesting (see Chapter 2) but that urban sites then lack the invertebrate foods needed by the resulting chicks, leading to lower levels of productivity. The associated question of whether the supplementary food enables females to achieve breeding condition earlier, or merely shapes the timing of breeding by acting as an indicator of food resources available within the environment, might be answered by our finding that clutch size was larger in non-urban sites. Since you might expect clutch size to be determined by the resources that a female has available, discovering that clutches were not bigger in urban areas might suggest that the supplementary food was not shaping breeding condition itself but merely indicating general feeding conditions in the environment, which might be the trigger to initiate a breeding attempt. Of course, supplementary food could enable females to attain breeding condition earlier, but it might be a different resource (such as calcium) that ultimately limits the number of eggs that a female can produce in an urban habitat.

There is also the possibility that other components of the urban landscape might influence the timing of breeding. Later in this book we will look at the impacts of heat pollution on songbird activity at garden feeding stations, but heat pollution also needs a mention here. Urban areas are often a few degrees warmer than the surrounding countryside and this additional warmth might result in birds nesting earlier in the year than they might otherwise do. It has, for example, been shown that nest boxes exposed to warmer temperatures result in earlier laying by Great Tits (Dhondt & Eyckerman, 1979).

As we noted earlier in this book, there is much variety between gardens, and between different types of urban landscape in terms of their suitability for birds. Consequently, we might expect to see variation in breeding success across different types of gardens and between different parts of a larger urban landscape. Using BTO Nest Record Scheme data, Gavin Siriwardena and Humphrey Crick found that the laying dates of House Sparrows and Starlings varied across the urban landscape, being the earliest in urban sites and latest in suburban sites – interestingly, rural sites were intermediate between the two (Siriwardena & Crick, 2002; Crick & Siriwardena, 2002). Siriwardena & Crick's work also revealed that Starling clutch size was significantly lower in urban sites, something also evident in the work of Mennechez & Clergeau (2001).

That gardens appear to be a sub-optimal habitat for many small birds, particularly those feeding their chicks on caterpillars, is perhaps not that surprising. The pattern of poor breeding success and low fledging weights seen in gardens is similar to that seen in other sub-optimal habitats, such as small and isolated woodlands (Hinsley et al., 1999). Blue Tits and Great Tits breeding in small woodland fragments tend to be less successful and rear lighter young; in

FIG 49. Nest survival rates for Blackbirds using rural gardens are higher than those in urban and wider countryside sites. (Jill Pakenham)

some years, the Great Tit populations using these woods suffer a high proportion of complete nest failures at the chick stage (something that also seems to occur in gardens), suggestive of starvation. This tendency is less evident in Blue Tits, which might help to explain why we see more Blue Tits breeding in gardens than Great Tits, despite the latter's ready use of garden feeding stations in winter and dominance at suitable nest sites.

It is worth just reiterating that gardens vary in their structure, location and in the resources they contain. The consequences of this for nesting birds can be seen quite clearly in a piece of recent work by colleagues at the BTO who have been developing new statistical approaches to look at nesting success (Miller *et al.*, 2017). This work, which uses Blackbird as its model species, has revealed that nest survival rates are higher in rural gardens than in either urban gardens or wider countryside habitats. This suggests that rural gardens offer a better balance between the lower availability of favoured food seen urban areas and the higher predation rates of the wider countryside. This underlines that we need to be careful not to generalise about gardens or to treat them as a single homogenous entity.

THE TIMING OF BREEDING

As we saw in Chapter 2, the presence of supplementary food can lead to earlier breeding, something we might therefore expect to see in the urban populations with access to garden feeding stations. There is evidence to support this from studies carried out here in the UK and elsewhere within Europe. Suburban Great Tit populations – but not the Blue Tit populations – in Cardiff were found to breed earlier than their woodland counterparts, something already alluded to when we discussed the meta-analysis carried out by Chamberlain *et al.* (2009a). This pattern of earlier breeding in urban environments has also been reported in other garden bird species. In Blackbird, for example, both male and female birds living in an urban area in Munich developed their reproductive organs some three weeks earlier than those breeding in a nearby forest. In both populations, regress in the reproductive organs took place at the same time during mid-summer, providing the urban birds with an extended breeding season (Partecke *et al.*, 2004). Urban Magpie populations have also been found to lay significantly earlier than those in rural locations (Antonov & Atanasova, 2003).

In woodland populations of Blue Tit and Great Tit, breeding early in the spring usually enhances breeding success (Nilsson, 2000). It has been shown, for example, that early hatched nestlings tend to grow more rapidly (Perrins & McCleery, 1989) and have better longer-term survival prospects (Norris, 1993) than those hatched later in the season. Of course, because these two species are so dependent on caterpillars, there is a limit to how early the nesting attempt can be; nest too early and the peak demands of your growing nestlings will fall significantly earlier than the peak in caterpillar abundance, greatly reducing the number of chicks that fledge. Some idea of the forward planning required can be seen from the time between when the decision to begin egg laying is made and when the first eggs hatch – in tits this interval is something like 26 days.

The timing of breeding is something that has been influenced by climate change, with UK birds now starting their breeding attempts earlier than they did just a few decades ago (Crick *et al.*, 1997). Climate change has also altered the arrival and departure dates of UK migrants (Newson *et al.*, 2016), and both of these factors may shape the timing of breeding events within gardens. While we see an earlier start to the breeding season in gardens, for the reasons already outlined in this chapter, we do not necessarily see this leading to increased breeding success. In fact, for most species, we see a lower breeding success than is the case in other habitats. We also see significant variation within urban areas in terms of the success of individual nesting attempts, something that may be shaped by the quality of the parents, by the nature of the nest site selected, or by the resources available to the birds. These are things that we will explore over the following sections of this chapter.

TERRITORY

Most garden birds maintain a defended breeding territory throughout part of the year; in some species this may only extend to the area in the immediate vicinity of the nest site, but for others it can extend over a much larger area. The distribution and size of these territories is typically driven by the availability of food resources, though it can sometimes be shaped by the availability of nest sites. Where food resources are spread relatively evenly throughout the landscape, then the pattern of territories is likely to be fairly regular, but if food resources are clumped or distributed in a way that leads to some areas or habitats holding more, then territory size and spacing becomes irregular. An area such as a small deciduous woodland, with an abundance of favoured caterpillar prey, will potentially support a higher density of breeding territories than an urban park,

FIG 50. Robin territories are defined and defended through a combination of song and display. (Jill Pakenham)

with few caterpillars. In addition to the territory-holding birds there will be other individuals, either those that have yet to reach breeding age or those that are of breeding age but which have been unable to secure a territory of their own. The presence of the latter group of individuals can be readily proved by removing territory-holding birds; such vacant territories are then quickly filled.

The ownership of a breeding territory is advertised and maintained through song and display, with individual birds only resorting to direct aggression if these behaviours fail to drive an intruding bird away. Behaviours associated with territorial defence can involve the adoption of particular postures, such as those that show off plumage ornamentation, asserting status and dominance. We will look at these in more detail in Chapter 5 when we examine garden bird behaviour. If resources are not distributed evenly, which is usually the case, then we might expect the most dominant birds to occupy the best territories and to then receive the benefits associated with this (such as increased productivity). A question that then arises is to what extent does territory quality, rather than individual quality, determine breeding performance? While some studies have suggested that territory quality is the more important, others suggest it is that of the individual. Teasing out these different components is difficult and what you really need is a study in which you can follow the fortunes of a series of individuals, nesting across a series of territories and sometimes using different ones in different years. This is something that has been examined on the outskirts of Sheffield for Magpie, with the aim of quantifying the separate effects of individual quality and territory quality on several different measures of breeding performance (Goodburn, 1991). The results of this study revealed that male quality explained 70 per cent of a breeding pair's success within a breeding season, with female quality explaining over 60 per cent of the variance in clutch size and in the size of the eggs laid. The timing of breeding, however, appeared to be controlled primarily by territory quality – though the effect was relatively weak. These results contrast with those of Högstedt (1980), who also studied Magpies, the different findings most likely the results of the greater variability in territory quality evident within Högstedt's study area and the more frequent occurrence of territory vacancies.

Garden birds, particularly those occupying gardens within larger urban areas, may have access to ready supplies of food (at least in terms of adults and fledged young). They may also have ready access to nest sites – though this clearly varies with species and the types of nest sites favoured. How then might the structure and distribution of territories within an urban area differ from those seen in other habitats, and how might the 'quality' of territory holders compare with those elsewhere? David Snow (1958), working in Oxford, found his Blackbirds to hold territories ranging in size from 0.16 to 0.24 ha, though it is worth just noting that Creighton (2001), working the same site, reported males holding territories of 0.54 ha. Elsewhere, urban Blackbird territories have been reported varying from 0.12 to 0.7 ha (Jackson, 1954; Lind, 1955; Ludvig *et al.*, 1994). By way of comparison, territory sizes in mixed deciduous woodland habitat are typically 2.2–2.7 ha (Tomiałoj , 1992). The smaller territory sizes of urban Blackbird populations are reflected in the very high densities reported in the work of Simms (1965), Batten (1973) and Mason (2000), documenting urban densities of 96, 246 and 186 territories per km^2 respectively.

Habitat structure appears to influence the settlement patterns of nesting Blackbirds in wider countryside habitats, with areas occupied by breeding pairs typically having greater habitat complexity than unoccupied sites (Hatchwell *et al.*, 1996b). Settlement behaviour may be important at a more general level; it has, for example, been found that Great Tits settling on urban territories may be smaller on average than those individuals occupying rural territories (Lehikoinen, 1986). Some of this may result from urban-born individuals being structurally smaller than their rural-reared counterparts, but it may also result from size-related success when competing for food resources within woodland during the winter months.

The results of our work on urban House Sparrow populations (Shaw *et al.*, 2011) help to draw out some of the landscape features important to this species during the breeding season. By mapping the presence of chirping male House Sparrows onto a detailed habitat map for each of our survey squares, we were able to determine which urban habitat features were favoured and which were avoided. Habitat use by House Sparrows within the core 50 m around their nest sites was significantly non-random with respect to the availability of habitat types within the survey squares as a whole. House Sparrows consistently selected residential areas with gardens over every other habitat type, regardless of the level of urbanisation in the area. Interestingly, the least preferred habitats were buildings without gardens and (perhaps surprisingly) urban green space.

The importance of houses with gardens (combining nesting and foraging opportunities) has long been recognised for House Sparrow, though it is only more recently that we have discovered that those properties in the more economically deprived areas of towns and cities offer better opportunities for House Sparrows than those in more affluent areas (Shaw *et al.*, 2008). Houses situated within more economically deprived areas are likely to offer more nesting opportunities for House Sparrows because their roofs are likely to be in a poorer state of repair, while their associated gardens are more likely to contain less well-managed vegetation and, potentially, a greater abundance of invertebrate prey. Detailed local work carried out in Oxford by Wilkinson (2006) suggests

FIG 51. Nesting opportunities for urban House Sparrows have declined with changes in building regulations and the nature of roof tiles and barge boards. (John Harding)

that gardens with a high density of bushes are more likely to support House Sparrows, as are gardens with a greater proportion of native vegetation. The aversion to green space found in our study was unexpected, given how important it appears to be to House Sparrow populations in other European cities (Murgui, 2009), where private gardens are sometimes less common, but it may be because urban green spaces in the UK tend to be open and rather homogenous in character, reducing their attractiveness to House Sparrows.

Nesting opportunities for urban House Sparrows in the UK appear to be mainly restricted to the cavity sites that form under roof tiles or behind wooden fascia boards, both of which have become increasingly scarce following changes to building regulations and the replacement of wooden fascia boards with those made from PVC. Such changes are also thought to have reduced nesting opportunities for Starlings and Swifts. John Tully (2000; 2001) found that the type of roofing tile used on a house influenced whether or not the property was used by breeding House Sparrows, and work on the BTO House Sparrow dataset also indicates that roof tile type, and restoration work on a property, are linked to whether or not the site retains breeding pairs.

You might imagine that the densities of birds breeding within the built environment would be lower than seen in other habitats; while this is true for some species, it isn't necessarily the case for all, as we have just seen for Blackbird. Great Tit and Blue Tit populations breeding in urban areas in southern Finland, for example, have been recorded breeding at densities of up to 50 pairs per km² and 14 pairs per km² respectively, while those breeding in wider countryside habitats are up to 20 pairs per km² and 5 pairs per km² respectively (Suhonen & Jokimäki, 1988).

SONG AND THE ADVERTISEMENT OF TERRITORY

The dawn chorus is a feature of the garden bird community that provides a welcome start to the day for many householders, though the extent to which it does this may sometimes be determined by the species that are singing; Blackbirds, Robins and Song Thrushes are typically favoured over Woodpigeon and Collared Dove. The question of why birds sing at this time of day has prompted a good deal of research. There are several theories, and supporting evidence, which coalesce around either energetic or behavioural hypotheses. Singing is energetically expensive, especially at dawn when a bird has been unable to feed for several hours and may well be eating into its energy reserves. Where a bird has greater reserves, it may be able to sing for longer, providing an indication of quality and/or condition (Thomas & Cuthill, 2002). The dawn chorus may also serve to support the defence of the territory and the attraction and protection of a mate. In male Wrens, for example, song output is increased when the song of another male (recorded the previous day) is played back from a speaker located in their breeding territory (Amrhein & Erne, 2006). This suggests that the song is a verbal warning to an individual making a territorial incursion. Work in North America on Black-capped Chickadees has revealed that each male is establishing a communication network, in which he is joined by two or three male competitors (Foote *et al.*, 2010). Jennifer Foote's work suggests that singing males are involved in high levels of song matching with their neighbours, and that they match multiple individuals both simultaneously and sequentially.

Dawn is the time of the day when vacant territories are most likely to be occupied by wandering individuals, perhaps reflecting overnight mortality of territory holders – Kacelnik & Krebs (1983) noted that *c.* 5 per cent of territory-holding male tits died between January and May, so singing at dawn provides an opportunity to advertise that a territory is still occupied. It is also just worth

FIG 52. Singing is energetically expensive, particularly so at dawn after a long night without feeding. (John Harding)

mentioning that singing at dawn may benefit from better acoustic conditions, because it is known that there tends to be less wind and turbulence at this time of the day in many habitats. Another feature of dawn is the low light levels, which may make this an inefficient time to seek food, opening up the opportunity to sing instead. Many individuals also sing at dusk, though the combined 'dusk chorus' is significantly reduced compared to that taking place at dawn.

If song is advertising that a territory is occupied, then it also says something about the singing bird, a characteristic that may be used by the female when assessing the quality of a potential mate. Lambrechts & Dhondt (1986) found that song capacity (which includes measures of song length and repertoire size) in male Great Tits correlated with both their lifetime reproductive success and their social dominance at feeding stations during the winter months. This underlines that song capacity is an honest signal of male quality in this species, something that has also been found in many other birds. An important question is whether song output is similar in urban and garden settings compared to other habitat types, and this is what we will examine next.

NOISE POLLUTION

Our towns and cities can be noisy places, the sounds of human activities sometimes proving a challenge to birds seeking to communicate with each other through song. If a bird cannot be heard, then it may be unable to attract a mate or successfully advertise and defend a breeding territory. This may make some urban areas unsuitable for birds, perhaps leaving gardens close to busy roads or factories, for example, without a resident Blackbird or Robin pair. The impacts of roads on the settlement patterns of small birds are well known, and a number of studies have demonstrated that male birds whose territories are close to noisy roads are unable to attract a mate (Reijen & Foppen, 1994). Traffic noise tends to be pitched at a relatively low frequency, and Rheindt (2003) found that those bird species whose songs were much higher-pitched were less sensitive to road noise than species with lower-frequency songs.

Birds may respond to the challenges of noise pollution by changing their behaviour or even the way in which they sing. Work on urban Blackbirds living close to Madrid Airport found that these birds modified their song, changed its timing and sang for longer in the presence of aircraft noise (Sierro et al., 2017). Although variable, Blackbird song is composed of two main components: a series of loud low-frequency whistles, followed by a final flourish. Javier Sierro and colleagues found that airport Blackbirds were more likely to sing songs without the final flourish than their rural counterparts. The airport Blackbirds sang earlier and increased the time they spent singing during that part of the season where the chorus of song and aircraft traffic noise overlapped; this effect then disappearing later in the season, when the chorus and aircraft traffic schedule became separated by the advancement of the dawn chorus. Great Tits, Blue Tits and Chaffinches exposed to considerable traffic noise also move the timing of their song, starting far earlier than populations in quieter locations.

Noise pollution may not just affect the ability of birds to advertise their presence, attract a mate and defend a breeding territory. A population of Great Tits exposed to traffic noise laid smaller clutches and fledged fewer young in the noisiest areas (Halfwerk et al., 2011), though it is not clear whether confounding factors – such as differences in NO_2 levels between the sites – were controlled for sufficiently robustly. A more convincing piece of work demonstrating impacts of noise pollution on reproductive performance comes from a House Sparrow nest box study taking place on the island of Lundy, located in the Bristol Channel (Schroeder et al., 2012). The island relies on a set of generators, running continuously between 6 a.m. and noon. Examination of the breeding success and breeding behaviour of individual pairs nesting at different sites on the island revealed that the noise from the generators was detrimental to those breeding attempts made in nest boxes located close by. House Sparrow chicks reared close to the generators had a lower survival rate between hatching and fledging, and a significantly lower probability of recruiting into the population; they also had a lower body mass at day 12. There are two important aspects to this work: first, the researchers used cross-fostering to control for any variation in the genetic quality of parents, and second, they also examined House Sparrow behaviour during periods when the generators were running and when they were switched off. The behavioural component of the study revealed that female House Sparrows nesting near the generators provisioned their young less frequently than those nesting elsewhere; they also fed their young less frequently when the generators were running than when they were switched off. Schroeder *et al.* suggested that the females fed their chicks less often when the generators were switched on because they could not hear the begging calls of their chicks, which is thought to provide a stimulus to bring in food. Without this signal, the chicks received less food and so did not develop as well as those from broods nesting elsewhere.

NEST SITES

Garden habitats and their associated buildings provide a range of nesting opportunities for birds, but importantly they lack much of the low scrubby cover favoured by certain species (e.g. Whitethroat *Sylvia communis*, Blackcap and Chiffchaff *Phylloscopus collybita*), and they lack the natural cavity sites favoured by others (e.g. Jackdaw, Stock Dove *Columba oenas* and Tawny Owl *Strix aluco*). To a certain extent, the lack of natural cavity sites has been addressed by the availability of nest boxes provided by keen householders, but many of these tend to be of a standard design, favouring nesting tits rather than those species that prefer a larger cavity or entrance hole. The presence of evergreen cover may make gardens particularly attractive to early season species like Blackbird and Song Thrush, while the presence of thorn-bearing bushes may help to reduce the unwanted attentions of potential nest predators.

Several studies have shown that bird nests placed higher in trees have a better chance of survival than those placed lower down (Croci *et al.*, 2008). However, this relationship is likely to be influenced by many other factors, including the type of predators present in the area, the availability of cover around the nest and local climatic conditions, meaning that other researchers have found contrasting results. Katherine Kelleher and John O'Halloran, for example, found that nest

FIG 53. Whitethroat and other species that nest in low cover are uncommon in gardens, even rural ones, because few gardeners tolerate the bramble or nettle beds which these species prefer. (Mike Toms)

height in Song Thrushes breeding in Ireland varied with season, and that nest failure rates were greater at nests built in trees than in those placed in hedgerows or bushes. Nest failure in this study was mostly linked to avian predators, raiding the nest at egg stage, so nests placed in trees may have been easier for these predators to find. Within gardens, Jay, Magpie and Carrion Crow are likely to be the main avian nest predators involved, often visiting early in the morning when small birds are active provisioning chicks left unfed overnight, or taking a break from incubation duties. Most small and medium-sized gardens lack taller mature trees and so may not provide the high nest sites favoured by species like Mistle Thrush *Turdus viscivorus*.

Nest site placement has also been shown to influence nesting success in Blackbirds; by measuring the height at which 430 Blackbird nests were placed, their bulk and the degree of cover around each nest, Ben Hatchwell and colleagues were able to determine that the degree of nest exposure was the only feature that differed significantly between successful and failed nests (Hatchwell *et al.*, 1996b). Successful nests were less exposed than failed ones; interestingly, nest exposure was only important during the laying and incubation period and not during the nestling period. Presumably, the presence of chicks in an active nest increases the chances that it will be found by a predator, reducing the beneficial effects of having cover around the nest.

It appears that the presence of people can also influence breeding success of those birds nesting within the built environment. A study of the Blackbird population breeding on the University of Exeter campus found that those nests placed closer to the paths used by students, staff and visitors, suffered lower rates of nest predation (from Jay, Magpie, Carrion Crow and Grey Squirrel) than those located further from away. This finding did not appear to be linked to differences in the vegetation planted on the campus, since nests at different distances had similar site characteristics, suggesting that the presence of people was responsible for keeping predators away from the nests (Osborne & Osborne, 1980).

Site selection may also be shaped by prevailing weather conditions, something demonstrated by work looking at whether tits, Nuthatch and Pied Flycatcher *Ficedula hypoleuca* show preferences for nest boxes whose entrances are orientated in a particular direction (Gaedecker & Winkel, 2005). Most of

FIG 54. Blackbird nests may be placed low down at the base of a tree but are more often to be found in a garden hedge or climber. (Mike Toms)

the nesting pairs tested by Gaedecker and Winkel selected boxes that faced an easterly direction, either northeast, east or southeast, with the strongest preference exhibited by nesting Pied Flycatchers. As the authors of this work noted, east is the weather-opposing side of a tree, with less moisture and heat inside the box. Interestingly, such preferences may be moderated by what sites are available; the same study found that Starlings using natural cavity sites tended to use those that were orientated southwest. Closer examination of the results revealed that this was a consequence of the high availability of natural sites facing southwest, with fewer facing towards the east.

NESTS

Nests are constructed in a particular way and the process of construction usually results in the development of four functionally distinct components: an attachment layer, an outer layer (often decorative in purpose), a structural layer, and a lining (Hansell, 2000). Not all of these elements are present in all nests. In the case of Blackbird, there are three components: an outer layer mostly composed of grass, moss and stems, a layer of mud, and a lining of grass (Biddle *et al.*, 2015). Bullfinch nests have just two layers: an outer layer of stems or small twigs, and an inner layer of fine rootlets and thin grass culms. The different components serve different purposes, delivering sufficient rigidity and support to the female bird and her eggs, providing camouflage and helping to insulate the nest contents. It is not always clear as to the function of particular components, a good example being the hard lining found in the nest of the Song Thrush. In this species, the outer layer of moss and grass is then lined with a smooth layer of wood pulp and mud or dung; there is no additional lining of grass so the eggs rest directly on the hard lining. It has been suggested that the lining might provide some additional insulative properties (Pikula, 1978) or that it might reduce the number of ectoparasites (Reicholf, 2003), but we don't as yet have a definitive answer.

Nest construction has also been found to vary between species, individuals within a species, within individuals between years and between locations (Biddle *et al.*, 2018). There is certainly evidence that the availability of local materials can shape those used in a nest's construction: Britt & Deeming (2011), for example, noted an increase in the use of wool by Blue Tits and Great Tits in a year when sheep were being kept within the area local to their study site. Some garden birds spend a significant amount of time constructing their nest; this is certainly true of Long-tailed Tit, whose beautiful domed nest, camouflaged with lichen and lined with very large numbers of feathers, can take a pair more than a month to

FIG 55. The nest of the Song Thrush is lined with a hard layer, made from mud and rotten wood. Its purpose is unclear. (Mike Toms)

complete (McGowan *et al.*, 2004). A Long-tailed Tit nest is built in two stages: the pair begins by constructing the outer structure – on average this takes 23 days – before turning their attention to lining the nest with feathers, the latter process taking a further 15 days on average. The length of time spent building a nest tends to decline later in the season, possibly because of the increased urgency to squeeze in a nesting attempt, but it may also reflect changes in environmental conditions, as is the case for Long-tailed Tits. At 11 days, the construction of second nests by Long-tailed Tits is much quicker than for first nests, with the birds reducing the number of feathers incorporated into the nest as the warmer conditions later in the season require less insulation.

An obvious question to raise is whether garden birds, and those living within a wider urbanised environment, use different materials in building their nests or build their nests in different ways from individuals breeding in other habitats. It is known that nests constructed in colder locations tend to be larger than those constructed in warmer locations, which might suggest that the warmer environment of urban areas should favour the construction of smaller nests (Deeming *et al.*, 2012). However, it has also been shown that nests built earlier in the year tend to be larger than those built later – again thought to be linked to temperature differences (Britt & Deeming, 2011); given that some urban birds breed earlier than their rural counterparts, might this counteract the effects of the comparative additional warmth felt in urban areas?

There is evidence from Reading that Blue Tit nests built in boxes in urban areas are lighter than those built in rural areas, but no difference in nest weight was found for the related Great Tit (Hanmer *et al.*, 2017a). Jim Reynolds and colleagues looked at whether the position of nest boxes, used by Blue Tits along an urban gradient in the city of Birmingham, influenced their composition. By taking apart 131 nests removed from nest boxes at the end of the breeding season, the researchers discovered that nest composition did vary significantly depending on where on the urban gradient the box was located. Boxes in areas with a greater degree of built cover contained fewer feathers, while those in areas with more connected tree cover contained more feathers. Perhaps unsurprisingly, given the nature of the habitat, anthropogenic materials were found in nearly three-quarters of the nests examined; however, the inclusion of such material was unrelated to the location of the box on the gradient. Hanmer and his colleagues found a similar pattern in their urban tit populations; both species

FIG 56. Great Tits may use wool, or the material used to coat tennis balls and dog toys in the construction of their nests. (Jill Pakenham)

used anthropogenic material – it was found in 77 per cent of Blue Tit nests examined and 94 per cent of Great Tit nests. Interestingly, roughly a quarter of the materials used by the Great Tits were anthropogenic in origin (highly processed cottons, for example) but the amount used was much lower in Blue Tit, being 16 per cent in garden nest boxes and just 1–2 per cent in areas of urban green space. Hanmer *et al.* (2017a) failed to find any link between the degree of urbanisation and the use of anthropogenic materials. That Blue Tits make less use of anthropogenic material than Great Tits, a finding also reported by Surgey *et al.* (2012), might reflect their preference for feathers when lining the nest, something that they do to a greater degree than Great Tit.

The inclusion of anthropogenic material might be harmful to nesting birds, perhaps increasing the chances of nestlings becoming entangled (Townsend & Barker, 2014) or suffering from toxic effects. Alternatively, such material might be beneficial, reducing the numbers of ectoparasites, such as fleas, found in the nest. Work on this in Mexico City has revealed that both House Finches and House Sparrows incorporate cigarette butts into their nests, and that this behaviour leads to a reduction in the number of ectoparasites within the nest (Suárez-Rodríguez *et al.*, 2012). Elsewhere, the addition of natural plant material to the nests of several different species has been shown to reduce ectoparasite numbers, so this might appear to be an extension of this behaviour. Worryingly, this behaviour comes with a cost, as more recent work by the same authors has shown (Suárez-Rodríguez *et al.*, 2017). Both the House Finches and House Sparrows studied in Mexico City show increased levels of genotoxic damage, seemingly linked to the amount of contact with cigarette butts.

How far garden birds will travel to collect nesting material is unclear, but work on woodland tit populations suggests that individuals do not always use material from the nearest source to their nest (Surgey *et al.*, 2012). By experimentally providing the tits nesting in Treswell Wood, Nottinghamshire, with a wool-like substance, Joanne Surgey, Chris du Feu and Charles Deeming were able to examine use of the material, colour preferences and the distance birds were willing to travel. Although individual birds might collect material from two, three or even four well-separated sources, very few individuals travelled further than 200 m from their nest box. In Great Tit, the most common species in the boxes, use of the material declined with distance to its source. Use of the material appears to be opportunistic, which might explain why we sometimes find material taken from lost tennis balls – popular with dog walkers – in the Great Tit nests built in our woodland Tawny Owl boxes. Another interesting feature of these boxes, which are significantly larger than the small hole-fronted boxes used by many of Great Tits nesting in gardens, is that the birds cover the

FIG 57. Male Wrens make a series of 'cock nests', one of which will be chosen by a prospective mate. The more nests a male builds, the more likely he is to attract a mate. (Mike Toms)

entire floor of the box with nesting material, placing the small cup in one corner. This must require significant investment on the part of the female.

Nest size in Great Tits has also been linked to the quality of the individuals involved in the breeding attempt. Female Great Tits are solely responsible for building the nest, and it has been found that the strength of a female's colouration is related to the size of the nest constructed. Since the strength of plumage colour comes from carotenoids within the diet, the colour serves to indicate an individual's condition. Perhaps most interestingly, the relationship between plumage colour and nest size is even stronger in the males, which suggests that the better-quality females who mate with brighter-coloured males invest more energy in nest construction (Broggi & Senar, 2009). A bigger nest might provide better insulation for the eggs and chicks.

The signalling of quality might manifest in nest construction itself, particularly in those species (such as Wren, Blackcap and Whitethroat) in which the male constructs a number of nests within his territory, one of which will then be selected by his mate. These male nests are known as 'cock nests' and are rarely fully finished. Nevertheless, the effort that a male Wren puts into constructing his nests is substantial, with some individuals building as many as 12 nests within a territory. Male Wrens with more cock nests are more likely to attract a female (Evans & Burn, 1996), and as a male ages so he builds more nests. This appears to be accomplished by starting nest building earlier in the season and by going on building for longer, rather than building the nests more quickly as he gets older. While you might assume that older individuals are more likely to attract a mate than younger ones, this is not necessarily the case. The number of nests constructed is also influenced by the habitat structure present on the territory and by male body mass, with heavier males starting nest construction earlier in the season than lighter males (Evans, 1997). While male Wrens do build more nests per season as they get older, the variation seen within a year between different males is much greater than that seen between years within a male's lifetime. As Matthew Evans notes in the conclusion to one of his papers, '*Some males are more accomplished nest builders than others and that while males do improve with age, age cannot compensate for lack of ability.*'

NEST BOXES

Nest box designs can be grouped into three main types: those with a small entrance hole ('hole-fronted'), those with a large, more open entrance ('open-fronted') and those of a specialist nature and usually designed for one particular species ('specialist boxes'). Many of the simple designs can be made yourself, following the cutting plans that appear in books (Cromack, 2018) or online, but more complex designs may be better purchased from specialist suppliers. Nest boxes for common garden birds are readily available from wild bird care companies, garden centres and even supermarkets, though the quality of the design (and indeed the product itself) can vary markedly. For this reason it is worth considering the species you wish to attract and noting down its requirements before you go out to purchase a nest box. Plenty of suitable advice can be found online but there are some general pointers worth following. For a hole-fronted box, check that the diameter of the entrance hole is the right size for the species you wish to attract (see Table 6) and make sure that the distance from the bottom of the entrance hole to the floor of the box is at least 12 cm; any less than this, then you may increase the risk of the nest being predated. Make sure that the box is made from wood that is at least 15 mm thick; the insulative properties of the box may be insufficient if the wood used is thinner than this and the chicks may chill or overheat. Avoid boxes that have a perch; small birds won't need a perch but a predator might be able to make use of it.

TABLE 6. Suggested box dimensions and entrance hole diameters for hole-fronted boxes used by garden birds. All measurements are in mm.

Species	Size of base	Size of front panel	Entrance hole diameter
Robin	150 × 120	150 × 100	—
Wren	150 × 120	150 × 140	—
Spotted Flycatcher	150 × 120	150 × 60	—
Blue Tit	150 × 120	150 × 175	25
Great Tit	150 × 120	150 × 175	28
Coal Tit	150 × 120	150 × 175	25
Nuthatch	150 × 120	150 × 175	32
Jackdaw	300 × 300	300 × 400	150
Starling	150 × 180	150 × 250	45
House Sparrow	150 × 120	150 × 175	32
Tree Sparrow	150 × 120	150 × 175	28

Do not purchase a box that is incorporated into the roof of a bird table; any bird that chooses to use the box will spend all of its energy trying to chase away all the birds that arrive to feed at the bird table below. A good nest box will be well made and allow access for cleaning it out at the end of the breeding season or for monitoring the progress of the nesting attempt if you are submitting data to the BTO Nest Record Scheme.

Davies *et al.* (2009) reported on data collected through the Survey of English Housing and other studies, suggesting that on average at least 16 per cent of UK households had at least one nest box associated with their property. Scaled up, this suggests a minimum of 4.3 million nest boxes are available to UK birds. Of course, not all of these nest boxes will be suitable, perhaps because the entrance hole or the box itself is too small to attract interest. Nest boxes are usually less well insulated than natural cavity sites – though the degree of insulation does vary substantially between different types or makes of nest box – and this may contribute to the finding that nest boxes are sometimes associated with lower rates of nestling survival during periods of inclement weather (Duckworth *et al.*, 2017). Nest boxes may – again depending upon type – suffer from higher levels of predation under certain circumstances. A review by Vincze *et al.* (2017) revealed that artificial nests (both nest boxes and nesting cups) placed in urban areas were more likely to be predated than was the case for natural nests. Interestingly, the reverse was found to be the case for less urbanised landscapes.

EGGS

The egg is a truly remarkable thing, containing as it does all of the nutrients (except for oxygen) necessary for the developing embryo. Its production requires a female bird to deposit sufficient fat, protein, water and calcium to make the egg viable; for a small bird, with a large clutch of eggs, the accumulation of these materials may be a substantial task. Some of these materials will be easier to secure than others; the 1.3 g of water needed for each Great Tit egg, for example, should not present too much of a challenge, but finding sufficient calcium (see below) may be more difficult. Because of their small body size, most garden birds will be unable to store these materials in the quantities required for a whole clutch of eggs, which implies that they must collect the materials during the period over which the eggs are being formed and laid. There is some evidence that certain materials, for example fat, can be stored in small amounts; it is thought that female House Sparrows can store sufficient fat to service some 30 per cent of the energy required for her clutch of eggs (Schifferli, 1980).

FIG 58. A clutch of eggs represents a serious investment of resources for a small bird – here those of a Linnet. (Mike Toms)

Small birds may counter some of the difficulties in sourcing sufficient nutrients by adopting different behaviours during the laying period or modifying existing ones. They may, for example, change the interval over which eggs are laid; this appears to be constrained in tits – which have a large clutch to lay – but is seen in the Swift, which usually lays its eggs two days apart but will increase this interval to three days if weather conditions are poor. Birds may also change the size of their eggs in relation to the available resources (see below); interestingly, female Goldcrests regularly produce larger eggs as the laying sequence progresses, resulting in the last egg being as much as 20 per cent larger than the first to be laid (Haftorn, 1986). A third option is for the male to provide his mate with additional resources, a behaviour referred to as 'courtship feeding'. This behaviour is seen in a number of garden bird species, and in Blue Tit these additional resources are estimated to match the increase in energy demand that the female experiences during the egg laying period (Krebs, 1970). In addition to providing extra resources for the female, courtship feeding may help to cement the pair bond or even provide the female with information about her mate's ability to provision nestlings.

CALCIUM AND EGG FORMATION

Snails are likely to be an important source of the dietary calcium needed by small birds for the formation of their eggshells, the importance of which is demonstrated by a piece of work carried out in the Netherlands. Drent & Woldendorp (1989), working in the Buunderkamp Forest, observed that about a third of the female Great Tits in their study population produced eggs with thin or porous shells, defects that were also evident from other forest study sites located on calcium-poor soils. Using an experimental approach, Drent was able to quantify the rates of eggshell defects and their impacts on breeding success, before going on to counter them through the provision of supplemented sources of calcium (Graveland & Drent, 1997). Providing some of the Great Tits with an additional source of calcium in the form of snail shells and chicken eggshells reduced the number of females who did not produce any eggs, lowered the frequency of clutch desertion – which had been as high as 48 per cent in females laying one or more defective eggs – and reduced the proportion of nests with defective eggs. A study of Great Tit populations breeding in mixed deciduous woodland here in the UK found that females nesting in low-calcium areas, where snails were known to be scarce, laid thinner-shelled eggs than did females breeding in high-calcium areas (Gosler et al., 2005).

FIG 59. Snail shells, such as these scattered on a Song Thrush anvil, may be an important source of the calcium used by small garden birds to form their clutch of eggs. (Mike Toms)

Human-induced acid deposition was thought to be responsible for the increased levels of defective eggs seen by Graveland and Drent – and presumably for a decline in the abundance of the small snails on which the Great Tits were dependent for dietary calcium. However, the availability of small snails may also vary between habitat types, with differences in underlying geology, or because of the chemical control of snail populations through the use of molluscicides. This could mean that some gardens – particularly those within highly urbanised landscapes – support fewer small snails and, as a consequence, have less dietary calcium available to small birds.

While larger birds may be able to utilise some of their skeletal calcium to produce eggshells in areas of low environmental calcium, this is not an option for a small bird like a Great Tit or Blue Tit. A Blue Tit will need to find 0.25 g of calcium for a clutch of eggs but has just 0.175 g present within her 0.5 g skeleton. Some 90 per cent of the calcium required by a female Great Tit for her clutch of 6–9 eggs is consumed during the egg laying period. Small birds may have to respond to a decrease in calcium supply by increasing the amount of time that they put into searching for suitable sources (Holford & Roby, 1993). Female Great Tits faced with such shortages may spend 43 per cent of available daylight hours searching for calcium during the egg laying period, almost double the amount of time spent by females with sufficient calcium available to them (Graveland & Berends, 1997). The presence of snail shells in the crops and gizzards of female House Sparrows during the egg laying period demonstrates that these birds take small snails for their calcium, because this a prey type that does not normally feature in their diet. Spotted Flycatchers appear to make use of calcium-rich woodlice, coming down to the ground to catch them. As we have just noted, experimental studies reveal that the addition of calcium-rich supplementary food can counter the impacts of calcium shortage in tits (Tilgar *et al.*, 2002). This is of particular relevance to gardens because some of the bird foods marketed by wild bird care companies include oyster shell grit, which may provide egg laying birds with a ready source of accessible calcium.

The eggshell thickness of Song Thrushes, Mistle Thrushes and Blackbirds in the UK has been examined by Rhys Green (1998). Using material from museum collections, Green found that there had been widespread declines in eggshell thickness in all three species since the nineteenth century. Although the cause of these declines is unknown, the evidence highlights that eggshell thinning in these species began before the widespread use of the organochlorine pesticide DDT, whose introduction led to eggshell thinning in birds of prey and fish-eating birds from 1947 onwards. Green suggested that the underlying cause may have been acid deposition, leading to a reduction in snail populations. Declines in the pH of undisturbed soil samples, taken from southern England and archived, provides supporting evidence for this (Goulding & Blake, 1993). The question of whether there are differences in eggshell thickness in populations of garden bird species living within urban and rural habitats has been little studied, though Bailly *et al.* (2016) found no difference in eggshell thickness for either Blue Tit or Great Tit when they compared urban populations with those in forest habitat. Brahmia *et al.* (2013) also failed to find any difference in eggshell thickness in their study populations of Blue Tits, again looking at rural and urban sites.

Eggshell thickness has also been examined in relation to the pigmentation that is found on the eggs of many garden bird species. Eggshell patterning is a feature of many small birds, though it is much less common in non-passerines, which typically have unpatterned eggs. Patterning may have a signalling role, revealing female condition or quality (Moreno *et al.*, 2004), or act to camouflage the egg against its surroundings. It may also be used by females to reduce the chances of successful egg-parasitism by a Cuckoo *Cuculus canorus* (Davies & Brooke, 1989). More recent work (Gosler *et al.*, 2005) has postulated that eggshell patterning may have a structural role, since the deposition of protoporphyrin pigments in Great Tit eggs correlates with shell thickness. Thinner areas of the shell are marked by the addition of pigment, and there is a relationship between the darkness of the pigment deposited and the degree of thinning. The pattern of pigment spread in Great Tit eggs from Gosler's long-running study has changed over time, matching a decline in soil calcium levels and a decline of 6.5 per cent in eggshell thickness, adding further evidence for a structural role (Gosler & Wilkin, 2017). Another response to reduced calcium availability may be a change in egg shape, with spherical eggs more common in Great Tit populations living in areas with lower calcium availability in the soil. A spherical shape is stronger than a less spherical shape.

Eggs are not just variable in their patterning and shape, they can also vary in size and not just between species. Variation in size (and patterning) within a clutch of eggs is common and while such variation is usually quite small, there can be significant differences. Perrins (1996), for example, reports on the variation in a sample of 4,752 Great Tits eggs, weighed before incubation had been initiated. The smallest egg recorded weighed 1.0 g, while the largest was 2.1 g. There are some general patterns relating to egg size, teased out from various studies across a number of species over many years. Eggs tend to be slightly smaller in larger clutches, in clutches laid early in the season and when formed during periods of low temperatures. They are also smaller when population density is high, which, in the case of Great Tit, can include the high density of competing species (in this case Blue Tit). In Great Tit, it also appears that egg size may be influenced by the nature of the nest box in which the bird is breeding, as Perrins (1996) found a stepped decline in egg size following the replacement of his project nest boxes with a new 'anti predator' design. Egg size is important because it has consequences for later life, having been demonstrated to influence hatching success, fledging success and fledging weight, the latter linked to subsequent recruitment into the breeding population.

CLUTCH SIZE, PARENTAGE AND LAYING ORDER

Clutch size is likely to be shaped by how many eggs a female bird can produce and incubate successfully; it is also likely to be shaped by the number of chicks that can be supported once the clutch has hatched. The typical clutch sizes of a range of garden bird species are shown in Table 7. Within single-brooded species, clutch size tends to decline over the course of the season (Kluijver, 1951), while for multi-brooded species it tends to peak in the middle of the season (Ludvig et al., 1995).

TABLE 7. The breeding traits of some common garden birds. Data derived from the BTO Nest Record Scheme.

Species	No. broods	Clutch size	Incubation (days)	Young in nest (days)
Feral Pigeon	2–3	2	17–19	c. 25
Stock Dove	2–3	2	16–18	27–28
Woodpigeon	2–3	2	17	29–35
Collared Dove	2–3	2	14–16	c. 18
Swift	1	2–3	19–20	37–56
Jackdaw	1	4–5	21–22	22–28
Blue Tit	1	8–10	12–16	16–22
Great Tit	1 (2)	6–9	c. 14	c. 19
Coal Tit	1–2	8–10	14–16	18–20
House Martin	2 (3)	4–5	14–16	19–25
Long-tailed Tit	1	6–9	14–16	14–17
Nuthatch	1	6–8	15–16	23–25
Wren	2	5–6	13–18	14–19
Starling	1 (2)	4–5	c. 12	c. 21
Blackbird	2–3	3–4	13–14	12–15
Song Thrush	2–4	4	13–14	13
Spotted Flycatcher	1 (2)	4–5	12–14	c.13
Robin	2	4–5	13–14	13–14
Dunnock	2 (3)	4–5	11–12	c. 12
House Sparrow	2–3	4–5	c. 12	14–15
Tree Sparrow	2 (3)	5–6	11–14	15–20
Chaffinch	1 (2)	4–5	11–13	c. 14
Greenfinch	2 (3)	4–5	c. 13	13–16
Goldfinch	2	4–5	12–13	14–15

Our meta-analysis of demographic differences between urban and rural populations included 46 clutch size comparisons across 19 different species. In general, we found that clutch size was larger in non-urban landscapes. The clutch sizes of Blackbird, Great Tit, Blue Tit and Starling were all consistently larger in non-urban than urban landscapes. However, no significant differences were

revealed in studies on Magpie (Eden, 1985; Antonov & Atanasova, 2003), Song
Thrush (Kelleher & O'Halloran, 2007) or House Sparrow (Crick & Siriwardena,
2002). Clutch size in urban Great Tit and Blue Tit populations within southern
Finland has been found to be some 9.8 to 17.3 per cent smaller in urban areas than
in rural habitats (Solonen, 2001), a pattern also seen within UK populations of
these species (Perrins, 1965; Cowie & Hinsley, 1987). While there is good evidence
to support the suggestion that urban-nesting attempts begin earlier because of
the supplementary food available at garden feeding stations, it is less clear as to
why urban clutch sizes are generally lower than those seen in wider countryside
habitats. Possible causes include a greater proportion of young/lower quality
individuals within the urban breeding populations or a lack of suitable foods for
the female birds producing the eggs. It is even possible that the smaller urban
clutch sizes are an adaptive response to the poorer feeding conditions faced by
birds seeking to rear chicks within this environment. Of these possibilities, it
is the greater proportion of young or lower quality individuals within urban
populations that is perhaps most likely to be driving the difference.

In many garden birds that appear to pair with a single partner – this is
referred to as being socially monogamous – it is often the case that the males will

FIG 60. Offspring quality may be shaped by the order in which an egg has been laid, by the
food provided at the nest and by the sex of the individual that has hatched. (John Harding)

seek to mate with paired females who are not their partner. Such matings are referred to as extra-pair copulations and they result in a brood of chicks of mixed parentage. Extra-pair paternity in birds has been investigated in over 150 studies, encompassing nearly as many species (see Griffith *et al.*, 2002 for a review). Females may also solicit extra-pair copulations, as we'll discover later in this book when we take a more detailed look at the sex life of the Dunnock. In Great Tit, the frequency of extra-pair paternity has been estimated at between 5.4 per cent and 14 per cent of offspring (Blakey, 1994; Lubjuhn *et al.*, 1999). In one long-term study of Great Tits, it was revealed that in each year 27.8–44.2 per cent of broods contained at least one nestling that derived from a male other than its social father. Work on Blue Tits in Belgium revealed that extra-pair paternity occurred in 31–47 per cent of all nests and accounted for 11–14 per cent of all offspring (Kempenaers *et al.*, 1997).

One other aspect of the reproductive behaviour of garden birds is worth a mention here and that is laying order. The order in which eggs are laid can have an effect on the survival chances of the chicks that will emerge. In a way, we have already touched on this in our discussions of egg size and the resources put into eggs. There can be another effect of laying order and that is offspring sex. It has been shown that some female birds can skew the primary sex ratio of their offspring in response to breeding conditions. Female Blue Tits, for example, tend to produce more sons when mated to attractive males (Sheldon *et al.*, 1999), while Tawny Owls produce more daughters when there is a high availability of food resources (Appleby *et al.*, 1997). In Tawny Owl the female is the larger sex, and a female chick may require more food resources than a male chick. More recently it has been found that female Blue Tits may adjust the sex of their offspring according to the order in which their eggs are laid (Cicho *et al.*, 2003). It appears that female Blue Tits may favour daughters in the first eggs laid, with the proportion of sons quickly increasing after this. There is a small size difference between male and female Blue Tits, and having the smaller sex (female) in the early eggs may balance out the relative disadvantage of being a smaller individual within a brood of nestlings.

INCUBATION BEHAVIOUR IN GARDEN BIRDS

Most small garden birds lay one egg each day, usually early in the morning. It has generally been assumed that cavity-nesting birds like Blue Tits and Great Tits remain in the nest cavity overnight, and there is good evidence that this is the case (Pendlebury & Bryant, 2005). Such behaviour probably helps to reduce the energetic costs to the female, because conditions inside the box will be better than those outside, and it probably also reduces her risk of being predated or of her nesting attempt being usurped by another bird. We know that tits do not begin to incubate their clutch until the last egg (or the penultimate egg) has been laid; if they did, then the eggs would all hatch at different times. So how does the female avoid initiating incubation while remaining in the box overnight? By filming nesting Great Tits, Chris Pendlebury and David Bryant were able to show that most female Great Tits spend the night settled in the nest cup, head pushed down into the nesting material or tucked under a wing. Temperature probes inserted into the nest revealed that the nest cup temperature did not increase above the value at which incubation would begin, so the females must have been able to prevent their body heat reaching the eggs. Whether they did this by placing nest material between the eggs and themselves, by not allowing their brood patch to come into contact with the eggs, or because the brood patch was not yet fully developed is unclear.

Another reason why female tits may remain within the nest box overnight is to prevent damage to the developing egg. The shell of each new egg is laid down over several hours, often beginning at midday and being completed by 6 a.m. the following morning (Schifferli, 1979). During the initial stages of this process, the shell is soft and less readily damaged, as Schifferli (1977) demonstrated for female House Sparrows – those handled during the day produced undamaged eggs, while a large proportion of those handled overnight produced damaged eggs. By remaining in the nest box and not moving around, the female tit may reduce the chances of damage to her developing egg. It should just be noted that not all birds lay at dawn; Blackbirds, for example, appear to lay somewhat later into the morning (Perrins, 1996).

Incubation is usually the responsibility of the female but in a few garden bird species the male may also get involved, though usually to a lesser degree. In Woodpigeon, the two sexes split incubation between them, with each sex taking a significant shift. In other species, males may cover the eggs while the female is away from the nest feeding, perhaps reducing the amount of heat lost but not actually incubating the eggs. The length of incubation bouts varies between species and in relation to time of day and weather conditions. Typically, an incubating female will leave the nest every 30–40 minutes in order to feed, returning some 5–10 minutes later. The male may accompany her or, as we have just seen, sit on the nest or remain nearby. Interestingly, the males of some garden birds provision the female while she is incubating, a behaviour seen in Long-tailed Tit during incubation but not during egg laying. It has been shown that the provision of food to incubating female Long-tailed Tits enables them to incubate for longer in a given incubation bout (Hatchwell et al., 1999a). Male

FIG 61. Bouts of incubation are typically broken by periods when the female leaves the nest to feed; in some species (including Collared Dove) both sexes may incubate the eggs. (Mike Toms)

Magpies meet most of the food needs of their mate while she is incubating, with urban males often relying on the availability of scraps and discarded food; this resource, which is common in most towns and cities, may be one reason why urban Magpies breed earlier than their rural counterparts (Antonov & Atanasova, 2003).

Incubation can be a dangerous period for nesting birds, with incubating females and their eggs facing obvious risks from nest predators. Rates of nest failure during the incubation period are very high for Long-tailed Tits, with Hatchwell *et al.* (1999) recording losses of 47 per cent for their study population, and this is also true of other garden bird species. Working in the Hungarian city of Pécs, Kornélia Kurucz found that the daily survival rates of her study Blackbird nests were significantly higher once the eggs had hatched than was the case during the incubation period; this appeared to result from a mixture of egg predation and clutch abandonment (Kurucz *et al.*, 2012). Apparent clutch abandonment may be the result of predation – the adult bird being taken from the nest or while away foraging – or it may be a genuine case of the parent bird deserting the eggs. It is known that short-term changes in food supply or weather conditions can result in a clutch of eggs being abandoned. Failure of the eggs to hatch may also result in clutch abandonment but, while a common problem, it is unusual for an entire clutch to fail to hatch when the incubation duties of the parent bird have been successfully delivered.

HATCHING SUCCESS

A study of House Sparrow populations along an urban gradient (Peach *et al.*, 2008) revealed that, from an average clutch size of 4.04 eggs, 77 per cent of eggs hatched and 65 per cent of chicks fledged. This resulted in an average of 2.02 chicks fledging from each nesting attempt. However, a quarter of the nesting attempts made failed to fledge any chicks. Examination of the eggs that failed to hatch suggested that in most cases this was due to the eggs being infertile. A more detailed study of egg and chick mortality in House Sparrow (and Tree Sparrow) revealed similar levels of egg mortality (30 per cent for House Sparrow and 25 per cent for Tree Sparrow). The same study also found that nestling mortality ranged from 24–30 per cent for both sparrow species (Pinowski *et al.*, 1994). A large proportion of both eggs and chicks from this study were found to be infected with disease microorganisms, with *Escherichia coli* (*E.coli*) predominating. Work in Norway has looked at the bacterial loads present on Magpie eggs, revealing that those laid in urban nests harbour a greater abundance of *E.coli* and other microbes than rural ones; the differences in microbial loads being related to the difference in hatching success and nestling survival in these two environments, with urban populations exhibiting generally lower hatching success (Lee *et al.*, 2017).

The presence of ectoparasites within the nest may also influence hatching success; work on a nest box population of Great Tits, for example, found hatching success to be lower in boxes with higher levels of ectoparasites present, something that individual birds attempted to counter by preferentially selecting boxes with lower numbers of parasites where they could (Oppliger *et al.*, 1994). Other external factors may also exert an influence on hatching success. Work examining the impacts of the Chernobyl nuclear accident have, for example, highlighted that elevated levels of background radiation can reduce hatching success in Great Tits (Møller *et al.*, 2008), and other work has demonstrated the impacts of heavy metal pollution on Pied Flycatchers and Great Tits (Eeva & Lehikoinen, 1995).

Other factors influencing hatching success may relate to the parent birds themselves, such as their age, condition or fertility, or to other aspects of the breeding attempt. Lower rates of hatching success have been reported in young

FIG 62. House Martin nesting attempts may fail for many different reasons, from the nest being taken over by House Sparrows through to the loss of the adult birds to Hobby. (John Harding)

individuals in a number of longer-lived species, but this is something that is less readily determined for short-lived garden birds like tits and thrushes. Condition, perhaps influenced by disease, parasite load or available food resources, may shape an individual's ability to produce viable eggs or alter the pattern of incubation behaviour in ways that reduce the chances of eggs hatching (Arcese & Smith, 1988). Clutch size may also play a role, as determined experimentally for Starlings by Reid *et al.* (2000), who found that eggs incubated within experimentally enlarged clutches exhibited lower levels of hatching success than those incubated within natural-sized clutches. Even within a breeding pair, hatching success may vary with the timing of their nesting attempt. It has already been noted that breeding attempts made in the middle of the season by multi-brooded species like Blackbird should be more successful, but this is not always the case. Working on an urban Blackbird population in Budapest, Hungary, Ludvig *et al.* (1995) found that while clutch size peaked during the middle of the breeding season, hatching success declined, reducing the potential productivity gain from having a larger clutch. Looking more closely at their data, together with that on local weather conditions, it became clear that food shortage during the period of egg formation (brought about by dry weather reducing earthworm availability) led to the production of lower quality eggs, resulting in lower hatching success.

BROOD SIZE

Brood size is influenced by the number of eggs laid, but it is also shaped by hatching success and subsequent levels of chick mortality. In particular, the lack of suitable invertebrate prey within gardens and the wider urban landscape may impact brood size during the latter stages of the nestling period. Nutritional stress has been put forward as the most plausible explanation for the reduction in average brood size in the extensive sample of House Sparrow nests monitored annually through the BTO Nest Record Scheme. Since clutch sizes tend to be smaller in urban populations than those of the wider countryside, it follows that brood sizes also tend to be smaller. The smaller clutch sizes seen in urban tit populations should make it easier for the parent birds to provision their chicks with sufficient food, thereby mitigating some of the negative effects of breeding within an urban environment and emerging through reduced clutch size. However, this does not seem to be the case, at least for some of the tit populations studied. Solonen's study in southern Finland, mentioned earlier in this chapter, revealed that urban clutches of Great Tit and Blue Tit were some 9.8 to 17.3 per cent smaller than those seen in rural areas; however, fledging success proved to be as much as 19.3 to 21.5 per cent lower, suggesting that the smaller number of chicks hatched did not compensate for the smaller clutch sizes. It seems that these urban breeding birds faced additional challenges.

It has been suggested that female birds might seek to manipulate the age structure of their broods in order to best meet the resource constraints faced during the chick-rearing period. Writing in 1947, David Lack suggested that differences in nestling size, resulting from asynchronous hatching, can lead to competitive differences which allow the efficient reduction of brood size during times of food shortage. This behaviour is well known in owls and other raptors, but it can also occur in small birds like Blackbird and Magpie (Magrath, 1990; 1992). If food proves to be scarce, then the smallest chicks, which are likely to be the ones last to hatch, are outcompeted by their larger siblings and quickly die. The brood size becomes reduced until it reaches the optimal size for the resources available. Were all of the chicks to hatch at the same time, they would be equally competitive, leaving a shortage of food to jeopardise the whole

FIG 63. The success of a breeding attempt may depend on an adult Great Tit's ability to find sufficient invertebrate prey from the garden and its surroundings. (John Harding)

brood rather than just the youngest nestling. While hatching asynchrony is well known, supporting Lack's hypothesis, there have been numerous studies which demonstrate that parents can successfully raise additional offspring to independence (e.g. Boyce & Perrins, 1987, for Great Tit).

There are, of course, trade-offs between brood size and offspring quality, such that while a pair of Great Tits may be able to rear a large brood, the quality of the individual chicks may be lower than would have been the case were the birds to have produced a smaller brood. Smith *et al.* (1989) demonstrated this by artificially manipulating the brood size of Great Tit pairs within their study population, finding that nestlings in enlarged broods grew more slowly in the nest and suffered higher levels of mortality, both within the nest and after leaving it. Raising a larger brood may also have implications for the parent birds, perhaps even reducing their future survival prospects. Smith *et al.*'s parent Great Tits, rearing the artificially enlarged broods, experienced higher levels of summer mortality than those with smaller broods; similar effects have been found for Blue Tit (Nur, 1984a; 1984b).

THE PROVISION OF PREY

It has been possible to examine the rates of food provision to broods of Blue Tits and Great Tits in suburban gardens through the use of nest box cameras (Cowie & Hinsley, 1988b). These reveal that, on average, Great Tits make 22.6 visits per hour, while Blue Tits average 50.9 visits per hour, both of which are comparable to the visit rates made by their woodland counterparts. It is also possible to calculate the weight of prey provisioned; in the case of the Great Tits studied by Cowie & Hinsley, the mean fresh weight provisioned is 105.1 mg, which again is comparable to woodland populations (105 mg: van Balen, 1973; 122 mg: Gibb & Betts, 1963). The mean fresh weight of prey delivered to Blue Tit nests studied by Cowie & Hinsley, which was calculated to be 32.0 mg, is substantially below that seen in woodland (65 mg: Gibb & Betts, 1963). Cowie & Hinsley's suburban tits were feeding mostly small invertebrates, with spiders (Great Tit) and aphids (Blue Tit) seemingly important, something that contrasts with the high proportion of caterpillars taken in the diets of both of these species when breeding within mixed

FIG 64. Bullfinches feed their young by regurgitation, so won't be seen carrying food to their nest site. (John Harding)

deciduous woodland (Riddington & Gosler, 1995). It would be valuable to secure additional studies on the visits rates seen in urban tits and other garden birds.

Both time of year and time of day can influence the prey delivered to nest boxes. Great Tits, for example, provision more craneflies and hoverflies early in the morning to boxes located in suburban gardens than is the case later in the day, presumably because these insects are more sluggish early in the day and become harder to catch as it warms up (Cowie & Hinsley, 1988b). Provisioning rates may also be shaped by the number of chicks in the brood, something evident from work on Blackbirds (Chamberlain *et al.*, 1999), which demonstrates that parental provisioning rates increase with brood size. The diet of suburban Blackbirds is dominated by earthworms, typically taken from areas of short turf, such as lawns. The availability of these worms close to the soil's surface – where they can be taken by the birds – is influenced by soil moisture, with recent rainfall greatly aiding the bird's chances of taking worms. During periods of dry weather, and with earthworms unavailable, provisioning becomes much more difficult and whole Blackbird broods may starve. Dry conditions of this kind appear to be less of an issue for Song Thrush, which is able to switch to snails. Recent work on Blackbirds, using new statistical methods (Miller *et al.*, 2017), underlines the importance of rainfall for urban populations feeding on soil invertebrates. Mark Miller and colleagues found that nest success was influenced by the amount of recent precipitation in urban habitats, but that it was the longer-term availability of soil moisture which was important in wider countryside habitats, suggesting that the urban environment is more challenging in this regard.

The delivery of prey to Long-tailed Tit nestlings is often boosted by the presence of 'helpers'; these are individuals who are usually a close relative of one of the parent birds (Russell & Hatchwell, 2001). About half of all Long-tailed Tit broods studied by Ben Hatchwell and his colleagues (Hatchwell *et al.*, 2004) had helpers, 86 per cent of which were male. The presence of the helpers has long-term benefits for the recruitment of young from these breeding attempts, thereby delivering indirect fitness benefits for the helpers, if related, though these are substantially lower than the benefits that the helpers would have achieved had they managed a successful breeding attempt of their own. This suggests that the helpers are making the best of a bad job, their own breeding attempt having failed. Other work by the team at Sheffield (McGowan *et al.*, 2003) has revealed that failed breeders who become helpers have a higher survival probability than those failed breeders who do not; however, they also have a lower probability of successfully breeding in a subsequent year, suggesting there are additional costs and benefits to becoming a helper. Interestingly, Hatchwell & Russell (1996) showed experimentally that parents with helpers reduce their own provisioning effort. The presence of helpers does not always result in a reduction in parental provisioning, as can be seen from work on Dunnocks (Byle, 1990), where 'beta' males only help to provision a female's chicks if they have copulated with her; in fact, the greater the access a 'beta' male has to the female, the greater proportion of feeds he will provide.

Garden birds exhibit a considerable degree of variation in the extent to which male parents contribute to the care of their young (Silver *et al.*, 1985). The need for male provisioning (and indeed social monogamy) may have evolved in circumstances where two parents are required to rear young successfully, perhaps because of the challenges in finding sufficient food. This being the case, one would expect paternal care to increase chick survival and/or growth (Aho *et al.*, 2009). The level of parental care invested can also be viewed as an evolutionary strategy, balancing the costs and benefits of parental investment. If a bird invests time and energy in parental care, then it may be sacrificing other opportunities to improve its reproductive success, such as by pursing other matings. If a species makes multiple breeding attempts in a season, then the costs and benefits of deserting a brood of chicks and an existing mate also come into play. This is something that has been examined in the Treecreeper (see Chapter 7).

FIG 65. Magpies provide a wide range of invertebrate prey to their chicks, with some prey items more likely to be prepared by the adult before feeding. (Jill Pakenham)

Some garden birds prepare food items before giving them to their nestlings, perhaps because some parts may be dangerous (e.g. the sting of a bee) or even toxic; others may be too large for the chick to consume and so need to be butchered to a more manageable size. A study of Great Tits, for example, has revealed that prey preparation is mainly focussed on larger prey items, with the degree of preparation falling as the chicks grow in size (Barba *et al.*, 1996). Blue Tit parents may prepare certain food types more than others, the work of Jerzy Bañbura and colleagues revealing that while caterpillars are processed quickly, spiders and grasshoppers receive much more detailed treatment (Bañbura *et al.*, 1999). Magpies also prepare some of the invertebrate prey that they feed to their nestlings more than others (Ponz *et al.*, 1999).

CHICK GROWTH

It is amazing just how quickly a tiny chick, fresh out of the egg, can grow; in Blackcap, for example, a chick is capable of leaving the nest at just over a week old, though it usually fledges at 11 or 12 days old. A Blackbird chick usually leaves the nest at 12 to 15 days of age, though will then follow its parent around for another couple of weeks before it gains independence. Woodpigeon chicks, on the other hand, don't fledge until they are a month old or more. The risk of predation places a selection pressure on time spent in the nest, with resources directed to those parts of the chick's body that will enable it to leave the nest as soon as it can. Investment in those parts of the body, such as body feathering, that are less important at this stage is reduced. The chicks of some birds are able to leave the nest immediately after hatching; this ability is a feature of gamebirds and waders, but is not generally seen in those species nesting within gardens – Pheasant *Phasianus colchicus*, Red-legged Partridge and Mallard being the obvious exceptions.

The growth rates of chicks are influenced by food availability and by the provisioning rates of their parents. When the weather is poor, such as during periods of rain, invertebrate prey may be harder to find and the female parent may have to spend time brooding the chicks rather than foraging. It has been shown that the presence of daytime rain, falling at above the rate of 1 mm per hour, results in a 10 to 20 per cent reduction in Great Tit chick growth rates compared to what it would have been had it been dry (Keller & van Noordwijk, 1994). Provisioning rates may also vary with the time of day, being greatest early in the morning. One of the drivers for provisioning rate is the level of begging behaviour of the chicks, something to which we alluded earlier in this book when discussing the impact of background noise on House Sparrow feeding rates. Higher rates of begging tend to lead to increased rates of food provision in garden birds like Blue Tit (Grieco, 2002).

In House Sparrow, the body mass of chicks at day 13 has been found to be a good predictor of post-fledging survival probability (Hole, 2001). Chick growth may be influenced by environmental conditions, including the weather and the possible effects of pollutants on prey availability. In one urban House Sparrow population, body condition at 2–6 days and body mass at 10–12 days of age were both found to be strongly and negatively related to the local NO_2 concentration (Peach et al., 2008). As we have seen, the weight at fledging is important for chicks because reproductive performance in later life has been found to be positively related to weight at fledging (Haywood & Perrins, 1992). Elsewhere, comparisons have been made between urban and rural populations of House Sparrows, examining the types of food provided and the patterns of nestling growth. These studies suggest that an inadequate diet is responsible for poor nestling growth and that where chicks are cross-fostered, or reared in captivity, these differences disappear.

CHICK MORTALITY

Chick mortality is a common feature of many nesting attempts, with much of this mortality occurring within the first few days after hatching. Levels of mortality at the chick stage appear to be lower than that seen at the egg stage, at least in the small number of cases where this has been studied in detail within urban populations (e.g. Ebenman & Karlsson, 1984). Most of the chick mortality seen in an urban House Sparrow population in Leicester was found to occur within the first four days after hatching, and appeared to be the result of starvation (Peach et al., 2008), a pattern also seen in a study of North American House Sparrows (Mock et al., 2009). Douglas Mock's study revealed that chick mortality occurred in 42 per cent of the broods studied, occurring more frequently in larger broods than smaller ones. The first chicks to die are typically the individuals that were the last to hatch (Veiga, 1990), and mortality appears to be linked to starvation, occurring most frequently when parents are only able to provision at low levels to large broods. Studies of Finnish Starlings found that chick mortality was greatest where mean chick weights were low and between-sibling weight differences large, indicating that small chicks are outcompeted by larger siblings (Tiainen et al., 1989).

These studies on House Sparrows and Starlings do not provide a full picture, however, because these species are cavity nesters and therefore less susceptible

FIG 66. Jay is major predator of open-nesting songbirds, often returning to a nest over several visits to remove all of the chicks in the brood. (Jill Pakenham)

to the levels of nest predation seen in open-nesting species like Blackbird. Typically, nest predation results in the loss of the entire brood rather than just some of the chicks. Predators like Jay, Magpie and Weasel *Mustela nivalis* may make several visits to a nest, taking one chick after another, resulting in brood reduction over a few minutes or hours. Chicks may die for other reasons, perhaps because of disease, injury or through an accident. Individuals may fall from the nest or, in the case of a Dunnock nest that has been parasitised by a Cuckoo, be deliberately ejected. Others may become entangled in nest material, such as horsehair, resulting in an individual developing normally but ultimately starving because it is unable to fledge from the nest.

NEST PREDATION

Nest predation by avian predators is the main cause of nesting failure for many garden bird species, particularly those that build open nests within vegetation. Avian predators like Magpies and Jays are likely to be more important nest predators than domestic cats, though the latter are likely to have a far greater impact on chicks once they have left the nest, at least in a garden setting. Nests may be located by visual or auditory cues and it has long been supposed that nests containing chicks are more likely to be predated than those containing eggs because of the increased levels of activity at the nest and the begging calls of the young. This is not always the case, however, since work by Will Cresswell on Blackbirds found no evidence that begging behaviour increased predation rates in his study population; nest conspicuousness appeared to be the more important factor (Cresswell, 1997). Other work on Blackbirds, this time by Ibáñez-Álamo & Soler (2017), has revealed how parents may respond to the threat of nest predation by reducing the number of visits they make to a nest containing chicks; this is a pattern of behaviour also documented for this species by the same researchers during the incubation period. Most garden birds are wary when they approach their nest and may avoid returning if they are aware of a potential nest predator nearby. Some species, such as Robin, greatly modify their nest-visiting behaviour in the presence of a potential nest predator. Robins will drop the food they are carrying or even make false feeding visits to an alternative site, well away from their active nest, if they believe they are being watched.

Research examining whether levels of nest predation vary in relation to the degree of urbanisation has yielded mixed results, with apparently contradictory findings evident between many studies. A meta-analysis, published in 2017 by Ernö Vincze, revealed the reason why such differences tended to occur. Vincze found that while the survival of natural nests tended to increase with the level of urbanisation, that of 'artificial' nests – well used by ecologists when studying nest predation – tended to decrease (Vincze et al., 2017). It seems that the methodology used has an effect, perhaps because artificial nests are not as well hidden as natural ones; perhaps because they do not have natural activities (such as nest defence) taking place at them; or possibly because artificial nest studies usually focus on open-nesting species rather than cavity-nesting ones – and we know that cavity-nesting and open-nesting species show different relationships between predation risk and the degree of urbanisation. Cavity nests are predated significantly less in urban sites than rural ones, but open nests show no such pattern.

So why should natural nests be less likely to be predated in urban areas than non-urban ones? Is it simply down to the greater numbers of cavity nesters breeding in nest boxes, or does the different suite of nest predators have a role to play? Certainly, urban sites tend to lack some key nest predators, such as Weasel and snakes, but they can have high densities of avian predators like Magpie, which is known to be a significant predator of urban Blackbird nests, for example (Groom, 1993). We will look at Magpies and their role in nest predation in more detail in the next chapter.

Levels of nest predation in urban areas appear to show a seasonal pattern with, for example, the first nesting attempts made by Blackbirds in April showing lower levels of nest predation than the second attempts taking place in June (Kurucz *et al.*, 2010). It is thought that this may be linked to the energy demands of the nest predators (notably Jays in this study), which peak in June when they have their own chicks to feed. Kathi Borgmann, working on Dusky Flycatchers *Empidonax oberholseri*, also found a seasonal effect linked to variation in the food available to nest predators, in addition to which the seasonal variation in foliage density (providing nesting cover) was apparent. We've already noted the importance of vegetation cover around the nest earlier in this chapter and the role that evergreen or non-native vegetation can play, particularly for early season nests. While non-native shrubs, in the form of ornamental conifers, may provide early season nesting cover in many UK gardens, the use of non-native vegetation is sometimes associated with increased levels of nest predation. Work in North America, looking at Northern Cardinal and American Robin nesting in non-native honeysuckles and roses, found that nests placed in these exotic shrubs suffered from higher rates of nest predation (Borgmann & Rodewald, 2004).

Energetic demands and food availability may also shape levels of nest predation via the behaviour of the birds whose nests are targeted. We have already alluded to the suggestion that chick begging behaviour might increase predation risk, though noting that Will Cresswell found no evidence for this in his Blackbird population. Work in North America on Song Sparrows has revealed a tendency for the vulnerability of active nests to diurnal nest predators to decrease when additional food is made available to the parent birds (Rastogi *et al.*, 2006). This may enable the parent birds to spend more time in anti-predator behaviours, such as nest defence or increased vigilance, but probably does not have an effect on chick begging rates, which did not differ between food-supplemented and non-supplemented nests in Rastogi's study. Anne Rastogi also found that food supplementation reduced the levels of nest predation during the incubation stage, by enabling incubating females to reduce the length of their off-nest foraging bouts and increase the time spent at the nest.

Birds may potentially reduce their exposure to potential nest predators by selecting breeding areas that have a lower abundance of such predators, or by reducing the investment they make in a nesting attempt made in an area with a high abundance of predators. This has been tested through work on Blackbirds breeding within the city of Sheffield. Colin Bonnington and colleagues found no evidence that these urban Blackbirds responded to variations in predator abundance by adjusting the location of their breeding territory or by reducing their clutch size. This could suggest that these urban Blackbirds were caught in an 'ecological trap' (Bonnington *et al.*, 2015).

FLEDGING AND GAINING INDEPENDENCE

The sight of young Great Tits being coaxed from their garden nest box by the calls of their parents is one of the most rewarding moments for those who have put up a nest box for these birds. Leaving the relative security of the nest box brings each chick into a more dangerous world, where it will need to gain its independence rather quickly. The weight at which a chick fledges has important consequences for its chances of survival as it gains independence, something to which we have already alluded in our discussions of chick weight in House Sparrows. Work on Great Tits also underlines the importance of leaving the nest at a good weight. The work of Chris Perrins, for example, has revealed that a greater proportion of the individuals leaving their nest box with a fledging weight of 19 g recruit into the breeding population, compared to those with a fledging weight of 18 g (Perrins, 1965). Young birds often leave the nest site in a staggered manner, with some individuals perhaps slow to leave because their development has been slower than that of their siblings. On occasion, all of the chicks may leave at the same time, a behaviour that may be seen in Blackcaps or Blackbirds

FIG 67. Once a young Great Tit has left the nest, it faces a whole suite of challenges as it moves towards independence. (Jill Pakenham)

when the nest has been disturbed by a nest predator. This latter behaviour is an anti-predator strategy, the chicks leaving the nest prematurely but having better survival prospects than had they remained in the nest to face the predator.

Once the chicks have left the nest, the amount of time that they then remain with their parents will be determined by a number of factors, foremost of which is species-specific behaviour. Some pairs may be waiting to begin another breeding attempt and so will drive their young away within a few days or even hours; in other species, the chicks may remain with their parents for much longer. We know from work with BTO Garden BirdWatchers that adult Great Spotted Woodpeckers guide their chicks to garden feeding stations, accompanying the youngsters as they first discover reliable sources of food, to which they will return on their own as they move towards full independence. Male Great Tits also guide their broods to good foraging sites, but the amount of time they then spend with them is shaped by individual personality traits – both of the parent and the chicks. 'Fast exploring' male Great Tits, for example, have been shown to be more aggressive towards their fledged offspring than slow-exploring fathers, resulting in the chicks moving away from their natal territory more rapidly (Dingemanse *et al.*, 2003).

Parent birds may divide responsibility for their brood between the two members of the pair, a behaviour sometimes referred to as 'brood division' and studied in several garden bird species, including Robin (Harper, 1985a), Blackbird (Edwards, 1985) and Dunnock (Byle, 1990). In both Robin and Dunnock, the incidence of brood division is greater later in the season than it is early in the season, with food availability thought to play a role in whether or not a brood is divided. Once this period of parental support comes to its end, the fledglings are on their own and likely to move away from their natal territory, a process that is termed natal dispersal. While the fledglings may endeavour to secure a territory of their own close to where they were raised, they will usually be disadvantaged in terms of age and experience when competing with those individuals already established as part of the local breeding population. In a non-migratory species like Great Tit, how far a chick disperses may well depend on the local availability of suitable breeding territories and whether or not they are already held by established birds. For those individuals raised as part of a genuine second brood, competition will not just be with established adults, it will also involve young birds from earlier breeding attempts. This may explain why young Great Tits leaving their nest later in the breeding season disperse a greater distance than chicks fledging earlier in the year (Dhondt & Huble, 1968). One of the main reasons for natal dispersal is the avoidance of potential inbreeding and the damaging effects that it can have on subsequent generations.

SECOND BROODS AND REPLACEMENT CLUTCHES

Many species will initiate a second nesting attempt if the first one fails, though the chances of this happening may depend on when the first attempt failed and for what reasons. A smaller number of species will make multiple breeding attempts during the course of their breeding season, and it is these attempts – rather than the replacement clutches just mentioned – that are referred to as 'second broods' (or 'third broods', etc.). Some species will almost always make several breeding attempts during the course of the season, while for others the usual number of breeding attempts is just one, with a second brood an exception rather than the rule.

Second broods are uncommon in UK Great Tit populations, perhaps because of the short period over which the peak availability of their favoured caterpillar prey occurs; however, Cowie & Hinsley (1987) found that 18 per cent of their study Great Tits in suburban Cardiff managed to attempt a second brood. This may have been facilitated by the earlier start to the breeding season noted in the Great Tits monitored in this study – the early start and finish to the first attempt opening up the opportunity to begin another one. To some extent there is the potential for having multiple broods to compensate for the lower productivity of individual nesting attempts seen in urban and garden habitats. This appears to have been the case in a study of urban Great tits, where Junker-Bornholdt & Schmidt (1999) found that despite the very low clutch size and breeding success of their study population (compared to those in nearby woodland), the urban population remained stable. In this case, the high proportion of replacement clutches and second broods, coupled with reduced levels of adult mortality, appeared to compensate for the low breeding success of individual nesting attempts.

One of the challenges faced by those monitoring the nesting attempts made by garden birds is the difficulty in determining the reproductive success of a pair of birds over the course of their breeding season. This isn't really an issue for those studying single-brooded species, unless they are unable to locate replacement clutches following a failed nesting attempt, but it can prove problematic for those working with multi-brood species. We have already touched on this in our discussions about the definition of breeding success, noting that what is often meant by researchers is the productivity of a single nesting attempt rather than for the season as a whole. Getting at season-long productivity is an interesting challenge, but one we have been able to look at in a slightly unusual way for House Sparrow. Using information from the weekly BTO Garden BirdWatch survey, and noting the sedentary nature of House

Sparrow populations, we were able to derive an index of annual productivity for this species by looking at the change in mean peak counts using garden feeding stations between the start of the breeding season and the time of the post-breeding season peak. Our measure of annual productivity was similar in both rural and urban gardens, but showed regional variation that matched what was happening to breeding populations. Our measure was lower in the south and the east of Britain (at 1.32 fledglings per adult), where Breeding Bird Survey data show populations are declining, than in the north and west where populations are stable (1.37 fledglings per adult). Comparison with data from the Nest Record Scheme also revealed similar regional variation in its per nesting attempt measure of clutch and brood size (Morrison *et al.*, 2014). It is not clear that this approach would work for other, more mobile species.

SENESCENCE

As noted already, the age and experience of an individual may have a bearing on its breeding success, something that is perhaps more apparent in longer-lived species than those typical of many garden bird communities. In general, those birds breeding for the first time tend start their breeding attempt later in the season; they also produce smaller eggs and smaller clutches, and have lower hatching and fledging success than older breeders (Dhondt, 1989; Saether, 1990). Work on Blackbirds breeding in the city of Cambridge, for example, has revealed that clutch-initiation date, breeding-season length and clutch size all vary with age. First-year females started breeding the latest, had the shortest breeding seasons and produced the smallest clutches.

Increasing reproductive success with age is thought to be the result of the early death of low quality individuals, coupled with improving experience and increased reproductive effort (Forslund & Pärt, 1995). However, those reproductive traits that improve with age at the beginning of life also tend to deteriorate as an individual approaches the end of its life (Dhondt, 1989), something referred to as senescence. In the Treecreeper, for example, senescence starts particularly early – this is a very short-lived species – and egg size in the second year of life is smaller than that seen in the first (Enemar & Nilsson, 2008). A recent study of the life histories of 431 urban Blackbirds has revealed evidence of senescence in this species. While the average life expectancy of individuals in this population was just 3.7 years, reproductive success in females was found to peak at 4 years – supporting what we were saying earlier about the short lives of many garden birds truncating possible evidence for senescence. Male

FIG 68. Treecreeper breeding success has been shown to decline rapidly with age, even though it is a short-lived species. (John Harding)

reproductive success remained stable until the fifth year of life, with subsequent breeding success beyond years four and five declining for females and males respectively (Jankowiak *et al.*, 2018).

CONCLUDING REMARKS

As this chapter has demonstrated, the success or failure of an individual nesting attempt may be determined by a range of different factors. Failure may happen at any point during the breeding attempt and for different reasons. A long-term study of tit populations breeding in nest boxes in a woodland site in central England has, for example, revealed that different tit species may suffer nest failure more often at different parts of the nesting cycle from one another. Deeming & Du Feu (2011) found that while Coal Tits tended to suffer the greatest losses because of unhatched eggs, the failures seen in Great Tits were more often seen during the chick-rearing phase; Blue Tits appeared to struggle with both incubation and chick rearing. Similar differences may be found within garden-breeding populations, but are more difficult to study here because of the reasons outlined in Chapter 6.

At the start of this chapter, we explored whether nesting within a garden was a good option for a breeding bird. We have seen that gardens provide some opportunities, such as the presence of nest boxes and the absence of certain nest predators, but they also present some significant challenges, not least the lower availability of those invertebrate prey species that are so important for growing chicks. The nature of the vegetation present within our gardens may alter the vulnerability of open nests, and our domestic pets may take an increasing toll on newly fledged young. The combination of these different opportunities and threats has led some authors to suggests that gardens may be an ecological trap, tempting birds to nest within them, or tempting them to nest earlier than they should, but then catching them out later in the breeding cycle through higher levels of nest failure and chick starvation. As we have noted elsewhere in this book, we still need to collect more information on the lifetime reproductive success of individuals before we can say for certain whether choosing to nest in a garden is a bad thing. Until then, all we can do is continue to collect the evidence and take advantage of emerging technologies that enable us to better study the individual birds with which we share our gardens.

CHAPTER 4

Opportunities and Risks

A LTHOUGH GARDENS PROVIDE MANY DIFFERENT opportunities for birds, such as access to high-energy foods at the times of the year when natural food supplies are low and energetic demands high, there are a number of risks that birds using gardens may face. These include predation by both wild and domestic animals, disease, and encounters with windows, netting and other objects that may bring about injury or even death. We have already looked at the opportunities associated with the volume of supplementary food provided by householders keen to help visiting wild birds, and at the nesting opportunities to be found in gardens, so this chapter examines a small number of other opportunities before the focus shifts to some of the risks.

THE BRIGHT LIGHTS – ARTIFICIAL LIGHT AND GARDEN BIRDS

Artificial light is one of the most significant anthropogenic changes associated with the built environment (Hölker *et al.*, 2010). Street, security and ornamental lighting now illuminate our towns and cities, penetrating the darkness of night and potentially altering the behaviour of birds and other urban wildlife. Light is a key behavioural cue for many species and artificial lighting has been shown to alter the timing of various activities, including those associated with breeding-season song, reproductive physiology and foraging behaviour (Ockendon *et al.*, 2009a; Dominoni *et al.*, 2013; Gaston *et al.*, 2013; Nordt & Klenke, 2013).

We saw in previous chapters how there is increasing evidence that birds living within urbanised landscapes have a longer breeding season, brought about by the earlier onset of reproduction. This has been linked to the provision of supplementary food (Chapter 2), to a warmer microclimate, to greater levels of social stimulation and to increasing levels of light pollution. Evidence for the latter comes from work on London's Starling population (Rowan, 1938) and from experimental studies of Blackbirds (Dominoni *et al.*, 2013). Observations have also revealed that Robins and Blackbirds frequently sing or even forage at night in those parts of UK towns and cities lit by street lighting (Hollom, 1966; Mitchell, 1967; Fuller *et al.*, 2007b), though the avoidance of daytime traffic noise may, as we have already seen, contribute to this.

Dominoni's work, carried out in Germany, involved the use of light loggers attached to free-living Blackbirds, the information collected revealing the levels of light that individuals encountered in the wild. Free-living forest birds were exposed, on average, to 0.00006 lux of light at night, with little variation witnessed between individuals. In contrast, free-living city birds were exposed to significantly higher levels of light, averaging 0.2 lux. The amount of light that the city birds encountered at night was highly variable, ranging from 0.07 to 2.2 lux. Dominoni and his colleagues used the measurements collected to examine the influence of these differing levels of light on captive Blackbirds, some caught in the city and some in the forest. Birds exposed to light at night developed their reproductive system up to one month earlier than birds kept under dark nights; they also moulted earlier. Perhaps most interesting of all was the finding that city birds responded to the presence of artificial light at night differently to birds that had been captured in the forest, suggesting that the process of urbanisation might alter the physiological phenotypes of birds.

The timing of reproduction in birds is thought to be controlled through the process of natural selection, with optimal timing likely to deliver fitness benefits. Birds living within the temperate zone have been shown to use photoperiod – the period of time each day during which an organism receives illumination – to predict the optimal timing of reproduction. In species such as Blackbird, it is the increase in day length in early spring that initiates a series of neurological and physiological changes that lead to the development of the reproductive organs (Dawson *et al.*, 2001). If the photoperiod is altered through the presence of artificial light, this can lead to the types of changes being seen in populations exposed to artificial light.

Light pollution has also been shown to alter the activity levels of garden birds, both in the breeding season and at other times of the year. Davide Dominoni's work on Blackbirds has, for example, revealed that the onset of daily activity is significantly earlier in urban populations than it is in rural ones – though the end of daily activity does not appear to vary between the two

FIG 69. Having a large eye relative to its body size may be one reason why the Robin is able to be active early at garden feeding stations during the winter months. (John Harding)

(Dominoni *et al.*, 2014). Much of the work on this topic has concentrated on the timing of the dawn chorus, an obvious component of the breeding season whose timing has already been explored in relation to a range of different factors, including the level of background noise (Fuller *et al.*, 2007a), female fertility (Mace, 1987), food availability (Saggese *et al.*, 2011) and foraging success (Kacelnik & Krebs, 1983). The timing of dawn song has been linked to male quality in Eastern Kingbirds *Tyrannus tyrannus* and to the level of extra-pair paternity in male Blue Tits (Murphy *et al.*, 2008; Kempenaers *et al.*, 2010), so any change in its timing that results from the presence of artificial lighting may have profound consequences for breeding birds (see Chapter 3).

Less work has been done on the influence of light pollution on the activity of garden birds during the winter months. This is something that we were able to examine through the BTO's Shortest Day Survey (Ockendon *et al.*, 2009a; 2009b), a citizen science survey which asked participants to record the time (relative to daybreak) at which birds first visited garden feeding stations during one particular December morning. At northern latitudes, the long winter nights, with their associated low temperatures, may place additional stresses on small garden birds. Energy reserves, expended maintaining body temperature

TABLE 8. Mean arrival time (defined as the time between first light and a species being seen at garden feeding stations) and mean eye diameter for 24 common bird species recorded in the BTO's Shortest Day Survey (Ockendon *et al.*, 2009a).

Species	Arrival time	Eye size (mm)
Blackbird	15.4	6.61
Robin	19.9	4.77
Blue Tit	23.2	3.27
Rook	25.9	8.57
Dunnock	27.0	4.06
Song Thrush	28.7	6.43
Great Tit	29.4	4.09
House Sparrow	30.8	3.78
Magpie	30.9	6.63
Yellowhammer	32.2	4.15
Coal Tit	33.2	3.45
Wren	34.9	3.41
Long-tailed Tit	36.8	3.36
Chaffinch	37.1	3.78
Blackcap	39.6	3.95
Greenfinch	40.4	3.11
Goldcrest	42.3	2.96
Nuthatch	43.2	4.30
Bullfinch	44.5	3.70
Greenfinch	45.8	3.76
Starling	46.4	5.00

overnight, need to be replenished come dawn and this may prompt small birds to visit garden feeding stations as soon as it is light enough to do so. If this dawn activity is limited by light intensity, then small birds living in areas illuminated by street lighting may be active earlier than those living in areas without such illumination. The data collected from 5,800 participants through the Shortest Day Survey revealed a clear relationship between the average time at which garden bird species were first seen at garden feeding stations and their eye size.

Species with larger eyes relative to their body size were active earlier (see Table 8), with Blackbird and Robin leading the way (Ockendon *et al.*, 2009a).

Although the degree of illumination at each site was not recorded during this study – all observations were made on the same winter morning – individual garden sites were categorised as being either urban or rural in nature, allowing us to explore an assumption that urban sites received more illumination than rural ones. Based on this assumption, it was hypothesised that, within a species, average arrival times would be earlier in urban gardens than rural ones. Surprisingly, the opposite pattern to that expected was found for nine of the ten species included in this aspect of the study; only Collared Dove matched the hypothesised pattern. This suggests that while the time at which garden birds begin to forage on winter mornings may be limited by their visual capabilities at low light levels, factors other than the degree of illumination must also play a role in shaping activity (Ockendon *et al.*, 2009b). As we shall see below, one such factor is heat pollution and the 'urban heat island effect'. An experimental approach to examining the effects of artificial lighting on foraging times in winter has been adopted by colleagues working at the Max Planck Institute in Germany, where Arnaud Da Silva, David Diez-Méndez and Bart Kempenaers used video cameras to study feeder use by six forest songbirds under different levels of artificial lighting (Da Silva *et al.*, 2017). The researchers found that while two early foraging species – Blue Tit and Great Tit – started foraging earlier during experimentally lighted mornings, Blackbird, Jay, Nuthatch and Willow/Marsh Tit *Poecile palustris* did not.

HOT IN THE CITY – TEMPERATURE AND GARDEN BIRDS

Ambient temperature can be of particular importance to garden birds during the winter months, when many individuals require additional energy in order to keep warm. Small garden birds, such as Blue Tits, only lay down small amounts of body fat, perhaps only enough to get them through a single night. This means that they have to spend a significant part of the day searching for food, something that may be less of an issue for individuals using garden feeding stations than it is for those living within the wider countryside – the latter may spend 85 per cent of the available daylight hours looking for food. While small birds may alter their roosting behaviour to minimise the impacts of low temperatures – perhaps by roosting communally in a nest box – most will lose weight overnight. Research has shown, for example, that Blue Tits and Great Tits are some 5 per cent lighter at dawn than when going to roost the previous evening (Lehikoinen, 1987).

FIG 70. House Sparrow plumage weight increases by as much as 70 per cent following the autumn moult, providing additional insulation during the cold winter months. (John Harding)

The insulation provided by a bird's feathers can also help to reduce heat loss, with the downy under-feathers the most important. Increasing the quantity of downy feathers during the winter may help. In the House Sparrow, plumage weight increases by 70 per cent following the autumn moult, helping to increase insulation. The plumage can also be fluffed up to increase the number of air pockets, something that again reduces heat loss. Other birds may roost communally, perhaps even occupying roosting pouches – a recent addition to the garden bird care product range – or nest boxes (see Chapter 5).

The temperatures encountered within urban environments may be several degrees higher than those of the surrounding countryside (Landsberg, 1981), a result of 'waste' heat escaping from offices, housing and factories. The magnitude of this effect is related to the size of the urban area, and in our largest cities the temperature may be as much as 5–8°C higher than that of the surrounding countryside. It is worth noting, however, that local temperatures within a large urban area can also vary considerable with location; vegetation cover has an important role in local daytime temperatures, and pavements and other human structures an important role in night-time temperatures (Buyantuyev & Wu, 2010). Higher temperatures overnight may mean that small birds can roost for longer, having used up fewer reserves maintaining their body temperature and with less urgency to feed come dawn. The effects of urban heat may interact with those of light pollution, the timing of dawn activity being pushed back by temperature but pulled forward because of light pollution. Ideally, these two processes would be investigated using an experimental approach, but in the absence of such work we can use the results of the BTO's Shortest Day Survey to get an idea of how their effects might influence the activity of small birds.

As we have just seen, analysis of the data collected through the Shortest Day Survey revealed that urban populations of nine of the ten species studied were active significantly later than populations located in rural areas. This was counter to the pattern expected if light pollution – which should be greater within urbanised landscapes than rural ones – was the sole driving factor. Instead, it seems to suggest that, while light levels may influence the timing of dawn activity, urban heat pollution plays a more significant role in shaping dawn activity during the winter months (Ockendon *et al.*, 2009a). In an attempt to explore these patterns in more detail, by seeking to quantify the degree of artificial light present at or close to sites, the survey was repeated in January 2014 (Clewley *et al.*, 2015). Additional information on local weather conditions, including temperature, was extracted from the MIDAS Land and Marine Surface Stations Dataset (UK Meteorological Office). Arrival times of the 10 species most commonly recorded during the study were found to be associated with a combination of the density of artificial lights, rainfall, temperature and urban land cover. However, the study failed to find any evidence that birds advanced the onset of foraging in those gardens with more artificial lights nearby. Clearly, there is more work to be done in this area.

THE RISKS OF URBAN LIFE

In addition to the balance of opportunity and risk associated with light and heat pollution, which may alter the longer-term fitness of individual birds, there are other components of the garden environment that may have more obvious and more immediate consequences. These may be revealed by the presence of dead birds, found within the garden. One of the challenges in understanding the levels of predation and disease-related mortality associated with gardens and garden feeding stations is that many dead birds go undetected, especially where scavengers – both avian and mammalian – are present and remove carcasses. It can also prove challenging to determine the ultimate cause of mortality; for example, a bird that is found dead on a patio may have died from colliding with a

FIG 71. Sparrowhawk predation is just one of the risks faced by garden birds. (Jill Pakenham)

nearby window or succumbed to disease picked up at a nearby bird table; equally, a bird suffering from the disease trichomonosis and reluctant to move away from a garden feeding station may be more readily taken by a visiting Sparrowhawk. Projects like Garden Wildlife Health, organised by the Institute of Zoology in partnership with the BTO, RSPB and Froglife, can provide some useful information in such cases, with post-mortem examinations revealing both the cause of death and the presence of other contributing factors.

Understanding which factors are the most important drivers of the mortality witnessed within the garden environment is currently hampered by a lack of appropriate data. This issue was first examined in a systematic manner as part of the Garden Bird Health initiative and, latterly, through Garden Wildlife Health (Lawson *et al.*, 2018). These two projects utilised a network of citizen scientists to collect systematic information on mortality incidents in a garden setting, information that could then be used alongside the opportunistic reporting from worried members of the public that has been the more traditional source for information, particularly that relating to disease.

DISEASE AND GARDEN BIRDS

Wherever individual birds congregate there is an increased risk of disease transmission. Because garden feeding stations typically provide a concentration of feeding opportunities within a relatively small area, they may potentially have a role to play in disease transmission (Lawson *et al.*, 2015a; 2018). Additionally, since gardens are a place where people are able to observe birds at close quarters, garden feeding stations may also provide an opportunity to identify the presence of emerging diseases and to assess their impact on populations of wild birds (Friend *et al.*, 2001). Being able to tap into established networks of citizen scientists (see Chapter 6), and to partner these with professional staff working within the fields of animal health, wildlife management and ecology, has facilitated the establishment of disease surveillance schemes, such as the Garden Bird Health initiative and Garden Wildlife Health (www.gardenwildlifehealth.org).

Many existing disease surveillance schemes rely on the opportunistic reporting of wildlife disease by members of the public, and such opportunistic reporting typically secures the greatest potential network of reporters, increasing the chances of identifying unusual, emerging or novel incidents. However, the lack of standardisation makes it difficult to secure important information on the spatial and temporal distribution of incidents, not least because opportunistic reporting is often triggered in response to media appeals, and these may hit one region or audience but miss another. An alternative approach is to secure the participation of citizen scientists in a structured, standardised process – much like the standardised approach used by the weekly BTO Garden BirdWatch survey. This approach also has the benefit that it is often possible to collect baseline information on species abundance (e.g. the host bird species) and on disease occurrence alongside that being collected on disease itself. This approach, sometimes incorporating an additional opportunistic component, has made important contributions to disease surveillance in relation to emerging infectious diseases, such as trichomonosis (Robinson *et al.*, 2010) and mycoplasmal conjunctivitis (Hochachka & Dhondt, 2000). Information on the diseases of garden birds may also be collected through other citizen science networks, such as the network of bird ringers operating within the UK; the availability of such highly skilled volunteers opens up the possibility for background swabbing and surveillance for emerging infectious diseases, and indeed for other types of non-infectious disease.

THE NUMBERS OF BIRDS AND DISEASE INCIDENCE

Work in North America, involving a questionnaire approach to members of the Wisconsin Society for Ornithology, revealed that reported levels of mortality were higher at sites with a large number of individuals using the feeders, and with a larger number of different species present (Brittingham & Temple, 1986; 1988b). Of course, it may simply be that as the number of individuals visiting a feeding station increases, so do the chances of encountering a sick, dying or dead bird. Brittingham and Temple's work also suggested that observed mortality levels were lower at urban sites than rural ones, and that mortality occurred most frequently at feeding stations where platform feeders were in use. It is likely that platform feeders, which allow birds to stand in food, increase the probability of disease transmission. Hurvell *et al.* (1974) found that incidence of salmonellosis declined when feeders were cleaned and disinfected regularly, and where the feeder designs used prevented faecal contamination of the food being presented. Regardless of the type of feeder used, it is inevitable that some contaminated food will end up on the ground below the feeders, where ground-feeding species like Chaffinch and Dunnock may be placed at risk. There is also evidence that faecal contamination of nearby vegetation may act as a pathway for disease transmission (Petrak, 1982).

Another approach to exploring the question of disease transmission at garden feeding stations is to examine the feeders and to swab and test for disease agents. Prescott *et al.* (2000) did this in response to an outbreak of salmonellosis at feeding stations in southern Ontario that occurred over the winter of 1997–98. Prescott

FIG 72. Poor feeder hygiene may increase the risk of disease transmission between infected birds. (Jill Pakenham)

and his colleagues scored each of 124 feeding stations for its state of hygiene and swabbed for *Salmonella*. In the event no *Salmonella* were isolated from faeces recovered from the feeders. While the research failed to identify any significant differences in the degree of contamination of different types of bird feeder, it did identify that feeder hygiene scores were significantly lower where responsibility for keeping them clean was shared equally between two different people.

SALMONELLOSIS

Salmonella, or more strictly speaking salmonellosis, outbreaks have been documented in wild birds from at least the middle of the twentieth century, with a suggestion that the prevalence of incidents has risen over the past 40 years because of the increasing trend for providing supplementary food at garden feeding stations (Wilson & MacDonald, 1967; Kirkwood *et al.*, 1995; Tizard, 2004). The disease is caused by a bacterium, *Salmonella enterica* subspecies *enterica* serotype Typhimurium, which is seen in a number of different forms, known as phage types; definitive phage type DT 40, DT 56 (variant) and DT 160 account for most of the isolates recovered from infected garden birds here in the UK. Prevalence of the disease tends to be greater in those species of garden bird that are granivorous and which forage together in flocks. Although salmonellosis has been recorded in Blackbird, Dunnock and even Green Woodpecker (MacDonald & Cornelius, 1969), such cases are rare.

Examination of a national dataset, largely comprised of reports contributed by the general public, has enabled the seasonal and longer-term patterns of salmonellosis outbreaks to be determined by a team of researchers (Lawson *et al.*, 2010). Some 698 garden birds were examined post-mortem from 1993 to 2003, inclusive. Salmonellosis was confirmed as the primary cause of death in a quarter of the birds examined, from 7 of the 45 different species represented. During the period of the Lawson study, salmonellosis was the most common infectious disease cause of death in garden bird species; this has since changed following the emergence of finch trichomonosis, and the number of salmonellosis outbreaks has reduced significantly since 2008.

Greenfinch and House Sparrow were the two species most commonly diagnosed with the disease by Becki Lawson and her colleagues. The 157 *Salmonella* isolates cultured through the study revealed the presence of 10 different phage types, with DT 40 and 56 the most common; most of the others were only found in a single individual or came from a single outbreak site. Incidents showed a pronounced seasonal pattern, with a peak in occurrence

FIG 73. House Sparrow is one of the species for which incidents of salmonellosis have been most commonly reported. (Jill Pakenham)

during the winter months – i.e. between December and February. Over the course of the study period, the prevalence of particular phage types changed; DT 160 was only found during the initial five years of the study, while DT 56 – which had been found sporadically up until 2000 – suddenly increased considerably in its occurrence (Lawson *et al.*, 2010) but then dropped away again. Looking back over a longer period of time, you do get a sense that phage types may come and go; for example, the phage type U 218 seems to have been prevalent within many of the outbreaks reported during the 1967–68 winter (Cornelius, 1969) but not since.

The Lawson study also suggests regional variation in the level of incidence, with incidents generally absent from across central England and East Anglia, even though House Sparrow and Greenfinch carcasses are regularly submitted for post-mortem analysis from these regions. Although the sample sizes are relatively small, there is evidence of regional variation in the prevalence of phage types within Scotland. Tom Pennycott and colleagues have found phage type DT 40 to predominate in the north of Scotland, while the DT 56 variant is more common in the south of the country (Pennycott *et al.*, 2010). How much this pattern might relate to the species affected – Greenfinch predominates in the north of Scotland, House Sparrow predominates in the south – is unclear.

There is a suggestion that birds in poor condition are more susceptible to the infection, with infected individuals often of low body weight. However, low body weight might instead be a consequence of becoming infected – the birds unable to feed. This needs further investigation, as does the North American finding that more strongly ornamented Common Redpolls *Carduelis flammea* were more likely to die in the outbreak studied (van Oort & Dawson, 2005). Ornamentation in this species, expressed through the strength of carotenoid pigments, is a signal of male quality – the more brightly marked individuals being of highest status. This being the case, their lower survival during a salmonellosis episode might well be linked to the priority access they are likely to have to food sources during difficult times. Such access might put them at greater risk of ingesting the bacterium.

Regional variation in the distribution of salmonellosis cases has been found within the United States, the authors of this work suggesting that increased human population density and reduced area of wild habitat might be linked to increased incidence. If birds do not have access to natural habitat, but instead forage at garden feeding stations, then there may well be an increased potential for disease transmission, as individuals congregate together to feed under crowded conditions (Hall & Saito, 2008).

One interesting question is the extent to which *Salmonella* is present in populations of healthy individuals, not least because there appear to be significant differences between samples obtained from healthy birds and those obtained from dead or dying birds. Tizard *et al.* (1979) isolated the Typhimurium serotype from 15 per cent of the healthy House Sparrows they sampled in Ontario, Canada, but Wobeser & Finlayson (1969) isolated the same serotype from 90 per cent of the dead and dying House Sparrows they sampled from the same area. Although studies of healthy populations have almost all taken place away from garden feeding stations, it does appear that the incidence of *Salmonella* in healthy populations is low, particularly where these populations exist away from sites of human activity. Here in the UK, Wilson & MacDonald reported on *Salmonella* infections over a 20-year period, from 1939 to 1959, isolating serotype Typhimurium from just 9 birds of 1,573 sampled. Between 1960 and 1966, the same investigators found an increased incidence, identifying 19 isolates, including 10 from House Sparrow and 4 from Greenfinch (Wilson & MacDonald, 1967; MacDonald, 1965). More recently, the work of Tom Pennycott and colleagues has highlighted the prevalence rates that may be encountered at garden feeding stations, where members of the public are alerted to the problem by the large numbers of birds found sick or dead (Pennycott *et al.*, 1998; 2002). Individual birds infected with salmonellosis collapse and die quickly, often within a few hours; those that survive for more than 24 hours appear lethargic and are reluctant to move away when approached.

One of the reasons for government interest in the diseases of garden birds is that in some cases wild birds may act as a reservoir for diseases that impact human, companion animal or livestock health. Salmonellosis is one such disease. As we have just seen, in garden birds the disease is predominantly caused by *Salmonella enterica* subspecies *enterica* serotype Typhimurium phage types 40, 56(v) and 160. While these phage types are considered to be highly host-adapted, with a high degree of genetic similarity among isolates and suggesting that there is only a low risk of transmission to humans or livestock (Hughes *et al.*, 2008), recent research has revealed that wild birds are the primary source of these phage types in some cases of human infection (Lawson *et al.*, 2014). Since most documented outbreaks in wild birds occur at or around garden feeding stations, there is a clear risk to people of coming into contact with sick birds or their faeces. A New Zealand study into an outbreak of *S.* Typhimurium DT 160 infection in humans revealed that, in addition to consumption of fast food and contact with people with gastrointestinal disease, contact with dead wild birds was a significant risk factor for infection (Thornley *et al.*, 2003).

That there is the potential for *Salmonella* to be passed on through contaminated faeces is underlined by the finding of the bacterium in 48 per cent of bird faeces collected from a bird table, 42 per cent of those collected from under a hanging bird feeder and from 33 per cent of those found under a House Sparrow roost, all at a garden site in Scotland (Pennycott *et al.*, 2002). It appears that infected birds may shed the *Salmonella* through their faeces over many days; an outbreak of salmonellosis in Australian sheep was traced to crows and magpies, which were found to have been shedding the bacterium for up to 27 days (Watts & Wall, 1952). James Kirkwood and colleagues have suggested that the winter outbreaks of salmonellosis previously witnessed in the UK were a direct result of the high densities of seed-eating birds seen at garden feeding stations (Kirkwood, 1998), although this is difficult to prove. It does, however, seem likely that the high densities of birds seen at feeding stations might lead to an increased risk of disease transmission.

One of the pathways that may be of particular concern in relation to gardens, bird tables and transmission to humans is the one that sees transmission through gulls. The large increase in gull numbers, and the increasing size of urban breeding populations of certain species, has its origins in the availability of anthropogenic food. Gulls make use of food scraps near fast-food outlets and around landfills, sources which place them at particular risk of ingesting

Salmonella bacteria. These may then be shed through their faeces at garden feeding stations, where Black-headed Gull tends to be the most commonly encountered gull species. Although the presence of *Salmonella* has been determined in a not insignificant portion of the UK gull populations (Williams *et al.*, 1976; Butterfield *et al.*, 1983), most infected individuals show few obvious signs of the infection (MacDonald & Brown, 1983). In fact, it appears that salmonellosis is primarily only a problem in young gulls.

Salmonella bacteria are found within the intestine and so may be spread to other individuals either through contaminated faeces or through predation, where the intestine is eaten by the predator. One Spanish study found that 4 per cent of sampled free-living birds of prey tested positive for *Salmonella* (Reche *et al.*, 2003), with the range of different serotypes indicating that the infections had been acquired from a number of different sources. Cats are thought to become infected with the wild bird strains of *Salmonella enterica* through the small birds they predate and there is some evidence that this is the case (Taylor & Philbey, 2010). Salmonellosis in cats has long been called 'songbird fever', which is suggestive of the link to the predation of infected wild birds. However, salmonellosis in cats is associated with a wider range of serovars than just S. Typhimurium – though it is the most frequent – and with a range of different phage types, not just those

FIG 74. Salmonellosis in cats has long been referred to as 'songbird fever', underlining the clear pathway from prey to predator. (Jill Pakenham)

associated with wild birds. Phage types DT 40 and DT 56 variant have certainly been isolated from domestic cats showing evidence of illness (Philbey *et al.*, 2008) but the consumption of raw meat is considered to be perhaps the most important source of the disease in domestic pets. Cats that have become infected display vomiting, anorexia and haemorrhagic enteritis, which usually lasts from two to seven days and follows on from an incubation period of two to five days. Full recovery may take up to three weeks, with a small proportion of individuals – those with impaired immunity – dying as a result of the infection.

TRICHOMONOSIS AND FINCHES

The impact that an emerging infectious disease can have on garden birds is perhaps best illustrated by the outbreak of finch trichomonosis first reported from the United Kingdom in 2005. Trichomonosis, which was already known as a disease of pigeons, doves and some raptor species, is caused by infection with the protozoal parasite *Trichomonas gallinae*. The parasite typically infects the upper region of the alimentary tract, where it causes lesions of necrotic ingluvitis or pharyngitis; these often result in death, perhaps through secondary infection, starvation or because of an elevated predation risk. Infected birds are unable to swallow food, become lethargic and fluffed up in their appearance, and are often reluctant to fly away from garden feeding stations. The parasite may be transmitted between individuals through shared food – for example, when adults feed their chicks or during courtship feeding – or water. The *Trichomonas gallinae* parasite cannot survive for long periods outside of the host body because it is vulnerable to desiccation but it has been found to survive for up to two days in moist birdseed (McBurney *et al.*, 2017). An infected bird, unable to swallow, may regurgitate contaminated food items that in turn are then taken by another individual, spreading the disease throughout the population. More widely, trichomonosis has been a significant cause of nestling mortality in the Madagascan Pink Pigeon *Nesoenas mayeri* and it has also been suggested as contributing to the extinction of the North American Passenger Pigeon *Ectopistes migratorius*. The disease is known by bird keepers as 'canker' (in pigeons and doves) and as 'frounce' in birds of prey; you sometimes see academics refer to it as trichomoniasis rather than trichomonosis.

An index case of finch trichomonosis was first documented in the UK in April 2005, emerging from a Chaffinch submitted for post-mortem examination from a garden site in Ayrshire, Scotland (Pennycott *et al.*, 2005a; Lawson *et al.*, 2012a). The following year, summer 2006, saw a dramatic increase in the numbers of

FIG 75. The outbreak of trichomonosis in UK Greenfinches was tracked through BTO Garden BirdWatch data and the Garden Bird Health initiative. (Jill Pakenham)

mortality incidents involving Greenfinches, Chaffinches and a number of other garden bird species. The Garden Bird Health initiative – a national monitoring scheme being coordinated by the Institute of Zoology, BTO, RSPB and others – reported 1,054 incidents between 1 April and 30 September 2006, involving a combined total of some 6,300 dead Greenfinches and Chaffinches. Confirmation that *Trichomonas gallinae* was the disease agent came from scanning electron microscopy and DNA sequencing, which later confirmed that a single clonal strain was involved (Lawson *et al.*, 2011a).

Fortunately, the disease monitoring work was running alongside the already existing BTO Garden BirdWatch survey, which enabled researchers, myself included, to explore the impact of this emerging disease on finch populations. Using data from both BTO Garden BirdWatch and the BTO/JNCC/RSPB Breeding Bird Survey, we were able to show that the disease outbreak had resulted in a significant decline of around 35 per cent of the UK's breeding Greenfinch population and around 20 per cent of the breeding Chaffinch population (Robinson *et al.*, 2010). This work used information on disease occurrence submitted by members of the public (classed as 'opportunistic' records) and those participating in the weekly BTO Garden BirdWatch (classed as 'systematic' records). These records also enabled us to identify regions where

the disease outbreak was most pronounced, and to chart the movement of the
outbreak between these regions over different years. The initial outbreak was
largely focussed on the West Midlands, southwest England and Wales during
2006, shifting first to East Anglia and the southeast of England and then Scotland
in subsequent years (SAC Veterinary Services, 2008; Lawson *et al.*, 2011a). During
this initial outbreak period, there was strong seasonality to the pattern of
incidents, with most reported between 1 April and 30 September – and with a
peak in late summer – a pattern quite distinct from that seen in salmonellosis.

The impact of the disease outbreak on Greenfinch populations is revealed
from the weekly BTO Garden BirdWatch results. When plotted as a reporting
rate – a simple measure showing the proportion of garden sites recording the
species during a given week – the sudden loss of Greenfinches is evident from
September 2006, the impacts carrying over into 2007 (see Figure 76a). When the
same dataset is viewed through the numbers of individual Greenfinches seen
at garden feeding stations, the longer-term consequences of the outbreak are
revealed (see Figure 76b).

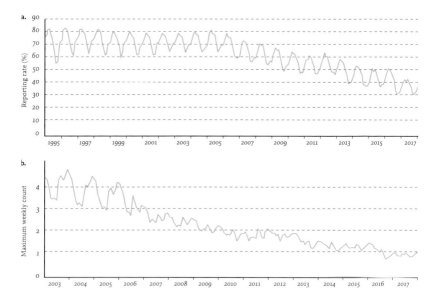

FIG 76. BTO Garden BirdWatch reporting rate data show the impact of trichomonosis on
garden Greenfinch populations, something that is evident in both (a) the weekly reporting
rate, and (b) the number of individuals visiting gardens. Data provided by the British Trust of
Ornithology with permission.

TABLE 9. Change in the breeding populations of Greenfinch, Chaffinch and Dunnock between 2006 and 2007, as revealed by the BTO/JNCC/RSPB Breeding Bird Survey, according to disease region. Disease regions were characterised by the number of cases of trichomonosis reported per thousand households and defined as 'high', 'intermediate' and 'low' incidence (after Robinson *et al.*, 2010).

Species	Low	Intermediate	High
Greenfinch	−10.9%	−15.2%	−35.5%
Chaffinch	+0.6%	−4.4%	−21.3%
Dunnock	−1.2%	−0.3%	+11.4%

BTO/JNCC/RSPB Breeding Bird Survey data were then used to look at the impact at a wider population level, the survey being the main mechanism for monitoring change in breeding populations for our most common and widespread breeding species. Data from regions with 'high', 'intermediate' and 'low' disease incidence were analysed separately for both Greenfinch and Chaffinch, the two species seemingly most heavily hit by the outbreak, with Dunnock also included in the statistical models as a control. Dunnock was not a species in which significant mortality was being reported, so if it had shown a similar pattern of population change to Greenfinch and/or Chaffinch, then this would have suggested that something else, other than the disease, was behind the changes observed. As hypothesised, Greenfinch and Chaffinch populations showed the most significant declines in the areas of high disease incidence, while Dunnock did not show any evidence of decline (see Table 9). The spatial and temporal changes in populations matched the pattern of disease outbreak and, coupled with the DNA work, strongly pointed to trichomonosis as the agent that had brought about the dramatic and rapid decline in finch populations.

The spread of trichomonosis within the UK was then followed by emergence of the disease elsewhere in Europe, with cases confirmed from multiple sites within southern Fennoscandia during the summer of 2008. Examination of the genetics of the disease agent revealed no variation between the British and Fennoscandian strains of the parasite, suggesting a direct link between the two outbreaks. Examination of ring-recovery data from the British and Irish ringing scheme suggests that a migratory Chaffinch may have been responsible for carrying the disease from its British wintering grounds to breeding sites in Fennoscandia. If we are correct in our assumption, then this would be the first case of a protozoal emerging infectious disease being transmitted by a migrating bird (Lawson *et al.*, 2011a). Both Greenfinch and Chaffinch are widespread across Europe and both undertake medium-distance migratory movements. Trichomonosis was first noted in Finland in 2008 and resulted in a significant (47 per cent) decline in breeding numbers from 2006 to 2010 (Lehikoinen *et al.*, 2013).

The presence of trichomonosis in Sparrowhawks submitted through the Garden Bird Health initiative and the scheme that has since replaced it – Garden Wildlife Health – suggests that these predators may have been exposed to the disease when predating infected finches. The disease has also been diagnosed in a small number of other garden bird species, including House Sparrow, Bullfinch, Siskin, Goldfinch, Yellowhammer and Great Tit (Lawson *et al.*, 2011a). Interestingly, in addition to what we have witnessed here in Europe, trichomonosis has since emerged in several passerine species within North America, with cases documented from 2007 onwards. These cases have largely involved American Goldfinch *Carduelis tristis* and Purple Finch *Carpodacus purpureus* (Forzán *et al.*, 2010).

Quite why trichomonosis brought about this novel disease outbreak in UK finches is uncertain, but comparison of the genetics of the parasite – recovered from infected finches and Sparrowhawks – with material held in a sequencing library suggests a spill-over event from a pigeon or dove (Chi *et al.*, 2013). The most likely candidate is Woodpigeon, a species that as we shall see later has been increasing in numbers at garden feeding stations across much of the UK. *Trichomonas gallinae* appears to be present in a sizeable component of the Woodpigeon population, something suggested by work on wintering Woodpigeons in Spain, where a third of sampled birds shot by hunters were found to be positive for presence of the disease (Villanúa *et al.*, 2006). Prevalence

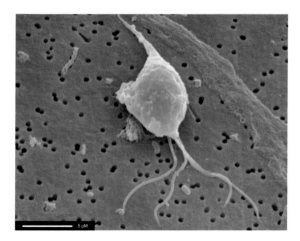

FIG 77. A scanning electron microscope image of the disease agent *Trichomonas gallinae*, found to be behind the UK finch trichomonosis outbreak. (Robinson *et al.* 2010)

was higher in birds from the south of Spain than the north, and higher in adults than in juveniles, but there was no significant difference between males and females. Parasitised birds exhibited lower body mass and had smaller fat reserves, indicating that they were in poorer condition than non-parasitised individuals.

There is also the question of why the Greenfinch appears to be so susceptible to the disease when other, equally common, garden bird species seem so much more resilient. The granivorous habits of Greenfinches, coupled with their gregarious nature, may result in high levels of contact between individuals and facilitate disease transmission, but this cannot be the only reason. Perhaps there is something about their morphology or physiology that may make them more susceptible. Jon Barrett, working at the School of Biological Sciences at the University of East Anglia, has done some initial work on this. His findings suggest that the way in which Greenfinches utilise hanging bird feeders may make them particularly susceptible to increased risk of disease transmission, with a suite of behaviours likely to result in transmission of the parasite between individuals (Barrett unpublished). It does, however, seem likely that controlled experiments using captive birds would be needed to take this area of work forward, and that is something that would be unpalatable to many of us working on garden birds and disease.

AVIAN POX AND GARDEN BIRDS

Avian pox is a well-known disease of both wild and captive birds, caused by viruses belonging to the genus *Avipoxvirus* and known from some 280 species of 70 different bird families worldwide (Thomas *et al.*, 2007). Within the UK, avian pox is considered endemic and has been reported from a number of garden bird species, including Woodpigeon, Jackdaw, Carrion Crow, Starling, House Sparrow, Dunnock, Blackbird and, more recently, Great Tit, Blue Tit and Coal Tit (Lawson *et al.*, 2012b). The virus causes discrete wart-like lesions on the featherless parts of the body, typically on the legs and feet or around the eyes. These lesions are described clinically as 'dry' pox, recognising the distinction from the 'wet' pox diphtheritic lesions that may form in the respiratory or alimentary systems. Wet pox lesions are rarely reported, presumably because they are significantly less obvious than the external dry lesions. Dry pox lesions are usually pink, red, yellow or grey in colour.

Most avian pox lesions are small and only rarely do they seem to impede the individual affected; in fact, most birds recover – the duration of the infection being from a few days to several months. More recently, since 2006, we have seen

FIG 78. An emerging form of avian pox has been reported in British tit populations, its spread charted through Garden Wildlife Health. (Hazel Rothwell)

Great Tits and Blue Tits with larger lesions, many of which impede vision to such an extent that they are likely to lead to higher levels of mortality. Another unusual feature of these lesions is the number of individuals affected at any given site; while reports of avian pox in birds other than tits usually refer to just a single individual, those linked to tits usually involve several. The reports suggest that Great Tit is the species of tit most likely to be affected – representing, for example, 90 per cent of the incidents reported by Lawson *et al.* (2012b). From those individuals submitted for post-mortem examination, including the index case from Sussex in September 2006, it has been possible to diagnose avian pox virus as the cause of the infection. The reports also indicate spatial clustering in the cases and a pattern of spread away from the south coast of England, from where the disease was first reported, to areas located further north and west within the UK (Lawson *et al.*, 2012b). As with the work on trichomonosis already mentioned, BTO Garden BirdWatch data have proved invaluable in helping to reveal the pattern of disease spread (Figure 79).

These reports of avian pox virus in UK tit species are not the first of their kind within Europe; Great Tits were first reported with avian pox lesions in the early 1970s in Norway, with others reported from Sweden in 2003 and the Canary Islands in 2006 – the latter incident involving an African Blue Tit *Cyanistes teneriffae*. There has been a marked increase in the numbers of reports of avian

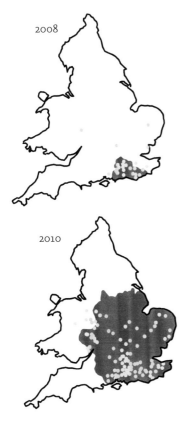

FIG 79. The spread of Paridae pox was mapped and modelled using data from citizen science schemes, demonstrating its origins on England's southern coast.

pox in Great Tits in several central European countries, including Austria, Hungary, Germany and the Czech Republic. Molecular examinations of the DNA extracted from the skin lesions of two dozen UK Great Tits has revealed that the avian pox virus present here is identical to that documented elsewhere in Europe. Coupled with the south coast origins of the UK outbreak, this points to the arrival of the virus from continental Europe. Since ring recoveries underline the sedentary nature of UK tit populations, leaving little opportunity for interchange between UK and continental tit populations, the question arises as to how this particular avian pox virus reached our shores.

It is known that the avian pox virus can be transmitted between individual birds through direct contact, through contaminated surfaces or via an intermediary insect vector – such as a mosquito. In this case, it seems likely that the virus arrived here via an insect vector, pushed across the English Channel within a plume of warm air, much like the way that Blue-tongue disease reached our shores. The seasonality of avian pox in UK tits is similar to that seen in finch trichomonosis, with a peak in records in August and September. The warmer months of summer might facilitate higher levels of disease transmission, since more mosquitoes are likely to be on the wing at this time, though it might also be linked to the entry into the tit population of a cohort of young, immunologically naïve first-year birds.

Although it is still too early to say what the impact of the emergence of this strain of avian pox within the UK might mean for our tit populations, thanks to the long-term monitoring work taking place at Wytham Woods in Oxfordshire, it has been possible to examine the impact on an established tit population (Lachish *et al.*, 2012a). Shelly Lachish and her colleagues were able to show that the pox virus reduced the reproductive output of infected individuals by reducing the ability of adult birds to feed their chicks. Furthermore, the researchers found evidence of transmission from parent birds to their young, leading to significant mortality of those chicks that became infected. Survival rates of individuals with avian pox virus were lower and this meant that the virus had the potential to reduce population growth rates, though not to the extent where a decline in overall population size would then follow. Its presence might, however, reduce the resilience of the population to other external factors that could reduce population size. The work at Wytham Woods also revealed that the avian pox virus became established at the site within two years, reaching a relatively high peak prevalence of 10 per cent of the 8,000 or so individuals caught and monitored by the research team (Lachish *et al.*, 2012b).

LEG ABNORMALITIES IN FINCHES

It is not unusual to see Chaffinches with legs that appear white, rough and thickened, sometimes to the extent that the entire foot is covered in a growth. These lesions have two main causes, the visible symptoms of both being similar in appearance. The first is Chaffinch papillomavirus, which can cause the skin disease papillomatosis, sometimes referred to as 'tassel foot' (Atkinson *et al.*, 2008; Gavier-Widén *et al.*, 2012; Prosperi *et al.*, 2016). As the name suggests, the resulting lesions are tassel-like or spiky, developing mostly around the foot and toes but sometimes spreading further up the leg. The second, producing crusty, scab-like lesions, is brought about by a sarcoptid mite belonging to the genus *Cnemidocoptes*. Several species are known to affect birds, with *C. mutans* known from poultry, *C. pilae* known from pet Budgerigars *Melopsittacus undulatus*, and *C. jamaicensis* and *C. intermedius* known from garden songbirds. Mite infestation

FIG 80. The leg lesions seen on Chaffinches have two main sources, one a virus and the other a mite. (John Harding/ Becki Lawson)

or cnemidocoptosis, which is sometimes referred to as 'mange' or 'scaly foot', often results in grey-coloured growths on the toes, feet and legs, very occasionally also appearing on the face.

The skin abnormalities resulting from both sources are thought to develop slowly over a period of time, from several weeks to several months; in the case of papillomatosis these may disappear with spontaneous recovery (Pennycott, 2003). Disease progression in cnemidocoptosis is not well understood and more research is needed to better understand its impacts on garden birds. In both cases, the extent of the lesions can be highly variable, from small discrete lesions through to much larger growths that can result in lameness or put the individual at risk of secondary infection. It is not unusual, for example, to see a Chaffinch that has lost digits or even an entire foot. Both conditions have been documented in the UK since at least the 1960s, with Chaffinch the species most commonly affected. Brambling and Bullfinch have also been reported displaying similar leg lesions, though the incidence of these is much less common than that seen in Chaffinch.

Within the UK, the two conditions appear to be endemic and long-established, with only a small proportion of individuals within any Chaffinch flock likely to be affected – a similar pattern has been noted elsewhere in Europe (Literák et al., 2003). MacDonald & Gush (1975) found a prevalence rate of 14 per cent in their Chaffinch population in Devon. However, epidemic disease has been reported elsewhere: for example, in American Robin in the mid-1990s, where a high proportion of the population was observed to have the lesions (Pence et al., 1999). Diagnosis of the two conditions requires laboratory tests since there is a significant overlap in their appearance and it is entirely possible that some individual birds may be suffering from a mixed infection, with both present.

OTHER DISEASES OF GARDEN BIRDS

Bacteria

Chlamydiosis

Chlamydiosis will be familiar as a disease of mammals – including humans – and birds that is caused by infection with bacteria in the genus *Chlamydia*. The specific strain known to infect garden birds is *Chlamydia psittaci* – a different species to that which causes venereal disease in people. It is often recognised as a disease of pet parrots, budgerigars and cockatiels, but is also seen as a disease of pigeons and doves (Thomas *et al.*, 2007). The disease is sometimes referred to as 'psittacosis' or alternatively 'ornithosis'. The first reported case of the disease in wild passerines in the UK came from a garden in the southwest of England, where it was confirmed in individual Robins, Dunnocks and tits (Simpson & Bevan 1989). Subsequently, it has been reported from finches, tits and Robins in a Scottish garden (2008) and from other sites in England during 2009 (one incident) and 2011 (five incidents) (Colville *et al.*, 2012). A review of archived tissues by Beckmann *et al.* (2012) revealed additional cases and suggested that chlamydiosis may be more common in British garden birds than previously

FIG 81. The first reported case of chlamydiosis in a wild bird in the UK came from a garden in southwest England. (John Harding)

suspected; the disease has also been recorded in a number of other bird species – including Barn Owl *Tyto alba*, Moorhen *Gallinula chloropus* and Herring Gull *Larus argentatus* (Sharples & Baines, 2009).

Birds infected with *Chlamydia* show the usual signs of ill health, being fluffed up and lethargic in appearance. On post-mortem examination infected individuals may show enlargement of the spleen and liver, together with infection of the respiratory tract. The bacteria are likely to be passed from one bird to another through direct contact, ingestion of infected secretions (e.g. faeces) or inhalation of contaminated dust – the bacterium can persist in the environment for many months. The strains of *Chlamydia psittaci* that affect wild birds do have the potential to cause disease in humans, where the resulting respiratory disease may be displayed through symptoms that can include those associated with a common cold; sometimes the disease may result in flu-like symptoms or more severe chest problems. There have been very occasional reports of disease in dogs and cats associated with *Chlamydia psittaci* infection, though in many of these cases the source is thought to have been a pet parrot rather than a wild bird.

Escherichia albertii

E. coli serotype O86 – now known as *Escherichia albertii* – is a bacterium belonging to the Enterobacteriacae which has been recognised in several species of garden bird, both here in the UK and elsewhere in the world. The bacterium may cause inflammation of the stomach and intestines, resulting in diarrhoea and, in some cases, accumulation of food in the crop and oesophagus. While some individuals may show no signs of ill health, others may appear lethargic with fluffed-up plumage. The disease caused by *E. albertii* infection, which is often referred to as colibacillosis, may result in death and there are occasional reports of epidemic mortality in small birds. Records of the disease from the UK have tended to refer to granivorous species like Chaffinch, Siskin and Greenfinch (Pennycott *et al.*, 1998; 2002; 2005b), with most of these coming from Scotland; it is unclear as to whether this is a genuine geographical pattern or an artefact of sampling effort. The sporadic outbreaks noted in Scotland since the 1990s have tended to occur during the spring months, with reports peaking between April and July.

Suttonella ornithocola

This recently discovered bacterium appears to occur most commonly in the Blue Tit (Kirkwood *et al.*, 2006), though it has also been seen in related Paridae species, such as Coal Tit and Great Tit, and in the Long-tailed Tit (Aegithalidae). It has yet to be diagnosed in other garden bird species. *Suttonella ornithocola* has been found to cause a pneumonia-like condition in affected individuals, resulting in breathing difficulties and general signs of ill health (Lawson *et al.*, 2011b). The most likely route of disease transmission, given that the bacterium causes a lung infection, is via aerosol or air-borne pathways (Foster *et al.*, 2005). Although the bacterium was first isolated in 1996, when 11 mortality incidents involving a range of tit species were reported from sites across England and Wales, it was not identified as a novel bacterium until 2005. The recent discovery of *Suttonella ornithocola* means that relatively little is known about it, but national surveillance through the Garden Bird Health initiative and, more recently, Garden Wildlife Health, has identified a small number of more recent incidents. This, coupled with the wide regional spread of the incidents, suggests that the infection is endemic within the British tit population.

Yersiniosis

The diagnoses of this bacterial disease, caused by the bacteria *Yersinia pseudotuberculosis*, requires culture of the disease agent from the sites of infection within the carcass. The presence of multiple pale areas within the spleen and liver are suggestive of its presence but are not conclusive. Available evidence suggests that the disease is sporadic in terms of its appearance but that it can cause mortality incidents of a localised nature. Infections have been identified in several species of tit and finch, together with Dunnock, Blackbird and Song Thrush (Kapperud & Rosef, 1983; Brittingham *et al.*, 1988b).

Mycoplasma gallisepticum

Although not directly relevant to garden bird populations within the UK, it is worth briefly mentioning mycoplasmal conjunctivitis, the disease caused by the poultry pathogen *Mycoplasma gallisepticum*, which is a bacterium. This was first diagnosed in North American House Finches in 1994 and it then spread rapidly throughout the eastern United States and Canada. The disease was particularly debilitating and caused very high levels of mortality within the House Finch populations affected. The disease outbreak is of interest because of its parallels with the outbreak of finch trichomonosis here in the UK; both resulted in high levels of mortality, both spread rapidly and both were studied by researchers who used networks of citizen scientists to collect information on the outbreak.

The mycoplasmal conjunctivitis outbreak reached epidemic proportions within three years of emergence, the scale and spread of which was then tracked by a network of citizen science observers coordinated by scientists at the Cornell Laboratory of Ornithology. These efforts were then brought in alongside finer-scale, intensive field studies, which together enabled the researchers to examine the effects of the disease on host behaviour and vice-versa (Dhondt *et al.*, 2005). In the late 1990s, the proportion of infected birds dying fell significantly and asymptomatic infection became more common within the population, though with continuing fluctuations in disease occurrence and annual outbreaks. We might, perhaps, be able to look to the patterns evident within the dynamics of House Finch/mycoplasmal conjunctivitis system – which appears to be density dependent – and learn lessons that might aid our interpretation of how the Greenfinch/trichomonosis system might play out (Hochachka & Dhondt, 2000). One other interesting aspect of the work on this disease relates to the risk factors associated with it; in addition to seasonal risk factors – an increased risk associated with the cooler non-breeding period from September through to March – there was an increased risk associated with the provision of food in hanging, tube-style feeders, suggesting that transmission rates might be higher where these were used (Hartup *et al.*, 1998). The role of food provision in disease transmission is something that we explored in Chapter 2.

A number of other bacteria have been reported from garden birds, which is unsurprising given the broad intestinal bacterial flora that one would expect to see. Those that tend to be mentioned are the ones that pose a potential threat to human, companion animal or lifestock health. These include various species of *Pseudomonas*, *Staphylococcus* and *Streptococcis*, all of which are of human and livestock health interest (Brittingham *et al.*, 1988b). Detecting the presence of these bacteria in live birds involves catching the birds to collect cloacal swabs, something that could be deployed within the UK at a wide spatial scale through the national ringing scheme, if needed. Bird ringers are highly trained and licensed to catch wild birds, making them an ideal group to involve in the collection of samples through swabbing.

Viruses

One of the groups of viruses that is giving particular cause for concern is the flaviviruses, which includes both West Nile virus and Usutu virus. These viruses show the ability to evolve rapidly when presented with the opportunity to occupy a new ecological niche, something that can lead to large-scale disease outbreaks (Vazquez *et al.*, 2011). The mosquito-borne Usutu virus neatly illustrates the threat that such viruses might pose. First isolated from mosquitoes in South Africa in 1959, it was not at that time associated with disease in humans or animals. However, when it emerged in Austria in 2001, it resulted in epidemic mortality in Blackbirds (Chvala *et al.*, 2007) and subsequent work has suggested an earlier arrival in Italy in 1996. The northward expansion of the virus has continued, reaching Germany in 2011 and resulting in large-scale mortality of wild birds in the Netherlands in 2016 – this time with at least 1,800 Blackbirds dying across eight provinces (Rijks *et al.*, 2016). Screening of wild birds here in the UK has yet to document the arrival of Usutu virus but given the scale of Blackbird and other bird movements between the UK and continental Europe, it is highly likely to reach us soon. Certainly, the species of mosquito involved in transmission elsewhere within Europe is present in the UK (Horton *et al.*, 2012).

UK researchers have also been screening for West Nile virus (Phipps *et al.*, 2008), a disease which has had a significant impact on the population trajectories of a number of North American bird species, including the American Crow, which declined by 45 per cent in the six years after West Nile virus arrived (LaDeau *et al.*, 2007). Should the virus reach the UK, then we might expect to see similar patterns of decline in garden corvids, like Jackdaw, Rook and Carrion Crow, plus possibly other species including thrushes and Blackbirds. This is another mosquito-borne virus, seemingly expanding its range in response to a changing climate.

Parasites

We have already seen the impact that a parasite – in the form of *Trichomonas gallinae* – can have on a wild bird population but this impact is small when compared with the impacts of another group of parasites, the *Plasmodium* species, which cause malaria. Transmitted by insect vectors, notably mosquitoes, malaria is widely recognised as a threat to human, animal and bird populations. The infection rate in bird species has been studied over many decades, avian malaria being a key model for researchers, and this information has recently been used to examine the extent to which a changing climate might alter malaria prevalence at a global scale (Garamszegi, 2011). The results of this work demonstrate that birds are at an increasing risk of malaria infection as a direct consequence of the changing climate, with the effects being felt most strongly within Europe and Africa. In addition to the impacts of a warming climate on the insect vectors, warming temperatures may also benefit the malaria pathogens more directly – the pathogen incubation period is blocked completely when temperatures drop below 15°C.

Of course, parasites are just as likely to be encountered on birds living away from gardens and the built environment. Some may show particular habitat associations, perhaps being more prevalent at sites close to water, but relatively little work has been done comparing the infestation patterns of parasites between urban (garden) and rural sites. Reporting on differences in the prevalence of tick infection across 11 paired urban and rural Blackbird populations from across Europe and North Acfrica, Evans *et al.* (2009b) found large and consistent reductions in both tick prevalence and intensity within urban areas. Grégoire *et al.* (2002) also found a difference between the infestation patterns of *Ixodes ricinus* ticks on Blackbirds living in urban and rural locations; infestation was much higher in rural populations (74 per cent) than urban ones (<2 per cent). The researchers attributed this to possible differences in tick survival between the two habitats or to differences in the availability of other hosts. Blackbird densities were higher in the urban habitat, suggesting that the density of this particular host was not related to the presence of the ticks. However, densities of final hosts – such as Hedgehog *Erinaceus europeaus*, Red Fox *Vulpes vulpes* and Roe Deer *Capreolus capreolus* – are likely to be significantly lower in gardens than they are in the wider countryside.

Tick infestation rates are important, not just because of the potential harm to host birds, but also because they may carry the bacterium *Borrelia burgdorferi*, the causal agent of Lyme disease. A study of 1,229 birds of 22 species, caught in a rural residential area in Scotland, found 29 per cent of the individuals examined were carrying larval ticks and 5 per cent were carrying nymphs (James *et al.*, 2011). Although the larval ticks were more difficult to remove to test for the bacterium, 8 per cent of the 24 sampled tested positive for *Borrelia burgdorferi*. At 20.6 per

FIG 82. Urban Blackbirds carry lower numbers of ticks than their wider countryside counterparts. (John Harding)

cent, prevalence of the bacterium was higher in the larger sample of 107 nymphs tested. Looking at what these results mean for the birds themselves, this suggests infection rates range from zero (Coal Tit) to 77 per cent (Blackbird), with ground-feeding bird species tending to show higher rates of infestation with infected ticks than those that feed arboreally in trees and shrubs.

Along with ticks, the other obvious external parasites of many garden bird species are fleas, which may be encountered when people come to clean out nest boxes at the end of the breeding season. The flea species found in nest boxes and natural cavity sites overwinter as pupae within cocoons, their emergence in spring triggered by rising temperatures and by the vibrations caused by visiting birds. After emergence, the fleas mate and the females then go in search of a meal of blood, necessary for the maturation of their eggs. Feeding throughout her life, a female flea will lay 2 to 5 eggs per day, resulting in infestations that can reach up to 800 fleas per nest box – though more typically averaging just 80.

The presence of fleas in an occupied nest box may reduce the growth, body mass and condition of nestling birds (Dufva & Allander, 1996), something that is usually compensated for by increased provisioning on the part of the parent birds. Tripet et al. (2002), working on Blue Tits, found that a high density of fleas reduced nestling weight during the early nestling stage but that these costs were fully compensated for by an increase in female feeding effort. Interestingly, the male Blue Tits did not increase their frequency of food provisioning to nestlings in heavily infested nests. The increased feeding effort put in by the female Blue Tits has consequences for their future reproduction (Richner & Tripet, 1999). In some years, however, where favoured invertebrate prey are scarce, the parents may be unable to provide sufficient food to counter the impacts of the fleas, resulting in chicks fledging in poor condition (Richner et al., 1993). There may also be an effect within a season, with second broods suffering more from higher levels of flea infestation as flea numbers increase throughout the summer.

Birds are not defenceless when it comes to those parasites that live on the outside of the body. The oily secretions of the uropygial gland, which are used to insulate and waterproof feathers during preening, have been found to also retard the growth of bacteria and fungi that may damage the plumage (Jacob & Zisweiler, 1982; Shawkey et al., 2003). Individuals may also modify their behaviour in response to the presence of ectoparasites: for example, by selecting nest and roost sites that hold fewer parasites (Christe et al., 1994; Merilä & Allander, 1995), by removing old nesting material from a newly secured nest site (Mazgajski et al., 2004) or by increasing their levels of grooming behaviour (Cotgreave & Clayton, 1995). Various bird species, including Starling, have also been recorded adding sprigs of green vegetation to their nests (Clark, 1990); one of the leading hypotheses explaining this behaviour is that birds preferentially select plant species that contain volatile chemicals with insecticidal properties and add these to the nest material in order to reduce the numbers of parasites. Work by Clark (1991) revealed that mite populations were significantly higher in Starling nests from which any greenery present was experimentally removed. A neat experiment looking at Yarrow *Achillea millefolium*, one of the plants sometimes added to Starling nests and known to be rich in volatile compounds, investigated this further (Shutler & Campbell, 2007). The experiment was carried out using nesting Tree Swallows *Tachycineta bicolor*, a species that doesn't add material to its nest – and thereby removing several potentially confounding effects linked to other hypotheses concerning the role of green material. Addition of the Yarrow was associated with a significant reduction in the numbers of nest ectoparasites.

PLUMAGE ABNORMALITIES

It is not unusual to see a garden bird showing some form of plumage abnormality; while many of these are simply the bird going through the normal process of feather replacement, there are occasions where disease, a parasite or some other factor is involved (Keymer & Blackmore, 1964; Blackmore & Keymer, 1969). Robins and Blackbirds are the two species in which, within the UK, plumage abnormalities are most often recorded. The degree of feather loss or damage may extend from just a few feathers – for example, around the beak or eye – through to the loss of feathers from the entire head and part of the neck (Soper & Hosking, 1961). A number of the cases examined to date – for which it was possible to carry out post-mortem examination – have revealed the presence of fungi. In one instance, the fungal hyphae were shown to have infiltrated the superficial layers of skin and the feather follicles, suggesting that the fungus was responsible for the observed feather loss (Keymer & Blackmore, 1964).

Feathers may also be damaged by the activities of ectoparasites, most notably chewing lice (Mallophaga, and part of the Phthiraptera), the damage sometimes sufficient to be seen with the naked eye on birds visiting garden feeding stations. Many different types of chewing lice are to be found on birds, and an individual bird is likely to be parasitised by a number of different species of louse. At least six different louse species, belonging to five different genera, may be found on a Rook. Some feed on both feathers and blood, the latter often obtained from developing feathers; others live within the feather quill and feed on the pith. Each species of louse tends to show adaption to living within the feathers of its

FIG 83. Plumage abnormalities may be seen in many garden bird species and may involve loss or damage to feathers or changes in plumage colouration, as in this House Sparrow. (John Harding)

host, sometimes even to particular feather tracts; for example, species found on the head and neck are typically more rounded in appearance than those species which live within the wing feathers, the latter being elongated and flattened dorso-ventrally. Such is the strength of the evolutionary relationship between louse and host that knowledge of louse taxonomy has sometimes been used to assess the taxonomic placement of its avian host.

PSITTACINE BEAK AND FEATHER DISEASE

Psittacine Beak and Feather Disease (PBFD) is caused by the Beak and Feather Disease virus, which is one of the Circoviridae viruses. It has been known from both captive and free-living parrots since at least the 1970s, with cases recorded from nearly 80 parrot species worldwide (Fogell *et al.*, 2016). The only UK species likely to be affected by PBFD is the Ring-necked Parakeet, an introduced species, and this was confirmed in 2012 when an infected individual, showing the characteristic feather loss across the head and body, was reported from London (Sa *et al.*, 2014). A small number of cases of Ring-necked Parakeets with plumage abnormalities have been reported through Garden Wildlife Health since then, with PBFD suspected as the causal agent. Further research is needed to establish whether BFDV is well established in the UK parakeet population – but with only infrequent disease – or is still emerging. Although there does not appear to be any risk to other UK bird species, it is worth noting that cases have recently been confirmed in a Rainbow Bee-eater *Merops ornatus* and a Powerful Owl *Ninox strenua* in Australia, where the disease is thought to have originated (Sarker *et al.*, 2015; 2016).

BEAK ABNORMALITIES

The avian beak is a key tool, its size and shape linked to the bird's feeding preferences, and so it is unusual to encounter an individual whose bill is substantially different from others of its kind. Such individuals can look very different and may show a degree of abnormality that reduces their chances of feeding successfully (Pomeroy, 1962). There are a number of recognised deformities that may occasionally be seen in those birds visiting garden feeding stations. These are usually described by the resulting appearance of the deformity, rather than the underlying cause.

Bill deformities arise in part because a bird's bill grows throughout its life, but the reason why this sometimes goes awry is often unclear. A number of possible reasons have, however, been put forward (Galligan & Kleindofer, 2009). Included within these is exposure to an environmental contaminant, such as an industrial pollutant, insecticide or herbicide. While such compounds have been implicated in the occurrence of bill deformities, strong evidence is lacking. Physical trauma, such as collision with a window, has also been suggested (Pomeroy, 1962; Olsen, 2003), but again clear evidence to substantiate this suggestion is lacking. Another possible cause is a nutritional deficiency (Tangredi, 2007) – particularly where related to calcium metabolism; nutritional deficiency could also include the absence of some textural component in the diet, since it is known, for example, that without access to bones, captive birds of prey may suffer from overgrowing mandibles – the bill tip is presumably shaped through abrasion when picking at a bone.

In excess of three dozen bird species have been recorded with beak deformities through the BTO's 'Big Garden Beak Watch' survey – an opportunistic reporting scheme collecting information on bill deformities in garden birds. Blackbird and Blue Tit are the most commonly reported species showing deformities, but others include Coal Tit, Goldfinch and Long-tailed Tit.

Types of deformity

Crossed mandibles are an infrequent abnormality – I have seen just three examples in two decades of catching and ringing wild birds – and result in the upper mandible becoming down-curved, while the lower mandible becomes up-curved, the two crossing each other. This gives the bird the appearance of a Common Crossbill *Loxia curvirostra*, where the crossed mandibles are an adaptation enabling the Common Crossbill to extract and feed on conifer seeds. Related to this abnormality is one where just one of the mandibles grows beyond the point at which it would normally meet the other mandible, resulting in an extended and curving shape. In many cases where just a single mandible curves well beyond its usual shape, there is evidence of damage to the tip of the other mandible (Pomeroy, 1962). Overgrowth of the upper mandible appears to be more common than overgrowth of the lower mandible. In a few cases, one or both of the mandibles may curve in the opposite direction, such that, for example, the upper mandible grows up and over the head. Pomeroy (1962) reports a Starling whose upper mandible was curved back so strongly over its shoulder that in flight it appeared as if it was carrying a stick.

FIG 84. Bill deformities are unusual but do get reported from time to time, often by garden birdwatchers or bird ringers, both of whom get to see birds at close quarters. (Mark Grantham)

Elongation of both mandibles is probably less common than the curving of one or other mandible. This is nearly always associated with a slight down-curving of the whole beak and usually involves the elongation of both mandibles equally. Starling appears to be the species in which this abnormality is most commonly reported. These elongated bills may be prone to damage, the end section breaking off. Not all of the abnormalities may occur along the usual angle of the bill. In some cases, there may be lateral curvature with one or other mandible growing to the right or to left.

It appears that in most instances the bony parts of the beak remain unaffected, the abnormalities occurring in the middle layer (the dermotheca) and the outer keratinous sheath (rhamphotheca). One of the most interesting developments in this area of research is the work that has been done recently in North America, where researchers have documented a significant cluster of cases in Alaska, the bulk of which are from just two species: Black-capped Chickadee and Northwestern Crow *Corvus caurinus*. Chickadees are the North American relatives of the tits, with the Black-capped Chickadee being similar in size and appearance to our Coal Tit. The discovery of this cluster in the 1990s, which could have signalled a wider problem within the region, prompted the establishment of a comprehensive research programme. The North American researchers coined the term 'avian keratin disorder' to describe what they were seeing. Alongside the beak abnormalities, they also noted abnormalities in the plumage, legs, feet and claws of some individuals (Handel *et al.*, 2010).

The Alaskan outbreak appears to have started in the early 1990s, increasing exponentially until about 2000, and then levelling off. With several thousand reports of chickadee beak deformities from the affected area – compared with just a few dozen from elsewhere in North America, this was a significant event. Examination of chickadees and crows by trained bird ringers (termed bird banders in the United States) suggests that the deformities do not begin to appear until individuals are at least six months old. The use of bird ringing also means that it has been possible to establish that individuals can suddenly develop a beak deformity after several years of seemingly normal fortunes. The levels of beak deformities being seen echo two previous instances in North America, both of which were associated with exposure to contaminants – selenium in California and organochlorine compounds in the Great Lakes. Having said this, the virtual absence of beak deformities among young birds in the Alaskan study area would seem to suggest a different proximal cause. Indications from the opportunistic work taking place here in the UK might suggest a recent increase in bill deformities in Blue Tits, making the Alaskan work all the more relevant.

The presence of a bill deformity can make it difficult for a bird to feed, or indeed to preen. Birds with damaged beaks may be attracted to garden feeding stations because of the easier foraging conditions. At least some individuals can compensate for their deformity, perhaps by feeding with their head tilted to one side. Difficulties in preening may lead to increased numbers of parasites, making the individual less efficient at flying or leading to a general deterioration in their health.

HYGIENE AND REDUCING THE RISK OF DISEASE TRANSMISSION

As we have seen earlier in this chapter, many of the common diseases of garden birds outlined above may be spread through food contaminated with the saliva or faeces of infected individuals. It follows that the risk of a disease being transmitted between individuals will increase where large numbers of birds gather together to feed at the same sites, day after day. In order to reduce the risk of disease transmission, you should use several feeding sites, so that the numbers of individuals at any one site are reduced. Rotating the sites, effectively splitting periods of use with rest periods, should also help to reduce levels of disease transmission, as should the regular cleaning of feeders and bird tables with an appropriate product. Such products include a weak solution of domestic bleach (5 per cent sodium hypochlorite) or professional veterinary products such as Ark-klens or Tamodine-E.

Feeder design may also influence disease risk, with the flat surfaces of bird tables and hanging feeder trays potentially posing a greater risk – through faecal contamination – than a hanging feeder alone. Feeder design can also determine how easy a feeder is to take apart and clean; if it is difficult or impossible to take apart, then the cleaning is unlikely to be thorough, leaving an increased risk of future infection (Feliciano et al., 2018). Some of the feeders now on the market have been designed with cleaning in mind, coming apart easily. Bird baths may also be a site for disease transmission and so should be cleaned and refilled regularly.

Albeit small, the risk to human health means that you should not use the brushes, cloths, buckets or other equipment used for cleaning bird feeders for any other purpose. They should be used and kept outside and you should wear rubber gloves when handling the feeders, washing your hands and forearms thoroughly afterwards. Feeding equipment should be rinsed after cleaning and then left to air-dry before being refilled. A similar approach should be adopted for birdbaths.

FIG 85. Garden feeding stations may increase opportunities for diseases to spread between individuals. Keeping feeders and bird tables clean should be a regular part of providing food for garden birds like these Tree Sparrows. (John Harding)

MYCOTOXINS AND GARDEN BIRDS

Detectable levels of aflatoxin – a type of mycotoxin – have been found in garden bird species, such as Greenfinch and House Sparrow, within the UK (Lawson *et al.*, 2006). These toxins are produced as secondary metabolites by several different species of fungus, some of which may be found in grain and other food crops (e.g. peanuts and maize) destined to enter the human, domestic animal or wild bird food chain. Aflatoxins are produced by *Aspergillus flavus* and *Aspergillus nomius*, and as a group include aflatoxin B_1 and aflatoxin B_2. Aflatoxin B_1 has been described as the most prevalent naturally occurring, acutely toxic and carcinogenic member of this group (Smith & Ross, 1991). While aflatoxins tend to be seen most often in peanuts and maize, they can also be found at high levels in wheat, barley and oats if the cereals are of low quality. Production of aflatoxins is influenced by storage and handling conditions, and by the local environmental conditions, such that it is greatest in the warm environments seen in many tropical areas. Interestingly, Thompson & Henke (2000) showed experimentally that the production of aflatoxin on maize could occur under the cool-dry conditions (a temperature of 14–18°C and a relative humidity of 35–40 per cent) typically witnessed within the UK. Testing for aflatoxins in foodstuffs is largely geared to the human and domestic animal food chain, with maximum permitted levels stipulated under core legislation and regulations. The maximum permitted level for aflatoxin B_1 in the UK is set at 20 ppb (parts per billion), so in theory the wild bird care products on sale in the UK should not contain levels above this.

The toxic effects of aflatoxins vary depending upon the toxin involved (for example, aflatoxin G_2 shows just 10 per cent of the toxicity of aflatoxin B_1) but are also determined by the size of the dose ingested and the species and health of the animal or bird involved (Gourama & Bullerman, 1995). The relative susceptibilities of different garden bird species to these toxins have yet to be determined, but experience for other species suggests that it can be difficult to predict whether or not a species will be particularly susceptible. The toxic effects are felt in the liver, with affected birds typically displaying the clinical signs associated with liver disease. They can also impact on the ability of the blood to clot (Pier, 1992) and lead to immunosuppression, weight loss and general ill health.

The significance of the aflatoxin residues found in House Sparrows and Greenfinches by Lawson et al. (2006) is unclear. Although no evidence of the liver disease consistent with aflatoxicosis was observed by Becki Lawson and her colleagues, most of the birds found to have the residues also showed signs of infectious disease (namely salmonellosis), something not seen in a similar sample of birds for which the cause of death had been determined as 'predation' or 'other trauma'. This might suggest that aflatoxin poisoning could weaken an individual's immune response but this is something that will require further investigation.

Another area where more work is needed is the presence of aflatoxins in the wild bird food chain. A small amount of work has already been done in this area, both here in the UK and elsewhere. Scudamore et al. (1997), for example, tested 15 samples of wild bird food purchased in the UK, of which one sample (some peanuts) was found to contain some 370 ppb of aflatoxin B_1. Killick et al. (unpublished) carried out a pilot study to test both branded and non-branded wild bird feed mixes for aflatoxins. This work tested the mixes when opened and, additionally, during exposure to UK climatic conditions. Aflatoxin concentrations of 24 ppb (aflatoxin B_1) and 5 ppb (aflatoxin B_2) were found in a sample of non-branded peanuts when opened. Higher levels, 341 ppb (aflatoxin B_1) and 49 ppb (aflatoxin B_2), were found in a sample of non-branded peanuts exposed to UK climatic conditions for two months. As part of our review of garden bird disease, we screened food residues from a sample of bird feeders and found detectable levels of aflatoxin in all seven samples (Lawson et al., 2018). Two of these greatly exceeded the maximum permitted limits set for such residues in peanuts destined for livestock feed – which includes wild bird food – and it therefore seems likely that garden birds may be exposed to these toxins at levels associated with the kinds of toxic effects noted in captive birds. A larger piece of work, looking across a wider range of the wild bird feeds on the market and covering some of the other climatic conditions experienced in the UK, would be timely.

A study of wild birdseed purchased in the US state of Texas revealed aflatoxins in 17 per cent of the 142 samples tested, with levels ranging from non-detectable up to 2,780 ppb (Henke *et al.*, 2001). Aflatoxin poisoning has been linked to mass mortality incidents in wild birds in North America, including Mallards in Texas in the late 1970s (Robinson *et al.*, 1982) and geese in Louisiana during the 1998–99 winter (Cornish & Nettles, 1999), the latter incident involving in excess of 10,000 individuals. Given the potential risks to wild birds associated with the mycotoxins this is an area where more research is urgently needed, once again underlining the need to better understand both the opportunities and potential risks associated with feeding wild birds.

WINDOW STRIKES

Collision with windows and other structures can cause significant mortality in some urban areas (Klem, 1990b; Ogden, 2002) but its impact on wider populations has yet to be determined. Daniel Klem, largely working in Illinois, estimates that the annual mortality resulting from window collisions in the United States is between 97.6 and 975.6 million individuals annually (Klem, 1990b) – we lack a corresponding figure for the UK. These are staggering figures and underline the urgent need to secure more information on both the scale of the problem and on opportunities to mitigate its impact. If correct, it is likely that collision with window panes is the second most important human-related cause of mortality in birds (after hunting).

The information that birds extract visually from the environment can be quite different from that which we humans extract, something that reflects the fundamental differences between birds and primates in terms of the structure and organisation of their respective visual systems (Martin & Osorio, 2008; Martin, 2011). There are, for example, significant differences in the perception of colour, the degree of resolution (acuity) achieved, determination of the position of an object relative to the animal, and in field of view.

The use of small sheets of glass as window panes can be traced back to at least 290 CE, but it was not until 1903 that the production of large sheets of glass for

FIG 86. Large patio windows, particularly those with bird feeders positioned close by, pose a risk to garden birds and can result in window strikes. (Mike Toms)

windows became commonplace. These appear to be effectively invisible to an approaching bird and many individuals collide with them at velocities that are likely to result in the collision being fatal. It has been suggested that fatal velocity may be reached at distances of substantially less than a metre (Klem, 1989). Although window collisions occur throughout the year, across many different types of window and under a range of different circumstances, there are some general patterns, providing insight into why such collisions can occur.

Examination of published studies suggests that half of all bird/window collision events result in mortality (Burton & Doblar, 2004; Gelb & Delacretaz, 2006; Bracey, 2011). Mortality rate does not appear to be influenced by the age or gender of the bird, but there is a suggestion that both behaviour and species – the two are linked – can play a role. For example, Drewitt & Langston (2008) found that species that are more active closer to the ground are more likely to collide with a window than those that are active higher within the canopy. Those (typically granviorous) species that are attracted to garden feeding stations, which are often positioned close to windows, are likely to be at greater risk of collision than insectivorous species that feed within vegetation.

Birds may not see a window, either because they can see straight through it to what is on the other side or because they can see the sky, vegetation or something else reflected in the window and fly towards this. It has been suggested that there are more collisions when the glass reflects nearby vegetation (Gelb & Delacretaz, 2009). The quality of this reflection will be determined by the nature of the glass itself and by local conditions, the latter including both local weather conditions and the degree of shading that the window receives. A particular problem may be where a bird can see through one window to another and beyond, thus establishing the illusion of a 'passageway' through the building. A special class of window strikes are those relating to birds attracted to lit windows at night – this particular problem is only really associated with high-rise office buildings (and lighthouses) and not with domestic properties, so will not be covered here. It is, however, likely to be an important cause of mortality for some species of nocturnally migrating bird.

If a bird moves towards a window, either from a starting position on a nearby bird feeder or from vegetation, then you might imagine that the distance from the bird to the window at the point at which it takes flight might influence whether or not a fatal collision will result. As we have already seen, Daniel Klem suggests that fatal velocity is achieved within a short distance (perhaps as little as 30 cm). Other researchers have found an increasing collision risk, and associated mortality, with distance from the window. Hager et al. (2013), for example, found an increase in collisions with feeders positioned from 5 to 10 m from the window, with a peak in fatalities when the feeders were positioned at 10 m from the window. Evans Ogden (1996) suggests a distance of from 4 to 10 m as being fatal for small birds.

Fatalities are thought to be the result of internal haemorrhaging, the bird typically striking the window head first (Klem, 1990b). Despite the 'loose-necked' appearance of a freshly dead bird, there is nothing to suggest that a broken neck is a common cause of death in such collisions. Of those birds that do survive the collision, at least initially, some may subsequently die from internal injuries, while others may be predated while they are lying prone and stunned on the ground beneath the window. It is likely that a sizeable proportion of window-strike casualties will be scavenged by predators; this suggests that the levels of mortality recorded in published studies are conservative estimates, with the true impact of window collisions potentially that much greater.

When it comes to attempts to reduce the incidence of collisions, there have been various recommendations and a number of commercially available 'solutions'. Avery (1979) concluded that the presence of drawn curtains and/

or net curtains could reduce collision risk, but the work of Evans Ogden (1996) and Stanyon (2014) suggests that this might not be the case. One of the most commonly used commercial 'solutions' is the use of sticker silhouettes, usually presented in the shape of a flying falcon or ultraviolet reflecting shape. The generally accepted wisdom within the published literature is that such devices are ineffective, the bird simply avoiding the sticker but still colliding with a different part of the window. There is even the suggestion that such stickers might make a collision more likely, since the bird will be distracted by the sticker and less likely to spot the presence of the glass (Stanyon, 2014). Other potential solutions, for example changing the angle of the window to 20–40° from vertical or adding a grid of dots or lines to the glass, may be more effective. While the former may cause engineering or design issues, the latter option could be more acceptable to homeowners, who see windows as a view into the outside world. Since humans cannot detect UV light but birds can, these patterns of dots or lines could be created from UV-absorbing or UV-reflecting materials, making them invisible to the human eye – unless light conditions inside the house are stronger than those seen outside (Buer & Regner, 2002; Klem & Saenger, 2013). Since the placement close to a window of features attractive to birds, such as bird feeders, berry-bearing vegetation or water, increases the risk of a window strike, it follows that removing such features should reduce the risk of a collision (Klem, 1991).

A special case of window collisions is those linked to anti-predator escape flights, where a bird is panicked by a predator and is flushed from its perch into the glass. Erica Dunn (1993) estimated that 16 per cent of the collisions documented in her study were the result of birds panicked by a predator. On some occasions, the pursuing predator may also collide with the window, something that is seen from time to time by those taking an interest in their garden birds here in UK gardens.

There are other objects with which birds may collide within gardens and the wider urban landscape that sits around many of them. Collision with motor vehicles, with wires, netting and with micro-turbines (generating wind energy) may also be responsible for mortality.

PREDATION

Garden birds are likely to experience predation in a similar way to that seen within the wider countryside. However, its impacts at the population level may differ because of differences in the predator species involved and in the degree of isolation of garden populations from those elsewhere. Predator populations tend to be limited by the availability of their prey but this isn't usually the case for domestic cats, which have a ready supply of food at home, and so their impacts may be greater than those of a Stoat *Mustela erminea* or Magpie, for example. Similarly, a population may be able to sustain high levels of predation under certain circumstances, perhaps where the population would normally be limited by some other factor (such as competition for food), or because it is sustained by recruits from elsewhere. As we shall see in this section, the interactions between garden birds and their predators may be complex, and there is still much for us to learn about the impact of predation on those birds using the garden environment.

While predator communities are likely to differ between urban and non-urban landscapes, it is important to recognise that not all gardens are urban; many are on the urban fringe and others are entirely rural in nature. It is not possible, therefore, to make generalisations about the levels of predation encountered within gardens and about how these might compare with the wider countryside. What we can say, however, is that the pattern of predation within an individual garden – and the predators responsible for that predation – is likely to be shaped by the nature of the surrounding landscape (Thorington & Bowman, 2003). There is good evidence, for example, that urban landscapes have higher densities of cats (Gaston *et al.*, 2005a; Sims *et al.*, 2008) and corvids (Jerzak, 2001; Antonov & Atanasova, 2003), and this might have an impact on the levels of predation experienced within this habitat.

SPARROWHAWKS

The Sparrowhawk is a specialist predator of small birds, whose English breeding population increased by 118 per cent between 1975 and 2014. This increase in abundance has been brought about through improved breeding success, following a decline in the use of those organochlorine pesticides linked to a reduction in eggshell thickness across a number of bird of prey species (Newton & Wyllie, 1992). The recovery of the Sparrowhawk population was largely completed by the mid-1990s, with recolonisation of its former breeding range (Balmer *et al.*, 2013) and an increased use of garden sites (Chamberlain *et al.*, 2005). Data from the BTO/JNCC/RSPB Breeding Bird Survey indicate that the breeding population has subsequently been in decline since 2006. The recovery of the Sparrowhawk population, and in particular its timing, has led some authors to suggest a causal link with the decline in UK House Sparrow populations (Bell *et al.*, 2010).

Sparrowhawks certainly do take House Sparrows and other garden birds, their presence in the vicinity of garden feeding stations sometimes triggering a strong emotional response from those garden birdwatchers who put out supplementary food to attract small birds into their gardens. On occasion, this has helped to feed the vigorous debate around the possible role of Sparrowhawk predation in the decline of urban House Sparrow populations. Although Sparrowhawk predation can remove a large number of individuals from a prey population, there is little evidence that this 'harvest' leads to any obvious depression of the breeding population the following year.

The effect of predators on their songbird prey has generally been assumed to compensate for individuals that would have otherwise succumbed to other forms of mortality. Evidence for a compensatory effect in relation to Sparrowhawk predation may be found through the analysis of data on post-breeding populations of tits, sparrows and other small birds. The work of Perrins & Geer (1980) and of Newton *et al.* (1998), for example, has revealed the local effects of an increasing Sparrowhawk population on non-breeding tits and other woodland species. These studies identified a shift in the seasonal pattern of songbird mortality, a reduction in the size of the post-breeding population and a change in the main agents of mortality, following recolonisation of sites by Sparrowhawks. Despite the Sparrowhawks taking up to a third of the young tits produced each year, their impact on the size of the breeding population in subsequent years was immeasurably small.

FIG 87. The Sparrowhawk is a specialist predator of small birds, and may visit garden feeding stations in search of prey. (John Harding)

Work looking at garden bird populations, and using data from the BTO's Garden Bird Feeding Survey (see Chapter 6), provides some additional insight into the question of Sparrowhawk predation and House Sparrow decline. Chamberlain *et al.* (2009b) and Bell *et al.* (2010) both analysed Garden Bird Feeding Survey data but found contrasting results, perhaps because of the different methods used or because of a failure on one or other part to properly isolate the impact of predation from other confounding factors. Chamberlain *et al.* (2009b) found no significant effect of Sparrowhawks on House Sparrows, when accounting for temperature and the number of bird feeders provided at the Garden Bird Feeding Survey sites studied. Bell *et al.* (2010) found significant negative effects of Sparrowhawks on House Sparrows but failed to account for any additional environmental covariates in their models. A piece of work by Newson *et al.* (2010), using a different modelling approach and a different dataset, also failed to find any evidence that House Sparrow breeding population declines were linked to an increasing Sparrowhawk population.

The development of new statistical approaches has enabled us to look again at the Garden Bird Feeding Survey data, which is probably the best dataset available to address the question of Sparrowhawks and garden bird populations (Swallow *et al.*, 2016a; 2016b). The results of this work suggest that, after controlling for the effects of environmental factors such as weather and surrounding habitat, there is still an additional negative effect of Sparrowhawks on House Sparrow populations using Garden Bird Feeding Survey sites (Swallow *et al.*, in prep). However, in practical terms the effect is extremely small and it is likely that Sparrowhawk predation is a very minor contributory factor to the decline of House Sparrows (and Starlings) rather than the main cause.

In addition to any possible direct effect of Sparrowhawk predation – i.e. small birds being killed – the presence of a Sparrowhawk in the vicinity of a garden feeding station may have an indirect effect on small birds by deterring them from accessing the food on offer. It is known that many small birds are reluctant to feed far from cover, something that has been attributed to the greater risk of predation facing birds feeding out in the open. Work in a Cardiff garden, for example, has found that the consumption of supplementary food provided in feeders adjacent to cover is double that of feeders placed 7.5 m away (Cowie & Simons, 1991).

A study by Hinsley *et al.* (1995) shows that older tits are more likely to use bird feeders positioned close to cover, forcing younger, subordinate individuals to take their chances on feeders positioned further away and at greater risk of Sparrowhawk predation. Similar findings have been found for other tit species and also in mixed-species flocks, where smaller and less dominant species are forced to feed in more exposed locations (Ekman, 1986; Suhonen *et al.*, 1993). Such studies underline that small birds are able to weigh up the risk of predation and to balance this against the need to feed. The vulnerability of particular species to Sparrowhawk predation has been found to be due to both the characteristics of the prey species themselves – such as habitat use and behaviour – and those of the predator (Solonen 1997; 2000).

Sparrowhawks deploy a number of different hunting techniques, the most commonly used of which is 'short-stay-perch-hunting' (Newton, 1986). This technique sees the Sparrowhawk make short flights from one perch to another, pausing on each to scan the local area from cover, before moving on. The use of cover, both while perched and during flight, underlines that the hawk is a stealth hunter, seeking to take prey by surprise in order to increase its chances of making a kill. Garden birdwatchers often report how hunting Sparrowhawks make use of the cover provided by hedgerows, fences, shrubby borders and other features in order to get as close as possible to hanging feeders or bird tables. The use of such features is sometimes referred to as 'contour hunting'. The difference in size between male and female Sparrowhawks – the female is the bigger sex – sees male Sparrowhawks typically take prey up to the size of a Mistle Thrush or Fieldfare, while females regularly tackle larger birds, such as Collared Dove and Woodpigeon. Although both sexes favour wooded habitats when hunting, females make greater use of open country than males and have larger hunting ranges (Marquiss & Newton, 1982). Whether this results in a greater use of gardens by females is unclear – this may be the case in rural gardens – and more work is needed to look at Sparrowhawks breeding within urbanised landscapes.

MAGPIES

The Magpie is a generalist and is known to use a broad range of food types. Animal prey, which is dominated by invertebrates, is most important during the breeding season when Magpies have young of their own to feed, while plant material dominates at other times of the year (Tatner, 1983). There are occasional records of Magpies killing frogs, moles and snakes, with small rodents and small birds taken more frequently – Magpies are even agile enough to catch adult birds, including House Sparrow and Dunnock. However, it is often the conspicuous predation of the eggs and young at songbird nests that has given rise to the assertion that Magpies might be responsible for the declines seen in certain songbird populations. There is relatively little quantitative information on the predation of songbird nests by Magpies, and even less on how such predation might impact on the breeding populations of the songbird species concerned.

FIG 88. Although happy to visit garden feeders in search of peanuts and suet pellets, Magpies may also visit gardens to search for the eggs and chicks of other garden birds. (John Harding)

Møller (1988), working on nest predation in Danish Blackbirds, found that the Magpies in his study area were responsible for 96 per cent of nest predation events recorded and that the presence of a breeding pair of Magpies in a wood resulted in an increased predation rate. In respect of urban Magpies, Mizera (1988) has suggested that Magpies were responsible for the breeding failure of most of the open-nesting songbirds in his Polish study area; as Magpie populations increased from 2 pairs in 1963 to 13 pairs in 1982, so the breeding success and numbers of Blackbirds declined. However, another urban study – this time in Berlin – found no evidence that increasing Magpie numbers had any effect on songbird numbers (Witt, 1989). There has been a small amount of work on urban Magpies and nest predation here in the UK. Groom (1993), working in urban Manchester, found that fewer than one in twenty of his Blackbird nests were successful, with Magpie thought to be the main nest predator. However, there was no apparent change in the numbers of breeding Blackbirds over the three years of this study, despite the high Magpie densities, and Groom concluded that habitat quality was probably the main factor determining the size of his urban Blackbird population.

The question of whether Magpies might be responsible for any of the widespread declines seen in songbird populations in the UK has been investigated by Gooch *et al.* (1991), who used BTO data for 11 common songbird species considered as being potentially vulnerable to Magpie predation. While these included several familiar garden bird species, such as Blackbird, Song Thrush, Dunnock, Robin and Chaffinch, the data were drawn mainly from woodland and farmland populations. Nest mortality was not related to Magpie density, nor did nest mortality increase with increasing Magpie density; in fact, the songbird populations actually did better (not worse) in regions where Magpie density was higher. A later study, using a larger dataset and a more advanced statistical approach, indicated that Magpie (and Sparrowhawk) was unlikely to have caused the observed songbird declines because the patterns of year-to-year population changes witnessed did not differ between sites with and without these predators (Thomson *et al.*, 1998).

These two pieces of work strongly suggest that, at a regional or national level, Magpies have no detectable effect on songbird breeding success. However, the same may not be true for urbanised landscapes, where both habitat structure and differences in food availability might alter the levels of predation risk for nesting songbirds. This is something that, as is indicated by Chapter 3, warrants greater study.

CATS

The presence within the UK of the cat as a domesticated animal extends back over many centuries, but it has only been relatively recently that its potential impact on populations of wild birds and other animals has been recognised (Matheson, 1944; Sims *et al.*, 2008). The large population of domestic cats present in the UK, estimated to number at least eight million pet cats and 800,000 feral individuals, coupled with frequent observations of their taking wildlife, reinforces the widespread belief that cats may have contributed to the marked declines seen in bird and amphibian populations. Despite the significant levels of bird mortality being linked to cat predation within some studies – Churcher & Lawton (1987) estimated that up to a third of the mortality they witnessed was linked to cat predation – we lack much-needed empirical evidence and simply do not know whether or not cat predation has any real impact on populations of wild birds. There is some evidence, for example, the recent work of van Heezik *et al.* (2010), to indicate that certain prey species may be unable to persist in habitats where levels of cat predation are high. Even within urbanised landscapes, such habitat effects may be of particular importance: there is, for example, evidence that predation rates on certain prey species may be higher within the urban/suburban fringe than they are within the core urban habitat (Gillies & Clout, 2003).

The nature of predation: compensatory or additive?

The very large figures quoted by the likes of Woods *et al.* (2003) and Loss *et al.* (2012), who estimated respectively that UK cats kill between 25 and 29 million birds annually and that US cats kill between 1.4 and 3.7 billion birds annually, may not translate into a decline in wild bird populations if this predation is 'compensatory' rather than 'additive'. Where predation is compensatory, the removal of part of the population serves to reduce the level of mortality that will be experienced by the surviving component. For example, if the size of a House Sparrow breeding population is ultimately driven by density-dependent competition for food during late winter, such that more individuals die when there is greater competition for a finite food source, then cat predation earlier in the year will simply reduce the number of individuals competing and result in a lower mortality rate from

FIG 89. Cat predation may be particularly problematic in some areas because of the numbers of free-living individuals present. (Mike Toms)

starvation than would have been the case in the absence of predation. The resulting breeding population would, in this instance, be the same regardless of whether or not the predation was taking place. Another way to think of compensatory predation is to view it as the predator taking part of the annual 'surplus'. Predation is 'additive' where its effects are additional to the other mortality causes.

Jarvis (1990) has argued that within the UK, cat predation is compensatory rather than additive; while there is some evidence to support this view (e.g. Flux, 2007; Lilith, 2007), it is important to recognise that birds are mobile and that the presence of a population at a given site may be maintained only by the arrival of individuals from populations elsewhere – something that has been studied by those looking at source-sink dynamics. This means that just because a garden bird population isn't declining in a locality where there is a high level of cat predation, this does not mean that predation by cats in this locality isn't having an impact at a wider population level.

One reason why cat predation may be particularly problematic is that domestic cats, living as companion animals, are supported with supplementary food by their owners. This means that their populations are not limited by the availability of wild prey, something that enables them to live at much higher densities than those seen in wild felids, living as part of a natural system (MacDonald & Loveridge, 2010). The provision of supplementary food no doubt reduces the level of predation that actually happens, but domesticated cats still maintain and implement their predatory behaviour (Fitzgerald & Turner, 2000).

It is also important to recognise a second component to many urban, and indeed rural, cat populations in the form of free-roaming individuals; these are cats that are not pets but neither are they truly feral (Calhoon & Haspel, 1989; Finkler et al., 2011). Instead, the animals take advantage both of handouts, in the form of supplemental feeding by people, and of other food scraps encountered within their foraging range. Densities of such individuals may range from 0.033 cats per ha (in rural Sweden – Liberg, 1980) to 7.43 cats per ha (Maryland, US – Oppenheimer, 1980). Dards (1979) reported densities of c. 2.00 cats per ha in urban Portsmouth. Urban densities of free-roaming cats are typically significantly higher than those of equivalent rural populations, with food availability and shelter both important in determining the densities attained. It is thought by some researchers that these un-owned, free-roaming cats are responsible for the majority of the bird and small mammal mortality linked to cat predation (Loss et al., 2012). If this is true, then most of the published figures for garden bird mortality resulting from cat predation will be significant underestimates.

Many of the studies to have examined the predation of garden birds and other wildlife by domestic cats have done so indirectly, asking cat owners to collect and record the numbers and identity of prey species taken. The successful application of this method necessitates the assumption that the prey items brought home are a representative sample of the total caught and killed; some items, such as larger invertebrates, may be significantly under-represented within the sample. There is also substantial variation between individual cats in the extent to which they kill prey and take it back to the household in which they live. Tschanz *et al.* (2011), for example, found that 16 per cent of the cats in their study accounted for 75 per cent of the prey returned. Some researchers have found that younger (and thinner) cats bring home more prey items than older cats (e.g. Woods *et al.*, 2003; van Heezik *et al.*, 2010).

The approach of asking cat owners to record the prey brought home by cats is certainly a better one than simply asking cat owners to estimate the number of birds and animals killed, since it has been shown that cat owners consistently underestimate predation levels, presumably because their judgement has in some way been clouded by the emotional aspect of their cat killing another creature (Barratt, 1998). Looking across the various studies using this approach for examining cat predation and its impacts suggests that, on average, domestic cats exhibit predation rates of between 0.58 (Baker *et al.*, 2005) and 6.57 prey items per cat per month (Calver *et al.*, 2007). Annual figures calculated by Loss *et al.* (2012) for the US and Europe combined are between 23.2 and 46.2 birds per cat per year; these compare to equivalent figures for mammal prey of 134.9–328.6, underlining the seemingly greater importance of small mammals in domestic cat diet. Such figures are often then used to produce estimates of the total number of prey items taken annually, the rate extrapolated up by the number of cats known to be resident within a particular city, region or country. While small mammals, such as mice, voles and shrews, tend to be the most numerous type of prey taken and brought home by domestic cats, small birds feature prominently (Churcher & Lawton, 1987; Woods *et al.*, 2003; Baker *et al.*, 2005).

The study carried out in Bristol by Phil Baker and colleagues (Baker *et al.*, 2005) used a diary approach, allowing cat owners to record what their cats brought home on a daily basis. In addition to the information collected on the species being brought home by the cats, Baker and his colleagues were also able to estimate from questionnaire returns that roughly one in five of the householders in the study area owned a cat. A Cats Protection League figure for the equivalent period suggests cat ownership could be as high as one in four homes. The most commonly recorded prey species was Wood Mouse *Apodemus sylvaticus*, while House Sparrow, Blue Tit, Robin and Blackbird were the most commonly taken birds (that could be identified to species). Using figures from the BTO/JNCC/RSPB Breeding Bird Survey for the Bristol region, Baker *et al.*

FIG 90. Cat predation may be particularly important in limiting the distribution of small mammals in some locations. (John Harding)

(2005) were able to calculate minimum predation rates for each species; these were found to be moderately high for three of the bird species considered, namely Dunnock (46 per cent), Robin (46 per cent) and House Sparrow (45 per cent), where the percentage represents predation as a proportion of the combined total of pre-breeding density and annual productivity. House Sparrow populations have previously been considered vulnerable to cat predation, most notably through the work of Churcher & Lawton (1987). Churcher & Lawton's work suggested that, within their English village study area, cat predation was responsible for up to 30 per cent of annual House Sparrow mortality.

While it might be assumed that there is a direct and negative relationship between keeping a cat and feeding wild birds in your garden, a national study by Woods *et al.* (2003) found evidence that cats living in households where owners fed the birds brought home fewer birds (and fewer reptiles and amphibians) than cats living in a house where food was not provided. The work of Dunn &

Tessaglia (1994) and of Lepczyk *et al.* (2004b) contradicts this, with both research teams finding that there was no difference in predation rates between households that fed wild birds and those that did not.

In addition to variation in the predatory activities of individual cats, there can also be variation in the impact that such predation has at the population level. It has been shown that birds are particularly susceptible to cat predation during the breeding season, and that the intensity of predation is at its peak during this period (Lepczyk *et al.*, 2004b; Baker *et al.*, 2005). This seasonal peak in predation may have a wider impact on the post-breeding population, the loss of an adult bird also potentially meaning the loss of its dependent young or its clutch of eggs. Domestic cats may impact garden bird populations in two ways: as we have already seen, they may kill birds but there may also be sub-lethal effects, with the presence of hunting cats preventing individual birds from foraging or from returning to an occupied nest. This 'fear of cats' has been investigated by researchers at the University of Sheffield, whose modelling approach suggested that such sub-lethal impacts could depress the size of urban bird populations (Beckerman *et al.*, 2007). Further work on this topic, also carried out at Sheffield, revealed that the brief presence of a model domestic cat at an active Blackbird nest led to a subsequent reduction in provisioning rates and increased levels of nest predation (Bonnington *et al.*, 2013). The latter effect appeared to result from the increased levels of nest defence behaviour directed at the cat model, which presumably alerted nest predators (Grey Squirrels and corvids) to the presence of the nest.

Reducing the impact of cat predation

Various attempts have been made to reduce the impact of cat predation on populations of wild birds. These have included curtailing the movements of domestic cats (including the enactment of legislation elsewhere in the world requiring that cats are kept indoors), the use of sonic and other devices to alert potential prey to a cat's presence (Clark & Burton, 1998; Clark, 1999; Ruxton *et al.*, 2002), and the deployment of 'bibs' and other restraints that limit a cat's ability to hunt effectively (Calver *et al.*, 2007). Since the time of day has an influence on the types of prey taken, it is possible for cat owners to reduce the impact of their pet on particular species by modifying the time periods when a cat is allowed outside – Barratt (1997) found that cats tended to bring home birds in the morning, reptiles in the afternoon and mammals in the evening, most likely reflecting peaks in the activity patterns of these different groups.

The addition of one or (better still) two bells to a cat's collar has been shown to reduce the number of prey items that a cat brings into its household. A study by Graeme Ruxton and his colleagues, in which 21 cats were monitored over eight weeks and carried a bell for four weeks within this period, saw the mean number of prey items delivered fall from 5.5 to 2.9 individuals. The bell had no effect on the relative numbers of different types of prey delivered and, within this study at least, no evidence that the cats adapted their hunting behaviour to reduce the effect of the bell over time (Ruxton *et al.*, 2002). The effectiveness of a not dissimilar device, in the form of a collar-mounted sonic apparatus, has also been shown to reduce the level of predation on birds – though not on mammals (Clark, 1999).

Working in Australia, Michael Calver and colleagues have investigated the effectiveness of a more substantial device, the CatBib^{TM}. The bib is a sizeable neoprene device that hangs from the cat's collar and is designed to interfere with the precise timing and coordination that a cat needs for successful bird catching. Alone, or in combination with bells, the bibs were found to stop 81 per cent of the cats studied from catching birds; cats wearing the bib caught only one in four of all birds (Calver *et al.*, 2007). While Calver found the device to be effective, continued use by those cat owners who trialled the device had dropped to 17 per cent eight months after the trial, despite nearly three-quarters saying they would continue to use the device.

In addition to the devices proposed for use on individual cats, there are also commercially available deterrents designed for use by people – typically non-cat owners – wanting to prevent cats from making use of their gardens. These range from cheap chemical sprays and pellets through to more expensive ultrasonic devices, such as 'Catwatch'. The ultrasonic devices work by detecting movement and body heat and using this to trigger an ultrasonic alarm operating at a volume of 56 decibels (at 7 m) and a frequency of 21–23 kHz. The results of a study examining the effectiveness of the 'Catwatch' device suggest that it does have a 'moderate deterrent effect' (Nelson *et al.*, 2006).

OTHER PREDATORS

Although a number of other predators may take the adults, young and eggs of garden birds, relatively less attention has been directed towards understanding either the scale of predation or its impact at the population level. One species that has been thought likely to be responsible for significant levels of nest predation – both to open nests and to those in nest boxes – is the Grey Squirrel. Squirrels, in general, are major nest predators, as revealed by studies in both Europe and North America (Martin, 1993; Nour *et al.*, 1993); however, much of this evidence is linked to species other than Grey Squirrel. While we know that Grey Squirrels do eat wild birds and their eggs in both woodland and garden habitats, there has been little work – either in the UK or North America – to quantify the numbers of birds and eggs taken. Anecdotal reports hint at local impacts within a handful of sites, but a study by Newson *et al.* (2010) failed to find any convincing evidence for an increasing Grey Squirrel population being behind an observed decline in woodland bird populations at a national level. Newson *et al.* (2010) did, however, find a positive association between nest failure at the egg stage in Blackbird and Collared Dove and squirrel abundance; this may mean that nest predation by Grey Squirrels had been depressing the populations of these two species.

The extent and pattern of Grey Squirrel nest predation may be very different in a garden setting to that seen within woodland or the wider countryside. Grey Squirrels are generalist feeders, exploiting a wide range of food types, and their populations may benefit from the presence of supplementary food, such as peanuts and sunflower seeds, provided at garden feeding stations. The provision of supplementary food may both increase the numbers of Grey Squirrels visiting a garden and the number of individuals foraging more widely within the garden setting. This is something that has been investigated by Hugh Hanmer, through his PhD at the University of Reading (Hanmer *et al.*, 2017b). Hanmer used cameras to monitor artificial nests that had been placed in the area around a series of bird feeders, some of which were empty and some of which contained food – the latter divided into those that were protected by a cage and those that were not. The work set out to establish whether Grey Squirrels – and other nest predators – were attracted to garden feeding stations providing supplementary food and, if so, whether this associated with differences in rates of nest predation. Grey Squirrels (and Magpies) were frequent visitors to those feeders containing food, and predation by Grey Squirrels (and Magpies and Jays) was significantly higher when nests were located close to filled feeders. Hanmer concluded that the increased predation on the artificial nests close to filled feeders was not simply a consequence of predators being attracted to a point source; instead, he thought that the predators were perhaps also being attracted by the presence of other feeder users in the vicinity. While Hanmer's work demonstrates the potential impacts at the level of individual nests, it remains to be determined if such predation affects the population dynamics of urban birds more widely.

Great Spotted Woodpecker, Jay, Weasel and Pine Marten *Martes martes* are known to be important nest predators within forest and woodland habitats across Europe, but they are unlikely to be important predators within a garden context – though all four species are regular visitors to some favoured gardens. Great Spotted Woodpeckers are known to feed on tit chicks extracted

FIG 91. Great Spotted Woodpeckers are known to predate the nests of other birds, even breaking in to nest boxes to take the chicks of Blue Tits. (John Harding)

from wooden nest boxes, the woodpecker either enlarging the entrance hole or – seemingly more often – drilling a fresh hole in the side of the box. Great Spotted Woodpecker predation of nest box contents appears to be linked to the presence of vocal chicks within the box. Weasels may also take young chicks from within nest boxes, a behaviour that may be more common in those years when favoured small mammal prey populations are low (Dunn, 1977). Jay, although a less commonly reported garden visitor than Magpie, appears to be an important nest predator targeting open-nesting species. Working in woodland in Germany, Schaefer (2004) used video cameras to monitor the fate of 132 Blackcap nests; Jays were responsible for 21 per cent of nest fates and 46 per cent of nest losses.

EXPOSURE TO ENVIRONMENTAL CONTAMINANTS

Many different types of environmental toxicants – which include insecticides, rodenticides, heavy metals and molluscicides – have been documented to cause mortality or bring about sub-lethal effects in wild birds. Such incidents have tended to be reported from bird populations living within the wider countryside – think of the impacts of DDT on bird of prey populations (Ratcliffe, 1967) or the presence of second-generation rodenticides in Barn Owls (Newton *et al.*, 1990; Gray *et al.*, 1994) – but individuals may also be exposed to such compounds within the garden environment. Urbanised landscapes are subject to higher levels of certain environmental pollutants than is the case within the wider countryside, with contaminants from industry, transport and other activities posing a potential risk to the wildlife using gardens, parks and other areas of urban green space. Chandler *et al.* (2004), for example, showed that the levels of lead found in an urban House Sparrow population in Vermont, US, were significantly higher than those from a wider countryside control group. Closer to home, a study looking at Finnish House Sparrow liver samples, sampled in the 1980s, found that heavy metal levels were higher in urban than rural areas (Kekkonen *et al.*, 2012).

Some heavy metals, including zinc, copper, manganese, chrome and iron, are essential to living organisms but become harmful if present in excess. Other heavy metals, such as cadmium, aluminium and lead, are usually not essential to living organisms. Heavy metal pollution has been shown to detrimentally affect key phases in the avian life cycle, including the development of the egg, chick growth and adult reproduction (Eeva & Lehikonen, 1995; 1996). Heavy metals and other airborne pollutants, such as combustion-derived hydrocarbon gases and biocides, are highly reactive elements which interfere with avian metabolism and key biochemical reactions. They can disrupt the activities of enzymes and alter the levels of free radicals – free radicals are by-products of cell metabolism and are usually balanced by a number of antioxidant elements. The antioxidant response to the oxidative damage caused by such pollutants has been used by some researchers as a biomarker, revealed through the blood sampling of key species – such as House Sparrow – and used to indicate the impacts of pollution on the wider environment (Herrera-Dueñas *et al.*, 2014).

The presence of lead within the urban environment has been linked to the use of lead-based paint and leaded petrol, the former banned from sale to the general public in 1992 in the UK – though continuing for some specialist uses – and the latter phased out from general sale from 1999. However, lead is persistent within the environment and concentrations in soil remain high in many urbanised landscapes. Birds may come into contact with this lead through inadvertent consumption of soil particles when feeding on soil-dwelling invertebrates, such as earthworms (Beyer *et al.*, 1988). Labere *et al.* (2004) reported that earthworms sampled from a lead-contaminated area at West Point, US, had up to 90 per cent higher concentrations of lead compared to an uncontaminated control site, while Weyers *et al.* (1985) found significantly higher levels of lead in the feathers and organs of Blackbirds feeding at contaminated sites in Germany. Lead poisoning in birds can have both physiological and behavioural effects: from anaemia, emaciation and brain damage, through to increased aggression and difficulties in walking, flying and landing. Work by Karin Roux and Pete Marra (2007) has revealed a gradient in lead pollution from urban to rural landscapes, which is matched by a similar gradient in lead levels within the blood of sampled adult and nestling birds, including American Robin, Gray Catbird *Dumatella carolinensis*, Song Sparrow, Northern Cardinal and House Sparrow.

The birds inhabiting gardens located closer to busy roads are likely to be at greater risk from pollutants associated with transport than gardens located within more leafy suburbs; it has also been speculated that changing levels of such pollutants might be behind the observed declines in urban House Sparrow populations. In addition to heavy metals like lead, other particulates, nitrogen oxides, polycyclic aromatic hydrocarbons and volatile organic compounds may also pose a risk to House Sparrows and other birds (Bignal *et al.*, 2004). There is also concern about some of the anti-knock agents – such as MTBE – introduced as a replacement to lead in petrol. Working along an urban gradient in Leicester, Kate Vincent and colleagues found that House Sparrow chicks reared at sites with high NO_2 levels tended to be smaller and lighter than those at other sites. The observed difference in body mass was sufficient to have had a relatively large impact on chick survival once they had left the nest (Hole, 2001; Peach *et al.*, 2008). The most likely route for emissions to impact on the growth of House Sparrow chicks is by reducing the availability of favoured invertebrate prey, and Vincent's work did find direct evidence for an influence of prey availability on reproductive success.

Large increases in the use of molluscicides in gardens, and more widely within lowland farmland (Garthwaite & Thomas, 1996), may have reduced prey availability for species like Song Thrush; they may have also caused direct mortality through secondary poisoning. However, despite the fact that snails form a large component of Song Thrush diet, particularly when other food is scarce, there has been little work done to evaluate the extent to

FIG 92. Song Thrushes may be exposed to environmental contaminants through their diet. (John Harding)

which molluscicides might have played a role in the decline of Song Thrush populations here in the UK. The use of other forms of pesticide within the garden environment may impact on garden birds by reducing the availability of favoured invertebrate prey, something that has already been demonstrated for some of the heavy metals already mentioned (Pimental, 1994; McIntyre, 2000).

OTHER CAUSES OF MORTALITY

A handful of reports suggest that ethanol poisoning may occasionally result in the deaths of berry-eating garden birds, which had presumably fed on fermenting berries or fruit (Fitzgerald *et al.*, 1990; Duff *et al.*, 2012). Cases of such mortality have been documented in Blackbirds and Redwings here in the UK, the former having fed on rowan berries *Sorbus* sp. and the latter on Holly. There are also a number of reports of birds being found drowned. In some instances, these incidents have involved multiple individuals of the same species. For example, Lawson *et al.* (2015b) reported on 12 incidents (from a 21-year period) of mass drownings with Starlings. These incidents always occurred in spring and early summer and usually involved juvenile birds. There was no evidence of underlying disease or other mortality cause and the authors concluded that the most likely explanation was that these were inexperienced birds getting into difficulty.

A small number of studies have highlighted a potential risk to urban bird populations from mobile phone base stations – a topic that has seen parallel concerns raised in relation to human health. Although more detailed work is needed, in part to control for other confounding factors, it would be wrong to dismiss the possibility of such effects out of hand. Non-thermal effects of microwaves on birds have already been documented (Tanner 1966; Fernie & Reynolds, 2005), suggesting, for example, that electromagnetic radiation from mobile phones may negatively impact on the development and survival of bird embryos (Farrel *et al.*, 1997) and disrupt magnetic navigation in several bird species (Thalau *et al.*, 2005). Demonstrating such effects within wild birds living within urban environments is likely to prove challenging.

CONCLUDING REMARKS

As we have seen through the work reported in this chapter, gardens have both opportunities and risks associated with their use. While we have a good understanding of some of these, our knowledge of others is far from complete. The challenges of working within the garden environment – something to which we will return in Chapter 6 – have been overcome in some of the areas of research (notably disease) that have been the focus of the current chapter. We have seen how risks and opportunities may vary between species and individuals, sometimes the result of physiology or ecology, sometimes shaped by behaviour. And it is behaviour to which we will turn our attention now.

CHAPTER 5
Behaviour

G ARDENS PROVIDE US WITH OPPORTUNITIES to watch birds at close
quarters, often from the comfort of an armchair, something that
can provide us with an insight into their lives and the different
behaviours that they exhibit. As well as being fascinating to watch, the behaviour
of garden birds can also provide clues to the ways in which certain species
have been able to exploit the opportunities that come from living within urban
landscapes. In addition to looking at behavioural responses to the characteristics
of the urban habitat identified in earlier chapters, through this chapter we will
also explore responses to the presence of humans and to the novel resources that
are so often associated with them. Some of these responses have already received
attention in earlier chapters, most notably those on feeding and nesting, but
there are many other fascinating behaviours for us to consider.

THE FEAR OF HUMANS

Most garden birdwatchers express delight at the opportunities that their bird
tables and hanging feeders provide for viewing birds at close quarters. On some
occasions, individual birds can become remarkably tolerant of their human
neighbours, perhaps taking food from the hand or even entering houses to
feed from the food bowls of domestic animals. Over the years that I spent
running the BTO's Garden Ecology Team, I regularly received photographs and
correspondence that underlined the amazing relationships that can develop
between people and 'their' garden birds. Such personal relationships underline
some of the well-being benefits that access to nature can provide.

A fear of humans is, however, common to most animals – except perhaps those that have evolved in isolation from predators on islands, or which have spent their lives living alongside us. Fear is difficult to measure in the field, so researchers often use the distance that a bird allows a human observer to approach to before taking flight as a proxy. This is known as the 'flight initiation distance' and has been widely studied. That those individuals living alongside humans become more tolerant than populations living within the wider countryside is evident from a growing body of research (Cooke, 1980). A field study of Burrowing Owls *Athene cunicularia*, carried out in the city of Bahía Blanca (Argentina) and its surrounding rural areas, found that urban-breeding pairs were more fearless towards human observers than was the case in the surrounding rural area (Carrete & Tella, 2017). Work by Samia *et al.* (2017) and Symonds *et al.* (2016), reviewing a broad range of studies, reported that the more urbanised a species is, the shorter its flight initiation distance, suggesting that living alongside humans within the built environment makes birds less fearful of us. Such relationships may sometimes be confounded by other factors; Sprau & Dingemanse (2017), for example, found that bold urban Great Tits occurred more frequently in areas where there were more cars but fewer humans, while shy individuals were mostly found in areas with few cars but more humans. While this might suggest that exposure to humans might not lead to bolder behaviour, the observed pattern could be explained by the differing levels of traffic noise, since Petrelli *et al.* (2017) found that noisy environments enabled a closer human approach to ground-feeding birds than was the case in quieter habitats.

One of the most interesting questions about the extent to which birds respond to human presence centres on whether species have become increasingly tolerant over time. Are species that have lived alongside humans for longer more tolerant of them? Research suggests that they are, with Symonds *et al.* (2016) reporting that urban populations with a longer history of inhabiting urban areas have lower flight initiation distances (i.e. they are more tolerant). This pattern is not seen in rural populations of the same species, suggesting that within the urban environment there may have been local selection of individuals with reduced responsiveness to the presence of humans.

While the birds foraging in our gardens may be bolder than those individuals living away from human habitation, they may also show a different reaction to any novel features that they encounter within the garden environment (Audet *et al.*, 2015). Certain individuals may be more willing to take the risk of exploring novel objects or opportunities than others. Anne Charmantier's work on Great Tits reveals strong differences in personality traits between forest and city habitats, with urban Great Tits faster to explore new surroundings than

FIG 93. Urban Great Tits are faster to explore their surroundings than their rural counterparts, and are usually bolder in their behaviour. (Jill Pakenham)

rural birds (Charmantier *et al.*, 2017). This finding supports that of earlier work demonstrating that urban birds are usually bolder in their behaviour and are less neophobic (Tryjanowski *et al.*, 2016; Ducatez *et al.*, 2017). They are also more tolerant of disturbance and show reduced levels of response to physiological stress (Lowry *et al.*, 2011).

The response to novel objects and opportunities may also be shaped by the degree of social behaviour exhibited within a particular species. It is well known that group living may offer benefits to birds and other species, including increased foraging success and better predator avoidance. It has been shown that groups of individuals may cope more effectively when faced with unfamiliar situations, something that is thought to be the result of larger groups containing a greater diversity of individuals with different skills and experiences (Liker & Bókony, 2009). Liker & Bókony's work focussed on House Sparrows and also revealed that, independent of group size, urban House Sparrow groups were more successful in dealing with novel tasks than their rural counterparts. Responses can also be shaped by prior exposure to novel objects, such that repeated exposure to bird feeders, for example, may lead to those individuals living in urban environments showing decreased levels of neophobia.

DEALING WITH NEW FEEDING OPPORTUNITIES

The foods presented at garden feeding stations are usually different from those that a bird would have encountered in the wild, even if they are of a similar general type, such as a seed. The ways in which supplemented foods are presented will also be different from how such foods occur naturally. This implies that at some point in the past an individual bird would have made the decision to explore a novel feeding opportunity, like a net bag full of peanuts. Exploratory behaviour is one of a suite of behaviours seen in most creatures, though the extent to which the behaviour is exhibited varies greatly between species. Defined as 'any behaviour that provides an individual with information about its environment', exploratory behaviour enables an individual to adapt to changing conditions and new opportunities. Individuals of the same species may differ in their exploratory behaviour, with those quick to explore novel environments also the ones most likely to explore novel objects introduced to their territory, home range or (in the case of laboratory studies) their cage. Exploratory traits may be heritable, learned, and selected for, such that behavioural responses may spread between individuals and throughout populations; one example of this is the way in which tits and several other garden bird species learned to exploit doorstep milk bottles, something to which we return in the next section.

Exploratory behaviour may also encompass problem solving and the use of tools, though the latter is particularly limited in birds. Various members of the crow family are known for their problem-solving skills, some of which approach those seen in primates in terms of the type of response and its complexity. It has been shown, for example, that Rooks will work together to solve problems; that Ravens *Corvus corax* will lead others of their kind away from boxes baited with food; and that Jackdaws will steal food more quickly from a human 'competitor' who either has their eyes closed or is looking elsewhere (Bugnyar & Kotrschal, 2004; Seed *et al.*, 2008; von Bayern & Emery, 2009).

Such problem-solving skills are supported by the fact that the corvid brain is significantly larger than predicted by body size and has a forebrain that is significantly larger, relative to whole brain size, than that of other birds (with the exception of parrots). While those corvids visiting UK gardens and bird tables may not demonstrate the tool-using skills seen in the New Caledonian Crow *Corvus moneduloides*, they have been observed practising behaviours that suggest a high degree of intelligence. For example, BTO Garden BirdWatchers have reported Rooks hauling up bird feeders and fat balls suspended from a branch by a piece of string. A Rook would pull up a length of the string with its bill,

FIG 94. Like other members of the crow family, Rooks are quick to exploit new feeding opportunities and show a high degree of intelligence. (John Harding)

before then clamping it to the branch with its foot; it would then pull up another length, repeating the process until it had the feeder on the branch. Corvids are also well known for the extent to which they cache food for future consumption – a behaviour seen in a number of other garden birds, including Nuthatch and Coal Tit. Caching behaviour requires good spatial memory. In corvids, however, individuals may also modify their caching behaviour in the presence of other individuals, something that is known to occur in wild Ravens, which avoid caching when they are being watched by other individuals who might then raid the cache and pilfer the contents.

The urban environment and its gardens present many novel opportunities and risks for visiting birds, suggesting that those species best able to adapt to these opportunities, and to take advantage of them, will be those best able to innovate. A study of the Barbados Bullfinch *Loxigilla barbadensis* found that urban individuals were better at problem solving than their rural counterparts (Audet *et al.*, 2016). The ability to innovate and to take advantage of new feeding opportunities is not without risks; in the previous chapter, we saw how the exploitation of garden feeding stations brings with it the increased risk of disease, something that may have implications for the development of innovation itself (Soler *et al.*, 2012). Research has revealed a positive link between brain size and feeding innovation and this might suggest that the two may have co-evolved. Work on captive Common Mynas, studied experimentally in outdoor aviaries, revealed differences between individuals in their foraging preferences: individuals that selected foods high in protein were found to be more exploratory in their behaviour and were able to solve experimental foraging tasks more rapidly than those individuals that favoured foods with a high carbohydrate component (Peneaux *et al.*, 2017). This underlines that the foods being provided at garden feeding stations have the potential to alter bird behaviour and may, over time, lead to more fundamental changes in the birds themselves.

THE CASE OF THE DOORSTEP PINT

Within the UK, milk has been delivered to household doorsteps in glass bottles since the beginning of the twentieth century. Initially, the milk bottles lacked tops and tits and Robins were sometimes seen to feed on the layer of cream present within. Later the tops of the bottles were sealed, initially with a waxed paper disc and later by an aluminium foil top, with a degree of regional variation evident in the timing of these innovations. In 1921, birds described as tits were seen to prise open the waxed paper tops of milk bottles that had been left on doorsteps at Swaythling, near Southampton (Fisher & Hinde, 1949) – the first documented case of such behaviour in the UK. Over the following years, the behaviour spread, with reports documented through a questionnaire survey carried out by the BTO.

The questionnaire was circulated to members of the BTO, to certain local natural history societies and through appeals placed in the *British Medical Journal*. This prompted some 200 or so responses, to which were added responses secured through articles placed in local and national newspapers. The resulting information was sufficient to provide an overview of the species of birds involved and to suggest how the behaviour was likely to have spread across the country. In 223 cases, observers were able to provide definitive information on the year in which the behaviour had first occurred at their premises. Fisher & Hinde then used this information to produce a series of maps revealing the pattern of spread.

The resulting distribution of records was consistent with the view that the behaviour emerged *de novo* within a small population of individuals at different localities across the UK, before spreading throughout the local population. In East Anglia, for example, the behaviour was first reported from Lowestoft, in 1941, before emerging in Norwich in 1943, King's Lynn in 1945, and by

1947 it was common in many districts across the region. In part of Llanelly (Monmouthshire), the milk bottle top opening habit was first noted in 1939, being reported from a single house in a wider group of 300 or so. By 1946, all of the houses to which milk was being delivered had had milk taken. The survey results also suggested that milk was more commonly taken during the winter months than the summer, and that bottles were attacked within a few minutes of being left on doorsteps by the milkman.

Of the 400 observations where identification of the tit species involved had been secured, the majority were Blue Tit (61.5 per cent) and Great Tit (35.5 per cent), with Coal Tit and a single observation of Marsh Tit making up the remainder. Other species seen opening bottles, as opposed to just feeding from them, were House Sparrow, Blackbird, Starling, Robin, Chaffinch, Song Thrush and Dunnock. An obvious omission from this list is Magpie, a species which took up the milk bottle top opening habit some time later. A subsequent paper by the same authors noted a series of records from other countries, including Sweden (Blackbird and Magpie), Denmark (Great Tit and Great Spotted Woodpecker) and the Netherlands (Great Tit).

In terms of behaviour, the tits usually started by puncturing the foil lids with a series of blows, before then tearing off the metal in strips. Waxed cardboard tops were treated in a similar manner, in terms of the initial blows, but appear to have been more challenging. The birds would sometimes have to remove several layers of board to access the contents, although on some occasions, where the lids were damaged, they were able to remove the lid from the side. The hammering behaviour employed by the tits was similar to that used to break into nuts and seeds. Sometimes the birds would remove the lid, taking it elsewhere to feed on the semi-solid cream stuck to its underside. This led to reports of piles of discarded tops deposited under nearby trees or hedgerows.

The tits and other birds were after the thick layer of cream at the top of the bottle, which sometimes extended down into the bottle by several centimetres. Accessing the last bits of cream led to a few unfortunate birds becoming stuck in the bottle and drowning, head first (Fisher & Hinde, 1949). Birds are unable to digest the lactose in milk and drinking milk is likely to result in diarrhoea and feeding aversion. Cream, however, is formed from a concentrated emulsion of fat globules and only contains a very small amount of lactose; this makes it an attractive lipid-rich food ideal for small birds during the winter months (del Rio, 1993).

As noted, Magpies seemed to cotton on to the opportunity that milk bottles provided somewhat later than tits, something that probably reflects the lower population of Magpies present at the time and (probably) a greater fear of humans and their habitation. Magpies were certainly still exploiting milk bottles in the early 1990s (Vernon, 1993). The practice of breaking in to milk bottle tops in this way, by both tits and Magpies, appears to have been an opportunistic response to a novel feeding opportunity. As consumer preferences began to change, purchasing more of their milk from shops and moving away from full-fat milk, so the opportunity began to disappear and it seems to have died out sometime in the late 1980s or early 1990s.

LOOKING AFTER YOURSELF

Another suite of behaviours evident in the birds using our gardens are those related to plumage maintenance, with bathing and preening readily observed by those watching the activities of familiar garden species. The water provided in a bird bath, or in the shallows of a garden pond, can prove highly attractive to birds like Starling and Blackbird, which may arrive to splash-bathe. Other birds may 'dew-bathe', using dew-covered vegetation to wet their plumage. Garden-visiting Woodpigeons sometimes adopt a curious pose when bathing, lifting one or other

FIG 95. Starlings regularly splash-bathe in bird baths in order to keep their plumage in good condition. (Jill Pakenham)

wing vertically to allow the water to reach the underside of the wing. This can result in the sight of several Woodpigeons sitting in a puddle, pond or bird bath during a rain shower, each with one wing raised in the air. Some species, notably House Sparrow, prefer to dust-bathe, working sandy or dry soil through their plumage and often with several individuals indulging in this behaviour together, before retreating into cover to continue preening.

Rather than washing the feathers, wetting with water may aid preen oil to spread across the plumage. This oil is produced from a gland located on the lower back of the bird towards the base of the tail. Although sometimes referred to as the 'preen gland', it is more correctly termed the uropygial gland; this is highly variable between species in terms of its shape and size. That the secretions produced by the uropygial gland serve to maintain feather condition can be seen from work on House Sparrows by Gregorio Moreno-Rueda (2011), who found that individuals with larger uropygial glands had less worn feathers. Preen oil has antimicrobial properties that inhibit the growth of feather-degrading bacteria, and insecticidal properties that work against chewing lice (Ruiz-Rodríguez et al., 2009; Moreno-Rueda, 2010).

Birds are sometimes seen sunbathing, adapting a posture in bright sunny weather that sees them spread-eagled on the ground, with tail and wings spread, body feathers ruffled and beak open (see Figure 96). It is thought that this behaviour has an important thermoregulatory role, something that is supported by the gaping behaviour that often accompanies the spread-eagled posture. However, the behaviour may also support feather maintenance, facilitating the spread of preen oil and forcing ectoparasites to become more mobile, and thus easier for the bird to locate and remove. Sunbathing is often accompanied by preening behaviour, so even if it is primarily a means of reducing body temperature, it does appear to deliver other benefits (Kennedy, 1969).

Something that has been viewed as an extension to sunbathing is 'anting', a behaviour that has been documented in more than 200 bird species worldwide, but which is seen primarily in Green Woodpeckers within the garden environment. An individual involved in anting tends to follow a series of stereotyped behaviours, adopting a characteristic pose that, like sunbathing, exposes as much of the plumage as possible. The presence of the bird at the ant nest provokes an aggressive response from the ants, which typically spray formic acid onto the bird. Ants belonging to the genera Formica and Lasius seem to be the ones most often targeted here in the UK. In addition to allowing the ants to move across the plumage, a bird may also pick up individual ants and wipe them through the plumage, prompting them to spray formic acid. Interestingly, despite the fact that it is possible to examine anting behaviour under laboratory

FIG 96. Robin is one of a number of species that may be seen to 'sunbathe' in a garden setting. (Mike Toms)

conditions, we remain uncertain as to its function. It seems most likely that the behaviour facilitates the removal of ectoparasites but it might also aid feather maintenance, decrease the level of skin irritation during moult, or even act as a form of sensory self-stimulation. Work on American Blue Jays indicates that while formic acid is the trigger for anting behaviour in this species – the jays select formic-acid producing ants over species that do not produce the substance – the levels of formic acid reaching the plumage are insufficient to have a significant antimicrobial effect against the common feather bacterium *Bacillus licheniformis* (Hutchinson & Kellam, 2015).

Another possibility, at least in relation to the Green Woodpecker and other ant-eating species, is that the behaviour helps in prey preparation by ridding the ants about to be eaten of their unpleasant defensive toxins (Morozov, 2015). There is some evidence to support this 'food preparation' hypothesis, with experimental evidence demonstrating that birds deprived of food are more likely to engage in anting behaviour than individuals that have been provided with food (Judson &

Bennett, 1992). A similar study, using Blue Jays, found that birds were more likely to eat ants that had had their formic-acid-producing sacs removed immediately, only eating intact individuals once they had been subjected to anting (Eisner & Aneshansley, 2008). The formic acid produced by ants can be deadly at high concentrations and when an individual has an empty stomach.

While the use of ants may serve a role in the maintenance of a bird's plumage, there is stronger evidence that birds may use plant material in an antimicrobial or insecticidal role in their nests (Clark & Mason, 1988); this is something that we touched on in Chapter 3. There is also some evidence that birds may adjust their selection of particular foods, or even ingest soil, in an attempt to self-medicate, maintain their physiological condition or to counter the effects of unsuitable foodstuffs (de Roode *et al.*, 2013). Perhaps the most well-known example of this practice is the Peruvian rainforest parrots that feed on a layer of clay soil, exposed on a river bend; this soil counters the effects of the alkaloids and other toxins present in the seeds and unripe fruits that dominate their diet (Diamond, 1999). While there is no evidence of self-medication in UK garden birds, many species do ingest grit as part of their daily routine. The importance of grit to certain garden bird species can be seen from work on House Sparrows carried out across

FIG 97. Dust-bathing is used by a number of species, including House Sparrow and Red-legged Partridge. (Jill Pakenham)

Europe and in North America. This work has revealed that House Sparrows use large amounts of grit throughout the year and that the amount carried in the gizzard consistently outweighs the amount of food present (Pinowska, 1975). The use of grit varies with diet, and granivorous species use grit to a far greater extent than those species feeding on invertebrates or fruit (Gionfriddo & Best, 1996).

The maintenance of flight feathers and body plumage, discussed earlier in this chapter, also extends to the annual moult, a process by which worn feathers are replaced and renewed. In addition to ensuring continued flight performance and energetic balance, the replacement of feathers also provides an opportunity to alter the signalling function of the plumage. This can involve moulting through from juvenile plumage into that of an adult, or a seasonal shift from non-breeding to breeding plumage. In a species like Robin, for example, where adult plumage carries a particularly strong social signal in the form of the red breast, having a different juvenile plumage reduces the chance of any unwarranted aggression being directed in the juvenile's direction. Before turning our attention to the behaviours associated with aggression and display, it is worth just noting that the process of moult may be associated with a change in behaviour, such that individuals undergoing their annual moult become more shy and retiring in habits. Presumably, this response reflects reduced flight performance and an increased risk of predation, countered by spending less time out in the open and more time within cover.

Garden birds display a range of different moult strategies, with this variation often linked to differences in the annual cycles of the different species; for example, those species that are summer visitors and which make long-distance migrational movements will be under different resource pressures to species that are resident within gardens throughout the year. The constraints placed by the need to migrate may shift the timing and pattern of annual moult so that it is very different from that of a related species that remains resident. Even within those species that migrate, there may be differences, some moulting before they begin their autumn migration and others after; some species may even make two complete moults during the year, one before migration and one after. Adult Blackbirds, which can look rather tatty as they come to the end of their breeding season, undergo their annual moult at the end of the summer, typically beginning two weeks after their breeding season has ended. Juvenile Blackbirds, born that year, undergo a partial 'post-juvenile' moult that sees them replace the soft and weaker juvenile body feathers, together with some of the covert feathers, on the wing; the main flight feathers are not replaced at this stage, which leaves young males with brown wing feathers but black body plumage through into the next breeding season.

The partial moult seen in juveniles, where the flight feathers and tail feathers are usually retained, is typical of most garden birds and is something that can prove useful when attempting to age a bird, either through binoculars or in the hand (in the case of bird ringers). A few garden bird species have a complete post-juvenile moult, however, with Long-tailed Tit and House Sparrow being perhaps the best examples. Once these individuals have undergone their complete moult, they will look just like their parents.

AGGRESSION, DISPLAY AND DOMINANCE HIERARCHIES

Wherever individuals compete for resources, be these feeding opportunities, mates or nest sites, there is the potential for conflict. If the conflict between two individuals leads to aggression and physical violence, then there is the risk of injury or even death. This results in a selection pressure for individuals to ascertain their competitive chances, relative to their opponent, prior to any aggressive encounter. If an individual can clearly see that it is outmatched by its opponent, then it is better not to resort to violence and simply admit defeat. This

FIG 98. Dominance hierarchies can often be seen at garden feeding stations and may help to explain why some species feed at different times, or in different ways, to others. (Jill Pakenham)

has led to the development of traits and behaviours that enable individuals to display their condition and/or status, through which other individuals can then make assessment of their competitive ability. Displays and behaviour may also be used by individuals to assess the status or suitability of a potential mate, or to identify an individual as being of the same species. Many of these behaviours are evident within garden birds, and indeed are often easier to study in a garden setting than within the wider countryside. We will come to courtship behaviour shortly, once we have taken a more detailed look at the behaviours associated with social status and dominance. We will also take a look at the dominance hierarchies that exist between species, evident at many garden feeding stations.

Signalling status

A degree of variability is evident within the plumage characteristics of individual species, most obviously between individuals of different age or sex classes, but importantly also within a class. Research across a range of garden bird species underlines that such variation within a class of individuals (typically adult males) may act as a badge of social status (House Sparrows, Møller, 1987; Greenfinch, Maynard-Smith & Harper, 1988; Great Tit, Järvi & Bakken, 1984). These badges of social status may be shaped by various factors, including access to particular pigments, nutritional condition, parasite load and the social environment within which the individual is living. In this respect, such badges may be viewed as an honest signal of status and/or individual quality, the latter perhaps being used by a potential mate to determine suitability.

Møller's work, for example, has found that the size of the male throat patch, termed the 'bib', may be used by females when selecting a mate; large-bibbed males are preferentially selected and tend to maintain the best territories and most secure nest sites, seemingly because they are dominant over other individuals. Bib size in male House Sparrows has been found to correlate with the age of the individual, his overall success in competitive interactions and his testosterone levels. Male House Sparrows also possess a 'secondary' badge in the form of their bill colour; this changes from horn-coloured to black with the arrival of the breeding season, with the strength of colour providing a measure of recent testosterone levels (Laucht *et al.*, 2010). In contrast, while female Great Tits use the size of the male's breast stripe as an honest signal of male quality – large-striped males being more attentive at the nest – stripe size does not appear to be a good indicator of male status (see Wilson, 1992).

David Lack's work on Robins, summarised in his book *The Life of Robin* (1953), underlines the strong signalling role of the Robin's red breast. The adults of both sexes share this feature, displaying it prominently towards intruders in year-round territorial disputes; Lack famously found that the red breast was sufficient to trigger an attack by a territory-holding bird. The size of the red breast has been found to vary with age, being smaller in first-year birds than those in their second year (Jovani *et al.*, 2012), and with sexual dimorphism in the size of red breast evident in the oldest Robins. When a territory-holding Robin encounters an intruder, the two birds will initially sing at each other, the territory holder attempting to sing from a perch above the intruder and seeking to show off his red breast to the full extent. If the territory holder finds himself positioned below the intruder, then he will adopt a different posture, throwing his head back and again emphasising the red breast. If this does not drive the intruder away, then the two may come to blows.

Dominance hierarchies

That individuals may signal their social status to others of their species can give rise to dominance hierarchies and a social structure to flocks. In Siskins, which advertise social status through their black bib, it has been shown that individuals can assess their position relative to that of another individual by using bib size. This assessment is done quickly and without the need to refer to other cues, such as overt aggression (Senar & Camerino, 1998). Interestingly, when joining others of their kind, individual Siskins prefer to join those who are subordinate to themselves.

Watch a garden feeding station and you will soon discover that dominance hierarchies also exist between different species, rather than just within a species. The detailed work carried out at New Zealand feeding stations by Galbraith *et al.* (2017b), reported on in Chapter 2, provides an interesting insight into the potential dominance hierarchies that exist between species. Using camera traps and PIT tags, Galbraith was able to demonstrate that feeding events were usually characterised by single-species visits, rather than those with multiple species present at a feeder simultaneously. This was despite the fact that individuals of multiple species were usually present in the vicinity of the feeders. If you look at the hanging feeders in your own garden, you will probably notice something similar, with certain species dominant over others. Greenfinches appear to be one of the most dominant species, while Coal Tits are one of the least dominant. Such hierarchies are also evident when birds compete for windfall apples, with Fieldfare and Mistle Thrush dominant over Blackbird, which is in turn dominant over Song Thrush and Redwing.

Dominant individuals displace subordinates from bird feeders, a behaviour that increases their access to garden food sources and which may, as we saw in Chapter 2, reduce their risk of predation because they can preferentially occupy

IG 99. Dominance hierarchies may explain the occasional reports of mixed broods of Great Tits and Blue Tits found in garden nest boxes, as in this instance. (Mike Toms)

feeders positioned closer to suitable cover. Being subordinate, therefore, carries a number costs and it is hypothesised that subordinate individuals should seek to carry larger body reserves and indulge more strongly in caching behaviour than dominant individuals or species. Evidence for this is somewhat mixed (see Lundborg & Brodin, 2003, for example), but Mikael Hake (1996) did find that subordinate Greenfinches carried larger fat reserves than more dominant birds within the winter feeding flocks that he studied.

Within the breeding season, dominance hierarchies between species may also shape nesting opportunities and nest box use. It is well known, for example, that dominant Great Tits may oust Blue Tits and Coal Tits from nest boxes, which is one reason why providing some nest boxes with smaller entrance holes is recommended, excluding the larger and more dominant species and providing an opportunity for the smaller tits. Competitive dominance of this kind may also be behind the occasional mixed broods found in Great Tit nests, where a brood of Great Tits includes one or more Blue Tit chicks, the parent Blue Tits presumably having been pushed out of the box part way through the egg laying period. This is something that I have encountered from time to time when checking boxes.

COURTSHIP BEHAVIOUR

Perhaps some of the most fascinating behaviour that can be seen within gardens is that associated with courtship. The increasing use of gardens by a growing Woodpigeon population, for example, brings with it a series of elaborate displays, which see the male courting his potential mate. Unmated female Woodpigeons, entering the territory of an unpaired male, initially adopt a submissive posture. If the male takes an interest in them, he will begin an elaborate bowing display, in which he dips his head, tilts his body forward and raises and fans his tail. This display is accompanied by a special call, phrased by R. K. Murton in his monograph on the species as 'co roo co co co coo'. Although the bowing display clearly has a courtship meaning, it is worth just noting that it may sometimes be directed at submissive males by a territory-holding bird. The female response to this display often involves retreat but since the display contains some submissive elements of its own (the bowed head and low body posture), she may overcome her fear and eventually allow his closer approach.

This then leads on to a second stage in the Woodpigeon's courtship display, where what can now be regarded as a pair begin to direct their attentions to a nest. The male makes a 'nest-call' and begins to show the female potential nest sites within his territory, some of which may be platforms of sticks used previously by nesting Woodpigeons. At this stage, as the pair come to settle on a preferred site, the pair bond is reinforced through caressing behaviours; these see the two birds engage in mutual preening, their attentions directed to the head and neck. This behaviour is reminiscent of a similar behaviour seen in Woodpigeon chicks, which nibble at the feathers around their parent's crop in order to solicit food. The display is then sometimes followed by courtship feeding, although this often happens independently, suggesting that it has its own role in courtship display in this species. What is evident from the sequence of displays seen in Woodpigeon is that the two birds have to overcome their initial fear and uncertainty around the presence of a potential partner; there is the transition from an initially aggressive response to behaviours that promote reassurance and seek to reinforce the pair bond. Such behaviours are evident in many of our other garden birds and are well worth looking out for.

As we saw in Chapter 3, song plays a central role in the establishment and maintenance of a breeding territory, and in attracting a mate. It may also be used to reinforce the pair bond, a behaviour that can also see male birds providing their mate with additional food. This latter behaviour is termed courtship feeding and has been documented in a large number of garden bird species, though it is more obvious in some than others. Courtship feeding is more obvious in Woodpigeon, in which the male feeds his mate by regurgitation, than it is in many of the smaller birds. Female Robins, for example, may be seen begging food from their mate while on the lawn, but such behaviour often takes place out of sight, even when she is sat on the nest incubating her eggs. In Robin, courtship feeding begins a few days after the nest has been built, the female initiating the feeding through her contact calls; these become a feature of this next phase of the breeding cycle, from the start of egg laying through into incubation during which the rate at which the male provisions his mate increases (East, 1981). As we saw in Chapter 3, in addition to reinforcing the pair bond, courtship feeding may provide the additional resources that a female needs to meet the energetic demands of producing a clutch of eggs. That this is an important driver for courtship feeding can be seen in the timing of such behaviour in Robins, starting as it does after the nest has been completed and immediately before the female begins to produce her clutch of eggs.

One particular aspect of courtship behaviour is that of mate guarding, where the male of the pair seeks to protect his interests by accompanying his mate when she is away from the nest, either foraging for food or actively collecting

FIG 100. Male Starlings guard their mate most actively during the period when she is at her most fertile. (John Harding)

nesting material. Such behaviour is particularly evident in the finches, the male often to be seen flying with his mate to and from the nest. Although mate guarding can extend over a significant period, it is most common in the period just prior to egg laying; given the high incidence of extra-pair copulations (see Chapter 3) seen in some species, it is easy to see why a male would want to pay particular attention to his mate during this period. Mate guarding has been well studied in the Starling, revealing that males target their guarding towards an 'insemination window' when their mate is at her most fertile (Pinxten & Eens, 1997). This is also when other males seek to copulate with females who are not their mate, the timing of which is late morning in this species. Ben Sheldon, working on Chaffinch, also found that males targeted their mate-guarding efforts towards particular periods (Sheldon, 1994), with guarding intensity increasing as egg laying approached; the males then reduced their level of guarding once the penultimate egg of the clutch had been laid and the female was no longer fertile. One other interesting figure to emerge from Sheldon's work was the frequency with which male Chaffinch copulated with their mate; this peaked at 4.4 copulations per hour three days before the first egg was laid and resulted in an estimated 207 copulation attempts for each clutch of eggs produced.

THE CURIOUS CASE OF THE DUNNOCK

The rather unassuming Dunnock exhibits a wide range of mating systems, which include monogamy (one male and one female), polygyny (one male and several females), polyandry (two or even three males and one female) and polygynandry (several males with several females). This complex set of relationships appears to be made possible because male and female Dunnocks maintain their own, largely independent, breeding territories. The larger size of the male territories provides potential overlap with the territories of other females, opening up the opportunity for additional pairings. Some male territories may be shared by two males, one of whom (the 'alpha male') is dominant over the other. This appears to be an uneasy arrangement, since the alpha male spends a great deal of time guarding his female(s) from the beta male, whose presence in the territory seems to be the result of persistence on his part. Both of the males will work together if another male intrudes on the territory.

Related to this complex social system is some equally complex sexual behaviour, which is accompanied by some characteristic displays. Prior to copulation, the female Dunnock will crouch low in front of the male, fluffing out her feathers, quivering and lifting her tail to expose her cloaca. The male then responds to this display by positioning himself behind his mate and then, while

FIG 101. Despite its rather unassuming appearance, the Dunnock has a particularly complicated and interesting social system. (John Harding)

hopping from side to side, he begins to peck at her cloaca. This pecking stimulates the female to eject some of the sperm from previous matings, increasing the male's chances of parenting any resulting offspring. The female may seek similar copulations with the beta and other males, hoping through her behaviour to secure the advantages that come from extra-pair copulations (see Chapter 3) or extra help provisioning the resulting brood. It has been shown that beta males will only help to provision the female's chicks if they have been able to copulate with her.

ROOSTING

Earlier on we noted how the waste heat that is characteristic of many of our larger urban centres can ease the challenges that small birds face keeping warm overnight during the winter months. While such heat pollution appears to offer some benefits, many small birds show additional behavioural adaptations to help them reduce overnight heat loss. One such behaviour is communal roosting, something that can see tens of thousands of Starlings gather together in huge communal roosts or a few Blue Tits or Wrens seek the shelter provided by a single garden nest box or roosting 'pouch'.

Through BTO Garden BirdWatch, we have been able to investigate the use of garden nest boxes for roosting by small birds during the winter months. This small-scale study revealed some interesting differences between the species using the 400 or so garden sites for which we received reports. Some 12 different species were recorded using the nest boxes and other cavity sites overnight, with Blue Tit and Great Tit most likely to be reported roosting alone. Others, however appeared to be much more likely to bed down in larger groups. Wrens, in particular, typically roosted in large numbers, with a maximum count of 51 individuals roosting together in a garden nest box in Dorset. The presence of several boxes with nest box cameras fitted was particularly helpful in revealing occupants and the numbers involved. It wasn't just nest boxes that were used, however, with roosting pouches also holding roosting birds; the rate at which these were used was lower than for nest boxes, with Wren really the only species to make use of them to any degree. It is not just cavities that are used for roosting; Blue Tits, for example, will often seek shelter within the porch of a house or other covered structure. Other garden birds may roost in bushes and other thick cover, either individually or in larger groups. Long-tailed Tits roost communally in a line along a branch or horizontal stem within a bush, the position of each individual determined by its status within the social group.

FIG 102. Prior to roosting, Starling flocks may come together to perform amazing displays, known as murmurations. (John Harding)

Roosting behaviour changes with season, such that individuals may roost on their own or with their mate in the breeding territory during the summer months, but as part of a larger communal roost during the winter. Such seasonal differences are shaped by other factors, such as food availability, the presence of eggs or young chicks, or climatic conditions.

UNUSUAL BEHAVIOURS

Gardens and garden feeding stations provide an excellent opportunity for those interested watchers to observe unusual or emerging behaviours. The reactions to novel feeding opportunities, for example, can lead to the development of new behaviours, as birds first explore and then respond to the challenges of a new food or feeder. It is from gardens that uncommon behaviours, rarely observed in the wider countryside, can be more readily observed and reported. Predation on newts and the tadpoles of Common Frog, for example, probably does occur within the wider countryside but is more evident in gardens, where ponds are often located close to the house from where human observers can watch the goings-on.

As we saw earlier, in our exploration of birds robbing milk bottles, some behaviours spread between individuals and between species. Pheasants, for example, unable to use hanging bird feeders, have learned that these contain food, presumably from watching other species using them; some individual Pheasants have worked out that they can jump up at the feeders, clatter into them and dislodge some of the seed contained within. This can then be eaten at leisure from the ground beneath the feeder. Other species have learned to exploit other opportunities, perhaps the most commonly reported of which is that of the Robin, which regularly follows the gardening activities of householders to take worms and other invertebrates disturbed when a piece of ground is being dug over. In a few extreme cases, individual birds (most commonly Blackbird it would seem) have come to associate a householder with the provision of food at a garden bird table. Such individuals have been reported to bang on the window, appear at the back door or even greet a householder arriving home from work, in order to prompt the provision of food. Sometimes, individual birds overcome their fear of humans to take food from the hand, a behaviour that can be developed with patience and a supply of mealworms in both Blackbird and Robin.

Some behaviours are a response to the garden environment, one of which involves attacking windows or car wing mirrors. This appears to result from the bird seeing a reflection of itself in the glass or the wing mirror; thinking it is another individual intruding upon its breeding territory, the bird first displays

FIG 103. Although the sight of adult birds feeding their recently fledged chicks is fairly common, such behaviour may sometimes be misdirected towards chicks that are unrelated, or even of a different species. (Jill Pakenham)

at the reflection, which displays back, and then escalates this to an attack. It can be difficult to halt such behaviour once it has started, the only option being to cover the window or mirror to remove the reflection. Such behaviour, most evident during the early part of the breeding season, is most commonly reported for Blue Tit, Great Tit, Chaffinch and Carrion Crow. Blue Tits commonly visit windows and brickwork to search for insects and small spiders and it may be this behaviour that first brings them into contact with their reflection, but how this arises in the other species mentioned is unclear.

Occasionally, over the years, I have received reports of young birds receiving food from an adult of a different species. Most commonly, this seems to involve fledged young, whose begging calls seem to coax unrelated birds into feeding them. On other occasions, the reports refer to adult birds feeding the young of other species at the nest, perhaps because they have their own nest nearby and have simply responded to the wrong set of begging calls. There are also reports in the literature of more unusual cases, even one where a male Blackbird adopted the young of another pair, whose own father had been killed. The visiting male contributed 50 per cent of the food received by the chicks. The female whose chicks these were would always fly off when the male (or his mate) appeared. The paired female started her own nesting attempt a metre above the occupied nest, but this failed before the clutch had been completed, at which stage she joined her mate in feeding the chicks, at least one of which fledged successfully (Dijkstra *et al.*, 1997). If you watch recently fledged chicks at a garden feeding station, they will frequently misdirect their begging behaviour to a bird that isn't their parent; they will also peck at items that are not food, underlining that they are going through a period of exploration and learning.

FIG 104. Gardens provide some of the best opportunities to watch birds and their behaviour at close quarters, something that provides a fascinating insight into their lives. (Jill Pakenham)

CONCLUDING REMARKS

There is much to learn about bird behaviour and, in particular, about how birds respond to the challenges and opportunities of garden living. As we shall see in our next chapter, it can be difficult to carry out research and experimental studies in gardens, but they do present a great opportunity to engage householders in collecting information. One of the best places to start if you want to kindle an interest is by looking at aspects of bird behaviour. In this respect, gardens are a microcosm of the wider behaviours that take place in other habitats. There are the behaviours associated with predation or attempts to avoid being predated, together with those centred on maintaining an individual (feeding and preening), and there are those that relate to courtship and reproduction. All of these may take place just a few feet away, on the other side of the window, providing a wonderful opportunity for those interested to develop an understanding of garden birds and their behaviour. The opportunities for studying garden birds is something that we will tackle in the next chapter, where we will also examine the benefits that we get from taking an interest in garden birds.

CHAPTER 6

Birds, Gardens and People

G ARDENS, BY DEFINITION, DEPEND ON people; they are an extension of our homes and our personalities, shaped by opportunities and social conventions. The extent to which we use them to engage with birds and other forms of wildlife will also be determined by these factors and this, in turn, will determine their wildlife value and the roles that gardens play in the lives of other creatures. In this, the final cross-species section of the book, we will look at the role that gardens and their birds play in our own lives. We will explore why we value some bird species over others and we will seek to understand the contributions that we, as individuals, can make to the conservation of garden birds, either through how we choose to manage our gardens or through active participation in citizen science projects, like the BTO Garden BirdWatch survey.

GARDENS AND PEOPLE

Office for National Statistics figures, published in 2017, reveal that there are some 27.2 million households in Britain. Roughly three-quarters of these are associated with a private garden, a figure that places Britain relatively highly when compared to other European countries. Access to a private garden may actually be somewhat greater than this when viewed at the level of the individual, with figures from commercial studies suggesting that nearly 90 per cent of adults have access to either a private or shared communal garden. As we saw in Chapter 1, a study by Davies *et al.* (2009), using data from a number of different datasets, put the proportion of households with an associated garden at 87 per cent. Of course, access to a garden does not necessarily mean access to,

FIG 105. While individual gardens may represent only a very small space, they provide a unique opportunity for us to engage with the natural world. (Mike Toms)

and engagement with, nature, since gardens may be used in different ways by different individuals (Bhatti & Church, 2004). A survey carried out in 1999 by the London-based research company MINTEL defined garden use according to five consumer sub-groups. The largest three of these were leisure gardeners (35 per cent) – people who enjoyed their garden but lacked the time and/or skills to do more with it; investors (35 per cent) – people who viewed their garden as adding financial value to their property; and horticultural hobbyists (23 per cent) – people who propagated plants from seed and were highly skilled and knowledgeable. It has been suggested that only horticultural hobbyists are likely to seek an understanding of nature, but there is a strong case to be made for including many leisure gardeners in with those who seek engagement with nature through their gardens.

Gardens themselves are just as varied as the people who own and manage them but there are some common patterns to garden use, and identifiable relationships linked to the class, gender, age and income of their owners. Over time there has, for example, been a shift within gardens away from the growing of fruit and vegetables towards the garden as an outdoor room, dominated by activities that are centred on sitting, looking and playing, and away from activities associated with cultivation. In part, this reflects changing social behaviour but it is also strongly influenced by changes in garden size. Pressures on land, and the almost total dominance of the private sector in the construction of new homes, has seen a significant fall in the size of the average garden plot. This is an ongoing pattern, with the density of new dwellings increasing by 72 per cent between 2001 (25 dwellings per h) and 2011 (43 dwellings per h).

The extent to which individuals engage with nature through their gardens is also shaped by other leisure uses and social issues: for example, certain wildlife-friendly gardening practices – such as the construction of a wildlife pond – may be considered unsafe by householders whose garden is used as a leisure space by young children. Individuals may also respond to the fashion of the day, be it the use of decking, prairie planting or, more recently, wildlife-friendly gardening. In many cases, however, the garden is viewed as being 'nature under control', which leaves many gardeners facing considerable ecological dilemmas in terms of how they balance competing garden uses and engagement with the plants and animals that are present (Bhatti & Church, 2001). In many ways, the garden and its biodiversity provide an opportunity for individuals to think about the balance that exists between 'human control on the one hand and wild nature on

FIG 106. Gardens are very personal spaces and their structure and function represents the balance that exists between 'human control on the one hand and wild nature on the other'. (Mike Toms)

the other' (Francis & Hestor, 1990). It presents a stage on which individuals can experience nature and ecological processes – such as predation and competition – and, in so doing, gain a better understanding of wider ecological communities and systems. In addition, we also need to understand that gardens are, like the home, a semi-private space and that they have a role in the construction of a domestic sense of place (Tuan, 1990).

As we saw in Chapter 1, private gardens differ from other forms of urban (and rural) green space in many functional aspects; this has consequences for the types of bird species that use them and for the ways in which particular ecological processes play out. They also differ because of the real and imagined connections to home and place that we have just touched on at the start of this chapter. In addition to influencing the bird communities present, and the ways in which individual gardens are used, the nature of garden ownership can also shape our ability to study and monitor the birds – and wider biodiversity – associated with them. If we want to study bird populations and behaviour within the garden environment, then we need to seek the help and support of garden owners. In some cases, this may just require seeking permission to access study gardens, but in other cases there may be a need to actively engage garden owners in the collection of ecological data. This latter point is something that we will explore later in this chapter when we look at citizen science schemes, such as the BTO Garden BirdWatch and Garden Wildlife Health.

ECOSYSTEM SERVICES

There is a growing body of evidence that interactions with birds and other forms of wildlife can provide people with feelings of being connected with nature. Such connections have been shown to have positive effects on human well-being and may be of particular importance within urbanised landscapes, where access to nature is often limited. Access to the natural environment can lead to faster recovery times following surgery (Ulrich, 1984) and to improved mental health and well-being (Kaplan & Kaplan, 1989; Hartig et al., 1991).

Private gardens may offer some of the best opportunities for such connections with the natural world to be established and maintained. The 'services' that the natural world provides to its human inhabitants are increasingly referred to as 'ecosystem services', some of which are more tangible than others. Tangible services include the pollination of crops and flood alleviation; less tangible services – such as the well-being benefits that come from seeing or hearing species that you like – are known as 'cultural services'. The

FIG 107. Gardens are one form of urban green space, contributing ecosystem services to the built environment and to the humans who live there. (Mike Toms)

ecosystem services approach is centred around identifying and accounting for the contributions that the natural world make to human health and well-being, the ultimately goal being to support better decision-making processes for the benefit of both people and the environment.

Not all interactions between birds and people are necessarily positive; birds are sometimes responsible for the contamination of water sources, for causing unwelcome noise and smells, or for disease transmission; these are referred to as 'cultural disservices'. Interestingly, the ecological traits of the bird species providing services and disservices tend to be quite different; those associated with cultural services tend to be insectivorous or granivorous and aesthetically pleasing, being interesting to watch, often colourful and small in body size (most garden birds), while those associated with cultural disservices tend to be larger and omnivorous (geese, pigeons and gulls). How the abundance and distribution of birds from these two groups varies across our urbanised landscapes might influence how different human communities experience birds and how this then shapes their wider appreciation of the natural world.

There is substantial variation in the 'likeability' of different bird species and most of the people watching garden birds will admit to favouring some species over others – large numbers seem to dislike Magpies, for example. Likeability has been tested here in the UK (Cox & Gaston, 2016), revealing both that people prefer to see greater variation in the species to which they are exposed, rather than a greater number of individuals of the same species, and that those who engage more regularly with wild birds through garden feeding show greater species likeability. Cox and Gaston found a strong correlation between the number of species that a person could identify and how connected to nature they felt when they watched garden birds.

Our understanding of likeability and the different groups of service and disservice birds has benefited from recent work, centred on the towns of Milton Keynes, Luton and Bedford (Cox et al., 2018). By carrying out extensive surveys of the bird communities in these towns, the researchers were able to measure the abundance and species richness of birds within both the cultural services (35 species) and disservices (9 species) groups. They then examined these findings alongside data on the human population, derived from the 2011 National Census and measures of socioeconomic status from the Office of National Statistics. Since, as we have already seen, bird diversity in urban areas is strongly associated with the structure and availability of urban green space, the team also had to take this into account. The results of this work demonstrate that the abundance of service and disservice birds varies with human population density, but each has its own distinctly different patterns. Service species are most abundant in areas of medium housing density (notably the suburbs), while disservice birds are most abundant in areas of dense housing (notably around urban centres). These patterns, which almost certainly result from differences in the pattern of urban green space and resource availability, underline that people living in different parts of the urban environment are likely to have differing relationships with wild birds. People living within the socially deprived parts of towns and cities (often located around urban centres) are exposed to bird species associated with more negative behaviours than wealthier communities, who tend to see more cultural service species.

Of course, we also need to understand how people perceive the bird species with which they share their gardens and the wider environment. Several pieces of research work provide insight here, documenting such perceptions and how they change with location, background and the bird communities to which people are exposed. Working in Rennes, France, Clergeau et al. (2001) found that the perception of birds varied depending upon where in the city people lived, something that was indeed linked to the species to which they were most commonly exposed. While bird diversity was highest within the suburbs, and

FIG 108. Colourful species with attractive songs, like Goldfinch, are well liked by people living in towns and cities; they are one of the 'cultural service' species recognised by researchers working on ecosystem services. (John Harding)

lowest in the most urban area, the density of birds was actually greatest in the urban centre; this was due to the abundance of particular species, most notably Feral Pigeon and Swift.

Elsewhere, Amy Belaire and colleagues have looked at the aspects of local bird communities that residents of Cook County, Illinois (US), most value, before going on to test residents' perceptions of the benefits and annoyances of local birds in relation to the characteristics of the species themselves (Belaire *et al.*, 2015). Residents of Cook County were found to value many aspects of their neighbourhood birds, especially those related to aesthetics and to the position that birds occupied within the local ecosystem. They did, however, note several key negative behaviours, most notably the presence of droppings and nests built on personal property. A small number of bird species, including House Sparrow, Blue Jay and Starling, were most commonly associated with the annoyances raised by residents, and it seems that these species are more likely to be noticed for their negative rather than positive qualities.

One of the most interesting things to emerge from the work carried out by Belaire *et al.* was the lack of a significant relationship between residents' perceptions of local bird richness and the actual (surveyed) richness of birds near their homes. Other studies, this time carried out in Europe, also underline that urban residents are largely unaware of the biodiversity around them (Dallimer *et al.*, 2012; Schwartz *et al.*, 2014). Two consequences arise from this inability of residents to correctly assess the levels of biodiversity or avian species richness that occur locally: first, individuals are more likely to link the cultural services delivered by birds with their own perceptions of local biodiversity, rather than with actual biodiversity. Second, if residents cannot identify the levels of biodiversity or richness around them, then there is greater likelihood that their experience of nature will be diminished. This latter point is linked to the 'extinction of experience' hypothesis, which concerns a theorised cycle of increasing separation between humans and nature over time (Miller, 2005).

'Extinction of experience' has been put forward as one of the factors behind the increasing levels of stress, anxiety and depression seen within society. The scale of the economic costs associated with such well-being problems can be

FIG 109. Starling is a species that many householders describe in negative terms, and it seems that this species is more likely to be noticed for its negative rather than positive qualities. (John Harding)

seen from the €187 billion figure that is thought to be the annual cost of dealing with anxiety and depression across Europe (Olesen *et al.*, 2012). Viewed alongside evidence that access to nature can reduce stress and anxiety (Maas *et al.*, 2009) and improve mood (Roe & Aspinall, 2011), this adds weight to the argument that interactions with birds, both within the garden and more widely, might be worth encouraging (White *et al.*, 2013). Several studies have already revealed that both watching birds (Fuller *et al.*, 2007b; Brock *et al.*, 2015; Cox & Gaston, 2016) and listening to them (Ratcliffe *et al.*, 2013) can be good for human well-being. Through the use of a questionnaire on urban lifestyle, shared with 1,023 adults living in the Milton Keynes, Luton and Bedford area, Daniel Cox was able to tease out links between particular landscape features (vegetation cover and bird abundance) and the prevalence of depression, anxiety and stress. Perhaps most interestingly, it was afternoon bird abundance, rather than early morning bird abundance, that was positively related with these measures of well-being. This underlines that researchers need to consider the timing of when human study subjects interact with wild birds, rather than using standard measures of bird abundance, which are invariably measured very early in the morning. By using dose response modelling, Daniel Cox and his colleagues were also able to determine the threshold exposure to vegetation cover above which the prevalence of these well-being issues was significantly lowered (typically 20–30 per cent).

The work of Cox *et al.* (2016), and others, increases our understanding of how humans and birds interact, and identifies opportunities to develop management and planning approaches that counter unfavourable relationships and nurture more beneficial ones. There are also opportunities to deliver beneficial relationships at the householder level, through practices such as wildlife-friendly gardening. These approaches are thought to be of particular importance, not least because of the wider benefits that can be delivered by a small number of people within a community adopting wildlife-friendly gardening approaches. The birds and wildlife using their gardens will also utilise neighbouring gardens, increasing opportunities for the broader community.

WILDLIFE-FRIENDLY GARDENING

We have already seen how the interaction between people and garden birds operates in both directions, with the provision of supplementary food and nest boxes regarded as generally positive for wild birds, and with human health and well-being benefiting from interactions with birds and other garden wildlife. Over recent decades, we have seen a growing interest in adopting approaches to

FIG 110. Wildlife-friendly gardening is becoming increasingly popular, providing the opportunity for householders to encourage birds and other wildlife into their own private spaces. (Mike Toms)

garden management that more directly benefit wildlife. This approach is known as wildlife-friendly gardening (sometimes 'wildlife gardening') and it has been defined as 'any actions conducted in private or domestic gardens to increase their suitability for wildlife' (Davies *et al.*, 2009).

The motivations for participation in wildlife-friendly gardening are similar to those behind the provision of food for wild birds, which is in itself a component of wildlife-friendly gardening. The Biodiversity in Urban Gardens in Sheffield project found, for example, that the prevalence of bird feeding and time spent gardening were both positively related to the proportion of cover by gardens and average garden size but independent of household density (Gaston *et al.*, 2007). However, most wildlife-friendly gardening practices require additional effort on the part of householders and so a higher level of motivation may be required. Work in Leeds also demonstrates that wildlife-friendly gardening is influenced by a combination of factors, some of which relate to the characteristics of the garden and landscape context, and some of which relate to the householders themselves (Goddard *et al.*, 2013). Respondents to a series of interviews and questionnaires highlighted personal well-being and a moral responsibility to nature as the key drivers. However, there were also barriers, such as the feeling of duty to maintain neighbourhood standards – which might run counter to certain wildlife-friendly gardening practices.

More widely, work in the US has sought to understand how wildlife-friendly gardening practices, particularly those aimed at birds, vary between different landscapes. Christopher Lepczyk and colleagues, working along a rural-to-urban landscape gradient, found that urban landowners planted or maintained vegetation in the lowest frequency but had the highest densities of bird feeders. In contrast, rural landowners provided more nest boxes but applied herbicides and pesticides more often (Lepczyk *et al.*, 2004a).

Wildlife-friendly gardening practices vary in the extent to which they are based on scientific evidence, with those directed towards wild birds seemingly better supported than those aimed at many other taxa groups (Gaston *et al.*, 2005b). In Chapters 2 and 3, we saw how gardening practices can influence the feeding and nesting opportunities available within gardens for wild birds. The extent to which the findings of scientific studies reach a wider public audience has depended to a large part on the efforts of organisations like the RSPB, BTO, the Wildlife Trusts, RHS and the Wildlife Gardening Forum. Popular publications, such as

FIG 111. It is not just birds that benefit from wildlife-friendly gardening practices; many other species, including this Common Toad *Bufo bufo*, do well where consideration is given to their needs. (Mike Toms)

those by Toms *et al.* (2008), Baines (2016), Thomas (2017) and Bradbury (2017), have supported those with a growing interest in helping wildlife. However, a look at garden centre shelves or online will reveal the continued presence of materials, particularly nest boxes, that have clearly been designed with people rather than birds in mind. Just as there is work to be done in supporting individuals in their choices, efforts are also needed to steer wild bird care companies towards evidence-based products of benefit to birds. Doing the science is the starting point for this process and one that has both advantages and difficulties that result from working within privately owned gardens.

SCIENCE AND GARDEN BIRDS

As recent academic books and special journal issues demonstrate (Niemelä, 2011; Murgui & Hedblom, 2017; Isaksson *et al.*, 2018), there has been a step-change in the effort directed towards the study of the urban environment and its biodiversity. One of the most interesting aspects of recent work on the study of urban birds is the finding that urbanisation not only affects the bird communities but also how researchers study them: the more urban a species, the more frequently it is studied (Ibáñez-Álamo *et al.*, 2017).

Despite this, working within the built environment can be challenging, particularly where that work has to take place within a multitude of privately owned gardens. Two of the biggest challenges for the researcher are securing access and controlling how resources – such as food provision – are managed, both within the garden and in the surrounding area. A few studies have, however, been able to secure access and control resources sufficiently to provide an insight into the ecology of the garden habitat – the Sheffield BUGS project is perhaps the best example of this (Gaston *et al.*, 2004). Fortunately, gardens are amenable to surveying and monitoring by the householders who own them (Cannon, 1999), something that has supported a suite of long-running projects studying garden birds, their behaviour, population dynamics and ecology.

Coordinated participation in garden-based experiments, monitoring and surveillance schemes has led to some of the largest and most successful examples of citizen science and mass-participation anywhere in the world. In addition to generating significant datasets and tackling important research questions, such schemes also facilitate public engagement with science, birds and bird conservation. There is, however, one caveat that requires mention: while participation levels in the schemes listed below reinforce the willingness to engage, this engagement is not equal across society. Instead, it tends to be associated with those who have the time and/or financial resources to participate.

FIG 112. Citizen science studies of garden birds have underlined the importance of gardens during periods of poor winter weather. (John Harding)

As we have seen already, gardens and their bird communities have been shown to vary in relation to their location within a city and with various socioeconomic factors. Because of this the results from most mass-participation surveys are biased towards certain kinds of garden, with others – typically small inner city gardens – under-represented. We must be careful, therefore, not to generalise about gardens and the birds when talking about the results of such schemes; nevertheless, they provide valuable and much-needed information that can help planners and land managers to make better-informed decisions about future land use and future urban landscapes. The following sections provide details about some of the citizen science schemes targeted at garden birds and operating here in the UK and elsewhere.

BIG GARDEN BIRDWATCH

The RSPB's Big Garden Birdwatch is the UK's highest-profile project linked to garden birds, receiving substantial media coverage and participation around its annual event. The project began in 1979 as a simple winter activity for junior RSPB members, attracting the attention of the children's programme

Blue Peter and leading to in excess of 34,000 submissions. The project, focussed on children, was relaunched in 2001 as an activity for the wider family and it has grown substantially since then, raising awareness and funds for the RSPB and its conservation work. That the project has been able to engage so many people in watching garden birds, and introduce them to the idea of citizen science, is a major achievement.

Big Garden Birdwatch works by asking participants to record the birds that they see visiting their gardens during an hour-long period over one weekend at the end of January. By asking participants to follow a series of simple and standard methods, it is possible to compare what is seen in different parts of the country, and indeed from one year to the next, to create a 'snapshot' of bird numbers across the UK. It is just a snapshot, however, the counts made over the weekend not just reflecting the number of birds visiting garden feeding stations more generally but also shaped by the weather conditions experienced over the short recording period.

The data collected through Big Garden Birdwatch are analysed and a set of results published within a few weeks of the survey being completed, enabling comparisons with previous years and across different regions. No peer-reviewed publications have, as yet, emerged from the study, but the data may be of value for broader analyses, looking at landscape scale patterns.

FIG 113. Long-term projects like the BTO's Garden Bird Feeding Survey have helped to document the changing status of species like Siskin. (John Harding)

BTO GARDEN BIRD FEEDING SURVEY

Launched as a pilot study in the July 1970 edition of *BTO News*, the BTO Garden Bird Feeding Study (GBFS) was designed to gather information on a national scale concerning 'which species are currently coming to garden feeding stations in the British Isles and when; what foodstuffs are being presented and which items consumed most readily'. The pilot, which covered the 1970/71 winter, was organised by Norman Pullen, working alongside Chris Mead and David Glue; David Glue was to take over the running of the survey longer term, something that he continued to do up until his death in 2014.

GBFS is restricted to approximately 250 gardens each year, chosen to ensure good geographical coverage across the UK and an approximately equal split between rural and suburban gardens. Each year a few participants drop out and suitable replacement gardens are identified from among the membership of BTO Garden BirdWatch. Participants make observations from October to March, their weekly observations split into two 13-week periods, with the maximum number of each species seen using provided food or water (or observed hunting

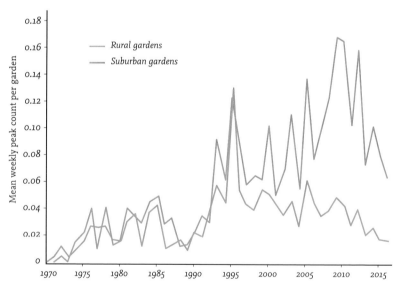

FIG 114. The increased use of garden feeding stations by Blackcaps during the winter months in urban areas is evident from BTO Garden Bird Feeding Survey data. Data used with permission from the BTO.

the birds that are using these resources) recorded on a weekly basis. Additionally, participants are asked to log the foods that they have provided in each week.

The weekly data provided by participants in the survey are used to calculate 'peak count indices', by week, habitat and species, that can reveal changes in the use of garden feeding stations by nearly 40 species, plus Sparrowhawk. Having been running since the 1970/71 winter, the survey provides important information on the broad-scale changes in the garden bird community over a substantial period. Its results reveal the timing and pattern of decline in House Sparrow populations, the increase in Woodpigeons and Goldfinches, and the development of the wintering Blackcap population (see Figure 114). It also reveals some interesting changes in other species, such as Blue Tit and Jackdaw, for example, which can be compared with long-term trends seen in these species within the wider countryside.

Data from the survey have been well used in peer-reviewed research, particularly in relation to work looking at how the size of tree seed crops influences the use of supplementary food (Chapter 2: Chamberlain *et al.*, 2005; 2007a) and in relation to the possible impacts of Sparrowhawks on garden birds (Chapter 4: Chamberlain *et al.*, 2009b; Swallow *et al.*, 2016a; 2016b). They are also being used by Kate Plummer and colleagues to examine how garden bird communities are being shaped by long-term feeding (Plummer *et al.*, in prep.). GBFS data have also been valuable in helping to document and understand the long-term population declines of House Sparrow and Starling (Crick *et al.*, 2002).

BTO GARDEN BIRDWATCH

Although launched in January 1995, BTO Garden BirdWatch (GBW) has its origins in an earlier study carried out by the organisation, namely the BTO/BASF Garden Bird Survey. This launched in June 1987 and ran for three full years, with data collected on a weekly basis using paper forms that could then be put through an Optical Mark Reader (OMR) machine. Some 6,500 people contributed to the study during the period of data collection, providing a valuable insight into what could be achieved by adopting a mass-participation, citizen science approach to the study of garden birds (Muirhead, 1990).

The BTO/BASF Garden Bird Survey approach underlined the very valuable information that could be gained from urban and garden habitats by engaging householders in the collection of scientific data. The challenge, however, was how to fund such a project when core funding from government was being directed towards the bird communities in other habitats. One option would have

FIG 115. BTO Garden BirdWatch volunteers have made a significant contribution to our understanding of how birds use gardens and how this use has changed over time. (Paul Stancliffe)

been to continue to seek commercial sponsorship, but one argument against this was the typically short-term nature of such funding and the likely wish of subsequent funders to want the project to be different from what had been run previously – with long-term monitoring, the goal is to maintain the methods used over time so as not to introduce bias. In the end, the decision was taken by Nigel Clark and Chris Mead, both key individuals driving forward the BTO's garden-based research agenda, to take the idea to the BTO leadership team of a survey funded by contributions from its participants. What was potentially a risky strategy was softened by the support of Chris Whittles and C. J. Wildlife Ltd, who offered to support the project financially, at least initially, so that it could test the willingness for participants to make a financial contribution. In the event, the decision backed by BTO management was a huge success, and by the end of the first year the scheme had received submissions from roughly 3,000 participants. Since then it has grown into a significant mass-participation survey, delivering weekly records of birds and other garden wildlife throughout the year.

During the initial years, Garden BirdWatch was entirely paper-based, with participants submitting records of 42 common bird species on special recording forms. Web pages offering online submission were trialled in 2001 and then launched, enabling greater detail to be collected across a broader range of species. The proportion of participants recording through the online system has increased over time but a substantial number of participants continue to make their submissions on paper. Following requests from participants, the recording of other taxa species was initially trialled, before being launched and becoming fully integrated in 2007.

Like any other mass-participation project, the size of Garden BirdWatch imposes some constraints on the way in which data can be collected and used. The use of OMR forms and data entry web pages minimises the effort required to get the data into a useable format and loaded into the core database tables that hold the vast numbers of observations of birds recorded since 1995. A central component of the recording methodology is that participants should be consistent in the way that they, as individuals, carry out their weekly recording. Participants are asked to make records from the same place (their defined 'recording area'), which could be their whole garden, at more or less the same time or times each week. Continuity of recording effort is more important than the quantity of recording carried out, since each weekly submission made by an observer provides a relative measure of garden use. Only species actively using the garden are recorded, so birds seen flying over the garden are excluded. Differences in effort between participants can be handled statistically during any subsequent analysis and modelling. Individuals are asked to record the maximum number of individuals of each species seen together at any one point in time during the recording period. Hence, if a participant recorded for an hour each day throughout the week and saw two Blackbirds together on the Monday, one each on the Tuesday and Wednesday, none on Thursday, three on Friday and two each on Saturday and Sunday, the maximum count for the week would be the 'three' from the Friday. This approach tackles the problem of double-counting individuals but only provides a minimum count for the number of different individuals using the garden and its resources over the course of the week. We know from bird ringing in gardens that up to 100 different Blue Tits may visit a garden feeding station during a single winter's day.

Data validation is often problematic for mass-participation surveys, and this is something that has been addressed for the online submissions made by participants but not to the same degree for paper submissions. As each participant enters their count details online, the data entered are checked against some simple validation tables. These warn observers of potential inputting errors by alerting them to unusually high counts, records that appear to fall outside of the known geographic range for a particular species or which are from

FIG 116. Garden BirdWatch records include those of less common visitors, something that can provide useful additional information for bird atlas projects and county bird reports. (John Harding)

an unusual time of the year (the latter particularly useful for migrant species). Alerted to a possible error, the observer has the opportunity to make a correction, but may choose not to. Since the paper recording forms rely on participants placing a mark in a box at a particular place on the form, there is the potential to fill in an incorrect box – for example, by ticking Tree Sparrow when you meant Treecreeper. While this is not a problem for the core national analyses of the most common species, where such an error just adds a very tiny amount of background 'noise' to an underlying trend, it can be a problem if the data are taken and used for county atlases or local projects. This is where the opportunity to use local volunteers, such as county bird recorders, could be particularly useful. Despite these small criticisms, BTO's weekly Garden BirdWatch continues to play a central role in helping us to understand how and why birds use gardens and how this use varies with season and location.

BTO Garden BirdWatch data have featured in several dozen peer-reviewed papers and have also been used in Wild Bird Indicators to provide a measure of change in urban bird communities. One of the first papers to emerge from the project was the work by Cannon *et al.* (2005), which reported on trends and seasonal patterns of garden use for the first time. This paper was important because it demonstrated ecologically important trends for wild bird populations in the UK's gardens and provided new insights into the seasonal cycles of garden use, additionally underlining the scheme's potential as a monitoring tool for a habitat that is both important in its own right and not adequately covered by other monitoring schemes. Other papers have since extended the peer-reviewed monitoring outputs of the survey, not just for birds but also for other taxa (Toms & Newson, 2006), or looked at garden use in relation to wider landscape features (Chamberlain *et al.*, 2004a; Mckenzie *et al.*, 2007), behaviour (Ockendon, 2009a; 2009b), disease (Lawson *et al.*, 2010; 2012b; 2018) and demographics (Morrison *et al.*, 2014).

GARDEN WILDLIFE HEALTH

Garden Wildlife Health (GWH) is a collaborative project between the Zoological Society of London, British Trust for Ornithology, Froglife and RSPB, which aims to monitor and identify disease threats to British wildlife, including birds. The scheme is comprised of two components: one that allows the opportunistic reporting of disease through an online system, and one that delivers systematic surveillance of disease by asking participants in the weekly BTO Garden BirdWatch to submit information on the presence or absence of disease in the wildlife being observed in their gardens. Participants in Garden BirdWatch seeing evidence of disease can then submit additional information through Garden Wildlife Health. The system effectively pairs citizen science observers with veterinary scientists, the latter also being able to request carcasses of birds found dead for post-mortem examination. Participants receive feedback from the veterinary scientists on the likely causes of death of any birds that have a post-mortem examination carried out on them. As with many of the other projects mentioned within this section, Garden Wildlife Health reports its findings back through web pages, some of which are interactive. In addition, the findings are shared with UK-wide disease surveillance networks and with government, alerting others to the potential risks of emerging diseases. The use of citizen scientists in this way is a hugely valuable and financially efficient way of securing national disease surveillance that can draw on the strengths of combining opportunistic reporting with systematic observations. The scheme has operated for a number of years, formerly under the name of the Garden Bird Health initiative, and thanks to the generosity of its funders – the organisations themselves, the Universities Federation for Animal Welfare, government, the Esmée Fairbairn Foundation and representatives of the wild bird care industry.

As can be seen from many of the papers mentioned in Chapter 4, the project has delivered a significant amount of new information on the diseases of garden birds, from the emergence and spread of finch trichomonosis and paridae pox through to beak and feather disease in Ring-necked Parakeets and drowning mortality in Starlings (Sa *et al.*, 2014; Lawson *et al.*, 2015b; 2018). In addition, the extensive sample and tissue archive allows current and future researchers to test for and study other disease-related topics going forward.

BTO NEST BOX CHALLENGE

Launched in 2007, Nest Box Challenge is an online survey offering interested nest box owners the opportunity to record simple details about their nest box, its location and use. The survey is essentially a cut-down version of the long-running Nest Record Scheme, collecting information on those demographic parameters relating to garden-breeding attempts. To date, 40,000 nests have been registered from just under 15,000 gardens, the bulk of which relate to species

FIG 117. Nest Box Challenge provides valuable information on garden nesting attempts by species like Spotted Flycatcher. This information feeds into the BTO Nest Record Scheme. (John Harding)

using the familiar small-hole boxes described in Chapter 3, notably Blue Tit, Great Tit and House Sparrow. Participants are asked to monitor the box across the season, noting occupancy and collecting information on the progress of any nest contents.

Monitoring visits follow the guidance provided to participants and a code of conduct, based on the premise that locating and observing a nest should not jeopardise its safety. Each observer is asked to exercise a sense of responsibility, always putting the bird's interests first, something that is important for both ethical and scientific reasons. By following the guidance and the code of conduct, possible disturbance at the nest is minimised. As noted in Chapter 3, it has sometimes been difficult to overcome people's nervousness about looking into occupied nest boxes, but Nest Box Challenge is helping to address this, as are the materials put out in support of this project and the BTO Nest Record Scheme. Research in the US underlines that citizen scientists involved in the monitoring of nests in their backyards have no negative effect on the nests that they monitor and provide estimates of nest survival comparable to those of professional ecologists (Ryder *et al.*, 2010).

A similar project operates in North America; called the Neighborhood Nestwatch Program, the project is driven by two goals: to collect data on the ecology and population dynamics of eight species along an urban-to-rural gradient in the Washington DC area, and to teach people about bird biology. Operated by researchers at the Smithsonian Conservation Biology Institute, Nestwatch began as a pilot project in 2000 with just 45 participants. The project has since expanded and now averages between 50 and 100 participants annually, across several regional centres, leading to a series of peer-reviewed papers and other publications (Evans *et al.*, 2005; Ryder *et al.*, 2010; Narango *et al.*, 2017).

PROJECT FEEDERWATCH

The North American Project FeederWatch began its life during the winter of 1976/77 as the Ontario Bird Feeder Survey, launched by researchers at the Long Point Bird Observatory with the aim of seeing which species visited garden feeding stations, in what numbers, and which foods they preferred. After a successful 10-year run involving more than 500 participants, the organisers determined that if the survey could be expanded to cover the whole of North America, then it would greatly add to the knowledge being gathered. It was at this point that the Cornell Lab of Ornithology became involved, and Project FeederWatch was launched. Cornell has a history of delivering mass-

FIG 118. The spread of the Collared Dove across North America is being charted through Project FeederWatch. (John Harding)

participation surveys through citizen science. From 1987 to 1988, more than 4,000 people enrolled, since when participation has grown to more than 20,000. Project FeederWatch continues to be a cooperative research project of the Cornell Lab of Ornithology and Bird Studies Canada (formerly the Long Point Bird Observatory).

This winter-only project asks participants to keep a simple count of the number of individuals of each species that they see, the counts being made several times throughout the winter. Participants are asked to count a portion of their yard (garden) that is easy to observe, and make counts on two consecutive days – with at least five days between subsequent counts. As with BTO Garden BirdWatch, it is the maximum number of each species visible at any one time during the recording period that is noted, and again the target is birds using the garden and its resources rather than birds seen from the property or flying overhead. The project always starts on the second Saturday of November and runs for 21 weeks.

As is the case with BTO Garden BirdWatch, Project FeederWatch data can inform us of changes in species populations, particularly when used alongside data from other schemes and habitats. For example, Project FeederWatch data from Florida revealed that the winter population of the Painted Bunting *Passerina ciris* had declined steadily since the 1980s, prompting an examination of complementary data from the US Breeding Bird Survey (which itself suggested a decline of 4 per cent per year) and leading to systematic monitoring of bunting populations and a programme of conservation work. A wider comparison of Project FeederWatch data with those from the US Breeding Bird Survey found significant correlations between the average percentages of garden feeders visited during winter and Breeding Bird Survey indices across 13 US states for nine species (Wells *et al.*, 1998). They have also been instrumental in revealing changes in the range of Northern Cardinal, Evening Grosbeak *Coccothraustes vespertinus*, Collared Dove and Anna's Hummingbird (Greig *et al.*, 2017), and for understanding the emergence and spread of mycoplasmal conjunctivitis in House Finch populations (see Chapter 4). Project FeederWatch has also been particularly useful in helping to recognise citizen science projects as a valuable research tool (Bonter & Cooper, 2012).

OTHER INTERNATIONAL GARDEN BIRD SURVEYS

Launched in 2007 and modelled on Big Garden BirdWatch, the New Zealand Garden Bird Survey operated by Manaaki Whenua Landcare Research currently involves *c.* 3,500 gardens annually, equivalent to 0.19 per cent of all New Zealand households. A one-hour count is made on one day within a week-long period within the New Zealand winter. BirdLife Australia and Birds in Backyards now operate the Aussie Backyard Bird Count, another single-session-based count, that takes place during late October. In this instance, the recording period is limited to a 20-minute session. Within France, a national garden bird survey is run by the Ligue pour la Protection des Oiseaux (LPO) and the Muséum National d'Histoire Naturelle. Participants are directed towards key periods: the last weekend of January (for wintering birds, and matching the UK's Big Garden Birdwatch weekend) and the last weekend of May (for breeding birds).

SHORT-TERM CITIZEN SCIENCE PROJECTS

In addition to the ongoing schemes already mentioned, there have been a number of large-scale one-off or short-duration projects providing valuable information on garden birds and their ecology. The results from several of these studies have already had a central place in some of the other chapters of this book, most notably the BTO Garden Nesting Survey (Bland *et al.*, 2004), the Shortest Day Survey (Ockendon *et al.*, 2009a; 2009b), the BTO House Sparrow Survey (Shaw *et al.*, 2011; Chamberlain *et al.*, 2007c), the London Bird Project (Chamberlain *et al.*,

FIG 119. The BTO's Garden Nesting Survey underlined that gardens make an important contribution to the breeding populations of species like Robin – here a juvenile. (Jill Pakenham)

2004b) and the Biodiversity in Urban Glasgow study (Humphreys *et al.*, 2013). The networks of volunteers established through such schemes also provide opportunities to ask research questions whose answers may support ongoing pieces of research work. The study of what has driven the increase in wintering Blackcap populations within the UK (Plummer *et al.*, 2015), for example, benefited from being able to go out at short notice and ask for additional information on the food preferences of this warbler. A central theme of all of these projects has been the willingness of garden owners to get involved in citizen science, something that underlines the place that garden birds play in many of our lives.

CONCUDING REMARKS

The conservation value of gardens

It can be difficult to imagine that a small private space, with its neat borders and lawns, perhaps with a bird table, hanging feeders and nest boxes, has any conservation value. It may be even more difficult for the owner of that space to see how they can deliver conservation benefit through the decisions that they make about how it is managed and used. Yet each of our small private spaces does not exist in isolation; they are part of a wider landscape and – if viewed as a whole – represent an important resource for other creatures. This suggests that despite their ecological limitations, the conservation significance of private gardens is substantially greater than their absolute value in terms of habitat for birds. Gardens provide experiences and opportunities, from those that build connections with other creatures through to those that enable us to recognise and understand processes that shape our planet and its resources. Andrew Cannon captured these opportunities well in an opinion piece delivered through the journal *Bird Conservation International*, when he saw gardens as providing *direct conservation value* as habitats and havens, and *indirect conservation value* through engagement and empowerment (Cannon, 1999).

As we have seen from earlier sections within this book, UK gardens are important for several bird species, from Starlings and House Sparrows through to migrant Spotted Flycatchers and wintering Blackcaps. UK gardens may also provide a refuge for species whose populations have declined markedly within other habitats. In the arable areas of East Anglia, for example, gardens appear to be an important refuge for breeding thrushes; Mason (2000) found that although

FIG 120. Gardens and the food resources they provided have almost certainly supported the range expansion seen in Nuthatch. (John Harding)

FIG 121. Rural gardens may well be providing farmland Tree Sparrows with a vital food resource during the difficult late winter period, something that may have helped to reduce the severity of their national decline. (Jill Pakenham)

farmland occupied 67 per cent of his study area, it held significantly fewer Blackbird and Mistle Thrush territories than expected, with many more of the breeding territories of these two species located within urban areas and gardens than predicted. Importantly, Mason failed to find any evidence of Song Thrushes breeding within farmland, only locating breeding Song Thrushes within the urban areas, where they favoured areas of scrubby vegetation.

The food provided at garden feeding stations is a significant resource and has the potential to support populations of birds that may be struggling to find natural foods in other habitats, but this may come at the cost of an increased risk of disease and carry-over effects, both into the breeding season and into subsequent generations. Garden nest boxes may provide alternative nesting opportunities for species whose favoured nesting cavities under roof tiles or behind barge boards have been lost to changing building regulations and the development of new materials for house construction. The birds nesting in these gardens may benefit from these new opportunities but some may struggle to find sufficient invertebrate prey for their chicks, something that might turn gardens into ecological traps. Alternatively, the birds nesting in our gardens may be less dominant individuals, unable to secure a nest site in a nearby piece of suitable wider countryside habitat; for these individuals, a garden nest box may be a choice worth making, perhaps leading to chicks that fledge successfully, perhaps helping them to gain experience that will provide them with better opportunities the following year.

This all suggests that while there is real conservation value in gardens for wild birds, there are also some challenges and it is essential that we should seek to understand what these are and what impact they might have in a wider context. We also need to recognise that lessons learned in one part of the world – or even one part of a city – may not necessarily translate elsewhere because of the variation seen in gardens and because of the complex interactions that exist between gardens and the landscapes within which they sit. Finally, we need to recognise that the European-style garden is very different from other, more common, forms of garden and that it is these latter forms of garden that may be most relevant in the context of urbanisation at a global scale. If gardens are to serve a role for engagement and empowerment, then we need to understand and tease out conservation messages that are relevant and correctly focussed for individual garden owners.

The future of gardens and birds

The world's population is growing at a rate of nearly 1 per cent per annum and our larger cities are expanding at a rate even higher than population growth, particularly within important biodiversity hotspots (Seto *et al.*, 2012). Such growth, and its associated expansion in urban landscapes, has profound consequences for biodiversity; this makes it all the more important to understand the role that private gardens and wider green space play in the ecology of our towns and cities. Not only will this enable us to understand how avian communities will change as land is converted from other land uses to a built environment, but it will also help us to plan our cities better, so that we can maintain as much avian biodiversity as is possible.

Recognising the role that access to nature and interactions with garden birds plays in human health and well-being is the first step towards building upon this knowledge to tackle the rising levels of anxiety, stress and depression being documented within our increasingly urbanised population. While gardens are private and personal spaces, they also have a wider societal role, often delivering benefits well beyond their boundaries. We must, however, recognise that not all of the interactions between householders and garden birds are necessarily positive. As we saw in Chapter 4, gardens present both risks and opportunities to

FIG 122. The appearance of a rare visitor, such as this Wryneck *Jynx torquilla*, can be the highlight of any garden birdwatcher's year. (Jill Pakenham)

wild birds, and not all birds respond in the same way to these different risks and opportunities; for example, finch trichomonosis has hit Greenfinch populations but not those of Goldfinch – why is this and what are its implications for the garden bird community? We also need to understand what a changing climate will mean for our garden birds: will we see more summer visitors staying to overwinter; will we see fewer winter visitors; will we receive new and exotic colonists? One thing is certain, we will need people's love of garden birds to support the research that is needed; some of this support will be financial and some will also involve participation in citizen science schemes. We have been able to do a great deal and learn a significant amount since the feeding of garden birds became a popular pastime here in the UK. We need to ensure that we continue to support this interest through the provision of appropriate, evidence-based advice, using the knowledge that we gain from scientific study to support those who watch garden birds and, of course, the birds themselves.

CHAPTER 7

Species Accounts

THIS, THE FINAL SECTION OF the book, takes a more detailed look at each of the bird species most commonly encountered in UK gardens. Each of the species accounts provides an overview of the species, with a particular focus on how and when it uses gardens, and highlights interesting behaviours and research that will add to the reader's appreciation of the birds visiting their own garden. Each species account is accompanied by a simple calendar wheel that shows how the presence of the species varies throughout the year, and a map showing its distribution. The calendar wheels are derived from the weekly data collected by participants in BTO Garden BirdWatch. The amount of the darker colour within each segment indicates the likelihood of seeing the species. Segments that are empty (pale grey) indicate that the species is not usually seen in gardens during that month. Note that a filled segment does not mean that the species is seen in all gardens in a particular month; instead, it is a relative measure, allowing the seasonal pattern of an uncommon species to be seen as clearly as that of a very common species. The figure in the centre of the wheel shows the peak reporting rate (proportion of gardens in which the species is seen) during the month(s) with the all dark segment. Hence, in the example given in Figure 123, the peak month is March and its full segment represents the peak reporting rate of 41 per cent.

The map included with each species account present the likelihood of seeing the species across different parts of Britain

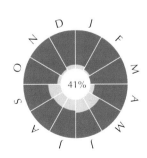

FIG 123. Calendar wheel for the Wren.

and Ireland. The data used for this map comes from *Bird Atlas 2007–11* (Balmer *et al.*, 2013) and combine both summer and winter data in a way that also reveals whether the species is a resident, a summer migrant or a winter visitor to that part of the region. In **purple areas**, the species is resident all year round, and is equally abundant in summer and winter. Where the colour tends towards **blue**, this indicates a species present only in winter (e.g. Fieldfare), whereas a change from **purple to red** indicates a tendency towards summer dominance; **pure reds** indicate summer visitors (e.g. House Martin). **Darker colours** indicate greater abundance, while **white areas** mean that the species is absent or very rare.

The species accounts all include a brief outline of key demographic information, including such things as clutch and brood size, the timing of breeding and typical lifespan, together with UK population size (Musgrove *et al.*, 2013) and current conservation status – the latter taken from *Birds of Conservation Concern 4* (Eaton *et al.*, 2015). The demographic data are derived from British Trust for Ornithology datasets, notably those of the Nest Record Scheme and the Ringing Scheme.

PHEASANT
Phasianus colchicus

Key facts:
Breeding season: April to September
Clutch size: 8–15 eggs
Incubation period: 22–28 days
Fledging period: 10–11 weeks
Number of breeding attempts: 1 per year
Typical lifespan: not known
Population size: 2.2 million females
Conservation: not listed

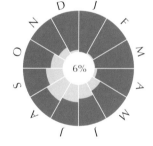

Pheasants are thought to have been introduced to Europe as early as 500 CE (Boev, 1997), the earliest introductions likely to be of the nominate subspecies *Phasianus colchicus colchicus*. Later introductions included birds of the Mongolian race *mongolicus* and the Chinese Ring-necked Pheasant *torquatus*. In addition to the introduced populations in Europe, the Pheasant has also been introduced to North America, New Zealand, Australia and Hawaii (Johnsgard, 1999). The species was probably introduced to England by the Normans, with the race *torquatus* dominating the population now present here (Yapp, 1983). It is thought that

Pheasant

somewhere in excess of 40 million pheasants are released into the wild each year, providing stock that forms the basis of a sport-shooting industry that harvests *c.* 12 million individuals per season (Tapper, 1999). These individuals contribute to an established wild population that makes this handsome gamebird a familiar sight across much of the countryside, leading to its regular appearance in many rural gardens and occasional suburban ones (Hill & Robertson, 1988).

Although the average weekly reporting rate from BTO Garden BirdWatch is just 6 per cent, the strong seasonal pattern to garden use – which sees a summer trough and a late winter peak – indicates that as many as one in five of the survey's gardens may be visited by the species during February or March. The timing of the late winter peak in garden use is interesting when viewed in relation to the shooting season, which runs from 1 October to 1 February. The hand-reared Pheasants important to delivering 'sporting birds' are typically provided with supplementary grain throughout the shooting season, something that is required in order to hold them in those areas used for shooting (Draycott *et al.*, 1998). The provision of this supplementary food usually ceases once the shooting season comes to an end, after which individuals are left to forage for natural foods. While this may create something of a 'nutritional bottleneck' and perhaps lead to increased levels of natural mortality, it might also lead to more birds entering private gardens in search of food.

Individuals may be attracted to garden feeding stations by the presence of fallen seeds and grain, though the omnivorous diet also sees them take plant material – including berries, leaves and roots – and small invertebrates. Very occasionally, they may supplement their diet with small vertebrates, which usually include Slow-worm *Anguis fragilis*, Common Lizard *Zootoca vivipara* and young Grass Snake *Natrix natrix* but may extend to young small mammals or birds. The food available at garden feeding stations may provide additional support to female Pheasants during the difficult later winter period, since it is known that food availability is a key factor influencing body condition of hen Pheasants in Britain (Draycott *et al.*, 2002).

FIG 124. Pheasants can visit gardens at any time of the year but there is a seasonal peak in late winter. (Jill Pakenham)

Something of the behavioural adaptability of the species can be seen from the habit of jumping from the ground to dislodge seed from bird feeders hanging overhead. This behaviour may be an extension of a behaviour in which individuals jump at overhanging berry bushes in an attempt to dislodge ripe fruit.

Very occasionally, a Pheasant may choose to nest in a rural garden, the less showy female choosing dense ground vegetation, often up against or within a hedge. Mature flowerbeds, with plenty of low cover, may be used and it is here that the clutch of 8 to 15 eggs is laid within the shallow scrape that serves as a nest (Robertson, 1991). This may be lined with grass and other plant material. Males are polygynous and establish large breeding territories within which they maintain a 'harem' of a dozen or more females. Each female is accompanied during the period in which egg laying takes place, the male mate guarding to protect his interests, but is then left once incubation begins. The female's plumage provides a high degree of camouflage from would-be predators, and her tendency to sit tightly on her clutch means that the first indication of her presence within a rural garden may be when she is disturbed by gardening activities or she brings her chicks out into the open. Pheasant chicks, which are born covered in down and with their eyes open, are precocial and able to leave the nest soon after hatching.

The young chicks remain with their mother for 9–12 weeks, after which time they become independent. However, individual chicks may continue to associate with their mother for a substantial period beyond independence, perhaps remaining with her through into the winter months when larger numbers of individuals come together to form winter flocks. These flocks, which can number 20 or more birds, tend to be formed of individuals of a single sex, the females typically forming larger flocks than the males. Although Pheasants are usually reported from gardens as single visiting birds, some rural gardens may be popular with larger winter flocks, where they can come to dominate garden feeding stations.

RED KITE
Milvus milvus

Key facts:
Breeding season: March to August
Clutch size: 1–3 eggs
Incubation period: 31–32 days
Fledging period: 50–60 days
Number of breeding attempts: 1 per year
Typical lifespan: 4 years
Population size: 1,600 pairs
Conservation: Green-listed

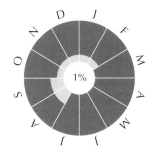

That such a large and predatory species can be considered a garden bird might seem surprising. However, Red Kites are now common visitors to some of the gardens located in areas, such as the Chiltern hills and Reading, close to where the species has been successfully reintroduced. Red Kites had been lost from England as a breeding species by 1871, and from Scotland by 1879, leaving only a small remnant population in Wales, occupying an area of largely sub-optimal breeding habitat. These losses were the result of persecution. A reintroduction programme initiated in 1989, coupled with the recovery and expansion of the population in Wales, has seen the return of the species to many of its former haunts and the Red Kite is now a familiar sight across large parts of southern Britain (Evans *et al.*, 1999).

The diet of UK Red Kites is dominated by food items that have been scavenged, and it is this scavenging lifestyle that saw the species associated with urbanised landscapes during the Middle Ages (O'Connor, 2000). Its role in consuming

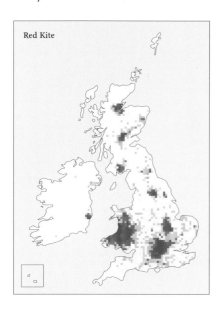

Red Kite

anthropogenic waste is recognised in the royal protection afforded to the bird at this time. Interestingly, the use of urban areas and scavenged food has become a feature of some of the birds that make up the current breeding population (Orros & Fellowes, 2014). This is despite the fact that such urban habitats no longer appear to hold the required amount of suitable food waste with, for example, the number of carcasses resulting from road kill thought to be very low within our larger conurbations (Orros & Fellows, 2015b). Instead, the food available in cities like Reading, where there is a sizeable Red Kite presence, is being

FIG 125. Red Kite is a very rare garden visitor unless you happen to live near one of the sites where these magnificent birds were reintroduced. (Jill Pakenham)

provided deliberately at garden feeding stations. Reading is just 20 km south of the site of the first English reintroductions.

The feeding of reintroduced kites appears to have begun soon after the reintroductions took place with, for example, villagers in the Chilterns regularly providing meat and other food scraps for the birds (Killick, 2006). Killick's work, which looked at the extent to which supplementary feeding by householders was helping or hindering the reintroduction programme, revealed that up to 10 per cent of the householders surveyed within the Chiltern study area were providing small animal carcasses, processed meats and leftovers for visiting kites. The quantities being provided were typically small and food provision was irregular. A more recent piece of work (Orros & Fellowes, 2014) looked more widely within the region at both food provision and the motivations of those providing it. This found a similar pattern of food provision, with just 12 per cent of respondents feeding daily, and 61 per cent feeding year round. Again, the quantities of food provided were low, with chicken the most commonly fed food of the 12 food categories reported. Those feeding the kites were motivated by seeing the birds close up, by a wish to help their conservation, by an interest in photographing the kites and by wanting to use up leftover food in a positive manner. Concerns over the impacts of providing such food prompted some individuals to cease feeding, while others stopped simply because they had moved house and were no longer visited by kites (Orros & Fellowes, 2014). The concerns about the provision of supplementary food are centred around its often low nutritional value (compared with natural foods), by the presence of additives in processed meat, and by the lack of bone and skin, which can lead to calcium deficiency – something that has been reported in young kites (Orros & Fellowes, 2014).

It is not just meat that Red Kites may take from the gardens they visit; those monitoring breeding kites have sometimes recorded the presence of human materials built into the nest. These include plastic bags, laundry and on at least one occasion a cuddly toy. Such behaviour is also alluded to in the writings of William Shakespeare, where the following lines are uttered by the rogue Autolycus '*My traffic is sheets; when the kite builds, look to lesser linen.*' It seems likely that we will see the use of garden feeding stations by Red Kites increase as the species continues to become more widely established. Future use of garden feeding stations will be shaped by attitudes towards whether or not providing supplementary food for these birds is considered appropriate. We will gain a better understanding of possible costs and benefits as more evidence is collected through the ongoing scientific research, but one thing is certain, however, and that is the rush of excitement that comes from seeing such a magnificent bird within a garden setting.

SPARROWHAWK
Accipiter nisus

Key facts:
Breeding season: May to August
Clutch size: 4–5 eggs
Incubation period: 32–36 days
Fledging period: 24–28 days
Number of breeding attempts: 1 per year
Typical lifespan: 4 years
Population size: 33,000 pairs
Conservation: Green-listed

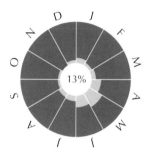

As evident from the section within Chapter 4, the presence of Sparrowhawks in gardens is linked to the availability of the smaller birds on which they prey. The use of gardens by Sparrowhawks increased from the 1970s, reflecting the recovery of the Sparrowhawk population from the impacts of persecution and the effects of organochlorine pesticides. The pattern of garden use seen in the BTO's Garden Bird Feeding Survey results indicates a difference between rural and suburban gardens in the timing of this increase, with that seen in suburban

Sparrowhawk

gardens showing a 15 to 20 year lag on the pattern seen in rural gardens. The increase appears to have halted abruptly in rural gardens in the late 1990s, a pattern reflecting the switch from population increase to population stability evident within the Common Birds Census/Breeding Bird Survey results from the wider countryside. These wider countryside results then show a period of decrease from 2006, which is thought to be linked to the emergence of finch trichomonosis (see Chapter 4), though it is difficult to secure hard evidence for this. Certainly, the pattern of decline can also be seen in both Garden Bird Feeding Survey and BTO

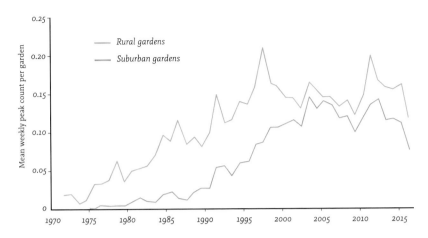

FIG 126. The long-term pattern of garden use by Sparrowhawk as revealed by the BTO's Garden Bird Feeding Survey. This survey runs through the winter months. Data used with permission from BTO.

Garden BirdWatch data for the period, and there is evidence from elsewhere in Europe that might suggest a link between predation on infected birds at garden feeding stations and *Trichomonas* infection in Sparrowhawks. Kunca *et al.* (2015) found that Sparrowhawk nestlings from an urban study area were more likely to be infected with the parasite than those from a rural area, though this pattern was reversed in the following year.

The colonisation of urban areas by breeding Sparrowhawks has probably also resulted in an increase in the numbers dying through collision with windows while chasing small bird prey, and there may be other hazards associated with urban living. However, the Sparrowhawks probably also benefit from the availability of smaller birds, gathered at garden feeding stations and making them a predictable resource, both in space and time. Individual Sparrowhawks appear to make good use of the available cover and select an approach route that often sees them emerge from behind a building or over a hedge close to the feeding station. Since they tend to follow a favoured route, you can tip the balance of favour towards the smaller birds by considering where best to place your feeders and by moving the feeders around the garden to reduce the predictability of where the smaller birds will be feeding.

The presence of a visiting Sparrowhawk may affect the behaviour of the smaller birds visiting a garden feeding station, perhaps leading to the avoidance

FIG 127. The Sparrowhawk is now a regular visitor to many garden feeding stations, attracted by the small birds that are likely to be present. (John Harding)

of gardens where predation risk is high or resulting in individual species forming larger flocks at sites where Sparrowhawks are present (Chamberlain *et al.*, 2009b). It has been shown that some songbird species are more prone to Sparrowhawk predation than others, perhaps because of behavioural traits (Götmark & Post, 1996) or the brightness of their plumage (Huhta *et al.*, 2003). Predation risk differences between habitats – such as those between urban and rural sites – have been examined in relation to the predation of birds by hunting Sparrowhawks, with Post & Götmark (2006) finding that birds in urban habitats are, on average, more exposed than birds in forest habitats and found closer to the ground, both features that may change with season and determine predation risk of the prey species.

There are also differences in the prey species taken by the two sexes, with the larger female Sparrowhawk able to tackle larger avian prey than her mate. Females, for example, may take birds up to the size of a Collared Dove or even Woodpigeon, while the smaller male typically takes birds up to the size of a Blackbird. The smaller male, whose size and agility is closer to that of the prey

taken, is largely responsible for hunting and prey delivery to the nest throughout
the whole breeding season (Andersson & Norberg, 1981). During incubation
the female is tied to the nest, leaving it only briefly to take and consume prey
delivered by her mate. The female is, however, responsible for preparation of
the prey and its presentation to the nestlings; she may occasionally hunt herself
during the latter stages of the breeding period, presumably to ensure that the
chicks are provided with sufficient food (Newton, 1978). Female Sparrowhawks are
the larger of the two sexes presumably because of the additional reserves required
to produce a clutch of eggs.

Work carried out in Scotland has examined the extent to which there might
be differences in breeding success and productivity between urban and rural
Sparrowhawk populations (Thornton *et al.*, 2017). This has revealed that urban
territories are occupied significantly more often than rural ones. Clutch size,
brood size and the number of fledglings produced per nest were not found to
differ between the two populations but because of a higher rate of nest desertion
in the rural population, the population breeding in urban Edinburgh actually had
a higher level of breeding success. Quite why these differences exist is unclear
and requires further research. Of course, urban and rural populations may react
differently to the presence of humans, something discussed in Chapter 5, but
there is no evidence that urban-nesting Sparrowhawks differ in their response to
those breeding in rural areas (Kunca & Yosef, 2016).

BLACK-HEADED GULL
Chroicocephalus ridibundus

Key facts:
Breeding season: April to August
Clutch size: 3 eggs
Incubation period: 23–26 eggs
Fledging period: c. 35 days
Number of breeding attempts: 1 per year
Typical lifespan: 11 years
Population size: 130,000
Conservation: Amber-listed

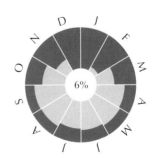

Gulls are generally rather uncommon visitors to UK gardens but some sites do
receive visits from Black-headed Gull and other species (notably Herring Gull
and Lesser Black-backed Gull, both of which have increasing urban breeding

Black-headed Gull

populations). All of these species prefer those gardens that have open areas of short turf or concrete, from which kitchen scraps can be snatched quickly. In more confined gardens, Black-headed Gulls may still visit, though in such circumstances they prefer to grab food while still on the wing and without landing.

BTO Garden BirdWatch data show that garden use peaks during the winter months, with much variation between years suggesting that garden use may be weather-related. Interestingly, the use of urban and suburban gardens appears to be greater than that of rural ones, a pattern evident in both Garden Bird Feeding Survey data and in our analysis of habitat associations evident within Garden BirdWatch data (Chamberlain *et al.*, 2004a). There is a suggestion that garden use in winter has declined somewhat since the mid-1990s, although whether this is due to less severe winter weather or the decline in national breeding populations is unclear – both may be important.

The distribution of Black-headed Gulls within the wider urban environment has been found to be linked to the availability of feeding opportunities; Maciusik *et al.* (2010), for example, found that the abundance of Black-headed Gulls across the city of Kraków in Poland was positively correlated with the distribution of litter bins, underlining that these provide good foraging opportunities for this species. The availability of anthropogenic food may influence breeding success in gulls and recent work has highlighted that Black-headed Gulls living in urban areas more readily select anthropogenic food over natural food. Through the use of a series of choice experiments, Scott *et al.* (2015) found that the food preference of Black-headed Gulls varied significantly along an urban–rural gradient. Natural food, provided by the researchers in the form of fresh Sprats *Sprattus sprattus*, was selected in 80 per cent of trials carried out in the most rural areas but decreased to just to 5 per cent in the most urban site.

Small urban-breeding colonies are a feature of some urban areas, for example central London, though at this time of the year the use of gardens is even less common. Another feature of urban Black-headed Gull populations is the degree to which they can be made up of individuals drawn from over a very large area.

FIG 128. Black-headed Gulls are primarily winter visitors to garden feeding stations, arriving in those periods when poor weather makes feeding conditions elsewhere more difficult. (John Harding)

During the winter months, the Black-headed Gull population here in the UK is joined by large numbers of immigrants, with individuals arriving from as far east as Russia. Examination of the birds visiting a garden, or sat loafing elsewhere within a town or city, will often reveal the presence of individuals carrying a leg ring. Careful use of a camera or pair of binoculars may reveal the ring number and lead to the determination of the individual's identity and its origins. Looking at individual Black-headed Gulls can also reveal their age; as with other gulls, these birds go through a series of plumage moults that over time lead to the development of the full adult plumage. The presence of brown feathers within the wings, for example, will indicate that a bird still retains some of its juvenile plumage.

FERAL PIGEON
Columba livia

Key facts:

Breeding season: March to October
Clutch size: 2 eggs
Incubation period: 17–19 days
Fledging period: c. 25 days
Number of breeding attempts: 2–3 per year
Typical lifespan: 3 years
Population size: 540,000 pairs
Conservation: not listed

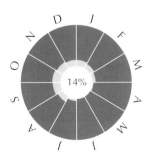

Descended from the Rock Dove, and possibly living in a semi-domesticated state since as early as 4500 BCE, the Feral Pigeon is a familiar urban bird, found in large numbers across most of our towns and cities. In some city-centre gardens,

Feral Pigeon

Feral Pigeon may be virtually the only bird table visitor and certainly the most numerous. Originally a cliff-nesting species, the Feral Pigeon is well adapted to the ledges of urban buildings and possesses a ready willingness to feed on scraps and bird table fare. Feral Pigeons often gather together in large flocks where good feeding opportunities exist; these may be in areas of public open space or at garden feeding stations, the preferred sites often have safe feeding perches located nearby. Tully (1993) has suggested that the higher perches are preferred, providing the birds using these with a better view of both feeding opportunities and potential dangers.

One of the characteristics of the long history of Feral Pigeon domestication is the presence of many different colour forms. Some of these resemble the wild type Rock Dove from which they are descended, but others come in a bewildering array of colours and patterns. The presence of particular colour forms has been found to vary between cities – for example, Tully (1993) found that most of the birds in Bristol (75 per cent) were of the light-blue chequered form, similar to wild Rock Dove, but these were joined by white birds (1–2 per cent), brown birds (1–2 per cent) and very dark birds (20–25 per cent); in London, Simms (1975) estimated the proportions at white (10 per cent), brown (10 per cent) and dark (5 per cent). One wonders if the return of urban Peregrines *Falco peregrinus* will influence these ratios.

Another feature is the level of ill health and deformities evident in Feral Pigeon populations. Indicative perhaps of the harsh realities of an urban existence scavenging scraps, the proportion of individuals within a flock showing signs of obvious injury may exceed 50 per cent. The level of injury can reflect local conditions with, for example, the high rate of injury to feet and legs noted in the flock using Bristol market thought to be the result of a high level of discarded nylon packaging (Tully, 1993). It is unclear how much interchange there is between the Feral Pigeon populations using city-centre spaces and those using small residential gardens and their feeding stations. However, it is likely that the birds present within an area will discover and learn the places where they can find food most readily, suggesting that there may be movements between the two.

FIG 129. Descended from the wild Rock Dove, the Feral Pigeon comes in many different forms, some of which are closer to the ancestral form than others. (Moss Taylor)

Feral Pigeon populations have been monitored since 1994 through the BTO/JNCC/RSPB Breeding Bird Survey, since when they have declined by 21 per cent. Declines are being seen in populations associated with urban and suburban habitat but not those associated with rural settlements (where numbers are low anyway). It is possible that the changing availability of food resources within our urban centres may be driving this decline; the development of better-quality seed mixes – lower in grain composition – might make garden feeding stations less attractive, and efforts are under way in many public open spaces to discourage or ban the feeding of Feral Pigeons. Work elsewhere suggests that a reduction in food availability may reduce productivity (Stock & Haag-Wackernagel, 2016) and that where people provide less food, pigeon densities may fall (Senar *et al.*, 2017). Despite the declines noted in the Breeding Bird Survey, data from BTO Garden BirdWatch show an increase in both the proportion of gardens reporting Feral Pigeons and the average flock size present for the period 1995–2017.

STOCK DOVE
Columba oenas

Key facts:
Breeding season: April to October
Clutch size: 2 eggs
Incubation period: 16–18 days
Fledging period: 27–28 days
Number of breeding attempts: 2–3 per year
Typical lifespan: 3 years
Population size: 260,000 territories
Conservation: Amber-listed

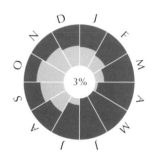

The Stock Dove is primarily a species of arable farmland and open woodland habitats, but it can be a regular visitor to feeding stations located within rural areas. Use of rural gardens appears to have increased, the species now visiting 12 per cent of the gardens monitored by the Garden Bird Feeding Survey and up from 9 per cent in 2008, something that reflects a wider population increase in arable areas. We know that Stock Dove was one of the species to suffer from the use of toxic seed-dressings in the 1950s and early 1960s, their subsequent

Stock Dove

recovery possible once the use of the compounds involved had been banned (O'Connor & Mead, 1984). One of the other reasons why Stock Doves might have been particularly hard hit by these pesticides is their sedentary habits, reducing the degree of immigration from populations elsewhere.

One of the interesting features of the period when arable Stock Dove populations were suffering from the use of toxic seed-dressings was an apparent increase in the relative frequency of nests recorded in urban and suburban areas (see O'Connor & Mead, 1984 – Fig. 5). This proportion rose sharply between 1950 and 1965

FIG 130. Similar in appearance to its larger relative, the Woodpigeon, Stock Dove has two short black wing bars, which also help separate the species from certain plumage forms of Feral Pigeon. (John Harding)

but then declined again, something that might be indicative of a population experiencing high levels of reproductive failure within rural areas but faring rather better in urbanised landscapes. O'Connor & Mead found that nests in suburban and urban areas were more likely to be successful than those in rural areas, the difference between the two habitats mainly a result of higher failure rates at the egg stage in rural nests. A further period of population increase, from 1995, was halted abruptly in 2004/05; while this could have been linked to the emergence of finch trichomonosis, cases of the disease in Stock Doves are rare.

Stock Doves can be nervous visitors to garden feeding stations and this, coupled with the similarity in their appearance to the larger Woodpigeon, means that they can be easily overlooked. Although similar in size, shape and general appearance to a Feral Pigeon, Stock Dove can be identified by the combination of short dark wing bars, iridescent green neck patch and dark eyes. Within their favoured farmland habitats, Stock Doves feed primarily on weed seeds, but they will also take cereal seed, something that also features in the supplementary foods taken from bird tables and the ground. Grains appear to be less important to Stock Doves than they are for Woodpigeon. The leaves, buds and fruits of trees do not appear to be an important food item, so we would not expect to see a similar pattern of garden use to that of Woodpigeon.

The species may also breed in rural gardens, occupying a suitable cavity, a ledge within a building or a nest box of acceptable size. The nest is usually made from a platform of small sticks, to which plant material may be added, but may sometimes just be a hollow scraped out of debris already present in the nesting chamber. Each nest may be used several times over the course of the nesting season, and pairs will also make use of the same site in subsequent years. Individual pairs are known to defend the nest site from other Stock Doves, and will also drive away other potential users, including Jackdaw and even Little Owl *Athene noctua*. Repeated use within a season can make the nesting chamber rather unpleasant, with droppings, unhatched eggs and the remains of chicks from previous nesting attempts all adding to the mess.

WOODPIGEON
Columba palumbus

Key facts:
Breeding season: April to October
Clutch size: 2 eggs
Incubation period: 17 days
Fledging period: 29–35 days
Number of breeding attempts: 2–3 per year
Typical lifespan: 3 years
Population size: 5.3 million pairs
Conservation: Green-listed

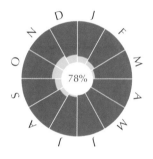

The increasing use of UK gardens by Woodpigeon, charted by BTO Garden BirdWatch and the Garden Bird Feeding Survey, is thought to reflect a change in agricultural practices and a wider increase in population size. The spread of intensive arable cultivation, most notably of winter-sown cereals and oilseed rape, has been linked to an increase in overwinter survival and better productivity, resulting in larger populations within favoured farmland habitats (Inglis *et al.*, 1997). One consequence of this appears to have been the movement into suburban and urban sites, which has been accompanied by a change in behaviour with urban populations seemingly more tolerant of the presence of people than their rural counterparts. Habitat-specific trends from the BTO/JNCC/RSPB Breeding Bird Survey demonstrate the substantial growth seen in urban and suburban populations since the mid-1990s. The increasing use of urban areas has also been seen elsewhere in Europe (Fey *et al.*, 2015). Slater (2001), working in Sefton Park in Liverpool, revealed that Woodpigeons in suburban

Woodpigeon

areas can breed at densities as high as or higher than those found in some farmland habitats; they can also have higher breeding success.

Within gardens and wider urbanised landscapes, Woodpigeons usually make their nests in tall shrubs and trees, a habit that shapes their urban distribution (Palomino & Carrascal, 2006), but they may also nest on buildings where suitable ledges occur. While O'Connor & Shrubb (1986) found that the Woodpigeon breeding season had advanced in response to the earlier sowing of cereals, Nest Record Scheme data suggest that the species is now nesting almost three weeks later than it did in the 1960s. Since Woodpigeons can make two or three nesting attempts per year, it is important to understand whether the number of breeding attempts, and how these are monitored by Nest Record Scheme volunteers, might also have changed. The Woodpigeon is one of a very small number of bird species that has been shown to feed its chicks on 'crop milk', a substance that is very similar to mammalian milk. Produced in the crop, this 'milk' forms the only source of nutrient that the chicks receive during the first few days after hatching.

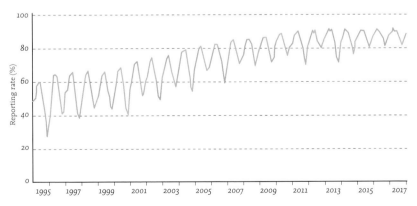

FIG 131. The long-term pattern of garden use for Woodpigeon, since 1995, as revealed by the weekly counts of BTO Garden BirdWatch participants. Data reproduced with permission from BTO.

FIG 132. Woodpigeons often bathe in bird baths, the shallows of ponds or temporary puddles. (John Harding)

Woodpigeons have been linked with the emergence of the parasite *Trichomonas gallinae* in UK finch populations (see Chapter 4) and it appears that the parasite is present within their wider populations too, its prevalence linked to migrational movements and the availability of supplementary food (Villanúa *et al.*, 2006). The Woodpigeon movements seen in continental Europe are tied to the size of the acorn and beechmast crops; while such movements are not well documented from within the UK, the importance of these seeds to Woodpigeons appears to shape the use of garden feeding stations. As Chamberlain *et al.* (2007a) found, the occurrence of Woodpigeons at UK garden feeding stations was lower in those years when beechmast was abundant within the wider countryside. Woodpigeon populations nationally have fallen back somewhat since the mid-1990s, which might suggest a link to the finch trichomonas outbreak, and this has resulted in the numbers present in gardens levelling off after a period of continued growth.

The Woodpigeon is certainly not favoured by everyone who feeds garden birds, something that no doubt reflects their ability to take large quantities of food from bird tables and ground-feeding stations. Woodpigeons struggle to take food from hanging feeders because of their size, but they have been seen to fly at hanging feeders in an attempt to dislodge food that can then be taken from the ground below. Some garden birdwatchers use a feeder guardian – a cage that allows small birds access but keeps larger birds out – to protect their garden feeding stations. Other garden birdwatchers are fascinated by their behaviour, two aspects of which are worth a mention here. When drinking, unlike most other garden birds, the Woodpigeon does not have to tip its head back to swallow. While happy to bathe in a bird bath or the shallows of a pond, Woodpigeons may sometimes shower-bathe in the rain, lifting first one wing and then the other to allow the water to access the underwing feathers.

COLLARED DOVE
Streptopelia decaocto

Key facts:
Breeding season: March to September
Clutch size: 2 eggs
Incubation period: 14–16 days
Fledging period: c. 18 days
Number of breeding attempts: 2–3 a year
Typical lifespan: 3 years
Population size: 990,000 pairs
Conservation: Green-listed

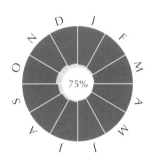

This delicate dove, with its creamy-grey-buff plumage and neat black-and-white half-neck collar, is a relatively recent colonist, whose colonisation of the UK has benefitted from an association with gardens. Collared Doves were first reported breeding in the UK in 1955, with at least two pairs present in north Norfolk, one of which bred in a small garden at West Runton (Richardson *et al.,* 1957). The next year another pair was found breeding in a large walled garden further along the Norfolk coast at Overstrand. These first breeding attempts were soon followed by others, the initial colonisation tending to follow the coastal towns and villages. By the mid-1960s, the Collared Dove had become established in over 80 Norfolk towns and villages and was now also established in other English counties. The initial period of colonisation was very clearly associated with human habitation and farmyards, particularly where spilt grain might be found, and it seems likely that the presence of poultry in many rural gardens helped the birds to become established. During this period, cereals formed an important part of Collared Dove diet, supporting large flocks of up to 200 birds that gathered at favoured sites during the winter months.

Collared Dove

The colonisation of Britain was part of a wider expansion in the Collared Dove's breeding range, an expansion that began on the other side of Europe (Fisher, 1953). As the nineteenth century reached its end, the Collared Dove was restricted to parts of Turkey and the Balkans, but just 30 years later it had reached Hungary as a breeding species. With the breeding range expanding northwest, Austria was reached in 1943, Germany in 1945 and the Netherlands in 1949. This rapid colonisation of Europe is one of ornithology's most remarkable events. That this rather unassuming bird had been able to break out from its established range and secure a much increased presence across Europe underlines the potential for rapid spread if conditions are favourable. Quite what had driven the expansion is unclear.

In addition to the food present in many gardens, another factor that may have been important is the Collared Dove's long breeding season. Pairs have been recorded breeding in every month of the year and may initiate a new breeding attempt before the last one has been completed. Although each nesting attempt only involves two eggs, pairs can squeeze as many as five attempts into a season. The nest, which is usually a rather flimsy platform of small sticks, may be built in a tree or shrub, placed on a ledge or balanced on the bracket holding a satellite dish or security light in place. Each male defends a small area around the nest, advertising ownership with his somewhat monotonous 'u-ni-ted' call, with emphasis on its second note.

Closely associated with human habitation, breeding densities appear to be at their peak in suburban habitats, with lower densities present in city centres and more widely throughout rural areas. Rural populations show a stronger association with gardens and farms, underlining the importance of foraging opportunities during the winter months. The trend of increasing numbers was halted in 2005, since when the breeding population has declined by 21 per cent, which suggests that the species might be suffering from the emergence of trichomonosis in garden-visiting finches (Robinson *et al.*, 2010). Another factor may be increasing levels of competition with the larger Woodpigeon, a species whose use of gardens has increased significantly over recent years.

FIG 133. Collared Doves may breed throughout the year, meaning that the 'u-ni-ted u-ni-ted' call can become all too familiar to householders. (John Harding)

It is not just Europe that has seen rapid colonisation by the Collared Dove; the introduction of the species to North America followed the escape of up to 50 birds, brought to the Bahamas by a pet breeder in 1973. Breeding was reported from the Bahamas the following year, and it appears that individuals from here then arrived in Florida during the 1980s. From there the further rapid spread has been documented through the North American Breeding Bird Survey (Hooten & Wikle, 2008) and the Christmas Bird Count (Scheidt & Hurlbert, 2014). The rapid spread may be facilitated by a pattern of longer movements to colonise new areas, followed by a process of 'backfilling' the gap between the old range edge and the new. Analyses of the colonisation patterns, both in the US and more recently in the Dominican Republic, have underlined the importance of garden feeding stations and suburban residential areas in the spread (Scheidt & Hurlbert, 2014; Luna *et al.*, 2018).

TAWNY OWL
Strix aluco

Key facts:
Breeding season: March to July
Clutch size: 2–3 eggs
Incubation period: 28–30 days
Fledging period: 32–37 days
Number of breeding attempts: 1 per year
Typical lifespan: 4 years
Population size: 50,000 pairs
Conservation: Amber-listed

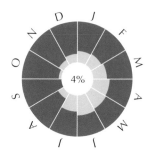

Tawny Owls do not appear to penetrate far into the urban environment within the UK, though they may sometimes occupy well-wooded city-centre parks. Most of the gardens visited by Tawny Owls, or indeed used for breeding, will be rural and close to areas of deciduous woodland. Pairs may also be found breeding in the well-wooded suburbs on the outskirts of towns and cities, where small birds join small mammals in the diet. Tawny Owls breeding in their favoured deciduous woodland habitats readily take small birds, with these contributing up to 5 per cent of the items found in a study of Tawny Owl diet carried out by

Tawny Owl

Southern (1954). The largest species taken was Woodpigeon, with several small and often flock-forming species, like Chaffinch, Greenfinch and Blackbird, the most important. Selection of such species could suggest that urban Tawny Owls might equally target these birds as they roost at night, though House Sparrow might also be an important prey for urban Tawny Owls. Tawny Owl diet has been studied in the Polish city of Kraków, where the proportion of different prey groups (e.g. invertebrates) and individual prey species (e.g. Wood Mouse) has been favoured to vary in importance along an urban–rural gradient (Grzędzicka *et al.*, 2013).

Along with Little Owl, Tawny Owls make greater use of invertebrate prey than other owl species breeding within the UK. Earthworms form an important component of woodland Tawny Owl diet, along with chafers and various dor beetles. This suggests that urban Tawny Owls may also make use of earthworms, taking them from the surface of garden lawns on those wet nights when the damp conditions tempt the worms above ground. Tawny Owls have also been recorded taking fish, including Goldfish *Carassius auratus*. Beven (1965) reported recovering the remains of Goldfish from pellets dropped by a Tawny Owl that regularly roosted close to a pond known to contain these ornamental fish.

FIG 134. Tawny Owls may breed in well-wooded suburbs, sometimes visiting garden lawns to take earthworms on damp nights. (Jill Pakenham)

The characteristic hooting calls of Tawny Owl pairs defending their breeding territories can be heard from early October and onwards through the winter. Late autumn is the period when young Tawny Owls, born earlier in the year, are dispersing and beginning to settle on territories of their own. This brings them into conflict with established pairs and leads to an increase in vocal activity. The calls of these young birds are less fully formed than those of the established adults and they can be picked out by those familiar with Tawny Owl calls. It is likely that many of the Tawny Owls heard calling from more urban gardens during late autumn and early winter will be dispersing young birds. Since these young birds are likely to move on, the calling features for just a few nights and then stops.

Tawny Owls are cavity nesters and take readily to suitable nest boxes, ideally placed high in a mature tree. Height is important – as is the amount of cover around the nest box – since it has been shown that chick survival is better at nest boxes placed high and surrounded by good cover. This is because Tawny Owl chicks leave the nest before they are able to fly and sit outside the box on a nearby branch, a behaviour that is known as branching. The chicks are very susceptible to predation at this age, with larger birds of prey and – for those chicks that end up on the ground – foxes known to be important predators.

It is unclear as to how well established Tawny Owls are within urban areas here in the UK, though this may be addressed soon thanks to a new BTO survey. Elsewhere, urban populations have been studied in Helsinki, Finland, where the timing of breeding was found to be significantly earlier in urban territories than in rural ones (Solonen, 2014). The earliest clutches recorded in this study were predominantly found in the city, rather than in its surrounding landscape.

SWIFT
Apus apus

Key facts:
Breeding season: May to August
Clutch size: 2–3 eggs
Incubation period: 19–20 days
Fledging period: 37–56 days
Number of breeding attempts: 1 per year
Typical lifespan: 9 years
Population size: 87,000 pairs
Conservation: Amber-listed

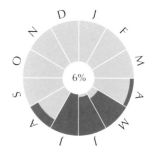

Swift

Despite the clear association between Swifts and the built environment, there is still a surprising amount that we have yet to learn about these summer visitors. Returning birds arrive in the UK from late April and depart in August, the journey to our shores made so that the Swifts can take advantage of the summer abundance of flying insects to support their single breeding attempt. With the exception of breeding, and the need to find a solid surface on which to build a nest, virtually the whole of the Swift's life cycle is spent on the wing.

While the nature of an individual garden is unlikely to have any

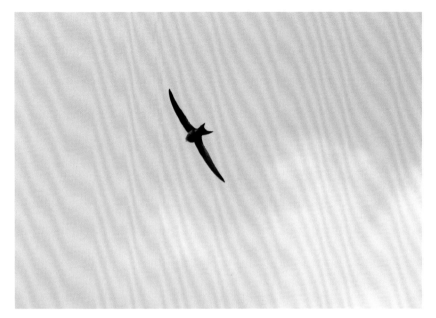

FIG 135. Unlike many other summer migrants, UK swifts have not extended the length of time spent in Britain. (Mike Toms)

influence on whether or not Swifts nest on the property, the characteristics of the house are important. Swifts generally favour older properties, yet to face refurbishment and the associated loss of the features they find important. Pairs typically nest on a flat surface within the eaves or in a hole in a wall but they will also take to suitable nest boxes, with these of particular importance where traditional sites have been lost to refurbishment or building regulations that have altered the nature of new housing and the nesting opportunities offered. The nest itself is a shallow cup of grass, feathers and other material collected on the wing, which is constructed by both members of the pair. Swifts do not begin breeding until they are at least two years old, and evidence suggests that many birds do not breed successfully until they are four years old. Breeding birds show strong fidelity to both their nesting colony and the nest site used the previous year; this is defended against younger birds attempting to establish themselves within a colony. These young birds are typically individuals from other colonies, with the young from the colony having dispersed elsewhere to breed.

Swifts are known to range over a significant area when searching for food, a behaviour that may take them away from the colony for substantial periods of time. If bad weather prevents the delivery of prey to the nest, then nestlings may enter a state of semi-torpidity, reducing their energy demands significantly (Lack & Lack, 1951; Thomson *et al.*, 1996). Even with this reduction in energy demands, chick mortality rates can be very high, and there is also evidence that growth patterns – potentially affected by periods of poor weather – might also impact on longer-term fitness (Perrins, 1964; Sicurella *et al.*, 2015). Given the short amount of time that Swifts are present on their breeding quarters, and the potential delays to the breeding cycle brought about by periods of bad weather, it seems that Swifts are somewhat up against it during the short summer months. Examination of data from two citizen science studies (the Inland Observation Points survey of the 1960s and today's BirdTrack scheme) have revealed that while many summer migrants are arriving earlier and leaving later now than they did in the 1960s, Swift is one species that has not extended the length of time spent here in the UK.

We are also learning more about the migration of Swifts from UK breeding colonies thanks to the development of tiny tracking devices called geolocators, which through the use of an internal clock, calendar and light-level monitor are able to record the location of a bird throughout its migratory journey. These have revealed that UK Swifts migrate south through France and Spain before crossing into North Africa. From here they cross the western end of the Sahara still heading south before turning east to a main wintering area in Central Africa. Some birds move further east and south from here as the winter progresses, before making an April movement back to West Africa, in preparation for the return to the UK breeding grounds. Despite this growing amount of knowledge, we still lack a reliable measure of the size of the UK breeding population; data from core monitoring schemes suggest that the UK breeding population has been declining since at least 1995 (when the launch of the Breeding Bird Survey allowed the Swift population trend to be monitored) and the population appears to have declined by 51 per cent between 1995 and 2015 (Massimino *et al.*, 2017). The loss of suitable nest sites is likely to have played a part in the decline, something that is being addressed by conservation action directed towards the provision of nest boxes within new building developments.

GREEN WOODPECKER
Picus viridis

Key facts:
Breeding season: May to June
Clutch size: 5–7 eggs
Incubation period: 17–18 days
Fledging period: 23–27 days
Number of breeding attempts: 1 per year
Typical lifespan: not known
Population size: 52,000
Conservation: Green-listed

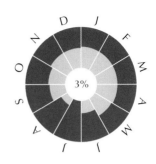

Although not attracted by the fare provided at garden feeding stations, the Green Woodpecker is a not uncommon visitor to rural and larger suburban gardens within its breeding range – the core of which is centred on southern and eastern England. When visiting gardens, Green Woodpeckers are most commonly encountered feeding on the lawn, where ants, together with their eggs and larvae, are the preferred food. This dietary preference is evident in the extraordinary long, mobile and sticky tongue carried by the bird. This is widened and flattened at the tip and lacks the barbs seen in many other woodpecker species. The

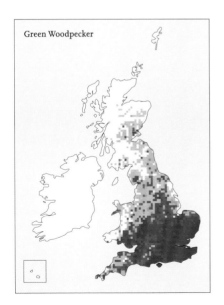

Green Woodpecker

tongue is used to probe into ant nests located within the soil of short-sward grasslands – hence why lawns are an ideal foraging ground – and the presence of enlarged salivary glands, which coat the tongue in sticky mucus, help the bird to capture the ants. A wide range of ant species has been recorded in the diet, but there is evidence that the species shows a preference for the larger species, presumably because they are energetically more rewarding (Rolstad *et al.*, 2000).

During the winter months, when ants are more difficult to locate, Green Woodpeckers may also take windfall apples, again from

FIG 136. Juvenile Green Woodpeckers can be distinguished from the adults by their more speckled plumage. (Jill Pakenham)

garden lawns. Although only a small amount of work has been done on the habitat preferences of Green Woodpeckers in the UK it, does appear that wider countryside short-sward grasslands, such as those grazed by sheep, and garden lawns are preferred as foraging sites over other habitats. A pair of Green Woodpeckers breeding within a farmland area in Dorset were radio-tracked by Danny Alder and Stuart Marsden, their results revealing that the birds spent most of their time feeding in sheep-grazed pastures and on garden lawns, with arable land and cattle-grazed pasture avoided. The sites used by the birds were found to hold high densities of ants, particularly *Lasius flavus* (Alder & Marsden, 2010).

The wider increase in UK Green Woodpecker populations evident from the mid-1960s through to 2008, coupled with considerable expansion in breeding range in central and eastern Scotland, has no doubt led to an increase in the use of gardens. While the range expansion has continued within parts of England and Scotland, recent atlas results (Balmer *et al.*, 2013) suggest that the species is being lost from parts of Wales and southwest England. This pattern may be a consequence of changing grassland structure or climate, perhaps resulting in reductions in the ant populations on which the Green Woodpecker depends; certainly, there is no indication that the availability of suitable dead trees for nesting is limiting (Smith, 2007).

Green Woodpeckers will occasionally use nest boxes of suitable size, typically filled with material that can be excavated to form a nesting chamber. There is also a record of an individual that took to a nest box erected in a Bournemouth garden and used it for roosting throughout the late autumn and winter of 1933/34 (Jourdain, 1936). Perhaps surprisingly given the reliance on ants and other invertebrates, the Green Woodpecker is extremely sedentary in its habits, remaining on its territory throughout the winter months rather than moving away. Records of ringed individuals moving more than 20 km are very unusual and there is no evidence of movements across the English Channel, to or from Europe. The sedentary habits may provide the woodpecker with valuable knowledge of the feeding opportunities within an individual's territory, and there is certainly good evidence that a bird will return to the same feeding site over a period of several weeks (Löhrl, 1977).

GREAT SPOTTED WOODPECKER
Dendrocopos major

Key facts:
Breeding season: April to June
Clutch size: 5–6 eggs
Incubation period: 10–13 days
Fledging period: 20–24 days
Number of breeding attempts: 1 per year
Typical lifespan: not known
Population size: 140,000
Conservation: Green-listed

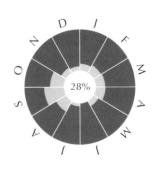

The Great Spotted Woodpecker is a species whose use of gardens has increased significantly since the 1970s, with rural sites seeing the biggest change. Greater use of gardens appears to be the result of an increasing population more widely, with periods of increase evident during the late 1970s and again from the late 1990s through to 2010. Examination of atlas data (Balmer *et al.*, 2013) indicates that the increase has been fairly uniform across the woodpecker's British range, with a degree of range expansion seen within Scotland and the unexpected colonisation of Ireland, which had previously lacked any resident woodpeckers.

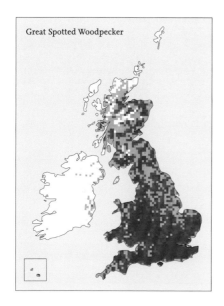

Great Spotted Woodpecker

Genetic studies of the birds in Ireland suggest a British origin, which is surprising given the sedentary nature of the British population (McDevitt *et al.*, 2011). This contrasts with Great Spotted Woodpecker populations in northern Scandinavia, which are prone to eruptive movements. Ken Smith has suggested that the increase seen within the UK, and the move into less wooded habitats, may be linked to the decline in Starling populations and an associated reduction in competition for nest sites, leading to better woodpecker breeding success (Smith, 2005).

As you might predict, the use of gardens by Great Spotted Woodpeckers is determined by the presence of mature trees and deciduous woodland nearby, something that favours rural and larger suburban gardens over those that are more urban in nature. Woodpeckers may utilise woodland patches within more urbanised landscapes, but patch area, canopy structure, species composition and the degree of nearby urbanisation all influence patch use and woodpecker abundance (Myczko *et al.*, 2014). The use of garden feeding stations, to which woodpeckers are attracted by peanuts and suet-based products, also has a strong seasonal pattern, with a summer peak. This peak matches the period when young woodpeckers leave the nest and are brought to feeding stations by their parents. It seems likely that feeding stations provide a reliable food source for young birds as they move towards independence.

Great Spotted Woodpeckers may also be attracted to gardens by nest boxes containing broods of Blue Tit or Great Tit chicks, which may provide much-needed protein for the woodpecker's own young. Individual woodpeckers may first tap a nest box before attempting to break in, and it has been suggested that this behaviour might be an extension of that used when testing dead wood for the presence of beetle larvae. If the chicks inside the box respond to the tapping, then the woodpecker will either enlarge the entrance hole or, more commonly, drill a fresh hole in the side of the box. The role of the Great Spotted Woodpecker as a predator of smaller birds has been examined by a number of researchers and it has been identified as one of a small number of specialist predators (in this context a reference to chick predation) to be found within the urban environment

FIG 137. Great Spotted Woodpeckers are known nest predators, breaking into wooden nest boxes to predate young chicks. (Jill Pakenham)

(Sorace & Gustin, 2009). Eggs may also feature in Great Spotted Woodpecker diet, but it is dead wood invertebrates that are the staple food during the breeding season, with tree seeds becoming more important during the autumn and winter months. The size of the autumn crop of tree seeds may, as for several other garden bird species, determine the extent to which garden feeding stations are visited during the autumn months (Chamberlain *et al.*, 2007a). It also determines the eruptive movements seen in northern European populations (Linden *et al.*, 2011). It is unusual to see more than one Great Spotted Woodpecker visiting a garden feeding station outside of the breeding season; this is because the birds maintain individual feeding territories. Where these territories provide access to fat-rich suet products, breeding females may initiate their breeding attempts earlier than they otherwise would; supplementary food may also lead to increased productivity (Smith & Smith, 2013).

Male and female Great Spotted Woodpeckers can be distinguished from one another on the basis of their plumage, the male sporting a small patch of red on the back of his head, which is absent in the female. Juveniles have an extensive red crown, a feature that can lead to them being misidentified as the much scarcer and smaller Lesser Spotted Woodpecker *Dryobates minor*, a species that only rarely visits garden bird feeders. All ages of Great Spotted Woodpecker have some red under their tail – this being more pronounced in adult birds than it is in juveniles – whereas in Lesser Spotted Woodpecker these feathers are white with black spots.

RING-NECKED PARAKEET
Psittacula krameri

Key facts:
Breeding season: March to June
Clutch size: 3–4 eggs
Incubation period: 22–24 days
Fledging period: 40–50 days
Number of breeding attempts: 1 per year
Typical lifespan: not known
Population size: 8,600 pairs
Conservation: not listed

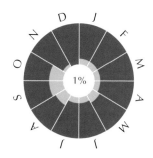

The sight of a Ring-necked Parakeet at a garden feeding station may deliver a sense of the exotic, welcomed by some but hated by others. This non-native member of the parrot family was introduced to the UK from its native range, which extends across subtropical Africa and Asia. It is thought that the current UK population is derived from two subspecies found on the Indian subcontinent (Pithon & Dytham, 2001). Popular as a caged bird, this parakeet has become established in a number of cities across the world, including London. Parakeets have probably been breeding in the wild in the UK since the late 1960s, and the species was added to category C of the British List in 1983 because of its feral and self-sustaining population. Since then, the population has expanded and huge roosting flocks may gather during the winter months at favoured suburban sites in Thanet (Kent), southeast London and to the west of London (Pithon & Dytham, 1999a; 2002).

Despite the increases in population size, we have yet to see any significant expansion in the range occupied; there is evidence that parakeets avoid areas of higher ground or those lacking in mature trees. Butler (2003) estimated

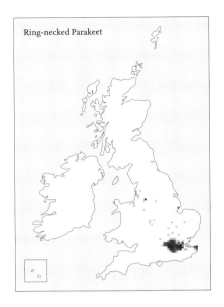

Ring-necked Parakeet

that over the previous decade the Ring-necked Parakeet population in Greater London had increased by 30 per cent per annum but that the range occupied had only increased at a rate of 0.4 km per year. Feeding opportunities do not appear to be a limiting factor, with birds taking a wide range of plant material in the UK and also making regular use of garden feeding stations. Similarly, nest site availability does not appear to be limiting (Pithon & Dytham, 1999b; Butler et al., 2013), so perhaps range expansion is inhibited by the communal roosting behaviour shown by this species. If communal roosting is important, and there is a strong tendency to use particular sites, then we may not see expansion until numbers at a roost become larger than the local feeding opportunities can support.

The presence of Ring-necked Parakeets could have consequences for native species, either through competition for nest sites or for feeding opportunities. A study on introduced Ring-necked Parakeets in Belgium suggests that they have the potential to reduce the abundance of Nuthatch through competition for nesting cavities (Strubbe & Matthysen, 2009). However, analysis of data from the UK Breeding Bird Survey failed to find any evidence for a significant impact on Nuthatch populations, or those of any other cavity-nesting species within the Parakeet's current range (Newson et al., 2011). It is possible, though, that competitive exclusion could be occurring at a minority of sites where the availability of suitable cavities is limiting, and this is something that needs further study.

Parakeet flocks can dominate garden feeders, which may reduce feeding opportunities for other garden birds through either the direct consumption of food or interference competition (where other species are less likely to feed at a site because of the presence of the parakeets). This is something that has been examined experimentally by researchers based at Imperial College and the Institute of Zoology in London. Using a combination of cage birds and broadcast calls, the researchers were able to test the potential impacts of the parakeets – and Great Spotted Woodpecker as a control – on the feeding behaviour of other species. The results demonstrated that the presence of parakeets significantly reduced feeding rates and increased the vigilance behaviour of smaller garden birds, compared with the woodpecker control. Perhaps most interestingly, of the visits made by smaller birds in the presence of a parakeet, feeding behaviour was more likely to occur at those sites within the parakeet's range than it was at sites elsewhere. This suggests that some degree of habituation has occurred within other garden birds living alongside these introduced parrots.

MAGPIE
Pica pica

Key facts:
Breeding season: March to June
Clutch size: 4–6 eggs
Incubation period: 21–22 days
Fledging period: 22–28 days
Number of breeding attempts: 1 per year
Typical lifespan: 5 years
Population size: 550,000 pairs
Conservation: Green-listed

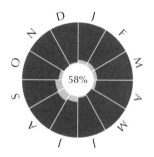

This bold and often conspicuous visitor greatly increased its use of garden feeding stations over a 20-year period from 1970 through to 1990, since when it has been largely stable. This pattern of change matches that seen within the wider countryside, with the recent period of stabilisation thought to reflect the saturation of suitable wider countryside breeding habitat. Over the longer term, we have seen the colonisation of urban habitats and Magpie populations appear to do well within our leafy suburbs, with their feeding and nesting opportunities. The distribution of Magpies within urban areas appears to be determined by the availability of nesting opportunities, the pattern and connectivity of favoured habitat, and the distribution of food resources (Tatner, 1982a; Kang *et al.*, 2012). Interestingly, a study of Magpie populations in France has revealed that the species is being lost from the wider countryside but is increasing in urban areas, leading to a rapid change in distribution (Chiron *et al.*, 2008).

Magpies are great opportunists, with a particularly broad diet, and they readily scavenge from the carcasses of animals and birds that have been the victims of road traffic. In this regard, Magpies play an important ecosystem service role; along with Carrion Crow and Red Fox, they remove carcasses from

Magpie

our streets. Research has shown that there is significantly greater depletion of urban carcass biomass in the presence of these three scavengers, removing up to 73 per cent of the carcass biomass present (Inger *et al.*, 2016). Magpies also take bird table scraps, invertebrates, fruit, seeds and small mammals (Tatner, 1983). However, it is their predation of the eggs and young of other bird species that attracts the most attention, leaving this member of the crow family unwelcome in many gardens. As we saw in Chapter 4, there is no evidence that Magpie predation has a significant impact at a wider level on songbird populations (Thomson *et al.*, 1998; Newson *et al.*, 2010; Madden *et al.*, 2015). Work in the suburbs of Paris has examined the extent to which Magpie predation impacts on urban songbird populations (Chiron & Julliard, 2007). François Chiron & Romain Julliard found that Magpies had a very limited effect on songbird productivity, even for those species known to be sensitive to predation by corvids.

Studies of Magpie diet in the city of Prague and the surrounding area underline that although nestling diet differs between urban and non-urban sites, it is still dominated by invertebrate prey (mainly beetles). Urban Magpies are active foragers, taking food while walking across short vegetation, but they will also use perches from which to target potential prey. Areas of short vegetation appear to be of particular importance to urban Magpies, more so than seen in rural populations. Food availability within urban areas may exert an influence on Magpie breeding success, as the work of Antonov & Atanasova (2003) demonstrates. Magpies in the city of Sofia, Bulgaria, were found to lay significantly earlier than those in a nearby rural area – suggestive of the similar effects of supplementary food on the timing of breeding seen in other species (see Chapters 2 and 3). However, while the probability of breeding success was significantly higher in the urban area – due to lower rates of nest predation – urban birds produced fewer fledglings per successful pair, suggesting that chick food supply may have been limiting (Antonov & Atanasova, 2003). It is worth just noting that the proportion of urban-nesting Magpies in Manchester that

FIG 138. Magpie diet is broad and this has allowed the species to adapt well to the offerings available at garden feeding stations. (John Harding)

renovate an old nest for a breeding attempt is much higher than seen in rural populations. Since it is quicker and easier to renovate an old nest than build a new one, the presence of this behaviour in urban pairs may be responsible for some of the difference in the timing of breeding attempts between urban and non-urban sites (Tatner, 1982b). Another aspect in which the breeding ecology of Manchester's Magpies differs from those of rural birds is in the high frequency and high success rate of repeat breeding attempts following an initial failure.

Urban-nesting Magpies show differences in the choice of their nest sites. The relative nest height of Magpies nesting in Finnish cities, for example, is lower than it is at rural sites, either suggesting that nesting opportunities in taller trees are more limiting in urban sites or that the species is reacting to the lower levels of persecution encountered here (Jokimäki *et al.*, 2017). Even so, Finnish city-living Magpies still prefer breeding sites with greater levels of green cover and which are less built up in nature, a pattern repeated here in the UK. The Magpie is a successful colonist of UK gardens and the wider built environment, and this is now a pattern that is also being seen elsewhere in the world.

JAY
Garrulus glandarius

Key facts:
Breeding season: April to July
Clutch size: 4–6 eggs
Incubation period: 16–17 days
Fledging period: 21–22 days
Number of breeding attempts: 1 per year
Typical lifespan: 4 years
Population size: 170,000 territories
Conservation: Green-listed.

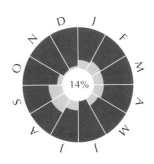

Although a resident species, the Jay is most noticeable in gardens during late autumn, when individuals travel over larger distances to collect and store acorns for the coming winter months. BTO Garden BirdWatch data also show a second peak in garden use during June. A preference for deciduous woodland is reflected in the greater use of rural gardens than suburban or urban ones, and the Jay's distribution at the national level also reflects this association, being scarce in upland areas and in the open landscapes of the Fens. National

Jay

populations have fluctuated over time, with a notable decline during the 1990s, but they have since recovered.

Jays are more secretive in their use of gardens than some of our other corvids, and many of their visits may go unnoticed. As alluded to above, acorns are an important component of Jay diet and individuals will spend significant amounts of time collecting acorns once they become available. Several acorns may be carried at once, the bird caching these in tree crevices, under roots and in small holes dug in the ground. Caching behaviour, as noted elsewhere, enables birds to take advantage of a seasonal abundance

FIG 139. The use of garden feeding stations by Jays varies with the availability of acorn crops more widely. (John Harding)

of a particular food type, providing that it remains edible when stored for a prolonged period. It is also important to cache food items where they are less likely to be found and taken by other birds, including other Jays. Experimental studies have found that Jays preferentially cache at a distance when they are being watched collecting acorns by others of their kind; presumably, this reduces the chance that they will be seen hiding the acorns, making the cache more secure (Legg *et al.*, 2016). The same researchers also found that Jays were more likely to hide an acorn behind an opaque object than a transparent one when being watched (Legg & Clayton, 2014).

It has been calculated that a single Jay may collect and cache 5,000 acorns during the period over which they are readily available. The fact that not all of these will be found means that Jays help in the dispersal of acorns and the establishment of new oak saplings some distance from their parent tree. Volatility in the size of the acorn crop appears to be behind the fluctuations seen in garden use through the weekly surveys of BTO Garden BirdWatch. Garden reporting rates in October can fluctuate between 10 and 20 per cent of sites. The availability of acorns is also behind the occasional eruptive movements common to Jay populations in parts of Scandinavia. In some years, a shortage of acorns can bring about large-scale movements of Scandinavian Jays across other parts of Europe, including to the UK (Selås, 2017). One of the most significant of such movements occurred in 1983, resulting in thousands of migrating individuals arriving here. When there has been a particularly large acorn crop, Scandinavian Jays stay put, using hoarded acorns not only during winter, but also as food for their young in the following breeding season. Nestling diet is more typically dominated by caterpillars and beetles, the former largely comprised of oak-feeding moth species (Owen, 1956). At other times of the year, garden-visiting Jays will feed on invertebrates, with small mammals and the eggs of other birds also featuring within the diet. Open-nesting species, like Blackbird and Song Thrush, may be susceptible to nest predation by Jays and it is likely that a proportion of the nesting attempts made by these species in rural gardens will be predated by Jays each year.

JACKDAW
Corvus monedula

Key facts:
Breeding season: April to June
Clutch size: 4–5 eggs
Incubation period: 21–22 days
Fledging period: 22–28 days
Number of breeding attempts: 1 per year
Typical lifespan: 5 years
Population size: 1.3 million pairs
Conservation: Green-listed

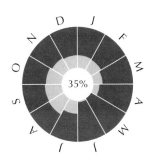

Jackdaw, the smallest member of the crow family in UK gardens, is a species that is commonly found breeding in a range of cavity sites, from chimneys to tree hollows. Although primarily a bird of the open countryside, the Jackdaw has made increasing use of gardens and garden nest sites over recent years. This is evident from both BTO Garden BirdWatch and Garden Bird Feeding Survey data. Despite their omnivorous diet, Jackdaws appear to have been less successful in penetrating the urban environment than either Magpie or Carrion Crow, something that is thought to be linked to a lack of the moth and fly larvae that are favoured when feeding their young. Interestingly, the BTO Garden BirdWatch reporting rate for the species shows a pronounced peak in May and June, when Jackdaws will be busy feeding their young.

Jackdaw

Another feature of Jackdaw breeding ecology linked to food availability is the pattern of incubation. While most garden birds initiate incubation with the last or the penultimate egg, Jackdaws initiate incubation part way through the laying period. This means that the eggs will hatch asynchronously, rather than all at the same time, resulting in a brood of chicks of mixed ages. If food conditions are poor during the chick-rearing period, then the smallest chicks will go unfed and potentially die, while the older chicks will be more likely to survive. The chances of a chick surviving through to fledging may also be shaped by its sex, particularly where there is a difference in size between the two sexes – something that is the case for Jackdaw. Work on a nest-box-using population in Wytham Woods, Oxfordshire, revealed a (statistically non-significant) female bias at both hatching and fledging, with broods produced late in the season significantly female biased. Female chicks, hatched towards the end of the season when conditions were poor, were more likely to fledge than male chicks, and overall male chicks had a higher mortality rate than females. The researchers concluded that the most likely cause of this difference was the higher energetic demands of the larger sex, resulting in increased levels of starvation (Arnold & Griffiths, 2003). One wonders if there might be larger bias evident within urban populations, where the availability of chick food may be more limiting than that seen in this wider countryside study population.

The challenges of rearing chicks may also be behind the long-term pair bond that is seen in Jackdaw. Birds usually pair for life, remaining together throughout the year, and are often easy to pick out when seen as part of a wider flock because paired individuals will tend to fly together. Both sexes invest in the pair bond by using various forms of social behaviour: males, for example, feed their mates throughout the year. Jackdaws nest semi-colonially, often resulting in birds occupying all of the accessible chimneys along a suburban street, and there is good evidence that the pairs come together to form a wider social unit. For example, work by Robin Kubitza has demonstrated that individuals actively seek out social ties and interactions with other members of their flock (Kubitza

FIG 140. Jackdaws are a familiar sight in many gardens, with pairs often nesting in house chimneys. (John Harding)

et al., 2015). It appears that there is a hierarchy to this wider social unit, something that has been studied in a semi-urban environment in the Netherlands (Verhulst *et al.*, 2014). Older Jackdaws often hold a higher rank within the group, their social status increasing with age but declining rapidly towards the end of their life. Other results from this study, namely those demonstrating that high-ranked individuals have a shorter lifespan, suggests that maintaining such status comes at a cost. It is not clear, however, whether the hierarchies differ between urban and non-urban environments.

The sharing of food between individuals is another interesting component of Jackdaw social behaviour, and one that is not limited to the form of courtship feeding discussed earlier. Work with captive Jackdaws suggests a level of food sharing that is greater than that reported for primates, with the behaviour most commonly seen in juveniles. The frequency of food sharing appears to decline as young birds age, stabilising at a low level at around four months old (de Kort *et al.*, 2003; 2006). Adult Jackdaws do, it seems, continue to share food, but this appears to be an infrequent behaviour. The sharing behaviour is directed most at individuals from whom food has been received previously, suggesting that it helps to build social bonds that may be important later in life.

ROOK
Corvus frugilegus

Key facts:
Breeding season: March to June
Clutch size: 4–5 eggs
Incubation period: 16–19 days
Fledging period: 30–36 days
Number of breeding attempts: 1 per year
Typical lifespan: 6 years
Population size: 990,000 pairs
Conservation: Green-listed

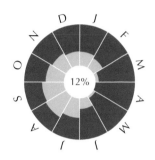

Of our widespread crows, the Rook is one that is least commonly reported from gardens. Where it does make use of gardens, these tend to be rural in nature, although there has been an increase in the use of suburban gardens during the winter months over the last few years. As a species of farmland and open grassland, with the habit of nesting colonially in the tops of mature trees, it is perhaps unsurprising that the Rook has not pushed far into the built environment. Where Rooks do appear in gardens, they have proved to be extremely

Rook

resourceful feeders, well able to pull up bird feeders or fat balls that have been suspended from a branch or bird table by string, or perhaps unhooking them so that they fall to the ground where they can be accessed. The colonial habits also mean that where a garden is visited, it tends to be visited by several individuals at the same time, something that can deter smaller birds from feeders.

There is a peak in garden use during March, April and May, a little earlier than the peak seen in Jackdaw and underlining the earlier nesting season of the former species. The communal nesting behaviour is focussed on rookeries, usually located

FIG 141. Not always welcome at garden feeding stations, these rather smart birds are resourceful and often entertaining visitors. (John Harding)

in farmland or woodland but which may sometimes be located in the mature trees found within larger rural gardens. The presence of a garden rookery can provide a fascinating insight into the lives of these birds and to the vast range of calls that they make throughout day and, to a lesser extent, night.

Urban populations occur in other European countries, with these being the particular focus of research work in Poland, where Rooks show a growing tendency to winter in cities. The Polish work has revealed how the use of urban food sources is shaped by weather conditions, with more birds feeding within cities during period of snow cover (Jadczyk & Drzeniecka-Osiadacz, 2013). Other work on these populations has explored the impacts of heavy metal and pesticide contamination (Orłowski *et al.*, 2009), and the risks to humans posed by diseases transmitted by the birds (Perec-Matysiak *et al.*, 2017).

Changes in Rook populations within the UK are now monitored annually through the Breeding Bird Survey, replacing the need for periodic surveys that attempted to count the number of occupied nests at rookeries. The Breeding Bird Survey data show a decline since 2000, although it should be noted that this comes after a long-term rise which, for example, saw a 40 per cent increase in abundance between 1975 and 1996 (Marchant & Gregory, 1999). There is evidence that some once larger rookeries have become fragmented because of persecution – Rooks are viewed by some farmers as an agricultural pest and their nests are shot out during the breeding season, something that may have facilitated the adoption of mature trees in gardens by smaller groups of birds. Whether we see a continued increase in the use of gardens is unclear, but given the habitat and dietary requirements of this bird, coupled with the declining rural population, this seems unlikely.

CARRION CROW
Corvus corone

Key facts:
Breeding season: April to July
Clutch size: 4–5 eggs
Incubation period: 18–19 days
Fledging period: 28–35 days
Number of breeding attempts: 1 per year
Typical lifespan: 4 years
Population size: 1 million territories
Conservation: Green-listed

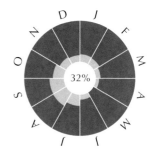

An ongoing and long-term increase in Carrion Crow populations within the UK has seen the expansion of crow populations in urban areas, bringing individuals into an increasing number of gardens. It is unclear as to why the population has increased so strongly year on year since the early 1970s, but it is thought that increases in breeding success, perhaps coupled with a reduction in the levels of persecution, may have been important. An omnivorous diet and the Carrion Crow's ability to adapt to a broad range of habitats may explain why this species has done so well within the built environment. There is good evidence that pairs with access to supplemented food produce more and heavier chicks (Richner, 1992), so it is tempting to speculate that new feeding opportunities have supported the period of population growth and colonisation of urban sites. Yom-Tov (1974), working around Newburgh in Aberdeenshire, demonstrated that provision of supplementary food led to improved chick survival, concluding that the spatial pattern of food availability was the most important factor in determining breeding success.

Another interesting feature to arise from the work of Heinz Richner and others working on Carrion Crows is the discovery of helpers at the nest. Richner

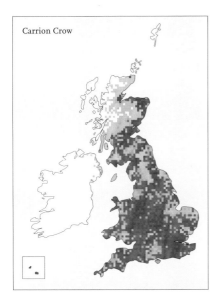

Carrion Crow

(1990), working on a population of marked individuals breeding in Lausanne in Switzerland, recorded three instances of helping at the nest, with each case occurring within his high-density urban study area. Cooperative breeding of this kind is known from about 3 per cent of bird species but the Carrion Crow is not considered a cooperative breeder across most of its range. In northern Spain, however, there is a well-studied population where cooperative breeding is widespread, with juvenile birds sometimes remaining on the natal territories until their second year and with groups of three or more birds

FIG 142. Many members of the crow family have adapted well to the built environment and the feeding opportunities that it presents. (Jill Pakenham)

found on nearly three-quarters of the territories (Baglione *et al.*, 2002). It isn't just juveniles remaining on their natal territory that is responsible for the helpers, since some individuals are immigrants to the territory on which they are helping. Baglione's study population is rural, rather than urban, so cooperative breeding in this species is clearly not restricted to the built environment. Baglione's review of published data on other European crow populations suggests that the occurrence of cooperative breeding isn't linked specifically to habitats containing a highly saturated set of breeding territories – which is what you might have predicted. Instead, Baglione *et al.* (2005) suggest that it is year-round residency that supports this cooperative behaviour. Territoriality in UK populations is principally a feature of the breeding season, but it would be interesting to see whether this remains the case for the growing urban population of Carrion Crows.

Outside of the breeding season, UK Carrion Crows often leave their breeding territories to feed elsewhere, sometimes forming small flocks or even joining larger mixed winter roosts with other corvids. A study carried out by the late John Harpum in Cheltenham found that the town's resident Carrion Crows tended to maintain their territories year round, but with the birds sometimes feeding in a communal area alongside other individuals that had arrived from the surrounding farmland. Attempts by individual birds to establish and hold breeding territories within the communal feeding area invariably failed, in part because of the levels of human disturbance but also because of the attentions of other crows (Harpum, 1985).

GOLDCREST
Regulus regulus

Key facts:
Breeding season: April to July
Clutch size: 7–12 eggs
Incubation period: 14–17 days
Fledging period: 16–21 days
Number of breeding attempts: 2 per year
Typical lifespan: 2 years
Population size: 520,000 territories
Conservation: Green-listed

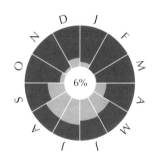

That Goldcrest is reported from just 6 per cent of the gardens participating in BTO Garden BirdWatch each week probably has something to do with this being a species that is easy to overlook, typically feeding within the canopy of trees and with a soft high-pitched song and call. Despite this, the Goldcrest is widely distributed across the UK and only absent from the open uplands and areas lacking suitable tree cover. There is a marked preference for mature conifer woodland during the breeding season, but individual pairs will also breed in solitary conifers present within other habitats, such as gardens, parks and churchyards. Gardens are visited throughout the year but it is during the winter months that this small bird is most likely to be seen.

Being so tiny presents significant challenges for this insectivorous bird, and UK populations are strongly shaped by winter weather. A run of cold winters can decimate the breeding population but the large clutch size, coupled with the potential for two breeding attempts per year, means that numbers can bounce back when conditions improve. UK Goldcrests are resident but a large influx of migrants

FIG 143. Goldcrests spend much of the day feeding high in the canopy, taking small insects and other invertebrates. (Mike Toms)

Goldcrest

reaches our shores from Scandinavia and Russia during the autumn months. That such a small bird can make such long journeys may seem incredible, and might have led to the unfounded belief that Goldcrests hitched a ride in the feathers of migrating Short-eared Owls *Asio flammeus* and Woodcock *Scolopax rusticola*. The speed at which Goldcrests make their migrations depends on the route used, the time pressure that they are under and the amount of fat reserves they are carrying. Those crossing the sea tend to travel more quickly, as do those migrating later in the autumn or carrying more fat reserves (Bojarinova *et al.*, 2008).

Garden use peaks during the second half of the winter and this is when individuals may turn to the suet-based products available at garden feeding stations. Data from the BTO's garden-based surveys underline the extent to which the use of gardens can vary from one year to the next, perhaps highlighting the volatility of Goldcrest populations and the impacts of winter weather. Surviving cold winter nights is a challenge for such a small bird and yet individuals have been recorded surviving temperatures as low as minus 25°C and fasting for at least 18 hours (Reinertsen *et al.*, 1988). It appears that rather than enter nocturnal hypothermia, as some authors have suggested, Goldcrests adopt a strategy of building up sufficient fat reserves during the daylight hours and then couple this with behaviours that reduce heat loss, such as roosting with other individuals and using cavities, roosting pouches and snow holes.

Gardens may also be used for nesting, the species attaching its deep, thick-walled cup of moss, lichen and spider webs to the underside of a conifer branch. Spruce and fir are preferred, though Yew and Ivy may also be used. The nest is lined with feathers, on which the large clutch of 7 to 12 eggs is laid. The clutch represents a significant investment for such a tiny bird, a feat made all the more remarkable by the fact that the female may initiate a second breeding attempt while her mate is still feeding the young from the first attempt.

BLUE TIT
Cyanistes caeruleus

Key facts:
Breeding season: April to June
Clutch size: 8–10 eggs
Incubation period: 12–16 days
Fledging period: 16–22 days
Number of breeding attempts: 1 per year
Typical lifespan: 3 years
Population size: 3.4 million territories
Conservation: Green-listed

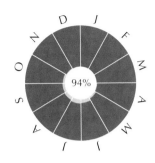

The Blue Tit is one of our most familiar garden birds, found in most gardens, including those located within our largest towns and cities. UK populations have undergone a long period of increase, though with occasional periods of stability, but since 2005 there has been something of a decline. Interestingly, Garden Bird Feeding Survey data show a long-term decline in the mean peak count for Blue Tits recorded using garden feeding stations during winter, a decline that extends back to when the survey started at the beginning of the 1970s. A pattern of decline is also evident within the weekly reporting rate figures produced from BTO Garden BirdWatch since 1995. The causes of the long-term increase at a

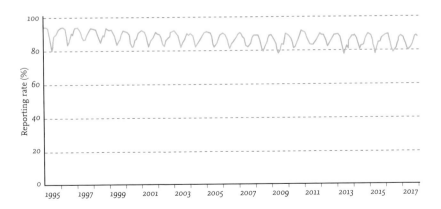

FIG 144. The consistency in garden use by this species, coupled with the strong seasonal pattern, is evident from the weekly records collected through BTO Garden BirdWatch. (BTO)

Blue Tit

UK level are thought to be linked to the increasing availability of food in gardens during the winter months, coupled with increased availability of nest boxes – the latter likely to have reduced levels of egg and chick predation. The different pattern being seen in gardens might reflect increasing competition at garden feeding stations from other species; we have, after all, seen the garden bird community using feeding stations increase significantly since the 1970s. Greater competition at feeders may have brought about a behavioural response, such that Blue Tits no longer dominate feeders in the way that they once did.

Another long-term change evident in Blue Tit populations is the advancement seen within the breeding season. BTO Nest Record Scheme data show that mean first egg dates have advanced by over a week since 1968, a pattern seen in a number of other garden bird species and linked to global climate change (Crick *et al.*, 1997). Our meta-analysis of how demographic parameters differed between urban and non-urban habitats (see Chapter 3) indicates that urban Blue Tits generally begin breeding earlier than their non-urban counterparts, and that they consistently have smaller clutches (Chamberlain *et al.*, 2009a). Cowie & Hinsley's 1988 study into chick provisioning in suburban gardens suggested that these birds brought back fewer caterpillars than those breeding in woodland (as reported by earlier studies). Cowie & Hinsley also noted that nestling diet changed with age; proportionally more spiders were fed to young nestlings, while older nestlings received more artificial food and aphids.

More recent work, by Christopher Pollock and colleagues, underlines that urban Blue Tit populations are less productive than their woodland counterparts and that this is due to a reduced availability of the caterpillar prey provisioned to chicks. Pollock *et al.* (2017) found that there was a significant reduction in the availability of caterpillars at urban sites, resulting in parent birds provisioning fewer caterpillars to their chicks, though suburban birds fared somewhat better. Nevertheless, the reproductive success of both urban and suburban birds was lower than that of the woodland populations studied, with reproductive

FIG 145. Young Blue Tits can be separated from their parents by the presence of pale yellow cheeks, as opposed to the white of adults. (John Harding)

success itself found to be positively associated with the volume of provisioned caterpillars. Stable isotope analysis work confirmed that the urban diet was fundamentally different to that of woodland populations.

Watch a garden feeding station and you may well see no more than half a dozen Blue Tits feeding at any one time; it would be easy to think that these same six individuals were the ones resident in your garden and the only ones to use the feeding station. However, those involved in bird ringing and setting nets at garden feeding stations would be able to tell you that 100 or more different individuals could be using your feeding station during the course of a single day. This underlines that individual Blue Tits move between feeding stations, travelling from garden to garden. Such movements are more pronounced during the winter months, when birds are not holding breeding territories, and recent work has determined that the extent of such movements, together with their spatial pattern, is shaped by the habitat connectivity present within the local area. Movement between gardens and across towns and cities is facilitated by the presence of suitable vegetation cover but reduced by the presence of roads or other unsuitable habitat (Cox *et al.*, 2016).

GREAT TIT
Parus major

Key facts:
Breeding season: April to June
Clutch size: 6–9 eggs
Incubation period: 14 days
Fledging period: 19 days
Number of breeding attempts: 1,
    sometimes 2, per year
Typical lifespan: 3 years
Population size: 2.5 million territories
Conservation: Green-listed

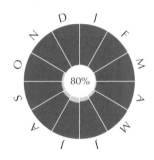

The Great Tit is another member of the woodland bird community to have taken to gardens and the feeding and nesting opportunities on offer, making this one of our most familiar garden bird species. Garden use is greatest during the winter months, though there is variation between years and this has been linked to the availability of beechmast within the wider environment (Chamberlain *et al.*, 2007b). In those years when the beechmast crop has been poor, garden use is increased. Great Tit populations have generally increased since monitoring began in the 1960s. As with Blue Tit, this increase has been punctuated with several brief periods of stability or even slight decline, and there is evidence of a more substantial decline since 2006. The timing of this decline matches the first record of an emerging form of avian pox (see Chapter 4), characterised by large lesions and seen to have spread northwards across the UK from a point of origin on England's south coast (Lawson *et al.*, 2012b). There is currently no evidence linking the emergence of this disease with the population decline seen, but this is something that could potentially be tested using data from Garden Wildlife Health and the Breeding Bird Survey.

Great Tit laying dates have advanced by 10 days since 1968, and we see a similar pattern of differences in the timing of breeding between urban and non-urban habitats to those seen in Blue Tit and mentioned earlier. Urban breeding may be more challenging for Great Tit than is the case for Blue Tit, presumably because of the additional resources required for the former species, with its larger body size. Paired studies of Great Tits nesting in urban and non-urban habitats have revealed that non-urban nestlings are significantly heavier than urban ones, suggestive of the lower availability of preferred prey within the built

Great Tit

environment. Since nestling weight has been shown to influence future prospects in Great Tit populations (Tinbergen & Boerlijst, 1990), you might predict garden-nesting Great Tits to be less successful than their woodland counterparts. However, the greater availability of food in gardens during the difficult winter months may balance things out or, perhaps, even tip the balance in favour of urban-born birds. This is something that requires further study.

One of the most interesting areas of recent study, in relation to the use of gardens and the wider urban environment by Great Tits, is that of the behavioural differences that exist between individuals. Great Tits have been used as a model for the study of personality in songbirds for some time, with the work revealing that individuals have distinct personalities; some individuals are bolder in their behaviour, quicker to explore new opportunities and more likely to take risks (Verbeek *et al.*, 1994). Individuals differ in the way they explore novel environments (termed 'fast' versus 'slow' by researchers), and individuals at the two extremes of the 'fast'–'slow' trait use different approaches when dealing with novel situations. 'Fast' explorers have an active coping strategy and are bold, aggressive and largely insensitive to external stimuli; in contrast, 'slow' explorers are shy, relatively less aggressive and sensitive to external stimuli. 'Slow' explorers are more readily able to adjust their behaviour to changes in their environment (Verbeek *et al.*, 1996; 1999; Marchetti & Drent, 2000). What is interesting about these different personality traits is that, within woodland populations at least, selection on a personality trait fluctuates across years, such that in some years one trait is favoured but in other years it is the other (Dingemanse *et al.*, 2004). Annual survival of adult individuals is related to this personality trait, which is heritable, resulting in differential survival between years. Examination of the environmental conditions placing selection pressure on the different traits suggests that food availability – in the form of beechmast – shapes the competitive regimes of individuals within the population and maintains genetic variation in personality types present. The question of whether such personality differences might be important in urban environments

FIG 146. Behavioural traits that differ between individuals have been found in Great Tits, with these traits shaped by environmental conditions. (John Harding)

has yet to be resolved; however, it has been demonstrated that that urban Great Tits are more aggressive than rural individuals, and show greater trait flexibility, features that may be important in securing and holding urban territories (Hardman & Dalesman, 2018).

It is also just worth noting the occurrence of a melanistic plumage abnormality that has been seen in some Great Tit populations here in the UK. These individuals tend to show black cheek patches and lack the usual white feathering seen in the wings and tail (Sage, 1994). There are records of such individuals extending back to the 1940s, with these early records centred on Esher in Surrey. More recent records show a wider distribution across Surrey and into neighbouring counties, but there is no evidence to suggest that the abnormality is increasing within the population. Instead, it appears to have persisted at a very low level for a number of decades.

COAL TIT
Periparus ater

Key facts:
Breeding season: April to June
Clutch size: 8–10 eggs
Incubation period: 14–16 days
Fledging period: 18–20 days
Number of breeding attempts: 1–2 per year
Typical lifespan: 2 years
Population size: 680,000 territories
Conservation: Green-listed

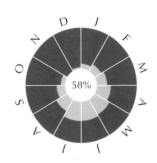

Coal Tits are most often seen taking food from hanging feeders and then retreating to eat it elsewhere, rather than remaining on the feeder's perch. This reflects their small size and low rank within the garden bird community – they are quickly displaced from feeders by larger and more dominant species. Widespread across the UK, their distribution reflects a clear association with coniferous woodland, which is their preferred breeding habitat. The population increase seen through to the mid-1970s probably results from an increasing area of mature conifer plantations, since when the population has been largely stable. There is evidence of a recent downturn in the population trend since 2011, something that is evident across all parts of the UK. Long-term changes in the pattern of garden use are similar, though with pronounced variation between winters that has been linked to the availability of Sitka Spruce seed in the wider environment (McKenzie *et al.*, 2007 – see Chapter 2).

Coal Tits are one of several species that regular take food from garden feeders and then cache it elsewhere for later use. This behaviour has been studied in detail in a laboratory-based experiment using wild caught

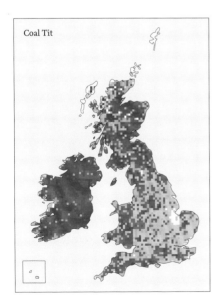

Coal Tit

FIG 147. The use of garden feeding stations by Coal Tits is strongly influenced by the availability of favoured conifer seeds within the wider environment. (Jill Pakenham)

individuals. The study, by Lucinda Male and Tom Smulders, demonstrates that the Coal Tit's ability to remember where it has cached seeds lasts for less than six weeks, a finding that is consistent with work on other tit species (Male & Smulders, 2007). It is known that cached seed can be important for tits much later into the winter, so how is this found? Male & Smulders' work indicates that Coal Tits have clear preferences for the types of site used to cache seed; while they may not be able to remember where all of their cached seed is located, they appear to be able to use knowledge of their site preferences to focus foraging efforts towards those sites more likely to contain cached food.

Food caches are likely to be important for Coal Tits living within forest habitats in the northern parts of their breeding range, particularly because their relatively small body size makes them vulnerable to periods of bad weather and the lack of foraging opportunities associated with short winter days. Examination of the daily pattern of feeding behaviour in individual Coal Tits, living in different parts of their breeding range, has highlighted that Spanish Coal Tits delay laying down additional body reserves until later in the day than is the case for Scottish Coal Tits (Polo *et al.*, 2007). These differences in fattening regime were linked to differences in day length, with individuals responding directly to the photoperiod experienced and making fine-scale adjustments to energy reserves on the basis of the external environment and their own body condition (lighter birds put on mass more rapidly at dawn than heavier individuals). The patterns of mass gain within urban populations, with access to predictable sources of food at garden feeding stations, are likely to differ from those of individuals living within the forests of northern Britain.

Coal Tits will occasionally use nest boxes located within the garden environment, something that is likely to be shaped by both the presence locally of coniferous trees and by competition from Blue Tits and Great Tits, both of which may exclude their smaller relative from suitable nest sites. Many of the natural nest sites used by Coal Tits tend to be located low to ground; experimental studies demonstrate that this is the result of competition, since Coal Tits prefer to use nest sites located 20 feet or more above the ground. The nest itself is similar to those of Blue Tit and Great Tit, though feathers are rarely used, and (on average) the cup is deeper with taller sides (Lambrechts *et al.*, 2016).

HOUSE MARTIN
Delichon urbicum

Key facts:
Breeding season: May to September
Clutch size: 4–5 eggs
Incubation period: 14–16 days
Fledging period: 19–25 days
Number of breeding attempts: 2, possibly 3, per year
Typical lifespan: 2 years
Population size: 510,000
Conservation: Amber-listed

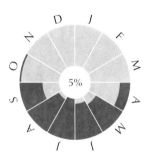

The House Martin has a very strong association with houses, other buildings and artificial structures, such as bridges. The broad range of structures used for breeding underlines that it is the buildings themselves, coupled with the local abundance of favoured invertebrate prey, that is important rather than the garden habitat itself. Nevertheless, the presence of a colony of breeding House Martins is something of which many garden birdwatchers are rightly proud, though not everybody views these summer visitors with the same level of respect. Despite the apparent accessibility of the species, House Martin populations are difficult to monitor accurately and there is a great deal of uncertainty around the size and trend of the UK population. Placement on the Amber List of Birds of Conservation Concern was triggered by figures from the combined Common Birds Census/

House Martin

Breeding Bird Survey datasets, which suggest long-term decline at a UK level. More detailed examination of the figures, coupled with information from Bird Atlas 2007–11, suggests that populations in Soctland may be increasing, while those in southern England are in sharp decline (Balmer *et al.*, 2013). The lack of certainty around these figures prompted the BTO to carry out a national House Martin survey in 2015, the results from which are due to be published soon. More widely, there appears to have been an ongoing and widespread decline in House Martin populations across Europe, evident since 1980.

These summer visitors return to the UK during late April or early May, with individuals occupying nest sites used the previous year. Such sites usually only require a few running repairs but where nests have fallen away or contain the dead remains of broods that failed to get away the previous season, birds will need to rebuild. Each nest, which is built from the base up using small pellets of mud, is constructed over a period of one to two weeks. Birds may have to collect up to 1,000 beakfuls of mud to make their nest and during periods of dry weather it can prove very difficult for them to find suitable sources. A detailed study of a House Martin colony at Gaast in the Netherlands (Piersma, 2013) found that the first nests to be occupied each year were those old nests that had survived the winter. Even though the use of these nests did not result in earlier incubation or chick rearing, they hosted a much higher percentage of multiple broods than was the case for newly constructed nests, and they were more likely to be claimed by older birds. Earlier nesting may not be possible in this species because of insufficient availability of favoured prey (Bryant, 1975). Interestingly, you would predict that old nests would contain a greater number of nest parasites, which should make them less attractive to the birds.

It has been found that conditions on the African wintering grounds can influence the breeding success of individuals during the following breeding season. Work in Spain revealed that more experienced males, which had wintered within habitats associated with high levels of rainfall, returned in better condition and produced more offspring, an example of 'carry-over effects' from one season

FIG 148. House Martin nests may be targeted by House Sparrows, with whom they compete. (Tom Streeter)

and location to another (López-Calderón *et al.*, 2017). Exactly where our breeding House Martins winter within Africa is unclear. It has been suggested that they primarily winter over areas of moist montane forest, but recent work looking at stable isotope ratios in House Martin feather samples suggests that this might not be the case. The stable isotope ratios found by Karl Evans and colleagues are similar to those found in several migrant species that use relatively dry and open habitats on their wintering grounds (Evans *et al.*, 2012).

Even once the nest has been constructed, breeding pairs face further challenges. It is known, for example, that House Sparrows will take over occupied House Martin nests, something that can be a particular problem at some sites. A number of other cavity-nesting species have been recorded using House Martin nests, including Blue Tit (Turzańska-Pietras, 2017). Others may be targeted by predators, including Tawny Owl, which pull open or dislodge the nest in order to access their contents (Zalewski, 1994). Another factor influencing the breeding success of House Martins is the availability of favoured invertebrate prey, such as aphids, small flies and other aerial insects. Clutch size, which declines through the breeding season, is correlated with the abundance of aphids in spring, and second clutches are more frequent when there is a high availability of invertebrate prey during June. Bryant (1975) found that House Martin pairs rearing only a single brood in a given year did so in July when food availability was greatest. Food availability is also the primary driver of chick growth, at least for first broods, and may also shape recruitment of these chicks into the population.

LONG-TAILED TIT
Aegithalos caudatus

Key facts:
Breeding season: March to June
Clutch size: 6–9 eggs
Incubation period: 14–16 days
Fledging period: 14–17 days
Number of breeding attempts: 1 per year
Typical lifespan: 2 years
Population size: 330,000 territories
Conservation: Green-listed

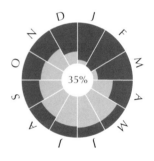

Long-tailed Tits almost invariably visits gardens in small groups and it is unusual to see an individual on its own. Garden use peaks during the second half of the winter and is at it lowest during the breeding season. The numbers using gardens during the winter months increased markedly from 1990 until 2008, according to data from the BTO Garden Bird Feeding Survey, since when they seem to have stabilised. This pattern reflects the wider national trend in breeding populations, which were at a low point following the severe winters of the early 1960s, and again during a run of cold winters in the 1970s, but which then increased through to 2010. As we have alluded to for several other species, cold winter weather can present a particular challenge for small birds, unable to lay down extensive reserves of fat.

The breeding behaviour of this species has already been touched upon in Chapter 3, where it was noted that Long-tailed Tits operate a kin-selected

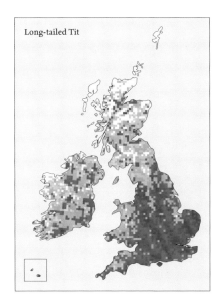

Long-tailed Tit

cooperative breeding system. Individuals that have failed with their own breeding attempts turn to help other, related individuals. This helping behaviour is most commonly seen between brothers, although a small minority of the helpers are female or may even be unrelated (Russell & Hatchwell, 2001; Nam *et al.*, 2010). Once the young have fledged, Long-tailed Tits may be encountered in small flocks, typically numbering from 5 to 25 individuals. These flocks forage widely during the day and then, come evening, huddle together in an overnight roost, the birds forming a linear group along a branch within suitable cover (Hatchwell *et al.*, 2009).

Flocks typically include individuals from several family groups, together with other, unrelated, individuals. Flock membership is not fixed and individuals (including both adults and juveniles) may switch between groups, with a tendency for dispersal into flocks containing fewer relatives (Napper & Hatchwell, 2016).

While kin selection appears to play an important role in many aspects of Long-tailed Tit ecology, it has been found to be of less importance when it comes to roosting behaviour. An individual's position within the roost is important, with Hatchwell *et al.* (2009) finding that those individuals occupying peripheral positions within a roost lose significantly more mass overnight than those occupying the more favourable central positions. Given that, on average, roosting Long-tailed Tits lose about 9 per cent of their body mass overnight, this represents a significant cost. Claire Napper and colleagues, working on a captive population of Long-tailed Tits, found that the location of an individual within the linear roost was dependent on an individual's position in the dominance hierarchy, with the effect of kinship dependent on an individual's size. Males were generally dominant over females, and individuals were more likely to occupy a preferred position if they were male and of high status (Napper *et al.*, 2013). One of the consequences of communal roosting is that it may facilitate the transmission of ectoparasites from one individual to another. That this is the case in Long-tailed Tits has been demonstrated by Roger Jovani and Guillermo Blanco, who found that feather mite abundance was more similar within flocks than between

FIG 149. Long-tailed Tits usually feed within the canopy of trees or hedgerow shrubs, but they may sometimes be seen feeding on the ground at garden feeding stations. (John Harding)

them (Jovani & Blanco, 2000). Within a flock, it was those individuals that were larger and in better body condition that had the greatest abundance of mites, perhaps reflecting their position at the centre of the roosting line.

Long-tailed Tits are more strongly insectivorous than the true tits, but they have been reported to take small seeds and fat from garden feeding stations. Small insects and spiders are taken from the canopies of trees and taller shrubs, the birds working through the leaves, buds and outer branches as they search for prey. While these foraging parties may cover a distance of 7 km or more during a day (Gaston, 1973), UK populations are largely sedentary in habits. Elsewhere within their wider breeding range, Long-tailed Tit populations may make massive eruptive movements or undertake more regular migrations (Bojarinova *et al.*, 2016). Very occasionally, such movements can result in the appearance of the 'white-headed' individuals of the race *caudatus* in the UK, including several records from gardens.

BLACKCAP
Sylvia atricapilla

Key facts:
Breeding season: April to July
Clutch size: 4–5 eggs
Incubation period: 11–12 days
Fledging period: 11–12 days
Number of breeding attempts: 2 per year
Typical lifespan: 2 years
Population size: 1.1 million territories
Conservation: Green-listed

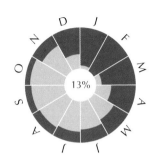

Although traditionally viewed as a summer visitor to the UK, the Blackcap is now a regular visitor to gardens during the winter months, a pattern supported by examination of data from BTO Garden BirdWatch, for which peak garden use occurs during February. The reason for the significant increase in our wintering Blackcap population, and its association with garden feeding stations, has been covered in detail in an earlier chapter of this book, but it is worth underlining the important role that the provision of supplementary food has played in

Blackcap

driving a microevolutionary change in migration behaviour. While some of the Blackcaps breeding in the UK do remain here in the winter, most depart for wintering grounds located in southern Europe and into North Africa; instead, it is individuals from the central European breeding population who dominate at UK bird tables during the winter months (Plummer *et al.*, 2015).

Blackcaps wintering within the UK favour gardens located in the southwest of Britain and those located within more urbanised areas, with a regular supply of food. Although it is not known whether the same individuals return to the same UK

FIG 150. Increasing numbers of Blackcaps now winter in UK gardens, the result of microevolution. (John Harding)

gardens in subsequent years, work in Spain demonstrates that fidelity to a wintering site does occur in this species (Cuadrado *et al.*, 1995), even though some individuals appear to adopt a more transitory approach (Belda *et al.*, 2007). Individuals frequenting hanging feeders and bird tables often show aggression towards other species, sometimes even taking on birds as large as Starling and Blackbird (Leach, 1981).

The Blackcaps wintering in UK gardens appear to arrive in the UK from October, though the main movement into gardens happens later in the winter. This suggests that birds feed within the wider countryside on hedgerow fruits and only move into gardens once the availability of these declines. Urban- and garden-using Blackcaps also feed on fruit and berries, though with those feeding at bird tables additionally taking suet products and sunflower hearts, and it has been shown that these wintering warblers are important seed dispersers for both native and non-native plants and shrubs (Cruz *et al.*, 2013). Additionally, there are records of Blackcaps feeding on the nectar of non-native plants, including Kniphofia, established in UK gardens. Feeding on nectar in this way appears to be a fairly common behaviour in some *Sylvia* warbler populations migrating through the Mediterranean, though with other plant species targeted, including *Brassica fruticulosa, Ferula communis* and *Anagyris foetida* (Schwilch *et al.*, 2001; Ortega-Olivencia *et al.*, 2005).

Small numbers of Blackcaps breed in UK gardens, typically favouring those that are rural in nature and which have areas of suitable scrubby cover in which to nest. Favoured nesting sites include brambles or nettle patches with sturdier vegetation growing through them. Urban gardens may sometimes be used – Blackcaps almost certainly bred within a large bramble and nettle patch that occupied the narrow town centre garden next to mine in two successive years, and in other years males regular sang for a few days when passing through on spring passage. Each male will build several rather flimsy 'cock nests', one of which will be selected and completed by his mate, assuming that he is able to attract one. The completed nest is a neat cup of grass, sometimes with added moss and often decorated with pieces of plant down; this is then lined with finer grasses, rootlets and hair. As with other *Sylvia* warblers, Blackcap chicks grow quickly and are able to leave the nest a week after hatching if disturbed by a predator. This behaviour is thought to increase the chicks' chances of survival if the nest is about to be predated.

NUTHATCH
Sitta europaea

Key facts:
Breeding season: April to June
Clutch size: 6–8 eggs
Incubation period: 15–16 days
Fledging period: 23–25 days
Number of breeding attempts: 1 per year
Typical lifespan: 2 years
Population size: 220,000 territories
Conservation: Green-listed

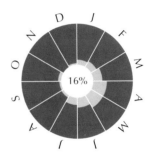

This striking garden visitor is most commonly reported from garden feeding stations located near to areas of deciduous woodland and within a breeding range that extends across most of England and Wales. Over recent years, there has been a northwards expansion in breeding range, seeing the Nuthatch arrive at bird tables and feeders in southern Scotland, something very evident from the weekly data collected by BTO Garden BirdWatchers living within the country. This pattern of change in garden use is supported by long-term trend data for wider countryside populations, where the species has been increasing steadily since the 1970s. Although the reasons for this increase are unclear, work elsewhere in Europe suggests that food supply might be important (Wesołowski & Stawarczyk, 1991). The availability of favoured tree seeds certainly appears to be important during the autumn months here in the UK, with the use of garden feeders found to be determined by the size of the beechmast crop elsewhere (Chamberlain *et al.*, 2007a). Treeless areas and larger urban centres are generally avoided, but the presence of urban parks may allow some pairs to

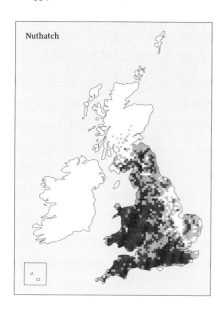

Nuthatch

establish themselves within larger conurbations, such as London. There is, however, concern that a growing Ring-necked Parakeet population might impact on Nuthatch populations by competitively excluding pairs from nest cavities (Strubbe & Matthysen, 2009).

Nuthatches may occasionally occupy garden nest boxes, typically plastering mud around the entrance hole if it is larger than they prefer. Some birds will also use mud to seal the lid of the box shut, preventing those wishing to monitor the nesting attempt from doing so. The nest itself is rather beautiful, being lined loosely with bark and dead leaves. The choice of materials (and also the extent to which mud is used) has been found to be determined by how available these elements are within 100 m of the nest site (Cantarero et al., 2015). The aggressive behaviour of this bird, sometimes evident at garden feeding stations, is also reflected in the strongly territorial behaviour exhibited by a breeding pair, who will additionally defend their territory throughout the year and drive newly fledged young out of the territory very soon after leaving the nest. Although the male takes the greater role in defence of the territory, both members of the pair play their part and females will readily call, display and attack intruders (Nad'o et al., 2018). Territory sizes tend to average between 1.46 and 2.93 ha in high-quality habitat (woodland), though comparable figures for pairs breeding in larger gardens are lacking. Pairs tend to occupy territories with higher densities of trees and tree cavities, presumably because these offer more foraging opportunities and reduce competition for nest sites (Kašová et al., 2014).

With their strong feet and claws, Nuthatches are able to forage on tree trunks and branches, searching for insects and spiders. During the autumn and winter, beechmast, acorns and Hazel *Corylus avellana* nuts become more important and this is when the strong chisel-like beak becomes particularly effective. Individual Nuthatches often wedge nuts and seeds in cracks and crevices, where they then become easier to smash open with strikes from the beak. Such behaviour has resulted in the Nuthatch acquiring several local names, including

'nuthacker', 'nut jobber' and 'jobbin' – 'job' is an old English word meaning to stab with a sharp instrument. The bill may also be used to chisel at loose bark when searching for invertebrates. Nuthatches will also cache seeds for later use, a behaviour that may sometimes extend to sunflower seeds and peanuts taken from garden feeders. Some recently published photographs show a Nuthatch in a London park apparently using a piece of bark to lever up other pieces of bark (Rutz & Deans, 2018), thus demonstrating a rather surprising piece of tool use – tool use by birds is rare, though there are at least three other anecdotal reports of tool use by other species of Nuthatch.

TREECREEPER
Certhia familiaris

Key facts:
Breeding season: April to June
Clutch size: 5–6 eggs
Incubation period: 14–15 days
Fledging period: 14–16 days
Number of breeding attempts: 2 per year
Typical lifespan: 2 years
Population size: 180,000 territories
Conservation: Green-listed

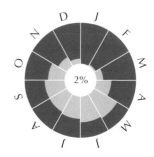

Small, delicate and mouse-like in its movements, the Treecreeper is an occasional garden visitor, easily overlooked and most likely to be seen during the winter months. Insectivorous in diet, the Treecreeper is most likely to be seen working its way up the trunk of a tree or along a branch, probing for insects and other small invertebrates within the cracks and crevices of the bark. The use of gardens has remained largely stable since the 1970s, though there is variation between years that is thought to be linked to the severity of winter

Treecreeper

weather conditions; like other small insectivorous species, Treecreeper populations are reduced by poor winter weather. The impacts of winter weather can be seen in the national population trend derived from the combined Common Bird Census/ Breeding Bird Survey. Research has demonstrated that both numbers and survival rates are reduced by wet winter weather (Peach *et al.*, 1995). When wet weather is accompanied by very low temperatures, the water present on the surface of a tree trunk may freeze, effectively sealing potential invertebrate prey behind the ice and leaving them out of reach for a foraging Treecreeper.

FIG 152. Treecreepers are occasional garden visitors, sometimes attracted to suet that has been pushed into the bark of garden trees during the colder winter months. (John Harding)

Individual Treecreepers may come together to roost in a suitable cavity, huddling to reduce heat loss. Early in the twentieth century, they were observed excavating small depressions in the soft bark of introduced Wellingtonia *Sequoiadendron giganteum* trees and then using these for roosting. This behaviour has spread through the Treecreeper population and now appears to be a not uncommon occurrence wherever these trees are present. Although unlikely to visit garden bird tables and feeders, Treecreepers may take suet products that have been pushed into the bark of garden trees. Providing such food during the winter months may be particularly valuable. During the winter months, Treecreepers may join tits in mixed-species flocks, a behaviour that is most common during the mid-winter period when temperatures are lower. Typically, only a single Treecreeper will be present in each flock and, as flock size increases, so this individual is more likely to narrow its foraging efforts to the trunks of trees, where the other members of the flock are less able to forage. This suggests that Treecreepers join these flocks to lower their predation risk, rather than to increase their foraging opportunities (Arevalo & Gostler, 1994).

Although the two sexes appear indistinguishable, the males are larger (on average) in all body measurements. They also have longer bills, a trait that may perhaps enable the two sexes to partition feeding opportunities and reduce competition between the two sexes (Tietze & Martens, 2009). Treecreepers are double-brooded and the males have been found to help their mate by provisioning the chicks, a not uncommon behaviour in garden birds. However, while paternal care is common during the first brood, male Treecreepers often desert their mate part way through the rearing of the second brood (Kuitunen *et al.*, 1996). Invertebrate prey are more readily available later in the season, so male provisioning is likely to be of greater importance for rearing of the first brood than the second. This is something that has been confirmed experimentally by Teija Aho and colleagues working in Finland (Aho *et al.*, 2009). By removing male Treecreepers from a breeding pair during the first brood, Aho demonstrated that 'widowed' females produced fewer fledglings than control pairs, where the male had not been removed; the fledglings were also of lower body weight than those of the control pairs.

The Treecreeper is a woodland species, with tree cover important to both territory establishment and breeding success. Research into the effects of forest fragmentation on Treecreeper breeding success provides some useful insights into the likely consequences of individuals breeding in woodland fragments adjoining or located within the built environment. One important consequence of woodland patch size on breeding success is that pairs breeding in small patches suffer from poor chick growth and higher levels of chick mortality than those breeding in larger woodland patches (Suorsa *et al.*, 2004). Treecreepers breeding in smaller patches also experience higher levels of nest predation, though this is likely to be less of a problem for the relatively small number of pairs breeding in rural gardens because the suite of predators is likely to be different.

WREN
Troglodytes troglodytes

Key facts:
Breeding season: April to August
Clutch size: 5–6 eggs
Incubation period: 13–18 days
Fledging period: 14–19 days
Number of breeding attempts: 2 per year
Typical lifespan: 2 years
Population size: 7.7 million territories
Conservation: Green-listed

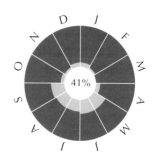

Wren

Although the bird itself is easily overlooked, the Wren's loud and penetrating song should ensure that its presence within a garden is known. This small, insectivorous bird has a very wide breeding distribution across the UK, being found in a wide range of habitats. Data from national surveys demonstrate that the UK Wren population is the highest it has been since monitoring began in the 1960s, making it our most numerous breeding bird. Numbers can, however, vary sharply from one year to the next, with cold winter weather known to have a significant impact on overwinter survival and population size (Peach *et al.*, 1995). Garden use peaks during the winter months and it is at this time of the year that individuals may sometimes use garden nest boxes for communal roosting. Most of these roosts just contain a small number of individuals, but up to 60 have been reported using the same nest box on a cold winter night. The birds arrive shortly before dusk and usually depart before first light.

Gardens are also used for breeding, the male constructing a series of 'cock nests' in order to attract a mate; his success is determined by the number of nests constructed (see Chapter 3). Some males manage to attract multiple females. Once a nest has been selected by the female it will be lined with feathers. Most nests are placed within a crevice or open cavity, but others may be constructed within trailing Ivy *Hedera helix* or bramble, in the nest of another bird (e.g. Swallow), or in an artificial hole provided by a man-made object (such as a wellington boot in a garden shed). Each male will make regular visits to the nests that he has constructed throughout his breeding territory, meaning that he will be aware of the progress of any nesting attempts underway with his mates. While he only rarely helps to provision the chicks, a male will take on the responsibility of feeding them if he loses his mate, perhaps even spending the night in the nest with them (Armstrong & Whitehouse, 1977).

The male's song plays an important role in advertising his presence, and you might imagine that the volume and frequency of this frees the male Wren from the challenges of urban noise pollution (which is usually of low frequency).

FIG 153. Wrens often roost communally during the winter months, using garden nest boxes and roosting pouches for shelter. (Jill Pakenham)

Work by Colino-Rabanal *et al.* (2016), however, demonstrates that Wren song differs between rural habitats (with an average of 43 decibels of background noise) and urban ones (mean of 66 decibels background noise). Urban Wrens have more complex songs, with higher frequencies and longer notes, than their rural counterparts. Male Wrens respond differently to the calls of known neighbours than is the case with certain other species of bird. In many species, territory-holding males are able to identify the songs of established neighbours and reduce the level of their own territorial response, presumably because established neighbours are not viewed as a threat. Territory-holding Wrens are also able to identify established neighbours and discriminate their songs from those of complete strangers. Interestingly, however, they continue to react as strongly to known neighbours as they do to strangers, which suggests that these established individuals still provide a threat, perhaps through competition for a mate or because territory size is of particular importance for a male Wren, who is attempting to secure multiple mates across a series of nests (Courvoisier *et al.*, 2014). One other interesting component of the territorial song in this species is that individual Wrens may share song components with their neighbours, suggesting that an individual's song develops and that birds adopt heard fragments from other birds.

A number of different Wren subspecies are known to occur in Britain, two of which are present on the mainland, while the others are found on particular islands. This means that the Wrens using the gardens on Shetland are noticeably different from those using a garden in southeast London. The nominate subspecies *troglodytes* is found in the southeast of Britain, grading into subspecies *indigenus* as you move north and west. The island forms are the Shetland Wren *zetlandicus*, the Fair Isle Wren *fridariensis*, the Hebridean Wren *hebridensis* and the St Kilda Wren *hirtensis*. The different subspecies are distinguishable on the basis of size, song, plumage colouration and the extent of barring on the upper and underparts (McGowan *et al.*, 2003). The island races have a tendency for shorter, simpler songs than the mainland birds. Examination of the genetics of these different races suggests a postglacial colonisation of these islands from mainland Britain and Europe, possibly with continued gene flow due to migration of birds from continental Europe (Shannon *et al.*, 2014).

STARLING
Sturnus vulgaris

Key facts:
Breeding season: April to June
Clutch size: 4–5 eggs
Incubation period: 12 days
Fledging period: 21 days
Number of breeding attempts: 1, sometimes 2, per year
Typical lifespan: 5 years
Population size: 1.8 million pairs
Conservation: Red-listed

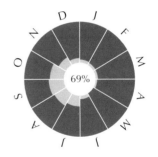

As is clear from the frequent references made throughout the book, the Starling is one of the species to have adapted well to gardens and the wider built environment. However, as we have seen, urban breeding populations are less productive than those living within other habitats, so maybe it is not such a clear-cut winner as its relative abundance at garden feeding stations may suggest. Both BTO Garden BirdWatch and Garden Bird Feeding Survey data show a long-term decline in the numbers of Starlings visiting gardens in the UK. Average peak counts in gardens have dropped from around 12 birds in the 1970s to just 5 birds today. These declines reflect the wider fortunes of the species, with breeding populations declining by 89 per cent between 1967 and 2015 (Massimino *et al.*, 2017).

Starling

The available evidence suggests that changes in first-year survival rates over the winter months are probably responsible for the change in Starling populations (Freeman *et al.*, 2007). Although we lack a complete understanding of the drivers behind this decline, it is likely that they are linked to changes in the management of pastoral farmland. During the spring and summer, Starlings feed predominantly on invertebrates taken from areas of short vegetation. Changes to the structure of these short grassland swards, brought about by changes in grazing management, may have made them less suitable for foraging. Within the UK, we have seen the shift from cattle to sheep grazing and increased stocking densities (Fuller & Gough, 1999). The drainage of wet meadows and damp grasslands may have also played a part in Starling decline (Newton, 2004), reducing the availability of craneflies – a favourite prey item – and wider foraging opportunities. Other potential factors include a warming climate – through its impact on soil-dwelling invertebrates – and the increasing use of insecticides (Vickery *et al.*, 2001). Craneflies appear to be of particular importance to Starlings when feeding their young (Rhymer *et al.*, 2012).

A changing climate and the use of insecticides may also be a problem for urban Starlings, which perhaps already face the challenge of finding sufficient invertebrate prey for their nestlings. Another issue within the built environment may be the lack of suitable nesting opportunities. Changes to building regulations and the switch from wooden to plastic barge boards is likely to have reduced the numbers of suitable cavities within our houses and other buildings. Starlings will, however, take to garden nest boxes, providing that these are of sufficient size. Box size has been found to influence breeding success in Starling, with birds seemingly doing better in boxes that were deeper, had a basal area of *c.* 310 cm^2 and an entrance hole diameter of no more than 45 mm (Moeed & Dawson, 1979).

Starlings are known for the complexity of their songs, which incorporate a high degree of mimicry and repertoire development. Each song sequence usually follows the same broad pattern, beginning with relatively simple and

FIG 154. Young Starlings, moulting through into adult plumage, can look rather odd, sometimes leaving garden birdwatchers uncertain over the identity of what they are looking at. (Jill Pakenham)

pure-sounding whistles, developing into a series of complex phrases and ending with a set of high-frequency subphrases; these are accompanied by wing flicking and waving, which is thought to have an important signalling function (Bohner & Veit, 1993). Starlings mimic a range of other bird species, together with other simple sounds and including some of human origin. Studies suggest that the phrases are taken from other bird species common in the area, and are usually simple in frequency structure with little amplitude modulation. This can lead to the develop of local 'dialects' (Hindmarsh, 1984). Those Starlings breeding in gardens are, therefore, more likely to exploit a greater number of artificial sounds, including car alarms and phones.

One of the features of Starling populations during the winter months is the formation of large roosts. Before entering these roosts, huge flocks – known as 'murmurations' – gather and swirl about in the sky, often delivering spectacular and pulsating displays. The birds attracted to these roosts may be drawn from over a very wide area, with individuals that had been feeding on farmland mixing with others from garden feeding stations and local parks (Peach & Fowler, 1989). The microclimate of urban roosts, which may be located on human structures such as bridges and piers, is more favourable than those located within the wider countryside, such as in reed beds (Clergeau & Simmonet, 1996). A dominance hierarchy exists within Starling roosts, with positions determined through competition; those positions towards the centre of the roost are preferred and these tend to be occupied by more dominant individuals (Feare *et al.*, 1995).

BLACKBIRD
Turdus merula

Key facts:
Breeding season: March to July
Clutch size: 3–4 eggs
Incubation period: 13–14 days
Fledging period: 12–15 days
Number of breeding attempts: 2–3 per year
Typical lifespan: 3 years
Population size: 4.9 million pairs
Conservation: Green-listed

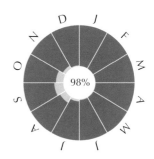

The Blackbird is one of our most familiar garden birds, found in just about every garden within the UK, and one whose urban population represents a significant proportion of the UK breeding population. While Blackbirds appear to be resident within gardens throughout the year, the detailed weekly observations collected through BTO Garden BirdWatch reveal a subtle shift in garden use during late summer and early autumn. At this time of the year, the Garden BirdWatch reporting rate for this species declines, leading to an autumn 'trough'. It is thought that this drop in reporting rate is brought about by the movement of some birds into the wider countryside, where they may exploit the autumn fruit and berry harvest, with others remaining in gardens but becoming less obvious while they undertake their annual moult. Some garden-breeding individuals may move away for the entire winter, as was revealed by a colour-ringed individual that bred in a Norfolk garden but spent successive winters in a Devon garden, returning to Norfolk in between.

Our resident population is joined by immigrants from elsewhere in Europe, with ring-recovery information underlining that our wintering population includes individuals from breeding populations across Fennoscandia and as far east as western Russia. It has been estimated that at least 12 per cent of our wintering population is made up of immigrants, with the arrival of these birds

Blackbird

very evident along the UK's eastern counties during the late autumn period. A changing climate may see fewer of these northern European birds migrate to Britain for the winter. The UK breeding population showed a long-term decline up until the mid-1990s, since when there has been a strong period of partial recovery; although this has since stalled, the recovery has been sufficient to see the species moved from the Amber List to Green List of Birds of Conservation Concern. It is thought that a reduction in survival rates was responsible for the decline (Siriwardena *et al.*, 1998a), but there is evidence that the processes involved may differ between the east and west of Britain (Robinson *et al.*, 2012). Research also indicates that the patterns of population change may also differ between habitats. Recent analysis of BTO Nest Record Scheme data indicate that different factors may be affecting nest survival rates in urban habitats from those seen within the wider countryside, with nest survival greatest in suburban sites (Miller *et al.*, 2017). Other demographic parameters also differ between urban and rural landscapes, as noted in some of our earlier discussions and the work presented in Chamberlain *et al.* (2009a). There is, for example, some evidence that Blackbirds are more productive in urban habitats, though the difference appears to be small, and that overwinter survival rates may be better in urban Blackbirds (Batten, 1978).

Some garden Blackbirds can become remarkably tame and there are numerous examples of birds that will approach a human observer for food, with some individuals venturing into kitchens to feed and even feeding alongside domestic pets from their bowls. Other Blackbirds have been observed to diversify their diet by taking Common Frog tadpoles and newts from garden ponds. These may be beaten against the ground before being eaten. More typical prey are earthworms and insects, largely taken from the ground. Earthworms are of particular importance in nestling diet and, since their availability is influenced by rainfall levels, this means that extended dry conditions can cause short-term difficulties for provisioning birds. In woodland habitats, caterpillars appear to make a significant, though short-term and early season, contribution to nestling diet, but

FIG 155. Over the course of the breeding season, a Blackbird may make three or even four nesting attempts. (John Harding)

the availability of these within most gardens is likely to make them less important in this habitat. Food limitation has been shown to be important in shaping breeding success in urban-nesting Blackbirds in Spain, with nest predation the more important factor in rural populations (Ibáñez-Álamo & Soler, 2010).

The failure of an individual nesting attempt may not prove catastrophic for a garden Blackbird pair, since they regularly make two or three nesting attempts during the course of a season. The parental investment in these attempts can take its toll and towards the end of the summer breeding adults can look rather tatty and well ready for their annual moult. Such investment can also have longer-term effects. A long-term study in Poland, carried out by Łukasz Jankowiak and colleagues, found that parental investment in the first two breeding seasons resulted in impaired breeding success later in life. However, the investment did not impact on lifespan, such that individuals that were highly productive in their early life still managed a higher level of lifetime reproductive success than those whose early life fecundity was low (Jankowiak *et al.*, 2018).

FIELDFARE
Turdus pilaris

Key facts:
Breeding season: May to July
Clutch size: 4–6 eggs
Incubation period: 13–14 days
Fledging period: 14 days
Number of breeding attempts: 1–2 per year
Typical lifespan: 2 years
Population size: a very rare breeder
Conservation: Red-listed

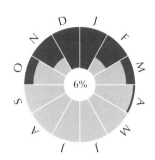

The Fieldfare is a winter visitor to the UK, with birds arriving to northern parts from mid-September and departing during April. These arrivals originate from breeding grounds that stretch across much of northern Europe and into northern Russia. Arrivals in the UK are influenced by food conditions on the breeding grounds, with the size of the Rowan *Sorbus aucuparia* berry crop determining when the birds begin to move south and west. Individuals are widely distributed across the UK during the winter months, though with a

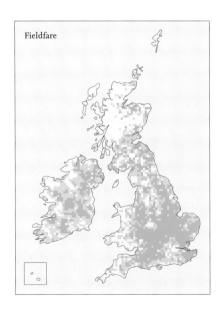

Fieldfare

clear preference for lowland areas of farmland, hedgerows and woodland. Significant movements into gardens only occur during periods of cold winter weather and snow. The fruits of *Sorbus aucuparia* may be taken from garden shrubs and trees, though these birds also show a preference for windfall apples. Berry depletion studies in Finland underline that urban berry crops are used after those available within the wider countryside have been depleted, suggesting that they may be important later into the winter where they are available (Suhonen & Jokimäki, 2015). This reliance on fruit and berries means that Fieldfares are perhaps less able

FIG 156. Winter-visiting Fieldfares make greatest use of gardens during periods of cold winter weather, when other feeding opportunities have been restricted by the conditions. (John Harding)

to withstand severe winter weather than other thrushes, something that may explain their often nomadic behaviour. Fieldfares ringed during the winter months in the UK have been found or recaptured in subsequent years, wintering on the Po and Rhône floodplains.

A very small number of Fieldfares are reported breeding in the UK on an annual basis, with most of these records relating to nesting attempts made in Scotland or northern England. During Bird Atlas 2007–11, 'confirmed' or 'probable' breeding was noted in 11 10-km survey squares (Balmer *et al.*, 2013). Within their core breeding range, Fieldfares often nest together in loose colonies, a behaviour that – while unusual in the thrush family – appears to reduce the number of nests lost to predation. Individual Fieldfares work together to drive off potential predators (Meilvang *et al.*, 1997).

The cooperative nest defence seen in breeding Fieldfares does not, it seems, always carry over to the winter months. Although less commonly observed than in some other thrush species, individual Fieldfares sometimes defend a group of berries or even a single windfall apple from others of their kind, and indeed from other thrush species (Skórka *et al.*, 2006). Larger rural and, to a lesser extent, suburban gardens are favoured, reflecting that flocks of visiting Fieldfare are more comfortable foraging within the wider countryside. Their English name derives from the Anglo Saxon word 'feldware', which roughly translates as 'traveller of the fields'.

SONG THRUSH
Turdus philomelos

Key facts:

Breeding season: March to September
Clutch size: 4 eggs
Incubation period: 13–14 days
Fledging period: 13 days
Number of breeding attempts: 2–4 per year
Typical lifespan: 3 years
Population size: 1.1 million pairs
Conservation: Red-listed

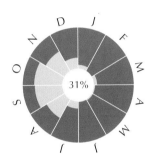

Song Thrush

As we have already seen elsewhere within this book, gardens now appear to represent an important habitat for UK Song Thrushes. Interestingly, however, Breeding Bird Survey habitat trends – which are produced for a small number of species – show a declining population trend for urban and suburban Song Thrush populations, while that for rural gardens shows a small increase, which is less than the increases seen in farmland habitats. The long-term national trend shows a substantial decline during the 1970s, since when populations have been largely stable. A similar pattern is seen in Garden Bird

FIG 157. Garden lawns and flowerbeds provide suitable foraging opportunities for Song Thrushes. (Jill Pakenham)

Feeding Survey data from the same period, although with the decline continuing (across both rural and suburban gardens) for far longer. Evidence of decline can also be seen in the BTO Garden BirdWatch data since 1995 – when the survey was launched. The reasons for the observed decline are thought to be linked to changes in survival rates during the post-fledging period and over an individual's first winter but there is some debate about the environmental drivers likely to be behind this. Changes in farming practices, changes in the availability of scrubby cover and increased levels of predation have all been suggested (Gill & Beardall, 2001; Peach *et al.*, 2004; Robinson *et al.*, 2004; 2014).

As is the case with Blackbird, earthworms are important to nesting Song Thrushes but many garden birdwatchers associate snails rather than earthworms with this small thrush. While Song Thrushes do feed on snails, leaving the remains of their shells around the 'anvils' on which they break them open, snails only become important during the dry conditions of late summer. At this time of the year, dry weather can make soil-dwelling invertebrates difficult to find. Song Thrushes deal with snails by grabbing them by the lip of the shell, before carrying the snail to a favoured stone or piece of hard garden path. Bashing the snail against the stone removes part of the shell, enabling the thrush to extract the unprotected contents, which are then wiped against the ground before being eaten.

Although this behaviour is particular to Song Thrush, there are occasional reports of Blackbirds attempting the same thing, presumably because they have watched a Song Thrush in action. Earthworms are, however, clearly the preferred prey, the thrushes only switching to snails when the conditions force them to adopt this behaviour. Interestingly, during prolonged dry spells, even snails become difficult to find and then spiders become important in Song Thrush diet. Work examining whether differences in the availability of earthworms and snails has any influence on breeding success or population trend has revealed a tendency for earthworms to form a higher proportion of the diet in stable populations, with snails forming a higher proportion of the diet in a declining population. However, the body condition of chicks appears to be unrelated to diet, at least in this study, since it did not differ between populations studied.

As we saw in Chapter 3, dense vegetation is important for nesting Song Thrushes, and those using gardens for breeding will take advantage of evergreen cover, such as Ivy, early in the season, perhaps moving into deciduous shrubs and bushes later in the year. There is also evidence that average nest height declines with season (Kelleher & O'Halloran, 2007). Both of these factors probably reflect the need to reduce the risk of nest predation, particularly from corvids, which have been identified as a problem during the incubation period (Paradis *et al.*, 2000). The nest, with its speckled, bright blue eggs and hard wood pulp lining, is characteristic and readily separated from those of our other breeding thrushes. While gardens appear to provide opportunities for Song Thrushes, they are not without their risks. In addition to the risks from predatory cats, Song Thrushes feature surprisingly often in reports of window strike casualties and concerns have also been expressed about their potential exposure to the molluscicides used in slug pellets. As we saw in Chapter 4, there is, however, little quantitative information on their impact on Song Thrush populations.

REDWING
Turdus iliacus

Key facts:
Breeding season: April to August
Clutch size: 5–6 eggs
Incubation period: 13 days
Fledging period: 12–14 days
Number of breeding attempts: 2 per year
Typical lifespan: 2 years
Population size: a handful of breeding pairs
Conservation: Red-listed

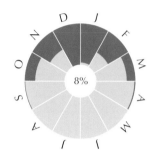

Some 10 to 20 pairs of Redwing breed in the UK each year, nesting in the north of Scotland, but it is as a winter visitor that the Redwing is better known. Large numbers of individuals arrive during autumn, the birds coming from two distinct breeding populations. Birds from Iceland dominate the populations wintering in Ireland and northwest Scotland, while individuals from Finland and Russia dominate across the south and east of the UK. Birds of these two races differ in both size and appearance, with those from Iceland being larger and darker in appearance. Individual Redwings are highly nomadic in their movements, a behaviour that can see an individual wintering in a Shropshire garden in one winter and be found in Syria the next. This nomadic behaviour reflects the vulnerability of Redwings to periods of cold weather, and the need to find food may see them move over very significant distances. Migrating Redwings are one of the first sounds of the approaching winter, with the soft flight calls readily heard on dark October evenings as birds overfly gardens.

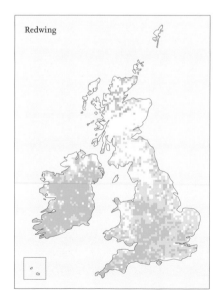

Redwing

As with Fieldfare, it is only during periods of cold weather that Redwings really turn to gardens, where they seek out the remaining berry crops on Holly, *Cotoneaster* and *Sorbus.* As with

FIG 158. Redwing are highly susceptible to poor winter weather, particularly lying snow and heavy frost, which is why they often move into gardens during the late winter months. (John Harding)

other berry-eating species, berry colour appears to determine berry preference, with black-coloured berries preferred over red ones, which in turn are preferred over white ones (Honkavaara *et al.*, 2004). This has relevance to those wishing to establish wildlife-friendly berry-producing shrubs in their garden and faced with a choice of cultivars, each with a different berry colour. Other berries may also be taken and individuals can sometimes be persuaded to feed from windfall apples placed at garden feeding stations. The pattern of garden use, seen in the weekly observations collected for BTO Garden BirdWatch, shows how Redwings may push into gardens in large numbers if the weather is poor. In most winters, garden use peaks at around 6 per cent but in February 1996 and January 1997 it jumped to roughly 25 per cent. Although berries are also important for those Redwings foraging within farmland and woodland, here they also take invertebrates from the soil's surface and from under leaf litter. Feeding Redwings appear to be active hunters, running or hopping in short bursts and then halting to scan the ground around them. Like Blackbirds and Song Thrushes, they may be seen to cock their head to one side as if listening for something moving within the leaf litter or grassy sward.

MISTLE THRUSH
Turdus visicivorus

Key facts:
Breeding season: March to June
Clutch size: 4 eggs
Incubation period: 13–14 days
Fledging period: 14–16 days
Number of breeding attempts: 2,
    sometimes 3, per year
Typical lifespan: 3 years
Population size: 160,000
Conservation: Red-listed

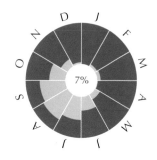

The loud rattling alarm call – think of an old-fashioned football rattle – is often the first indication that you have Mistle Thrushes breeding nearby. This large, resident thrush is less common in gardens than its smaller relatives, preferring urban parks and open woodland to the more confined spaces of urban lawns. Having said this, Mistle Thrushes will make greater use of gardens during the winter months, when individuals may vigorously defend a Holly or other shrub

Mistle Thrush

for its berry crop. The scientific name 'viscivorus', given by the Swedish biologist Linnaeus, recognises the association with mistletoe berries, though Linnaeus took the Greek word used by Aristotle for this thrush, and Aristotle had witnessed them feeding on the red fruits of the mistletoe *Viscum cruciatum* and not the white-berried species *Viscum album* that is familiar here in the UK.

Mistle Thrushes are usually quite selective in the berry patch that they choose to defend, favouring Holly over other species and selecting a tree that is isolated and of moderate size – it has to be worth the investment. Individuals in possession of a

FIG 159. During the late summer months, family parties of Mistle Thrushes may visit garden lawns and urban parks. (John Harding)

suitable Holly attempt to conserve its crop by feeding on other undefended bushes nearby, only turning their attention to 'their' tree once other berry stocks dwindle. Although berry crops can be defended and last right through the winter, the defender may be overwhelmed by other thrushes if the wider berry crop is all but gone. Holly lends itself to long-term defence because the berries are robust and do not deteriorate quickly.

Less obvious than the rattling alarm call is the territorial song, which may be confused with that of Blackbird, though in Mistle Thrush the phrasing is shorter. Mistle Thrush song is often delivered from the highest branches of tall trees, the early nesting season resulting in the song being heard from February or even earlier. These birds seem quite happy to sing during periods of poor weather, a behaviour that has earned them the local name of 'stormcock'. Nesting densities are lower than those of Blackbird or Song Thrush, and the preference for taller trees tends to see them associated with urban parks and large mature gardens rather than smaller plots. Early season nests are often placed within evergreen cover, such as that provided by Yew or Ivy, but later nests are more often located in the fork of a deciduous tree. Although nests are usually placed at heights of

2–10 m off the ground, some have been recorded at 17 m or more. Occasional pairs will build their nest on human structures, with some urban nests reported annually from traffic lights positioned on busy city-centre roads. Being multi-brooded, up to three broods may be raised during the breeding season; family parties can be seen and heard widely once the young have left the nest, through into June or July, and sometimes visiting larger garden lawns.

Mistle Thrush populations have declined significantly since the mid-1970s, a national trend that is also reflected in figures from BTO Garden BirdWatch and the Garden Bird Feeding Survey. The regional pattern of decline, as evident from the Breeding Bird Survey, suggests that while populations in the southeast are in steep decline, those in the northwest are actually increasing. The pattern is largely repeated in data from Bird Atlas 2007–11 but with the exception of Ireland, where population figures suggest decline while atlas data suggest increase. There has been a widespread but moderate decline evident elsewhere in Europe since 1980. Within the UK at least, the available evidence suggests that the population decline has been driven by a reduction in annual survival rates (Siriwardena *et al.*, 1998b).

SPOTTED FLYCATCHER
Muscicapa striata

Key facts:
Breeding season: May to August
Clutch size: 4–5 eggs
Incubation period: 12–14 days
Fledging period: 13 days
Number of breeding attempts: 1,
    sometimes 2, per year
Typical lifespan: 2 years
Population size: 33,000 territories
Conservation: Red-listed

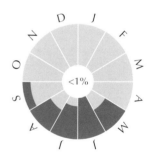

Although predominantly a bird of woodland edge, the Spotted Flycatcher also breeds regularly in rural and suburban gardens. This rather drab bird, with its soft song, is easily overlooked and it is likely that many garden-breeding pairs go unnoticed by the human residents with whom they are sharing the property. Spotted Flycatchers are one of the last summer migrants to arrive, typically reaching favoured gardens from the middle of May. The limited amount of information from ringed individuals recovered in Africa, coupled with data only

Spotted Flycatcher

just emerging from a new generation of tracking technologies, suggests that our Spotted Flycatchers spend the winter in Central Africa, south of the Congo Basin and within the Humid Zone. Like other many other migrants passing through West Africa, Spotted Flycatcher populations are in decline; with numbers having declined by 87 per cent between 1967 and 2015, the species now appears on the Red List of Birds of Conservation Concern.

Breeding Bird Survey data suggest that declines in rural gardens may have been greater than those seen in deciduous woodland or pastoral farmland habitats, though the difference is not statistically significant (Massimino *et al.*, 2017). In terms of breeding success, however, woodland and farmland appear to be sub-optimal to gardens (Stevens *et al.*, 2007; 2008). Analysis of core BTO datasets, carried out by Steve Freeman and Humphrey Crick, suggests that decreases in the survival rates of birds during their first year of life are more likely to have driven the observed decline than a change in breeding parameters (Freeman & Crick, 2003). However, these analyses are based on small sample sizes and there is an urgent need for more detailed work to be carried out on this species. If survival is the problem, then this could operate anywhere during that first year of life, either once the birds leave the nest, while on migration or while on their wintering quarters. Conditions away from the breeding grounds, particularly during spring passage through the Mediterranean, may influence breeding parameters once Spotted Flycatchers reach the UK; Finch *et al.* (2014) found that warmer conditions during the period of Mediterranean passage led to increased brood size.

Within gardens, Spotted Flycatchers often place their nests against a wall, perhaps within the fork of a climbing shrub or trained fruit tree (Kirby *et al.*, 2005). Other ledges may also be used, from that provided by a missing brick through to a piece of old metalwork once supporting a now missing door. An open-fronted nest box may be used, though this needs to be mostly open since Spotted Flycatchers like to be able to see out of the nest. Birds are more likely to be observed when fly-catching, using a perch and then sallying forth

FIG 160. Spotted Flycatcher populations declined by 87 per cent between 1967 and 2015. (John Harding)

to capture a large insect, sometimes with an audible snap of the bill. Large flies are the preferred prey, though day-flying moths and butterflies may also be taken. Spotted Flycatchers will take wasps and bees, removing their stings before swallowing them (Davies, 1977). If the weather is cool or wet, then large flying insects tend to be less available and flycatchers may turn to smaller insects taken from vegetation. These are often eaten directly, resulting in fewer prey items reaching hungry chicks if the weather conditions are poor. First-brood nestlings, being raised during June, do significantly better when conditions are warm and sunny, presumably because this ensures a greater availability of insect prey (O'Connor & Morgan, 1982). Breeding may continue through into August for those pairs that move on to have a second brood. Spotted Flycatcher chicks leave the nest before they are fully grown and at this stage they are unable to fly far. Although they may attempt to catch some insects themselves, they rely on their parents for food as they begin the transition to independence (Davies, 1976a).

It has been suggested that Grey Squirrels might be an important predator of Spotted Flycatcher nests, but there is no evidence to support this assertion. Danae Stevens, working with nest cameras on 141 Spotted Flycatcher nests, did not record any nests being lost to Grey Squirrels. Most of the nests lost to predation were predated by corvids, with Jay the main nest predator. The only mammalian predator reported was a cat (Stevens *et al.*, 2008). Danae's study encompassed a mix of habitats, including farmland, woodland, villages and rural gardens. The results of a different study, using the experimental removal of woodland predators, suggests that predation may limit the abundance of Spotted Flycatcher populations living within woodland habitats (Stoate & Szczur, 2006).

ROBIN
Erithacus rubecula

Key facts:
Breeding season: March to July
Clutch size: 4–5 eggs
Incubation period: 13–14 days
Fledging period: 13–14 days
Number of breeding attempts: 2 per year
Typical lifespan: 2 years
Population size: 6 million territories
Conservation: Green-listed

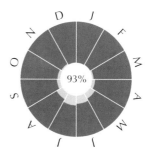

Voted Britain's national bird, the Robin is perhaps the most recognisable and familiar of our garden birds, being found in most gardens throughout the year. Data from BTO Garden BirdWatch indicate that rural gardens are more widely used, on average, than suburban ones and that these in turn are more widely used than urban gardens. These results are supported by work looking at the density of breeding Robins across different habitats in Ireland (Fennessy & Kelly, 2006). The seasonal pattern of garden use is consistent across the three garden types (see Goldfinch for a species where the pattern differs), underlining the year-round territoriality seen in this species. The long-term trend for gardens is stable, with a suggestion of a slight increase in winter use since the 1970s. National populations have shown a marked increase since the middle of the 1980s, something that probably reflects recovery from an earlier run of poor winters and which is also mirrored at a wider European level. Interestingly, Breeding Bird Survey data show the strongest positive habitat trend for suburban and rural gardens, suggesting that increases in this habitat have been particularly pronounced.

Within the garden environment, Robins may occupy open-fronted nest boxes, preferring those with a relatively small opening and within which they

Robin

can construct their nest. This is made from a foundation of dead leaves onto which is built a cup of grass and moss, lined within hair and fine plant fibres. Robins are extremely adaptable when it comes to nest sites and utilise a very wide range of cavities, from holes in walls and stumps through to human objects. Many nests are placed low to the ground, the bird relying on the cover around the nest to keep it hidden, and some may even nest on the ground itself, either within a grass tussock or under a fallen branch that has been largely covered by leaf litter. Around the nest site, Robins can be particularly wary in their behaviour, being reluctant to visit the nest if they feel that they are being watched by a potential predator, or human observer. On occasion, if carrying food for hungry chicks, an individual might drop the food if it is being watched or even make a 'false' visit to a site some distance from the nest. BTO Nest Record Scheme data show that the number of fledglings produced per breeding attempt has been increasing, with an associated reduction in the nest failure rates. There has been a widespread moderate increase across Europe since 1980.

As we saw in Chapter 5, territorial display plays a strong and well-studied role in the life of the Robin, the red breast used to threaten territorial intruders and the resident bird typically positioning itself so that this is displayed to its best advantage. If two individuals are unable to resolve their dispute through such posturing, then a fight may ensue, something that may sometimes result in the death or severe injury of one of the combatants. Territorial aggression may sometimes be directed towards other species, with Dunnock a frequent recipient of this misplaced behaviour. Outside of the breeding season, a Robin will sing and display to defend a feeding territory, a behaviour in which many females also indulge if the breeding territory has insufficient feeding resources to support both birds through the winter months.

Robin diet is dominated by invertebrates, with most of these collected through active foraging. Berries become important during the autumn and winter months when invertebrates are less readily available; some individuals will

FIG 161. Although Robins spend most of their time foraging on the ground, they have learned to take bird table fare. (John Harding)

take bird table fare, including mealworms, suet-based products and small seeds. Garden Robins can become remarkably confiding, perhaps feeding around the feet of a gardener turning up worms and other soil-dwelling invertebrates when weeding a flower border, or coming to take live mealworms from the hand of a patient garden birdwatcher. The confiding nature appears to differ from that which is typical on the continent.

UK Robins are fairly sedentary in habits, and many of the youngsters dispersing from the gardens in which they were raised will go on to set up a breeding territory of their own within just a few kilometres of their birthplace. Those adults that move off their suburban breeding territories for the winter do not appear to go far either, since most individuals are back on the same territories very early the following year (Harper, 1985a); those departing rural gardens may move further afield – or stay away for longer – as they do not return to the breeding territories until March or even April (Harper, 1986). Certain populations elsewhere in Europe undertake annual migrations over much greater distances, with data from bird ringing indicating that individuals from Scandinavia may pass through Britain on autumn passage.

Our understanding of how Robins cope with the urban environment has been
highlighted at various points throughout this book, from the work looking at
changes in singing behaviour in response to light and noise pollution, through
to the impacts of disease and daily body mass regulation. While Robins have
done well within gardens and the built environment, living here is not without
its challenges. Cat predation is a likely problem for Robins, something flagged
up by Baker *et al.* (2005), who noted that Robin was one of three bird species – the
others being House Sparrow and Dunnock – for which estimated predation rates
are particularly high relative to annual productivity, suggesting that urban areas
with high cat densities may be a sink for juvenile Robins moving out of more
productive areas nearby.

DUNNOCK
Prunella modularis

Key facts:
Breeding season: April to June
Clutch size: 4–5 eggs
Incubation period: 11–12 days
Fledging period: 12 days
Number of breeding attempts: 2,
sometimes 3, per year
Typical lifespan: 2 years
Population size: 2.3 million territories
Conservation: Amber-listed

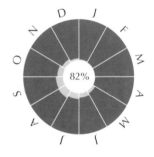

Easily overlooked, and sometimes wrongly identified as a sparrow, the Dunnock
is one of our most fascinating garden birds. As we saw earlier, the breeding
behaviour of this small brown bird has been well studied, revealing much
fascinating information and some surprising insights. Dunnock populations
underwent a period of significant decline from the mid-1970s through to the
mid-1980s, since when there has been a partial recovery. Habitat-based trends
from the Breeding Bird Survey demonstrate increases in abundance across
most habitat types, including gardens, since 1995. This, however, has not seen
the species return to former levels and so it remains on the Amber List of Birds
of Conservation Concern. Although the drivers of these declines are not fully
understood, it appears that different factors may be operating on populations
using different habitats; farmland Dunnocks are known to make use of the

Dunnock

experimental feeding stations used in studies of winter food availability for farmland seed-eaters, suggesting that a lack of seed during the late winter period may be an issue; woodland Dunnocks are thought to have been hit by the loss of low cover within woodland, following increasing grazing pressure from expanding deer populations (Gill & Fuller, 2007).

Dunnock is one of the main hosts of Cuckoo in the UK. The species appears to be a relatively recent host though, because it does not seem able to recognise the very different-looking Cuckoo egg from one of its own (Davies & Brooke, 1989). Interestingly, references to Cuckoos parasitising the nests of Dunnocks appear in Chaucer, in the writings of Gilbert White and in Shakespeare, the latter reference coming in King Lear (Act 1, Scene IV) with the lines 'The hedge-sparrow fed the cuckoo so long, that it had it head bit off by it young.' Dunnock eggs are a striking pale blue in colouration, which you might think would make the nest prone to predation during the period when the eggs are being laid. However, Dunnocks place their nests in thick cover, selecting sites that are surrounded by thicker vegetation than present at other potential sites (Tuomenpuro, 1991). Like other small garden-nesting birds, parent Dunnocks will eat the faecal sacs produced by young chicks, thereby removing what might become obvious white marks from around the nest. This behaviour, which is known as coprophagy, is common in female Dunnocks but rare in males (Lamb et al., 2017).

As noted in the Robin species account, Dunnock is one of three species for which the level of cat predation documented by Baker et al. (2005) is considered to be greater than annual productivity in some areas, suggesting that some suburban populations may only be sustained by immigration. Garden Dunnock populations may also suffer from disease, with chlamydiosis more common than previously recognised (Beckmann et al., 2014) and avian pox virus regularly reported over at least the last 60 years (Edwards, 1985). The latter does not appear to have any significant effect on Dunnock populations or affected individuals.

Dunnocks are primarily ground-feeders, often foraging with mouse-like movements under bushes and shrubs, perhaps venturing to feed under bird

FIG 162. Sometimes incorrectly referred to as a hedge sparrow, the Dunnock is actually a member of the accentors. (Jill Pakenham)

tables or, less often, on them. Their diet is dominated by small invertebrates but small seeds become more important during the winter months, when feeding conditions can become more challenging. Beetles and flies make a significant contribution to nestling diet, and it is thought that flies may be taken early in the morning while they are still sluggish (Bishton, 1985). Peanut fragments, finely grated cheese and breadcrumbs may be taken where these are presented at garden feeding stations. Despite the more challenging conditions of the UK winter, our Dunnocks are largely sedentary in habits; there are rare reports of autumn eruptions, resulting in large numbers of seemingly British-bred individuals being seen or captured by bird ringers within a small area (Taylor, 1984). Populations elsewhere in northern Europe are migratory – a behaviour that brings small numbers of continental birds to east coast sites during the autumn migration period (Wernham *et al.*, 2002). These largely go unnoticed, apart from places like Fair Isle where resident Dunnocks are absent.

HOUSE SPARROW
Passer domesticus

Key facts:
Breeding season: April to August
Clutch size: 4–5 eggs
Incubation period: 12 days
Fledging period: 14–15 days
Number of breeding attempts: 2–3 per year
Typical lifespan: 3 years
Population size: 5.1 million pairs
Conservation: Red-listed

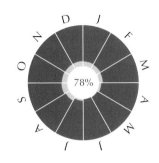

The decline of the House Sparrow, and its loss from many urban centres, provides some of the strongest evidence for the changing nature of urban landscapes and their suitability for once common species. Although granivorous for much of the year, House Sparrows depend on invertebrate prey during the breeding season and it seems highly likely that the loss of these is impacting on breeding success and recruitment into shrinking populations. Other factors are also likely to be involved, and it is worth noting that farmland House Sparrow

populations have also undergone significant levels of decline. Some birdwatchers are still fortunate enough to have House Sparrow colonies using their gardens, perhaps breeding in nest boxes or under roof tiles, visiting feeders to take grain and sunflower hearts, or indulging in social singing from within thick bushes and hedges.

The changing fortunes of the House Sparrow have been documented by the long-term garden-based surveys operated by the BTO, with the Garden Bird Feeding Survey revealing the pattern of decline across different types of garden since the 1970s. Since 1995, BTO Garden BirdWatch has enabled the regional pattern of decline within gardens to be examined and data from this large-scale citizen science project have also been analysed in an attempt to measure the annual productivity of garden House Sparrow populations. Because House Sparrows are very sedentary in their habits, it has proved possible to look at the change in the numbers visiting garden feeding stations over the course of a summer to derive an index of annual productivity (Morrison *et al.*, 2014). This work has revealed regional patterns in annual productivity that fit the regional changes evident in population trajectories.

The UK suburbs support some 35 per cent of the British House Sparrow population, the birds here occurring at much higher densities than is the case in urban or rural areas. However, as we saw in Chapter 3, they also have some of the lowest levels of breeding performance, at least at the level of each individual nesting attempt (Crick & Siriwardena, 2002), and it is evident from the work of Will Peach and colleagues that poor breeding success has played a role in the observed decline. Interestingly, however, analysis of BTO Nest Record Scheme data suggests that the earlier decline in House Sparrow populations was brought about by a fall in the survival rates of first year birds and, later, adults. More recent work on a declining House Sparrow population in Leicester very clearly indicates that poor breeding performance, and the low survival rates of fledglings (predicted from measures of nestling body size prior to fledging), are behind the decline seen there (Peach *et al.*, 2008).

House Sparrow society is centred on a loose colony of individuals, with individual males defending their nest hole and the immediate area around it. Once birds join a colony, most remain faithful to it for life. Dominance in male House Sparrows is choreographed by the size of a male's black bib. The higher up the social hierarchy, the larger his bib. Larger-bibbed males fledge a much

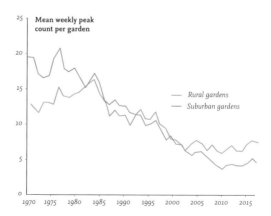

FIG 163. The long-term decline of House Sparrow is evident from the weekly winter counts collected through the BTO's Garden Bird Feeding Survey. Note the different pattern of decline seen in rural and suburban gardens. Data used with permission from BTO.

FIG 164. The size of the black bib on a House Sparrow has been shown to demonstrate social status. (John Harding)

higher proportion of the young in their nests than those males with a smaller bib (Voltura *et al.*, 2002), something that appears to be linked to the division of labour between the male and his mate – male House Sparrows help to build the nest, incubate and provision the young. Large-bibbed individuals do proportionally more of the work than is the case in small-bibbed individuals. Interestingly, they also perform a greater proportion of the behaviours (such as nest defence) that are considered the most risky, potentially indicating another reason why a female should choose to mate with a male sporting a large bib (Reyer *et al.*, 1998).

House Sparrows favour bird tables and feeders that are positioned close to cover, often taking small amounts of food and then retreating to a nearby bush or hedge. They can be wary birds and are often slow to take to new feeding opportunities, such as a new food. This wariness also extends to other objects and many a bird ringer will tell you how House Sparrows are not hard to catch once, but almost impossible to catch a second time. Cover is clearly important for urban House Sparrows, and not just for the invertebrate populations that it can support. Flocks frequent favoured bushes and may use these to roost, sometimes indulging in a bout of what has been termed 'social singing'. The 'chirrup' call that is a feature of House Sparrow flocks is also given by individuals when they are on their own. Experimental studies suggest that solitary House Sparrows, discovering a food source that is divisible, will make the call to recruit other individuals. However, where an individual locates a food source that is not big enough to share with others, it remains silent. The availability of cover may also determine whether or not local House Sparrows will reach and use a particular garden. A House Sparrow flock living just 20 m from a house I once owned, almost never visited our feeding station and the only explanation appeared to be the gap of three intermediate gardens that lacked any cover.

TREE SPARROW
Passer montanus

Key facts:

Breeding season: April to August
Clutch size: 5–6 eggs
Incubation period: 11–14 days
Fledging period: 15–20 days
Number of breeding attempts: 2, occasionally 3, per year
Typical lifespan: 2 years
Population size: 180,000
Conservation: Red-listed

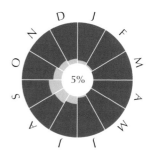

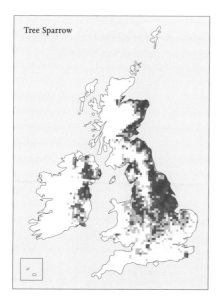

Tree Sparrow

The dramatic decline in farmland Tree Sparrow populations, which fell by 96 per cent between 1967 and 2015, has been one of the biggest seen for any UK breeding bird, resulting in its placement on the Red List of Birds of Conservation Concern. Although the reasons for the decline are unknown, the available evidence points to the intensification of agriculture. Tree Sparrows made extensive use of overwinter stubbles, the loss of which is likely to have greatly reduced favoured seed supplies during the later winter months (Siriwardena *et al.*, 1998a; Hancock & Wilson, 2003). As seen for House Sparrow, a lack of

FIG 165. Male and female Tree Sparrows are similar in appearance, their dark cheek spot and neat chestnut cap aiding separation from the more familiar House Sparrow. (John Harding)

suitable invertebrate prey may also be having an impact on the breeding success of Tree Sparrow populations, potentially adding to the problems faced during the winter months (McHugh *et al.*, 2017).

Only those rural gardens located in farmland habitats within the Tree Sparrow's shrinking breeding range are likely to be visited by this species. In addition to the use of garden feeding stations, Tree Sparrows will also nest on such properties, either under tiles in the roof or in nest boxes, the latter requiring a 28 mm or larger entrance hole. Tree Sparrow populations at individual sites are known for their sudden appearance and/or disappearance, something that has been linked to the provision of new feeding opportunities during the winter months (Field & Anderson, 2004). The role that garden feeding stations may play in the establishment or maintenance of Tree Sparrow breeding colonies is unknown, but some garden sites clearly support small breeding colonies. Elsewhere in Europe, Tree Sparrows are often found breeding within towns and cities, though typically at a lower density than House Sparrows and with a stronger association towards greener and less urbanised areas (Šálek *et al.*, 2015). New breeding colonies tend to be established by young birds dispersing from their natal colonies and establishing themselves where feeding opportunities are favourable.

Breeding begins early in the year, with the first eggs appearing during April, and pairs may go on to rear two or even three broods over the season, which extends through into August. Both sexes contribute to nest building, incubation and chick rearing, the pair tending to remain together for life. Unlike the more familiar House Sparrow, male and female Tree Sparrows look similar in their appearance, with a characteristic warm chestnut crown and small black cheek patches. The black bib, which is much smaller than that seen in House Sparrow, signals the status of an individual and males with larger bibs have been shown to be of better-quality, according to a series of different measures (Matsui *et al.*, 2017; Mónus *et al.*, 2017). Outside of the breeding season, pairs join with other birds from local breeding colonies to feed at scattered sites over a wider area, returning to the breeding colony to roost. From October through into early December, colony attendance is associated with display, as young birds seek to acquire a nest site and established birds defend theirs. At this stage new nests may be constructed, often built over the top of those from the previous breeding season. During the second half of the winter, the colony continues to be the focus for roosting birds but individuals disperse during the day to form foraging flocks – often in the company of finches and buntings – that seek out feeding opportunities within favoured farmland habitats (Pinowski *et al.*, 2009). The annual pattern of garden use documented by BTO Garden BirdWatch reveals a late summer trough in garden use, perhaps indicating the movement away once breeding has been completed.

PIED WAGTAIL
Motacilla alba

Key facts:
Breeding season: April to August
Clutch size: 5 eggs
Incubation period: 12–14 days
Fledging period: 13–16 days
Number of breeding attempts: 2, sometimes 3, per year
Typical lifespan: 2 years
Population size: 460,000 pairs
Conservation: Green-listed

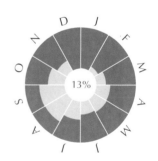

Pied Wagtails favour open ground with areas of short vegetation, often located close to water. Because of this they are found across a range of habitats, often penetrating the urban environment, where they may be seen feeding on areas of short grass, such as lawns and parks. The insectivorous diet of this species

Pied Wagtail

means that it is a rare visitor to garden feeding stations, only visiting during poor winter weather to take small seeds and bread. The winter months can be challenging for a small insectivorous bird, which explains why northern Pied Wagtail populations are partial migrants, wintering as far south as France, Spain and Portugal. UK populations show a similar pattern, with birds from northern England and Scotland wintering in southern England or pushing further south into Spain and France. Our Pied Wagtail *Motacilla alba yarrellii* is actually a race of the nominate White Wagtail *Motacilla alba* found more widely across Europe. Individuals of the nominate race do reach Britain, though it is our race, with its darker back, that is almost always the one encountered within gardens.

While migration is one option for Pied Wagtail populations during the winter months, other individuals may remain here, coping with the changing conditions by altering their feeding behaviour (Davies, 1976b). The use of a defended territory during the winter is one option, with territory-holding individuals securing increased local knowledge of where to find food and defending these resources against other individuals. If feeding conditions deteriorate within the territory, then an individual will move elsewhere and join a larger foraging flock. Equally, a territory holder may sometimes find itself overrun by other birds if it happens to be defending a particularly good feeding site during a period when other sites offer poor returns. Garden use peaks during the mid-winter months, with the weekly reporting rates recorded through BTO Garden BirdWatch suggesting a movement into gardens during periods of poor weather.

Another feature of the winter months is the large communal roosts, which can number up to 4,000 or more individuals. Within the wider countryside, the birds roost in reed beds, but within urban areas the roosts may be associated with city-centre trees or with buildings. Urban roosts are warmer than those available elsewhere, suggesting that the wagtails benefit from the heat pollution that has become a feature of our urban landscapes. Communal roosting may provide other benefits, either by reducing an individual's chances of being taken by a

FIG 166. During periods of cold weather and snow, Pied Wagtails may turn to garden feeding stations to take small seeds and suet. (John Harding)

predator or by acting as 'information centres'. In the latter case, an individual may be able to assess the condition of other birds in the roost and make a decision as to where it might feed the following day.

Smaller numbers of Pied Wagtails may breed in gardens, favouring fairly open cavity sites and covered ledges. Although they may take to an open-fronted nest box, they are more likely to use some other human structure, such as an outbuilding or log pile; such sites may be used in consecutive years. Studies in Ireland indicate that the male and female may share incubation duties, typically with the female incubating throughout the night and for the greater part of the day, and the male taking on a smaller role. The male's contribution appears to be highly variable, with some individuals not contributing to incubation at all; in some cases, the extent of the male's contribution may be associated with whether or not he has another mate nearby (Fitzpatrick, 1996b).

BRAMBLING
Fringilla montifringilla

Key facts:

Breeding season: May to July
Clutch size: 5–7 eggs
Incubation period: 11–12 days
Fledging period: 14 days
Number of breeding attempts: 1 per year
Typical lifespan: 3 years
Population size: very occasional pairs
Conservation: Green-listed

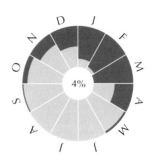

A male Brambling in breeding plumage makes a stunning spring visitor to a garden feeding station, a sight only likely to be seen during those years when individuals are late to depart our shores. This is a winter visitor, whose numbers vary greatly from year to year in response to the availability of beechmast elsewhere in Europe. Although a small number of pairs have been recorded breeding in the UK, our wintering Bramblings originate from breeding grounds that extend across large parts of Fennoscandia and northern Russia. The birds leave these breeding areas in autumn, moving south and west towards southern Europe, where they seek out beechmast. If this is in short supply, then they will move further west, and it is this movement that brings them to the UK (Wernham *et al.*, 2002). Arrivals usually coincide with those of migrant Chaffinches, with the mixed flocks visiting garden feeders likely to be dominated by the latter species. The use of garden feeders tends to increase through the winter, as beechmast crops in the wider countryside are depleted. Like Chaffinch, they prefer to feed on the ground, but will use hanging feeders.

Brambling

FIG 167. This wintering finch is closely related to the more familiar Chaffinch and the two species may be seen together in mixed flocks. (Jill Pakenham)

One of the features of the autumn and early winter movements is the formation of huge communal roosts, something that is more often seen on the continent than here in the UK. Some of these roosts can number tens or even hundreds of thousands of birds. Roost sites tend to be located within thick vegetation. An individual's location within a roost appears to be determined by its sex and body condition, with females and low-weight individuals more likely to be found on the edge of the roost rather than towards its centre (Jenni, 1993). While UK roosts tend to be much smaller, there is a record of a roosting flock in Merseyside that numbered 150,000 birds; unfortunately, many of the birds were killed by traffic, having first become incapacitated by salt applied to the icy road surface from which they were feeding on beechmast.

The presence of one or more Bramblings within a mixed flock, taking food from beneath garden feeders, may easily go unnoticed, the two species being similar in size, shape and general appearance. The most obvious feature is the white rump revealed in flight; this is green in Chaffinch but the more strongly patterned plumage and buff-orange flush on the chest and shoulders of Brambling are useful additional features. During the course of the late winter months, the male's breeding plumage begins to emerge. This is not the result of feathers being replaced by new plumage but instead comes about through feather wear. The glossy black head feathers have pale fringes which wear away with time, leaving the glossy black lower portion on show. This does not usually happen until the birds are back on the breeding grounds but occasional late-departing individuals may have just about completed this process before they leave. Departures usually happen in March, the first birds having moved into gardens the previous October.

Sunflower hearts appear to be popular with Bramblings, but they will also take other seeds and peanut granules. The use of garden feeding stations may, as we have seen in Chapter 4, lead to an increased risk of disease transmission and individuals may sometimes be noted with growths on their legs and feet.

CHAFFINCH
Fringilla coelebs

Key facts:
Breeding season: April to July
Clutch size: 4–5 eggs
Incubation period: 11–13 days
Fledging period: 14 days
Number of breeding attempts:
   1, sometimes 2, per year
Typical lifespan: 3 years
Population size: 5.8 million territories
Conservation: Green-listed

80%

The Chaffinch is one of the most common breeding birds in Britain. Despite a preference for deciduous or mixed woodland, substantial numbers also breed within gardens, where a tree, bush or shrub may be used for nesting. Chaffinch numbers increased rapidly from the 1970s through until 2006, something also evident in the data collected by the BTO's Garden Bird Feeding Survey. Garden Bird Feeding Survey data reveal that the increase in garden use during the winter months was significantly greater in rural gardens than suburban ones. Data from both this survey and BTO Garden BirdWatch, which started in 1995, indicate a period of stability during the 1990s, which is more pronounced than that evident within the breeding season data collected by other surveys. All of

Chaffinch

the surveys show a period of decline since then that has been linked to finch trichomonosis, the emergence of which is calculated to have reduced the Chaffinch breeding population within affected areas by as much as a fifth (Robinson *et al.*, 2010).

Chaffinches are also affected by the presence of skin abnormalities on the legs and feet. As we saw in Chapter 4, these white, rough and thickened growths are caused by both Chaffinch papillomavirus and *Cnemidocoptes* mites. It has been suggested that garden feeding stations may increase the risk of disease transmission for these diseases, either through increased levels of individual contact or through the contamination of food and feeding surfaces. The presence of affected birds, some of which may have significant growths or have lost digits, can be disturbing, reminding garden birdwatchers of the importance of good hygiene practices and their responsibilities when providing feeding opportunities for these and other wild birds.

Chaffinches seem well adapted to the garden habitat and are regular visitors to garden feeders, where sunflower hearts and other seeds are readily taken. Seeds dominate Chaffinch diet, with beechmast of particular importance to wider countryside populations. As we saw in Chapter 2, the size of the beechmast crop can determine the extent to which these finches turn to garden feeding stations (Chamberlain *et al.*, 2007a). Invertebrates, particularly caterpillars, spiders and small flies, become more important during the breeding season. These are usually taken from within trees and shrubs, where the Chaffinches spend more time foraging during spring and summer. Invertebrates are of particular importance to developing chicks, dominating their diet. The availability of favoured invertebrates is likely to influence breeding success, something evident from the finding for farmland Chaffinch populations that nestling growth was affected negatively by rain but positively by increasing minimum temperatures and daily hours of sunshine (Bradbury *et al.*, 2003). Given the lower availability of invertebrate prey within the garden environment noted in Chapter 2, it seems likely that breeding success is lower here than in other habitats, though differences in predation rates may perhaps compensate for this.

FIG 168. During the winter months, the UK Chaffinch population is joined by individuals from populations breeding further north and east. (John Harding)

Given the numbers of garden-breeding Chaffinches, it is perhaps unsurprising that the Chaffinch's song is one of our most familiar. A series of short phrases, ended with a terminal flourish, forms the basic song structure, which is fairly stereotyped across the UK. This is learnt during the first year of life, being developed from an innate framework onto which is added a learnt component (Poulsen, 1951; Thorpe, 1958). Once a young Chaffinch has heard the adult song, it appears to have learnt enough to fix the structure; only very rarely will an individual incorporate any other source into the song. While this appears to leave Chaffinches with a rather fixed and narrow song, individual males tend to have a repertoire of half a dozen or so variants on the central structure. A male will sing one variant before following this with a different one from his repertoire. When 'counter-singing' with a neighbouring male, an individual will tend to respond with that song from his own repertoire which most closely resembles that of his rival (Thorpe, 1958). Subtle regional differences in these repertoires lead to the formation of local dialects.

BULLFINCH
Pyrrhula pyrrhula

Key facts:
Breeding season: May to August
Clutch size: 4–5 eggs
Incubation period: 12–14 days
Fledging period: 14–16 days
Number of breeding attempts: 2,
    sometimes 3, per year
Typical lifespan: 2 years
Population size: 190,000 territories
Conservation: Amber-listed

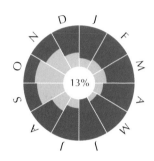

An increase in the use of garden feeding stations by Bullfinches has been evident within BTO Garden Bird Feeding Survey and Garden BirdWatch data since the mid-1990s. Wider countryside populations have increased over the same period, but possibly at a somewhat lower rate, suggesting that there may have also been a behavioural response to changing feeding opportunities at garden feeding stations. The increase seen in wider countryside populations needs to be viewed

against a longer-term trend, with a substantial decline evident during the late 1970s; populations remain well below the level present at the end of the 1960s. Although the underlying reasons for the decline seen in the 1970s have yet to be determined, there is evidence to implicate changes in adult survival rates (Robinson *et al.*, 2014). Changes in the structural diversity of woodland may have reduced available nesting cover, and a decline in floristic diversity may have reduced feeding opportunities (Fuller *et al.*, 2005). Declines within farmland habitats have been more severe than those in woodland and there is also the possibility that recovering

FIG 169. Bullfinches sometimes visit gardens to feed on the seeds of wild flowers, including dandelion, but they may also take food from bird tables and hanging feeders. (Jill Pakenham)

Sparrowhawk populations may have reduced the ability of Bullfinches to exploit certain habitats (Proffitt *et al.*, 2004; Marquiss, 2007).

Bullfinches are easily overlooked when on the breeding territories, the species having a rather soft call and favour woodland and scrub sites with thick vegetation. This preference for thick vegetation means that very few pairs nest within gardens, with those used typically rural in nature and well-connected to small woodlots and other suitable habitat by connecting hedgerows and scrubby cover. The nest itself is formed from an untidy foundation of small twigs, onto which is built a rather neater shallow cup lined with fine rootlets, usually dark in colour.

The use of gardens increases in early summer, with pairs arriving with their young in tow. At this time of the year, they may seek out the seeds of garden plants, particularly the dandelions, with individuals sometimes hovering to pluck the seed heads from the plant. Individuals may also make use of garden feeders, taking sunflower hearts and smaller seeds. The increasing use of garden feeders is something that has been commented upon by those participating in BTO surveys. Garden-visiting Bullfinches may also feed on the buds of fruit trees early in the season, a behaviour that led to the species being regarded as a serious pest of commercial fruit trees in some parts of the UK. Part of the problem was the preference for flower buds over leaf buds, the former being nutritionally more rewarding (Newton, 1964).

Bullfinches are regarded as being largely sedentary in their habits, with most individuals recovered within 20 km of where they were ringed (Wernham *et al.*, 2002). However, there is evidence that at least some individuals make significant movements within the long breeding season – which can extend from April through to September. It is possible that some of these longer movements might involve pairs moving between breeding attempts, something that would explain the appearance of individuals during July and August at sites where no breeding pair had been evident earlier in the year (Newton, 2000). If such movements do reflect a change in breeding location, then this may suggest that the birds are responding to changes in food availability. Young Bullfinches remain with their parents for a short period after leaving the nest, and it is at this stage that they may be seen to accompany their parents to gardens close to where they had been raised.

The populations of Bullfinches breeding further north within Europe make longer movements, migratory in nature, and these appear to be linked to variation in the availability of favoured food supplies, including the berries of Rowan (Fox *et al.*, 2009). In some years, large numbers of individuals may be on the move, sometimes pushing into eastern parts of the UK. These immigrants, which are structurally larger and more brightly coloured than our resident birds, are often referred to as 'Northern Bullfinch'.

GREENFINCH
Chloris chloris

Key facts:
Breeding season: April to July
Clutch size: 4–5 eggs
Incubation period: c. 13 days
Fledging period: 13–16 days
Number of breeding attempts: 2,
    sometimes 3, per year
Typical lifespan: 2 years
Population size: 1.7 million pairs
Conservation: Green-listed

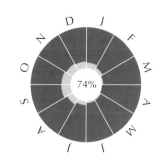

The loss of Greenfinches from many gardens from 2006 onwards has been well documented through the weekly figures collected by participants in BTO

Greenfinch

Garden BirdWatch. The loss of one in three individuals in the years following the emergence of finch trichomonosis underlines the impact that an emerging infectious disease can have on a population (Robinson *et al.*, 2010). As is clear from the latest Garden BirdWatch figures, the decline appears to be ongoing, something that is also evident within the data collected on UK breeding populations. It is likely that garden feeding stations have played a role in the emergence and spread of this disease, but it is also interesting to note the greater extent to which Greenfinches have been affected by the disease compared to other species.

While the emergence of finch trichomonosis has had significant impacts on the Greenfinch population, it is important to view this recent decline against the longer-term picture. Greenfinches were rarely seen in gardens at the turn of the previous century, their populations largely restricted to woodland and scrub habitats. Garden feeding appears to have supported a wider population increase during the 1990s, with sunflower seed and sunflower hearts supporting increased use of garden feeding stations. In addition to food taken from bird tables and hanging feeders, Greenfinches take a range of plant material; seeds are of particular importance with the larger seeds of elm and Dog's Mercury *Mercurialis perennis* joined later in the year by those of Yew, hawthorn and bramble. Rosehips appear to be a particular favourite, the birds often ignoring the fleshy fruit and just eating the seed.

Greenfinches are fairly common as a breeding species within gardens and the green spaces of the wider urban environment. The nest is usually placed just inside the canopy of a suitable bush or shrub, but it may also be placed against the trunk or in a fork between branches. Early season nests are more likely to be placed within evergreen cover, with introduced and ornamental conifers readily used within the garden environment. The nest, which is built by the female, is a surprisingly bulky affair, a cup of moss and plant material placed onto a foundation of twigs. This is then lined with finer material, plant down and hair. Each pair may have several broods, the young of which appear at garden feeding stations from early summer.

FIG 170. As recent research has shown, larger species like Greenfinch can dominant bird feeders to the exclusion of smaller birds. (John Harding)

Most of the Greenfinches breeding in UK gardens will be fairly sedentary in habits, remaining close to where they were born. Some, perhaps as many as 2 per cent, make longer movements at the end of the breeding season, with a few individuals wintering in northern France and Belgium (Wernham *et al.*, 2002). Alongside these movements, we also see the late autumn arrival at garden feeding stations of Greenfinches from the Norwegian breeding population. These movements into the UK do not appear to be a regular annual occurrence, but instead seem to reflect changing conditions on the Norwegian wintering grounds. In years when either the weather is poor, or favoured berries less available, more individuals migrate to the UK (Main, 1999). Others, presumably from further south in Norway, appear to reach East Anglia by being drifted across the North Sea by the prevailing weather conditions encountered during a southwards migration to Denmark and Germany. Since these individuals look identical to the birds breeding here in the UK, their presence has only been revealed through the efforts of bird ringers, operating both here and in Norway.

GOLDFINCH
Carduelis carduelis

Key facts:
Breeding season: April to August
Clutch size: 4–5 eggs
Incubation period: 12–13 days
Fledging period: 14–15 days
Number of breeding attempts: 2 per year
Typical lifespan: 2 years
Population size: 1.2 million pairs
Conservation: Green-listed

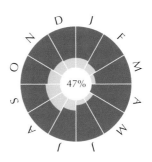

Goldfinches have increased dramatically in their use of gardens and garden feeding stations, something that is evident from the long-term data collected through the BTO Garden Bird Feeding Survey. This shows that the use of gardens first began to increase in the early 1990s, with similar patterns (and numbers) seen in both rural and suburban gardens. The increase in garden use is thought to have been supported by the introduction of sunflower hearts and Niger seed to garden feeding stations. As noted in Chapter 2, the fine-billed Goldfinch specialises in seeds of the Compositae family, particularly the thistles and dandelions, and it is thought that this habit first brought them into gardens to feed on ornamental thistles, lavenders and cornflowers (Glue, 1996). They then learnt to exploit the foods being provided in hanging feeders, with Niger seemingly more important in the earlier years than it is now – though this shift may also reflect a reduction in competition from the larger Greenfinch, whose populations have declined because of disease. It is worth just noting that within the wider countryside Goldfinches favour seeds that are not yet fully ripe, but which are still in what is termed their 'milky' stage.

Goldfinch

FIG 171. With its delicate bill, the Goldfinch is able to handle smaller seeds. (John Harding).

Goldfinch populations within the wider countryside have also increased over the longer term, at least since the mid-1980s, though this increase has come off the back of a decline evident over the previous decade and thought to be linked to the effects of agricultural intensification and the loss of favoured arable weed seeds. There has also been a moderate, but widespread, increase in Goldfinch populations more widely across Europe since the 1980s. The use of garden feeding stations shows a strong seasonal pattern, with a pronounced peak during April. A small secondary peak, which follows a few weeks later, is present in most (but not all) years and the timing of this in relation to the timing of the breeding season is interesting. There appears to be an increase in garden use during the period over which eggs are being laid, but we currently lack the evidence to prove this.

Patterns of garden use are complicated by the fact that the Goldfinch is a partial migrant, with a component of the UK breeding population wintering in France, Spain and Portugal (Wernham et al., 2002). It has been shown that female Goldfinches are more likely to move south than males, and winter further south, suggesting that individuals make a decision based on the availability of food resources and their ability to compete for these (Asensio, 1986). Information from the recoveries of ringed birds indicates that not all of these partial migrants have returned to the UK by May, so it may be that the April peaks in garden use might involve returning individuals rather than simply those breeding locally.

Goldfinches breed across a range of habitats and will penetrate into the centres of major conurbations. Nests are often placed in a fork towards the outermost branches of a suitable tree or bush, but others may be built in a hedge, within a creeper or (sometimes) in an ornamental conifer. Although the nest may be placed quite low, down to 1.5 m, many are located much higher, even up to 15 m above the ground. These neat cups of moss, grass and rootlets are usually lined with plant down, wool and cobwebs. Chicks are fed on a mixture of seeds and invertebrates, with early season broods receiving a greater proportion of invertebrates than those raised later in the year (Newton, 1972; Gil-Delgado & Guijarro, 2008). The presence of the breeding pair may only be confirmed with the arrival of newly fledged young at a garden feeding station; these initially lack the facial markings of their parents, only gaining them when they undergo their first moult of the body feathers.

SISKIN
Spinus spinus

Key facts:
Breeding season: April to August
Clutch size: 4–5 eggs
Incubation period: 12–13 days
Fledging period: 13–15 days
Number of breeding attempts: 2 per year
Typical lifespan: 2 years
Population size: 410,000 pairs
Conservation: Green-listed

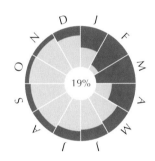

This small finch is a winter visitor to favoured gardens, whose presence owes much to the widespread establishment of conifer plantations across marginal upland areas of the UK. The introduced Sitka Spruce has been one of the main tree species used in the afforestation programme and it is the seeds of this tree that have enabled the UK Siskin population to increase significantly. The breeding population has increased by 61 per cent since 1995 (which is when it first became possible to monitor annual population trends for this species), with the population increase certainly beginning well before this. During the 1950s, Siskins were largely restricted to the Highlands of Scotland as a breeding species, with populations moving to forested lowland areas during the winter months. The movement into gardens is a more recent phenomenon and one that data from the BTO Garden Bird Feeding Survey suggests began in the mid-1980s.

The close relationship between Siskins and the availability of their favoured conifer seeds is something that we explored in Chapter 2 through the work that we carried out with Ailsa McKenzie (McKenzie *et al.*, 2007). This revealed that

Siskin

the use of garden bird feeders, as tracked by BTO Garden BirdWatch participants, was related to the size of the Sitka Spruce seed crop. In those winters when the crop was large, garden use was low; in years when the crop was poor, the use of gardens increased significantly. This results in a pronounced peak in garden use during late February and early March that, for those gardens located away from the conifer forests in which these birds breed, may be the only time Siskins appear. Movement away from the conifer forests sees birds move some distance; while some may settle in an area where food is readily available, others become more nomadic, ranging widely and resulting in a succession of small flocks passing through the gardens of suburban southern England. This pattern of movements sees both 'resident' and 'transient' individuals using the same wintering area. Most individuals appear to be transients, staying in one place for only a short period and typically making movements of up to 40 km in a single day (Senar *et al.*, 1992). Residents remain in an area for extended periods and rarely move more than 3 km during a single day. What is particularly interesting about this pattern of behaviour is that the split between residents and transients does not appear to be linked to age, sex or social status, all of which may explain differential movement patterns in other small birds. The one difference that has been found between the two groups is in wing shape, with transient birds having more pointed wings (more efficient when flying long distances) and resident birds having more rounded wings (probably more suited to other needs, such as predator avoidance).

Siskins were first reported taking food from garden feeding stations in 1961 (Spencer & Gush, 1973), the birds initially feeding on fat but then learning to exploit peanuts and seeds (Davis, 1977). Their fine bill also enabled them to feed on Niger seed following its introduction to the UK bird food market. The February/March peak in garden use falls just before the start of the Siskin breeding season, the timing of which is influenced by the size of the conifer seed crop; breeding begins in April in good cone years but can be delayed to May or even June when the crop has been particularly poor. Siskins are one of the garden bird species

FIG 172. The use of gardens by Siskins peaks during late winter, with garden use increasing during those years when conifer seed is less readily available. (John Harding)

known to suffer disproportionately from salmonellosis, with outbreaks at garden feeding stations often resulting in the mortality of numerous individuals. Fortunately, salmonellosis is now less common at garden feeding stations.

YELLOWHAMMER
Emberiza citrinella

Key facts:
Breeding season: May to August
Clutch size: 3–4 eggs
Incubation period: 13 days
Fledging period: 16 days
Number of breeding attempts: 2, sometimes 3, per year
Typical lifespan: 3 years
Population size: 700,000 pairs
Conservation: Red-listed

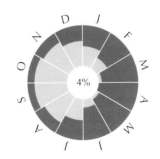

This familiar farmland bunting is an occasional garden visitor, most likely to appear in late winter and virtually restricted to rural sites. The use of garden

Yellowhammer

feeding stations has declined since the 1970s, a reflection of the dramatic long-term decline seen in UK breeding populations; these declined by 56 per cent between 1967 and 2015, the species now placed on the Birds of Conservation Concern Red List. Although the period of population decline falls a little later than that seen in other farmland species, the available evidence points to similar ecological drivers and it seems likely that the loss of overwinter stubbles and the intensification of grassland management have reduced food availability, while the loss farmland hedgerows has reduced nesting opportunities (Kyrkos *et al.*, 1998; Bradbury & Stoate, 2000; Gillings *et al.*, 2005). One interesting impact of the timing of Yellowhammer decline within farmland is that during the period of decline there was an initial increase in the use of garden feeding stations in the late winter months. This is the period when farmland seed supplies are at their lowest and the increased use of bird table fare might indicate that the birds were experiencing a particularly challenging time.

Away from lowland farmland, Yellowhammers may be found breeding in other habitats, including shrubby scrub and the early successional stages of plantation forestry. Gardens located alongside such habitats may also be visited by Yellowhammers during the winter months. Sunflower hearts and larger seeds are taken, mostly from the ground but individuals may also feed from bird tables. Visiting flocks can reach double figures, with the Yellowhammers feeding alongside sparrows, finches and Reed Buntings. Elsewhere within Europe, Yellowhammers can be regular visitors to rural gardens during the winter months, being one of the more dominant rural garden species in one Polish study (Ciach, 2012). Ring-recovery data from Yellowhammer populations breeding within the UK underline that the species is essentially sedentary in habits, with 95 per cent of the individuals recovered being found within 25 km of where they had been ringed. While some birds appear to move to lower ground during the winter months (Wernham *et al.*, 2002), others only range over a small area of farmland, the extent of such movements presumably shaped by local food availability.

FIG 173. Although a bird of farmland, heathland and scrubby woodland, the Yellowhammer makes use of many rural gardens during the later winter months. (John Harding)

The expansion of rural villages, coupled with wider urban sprawl onto former agricultural land, may well see the arrival of Yellowhammers at the garden feeding stations associated with these new properties. Understanding the extent to which locally breeding Yellowhammers (and other farmland species) move in to exploit this new food resource is something that requires further study – there has been a small amount of work on this in the UK (Siriwardena & Stevens, 2004; Calladine *et al.*, 2006). If the availability of seeds during the late winter period is a particular problem for farmland Yellowhammers, as is suggested by the work of Gavin Siriwardena and colleagues, then garden feeding stations may have an important role to play, supporting overwinter survival. However, if breeding success is also a problem, because of a lack of suitable nest sites and favoured foods, then the provision of supplementary food at garden feeding stations can only be part of the solution and not the whole.

REED BUNTING
Emberiza schoeniclus

Key facts:
Breeding season: May to July
Clutch size: 4–5 eggs
Incubation period: 13 days
Fledging period: 14–16 days
Number of breeding attempts: 2,
    sometimes 3, per year
Typical lifespan: 3 years
Population size: 230,000 pairs
Conservation: Amber-listed

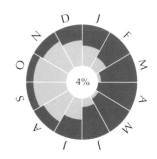

Like its relative the Yellowhammer, the Reed Bunting is primarily a late winter visitor to garden feeding stations, favouring those that are rural in nature. The use of these appears to be linked to the availability of farmland seeds, which are at their lowest abundance during the late winter period. According to data from the BTO Garden Bird Feeding Survey, garden use peaked during the early 1980s. This was the period when Reed Bunting populations in the wider countryside were in decline, suggesting that a lack of overwinter seed had prompted birds to forage more widely and to turn to the foods available at garden bird tables. The national decline is thought to have been driven by agricultural intensification, impacting on over-winter survival rates (Peach *et al.*, 1999).

Reed Bunting

Although to be found breeding on farmland, particularly in association with crops of oilseed rape, Reed Buntings are primarily associated with wetland habitats. Prior to the decline in national populations, the species had been increasing, its populations expanding into drier habitats from their wetland strongholds. Wetlands are also used during the winter

FIG 174. Reed Buntings only rarely visit gardens outside of the late winter period, but a late spring can see the presence of adult males in their breeding plumage. (Jill Pakenham)

months, when large flocks of Reed Buntings may gather together to roost in reed beds; this behaviour provides additional protection from likely predators. After emerging from the roost, individuals forage more widely, with rural bird tables sometimes attracting double-figure counts. Sunflower seed, sunflower hearts and other mixed seed are the foods of choice at garden feeding stations. Individuals often feed on the ground but readily take to bird tables and hanging feeders.

During the winter months, the striking black head plumage of the male Reed Bunting is hidden by paler feather tips, and the two sexes are fairly similar in their appearance. As winter nears its end, so the brown tips to the male's head feathers wear away, leaving a shadow of the coming breeding plumage to slowly appear. It is at this time that garden feeding stations are abandoned, the birds returning to their breeding sites, where they may go on to raise two or even three broods of chicks in well-hidden nests that are usually placed within a few inches of the ground and covered by vegetation.

References

Note that the scientific names used in the main text follow Gill, F. & Donsker, D. (2018). *IOC World Bird List* (v 8.1). Doi 10.14344/IOC.ML.8.1. http://www.worldbirdnames.org

Aho, T., Kuitunen, M., Hakkari, T., Suhonen, J. & Jantti, A. (2009). Effects of male removal on reproductive success and provisioning in the Eurasian Treecreeper (*Certhia familiaris*). *Ornis Fennica* **86**: 1–10.

Alder, D. & Marsden, S. (2010). Characteristics of feeding-site selection by breeding Green Woodpeckers *Picus viridis* in a UK agricultural landscape. *Bird Study* **57**: 100–107.

Allen, D. E. (1967). J. F. M. Dovaston, an overlooked pioneer of field ornithology. *Journal of the Society for the Bibliography of Natural History* **4**: 277–283.

Amrhein, V. & Erne, N. (2006). Dawn singing reflects past territorial challenges in the Winter Wren. *Animal Behaviour* **71**: 1075–1080.

Andersson, M. & Norberg, R. Å. (1981). Evolution of reversed sexual size dimorphism and role partitioning among predatory birds, with a size scaling of flight performance. *Biological Journal of the Linnean Society* **15**: 105–130.

Antonov, A. & Atanasova, D. (2003). Small-scale differences in the breeding ecology of urban and rural Magpies *Pica pica*. *Ornis Fennica* **80**: 21–30.

Appleby, B. M., Petty, S. J., Blakey, J. K., Rainey, P. & MacDonald, D. W. (1997). Does variation of sex ratio enhance reproductive success of offspring in tawny Owls (*Strix aluco*). *Proceedings of the Royal Society*, London (B) **264**: 1111–1116.

Arcese, P. & Smith, J. N. M. (1988). Effects of population density and supplemental food on reproduction in Song Sparrows. *Journal of Animal Ecology* **57**: 119–136.

Arevalo, J. E. & Gosler, A. G. (1994). The behaviour of Treecreepers *Certhia familiaris* in mixed-species flocks in winter. *Bird Study* **41**: 1–6.

Armstrong, E. A. & Whitehouse, H. L. (1977). Behavioural adaptations of the Wren (*Troglodytes troglodytes*). *Biological Reviews* **52**: 235–294.

Arnold, K. E. & Griffiths, R. (2003). Sex-specific hatching order, growth rates and fledging success in Jackdaws *Corvus monedula*. *Journal of Avian Biology* **34**: 275–281.

Aronson, M. F. J., La Sorte, F. A., Nilon, C. H., Katti, M., Goddard, M. A., Lepczyk, C. A., Warren, P. S., Williams, N. S. G., Cilliers, S., Clarkson, B., Dobbs, C., Dolan, R., Hedblom, M., Klotz, S., Kooijmans, J. L., Kühn, I., MacGregor-Fors, I., McDonnell, M., Mörtberg, U., Pysek, P., Siebert, S., Sushinsky, J., Werner, P. & Winter, M. (2014). A global analysis of the impacts of urbanization on bird and plant biodiversity reveals key anthropogenic drives. *Proceedings of the Royal Society* (B). **281**: 20133330.

Asensio, B. (1986). Migration of Goldfinches (*Carduelis carduelis*, L.) to Spain according to ringing recoveries. *Ardeola* **33**: 176–183.

Atkinson, C. T., Thomas, N. J. & Hunter, D. B. (2008). *Parasitic Diseases of Wild Birds*. Wiley-Blackwell, Oxford.

Audet, J. N., Ducatez, S. & Lefebvre, L. (2016). The town bird and the country bird: problem solving and immunocompetence vary with urbanization. *Behavioural Ecology* **27**: 637–644.

Avery, M. L. (1979). Review of avian mortality due to collisions with man-made structures. *Proceedings of the 8th Bird Control Seminars*. http://digitalcommons. unl. edu/icwdmbirdcontrol/2/

Baglione, V., Marcos, J. M. & Canestrari, D. (2002). Cooperatively breeding groups of Carrion Crow (*Corvus corone corone*) in northern Spain. *Auk* **119**: 790–799.

Baglione, V., Marcos, J. M., Canestrari, D., Griesser, M., Andreotti, G., Bardini, C. & Bogliani, G. (2005). Does year-round territoriality rather than habitat saturation explain delayed natal dispersal and cooperative breeding in the Carrion Crow? *Journal of Animal Ecology* **74**: 842–851.

Bailly, J., Scheifler, R., Berthe, S., Clément-Demange, V. A., Leblond, M., Pasteur, B. & Faivre, B. (2016). From eggs to fledging: negative impact of urban habitat on reproduction in two tit species. *Journal of Ornithology* **157**: 377–392.

Baines, C. (2016). *RHS Companion to Wildlife Gardening*. Frances Lincoln, London.

Baker, P. J., Bentley, A. J., Ansell, R. J. & Harris, S. (2005). Impact of predation by domestic cats *Felis catus* in an urban area. *Mammal Review* **35**: 302–312.

Baker, P. J., Thomas, R. L., Newson, S. E., Thompson, V. & Paling, N. R. D. (2010). Habitat associations and breeding bird community composition within the city of Bristol, UK. *Bird Study* **57**: 183–196.

Balen, J. H. van (1973). A comparative study of the breeding ecology of the Great Tit *Parus major* in different habitats. *Ardea* **61**: 1–93.

Balen, J. H. van (1980). Population fluctuations of the Great Tit and feeding conditions in winter. *Ardea* **68**: 143–164.

Balmer, D. E., Gillings, S., Caffrey, B. J., Swann, R. L., Downie, I. S. & Fuller, R. J. (2013). *Bird Atlas 2007–11: the breeding and wintering birds of Britain and Ireland*. BTO Books, Thetford.

Bañbura, J., Lambrechts, M. M., Blondel, J., Perret, P. & Cartan-Son, M. (1999). Food handling time of Blue Tit chicks: constraints and adaptation to different prey types. *Journal of Avian Biology* **30**: 263–270.

Barba, E., López, J. A. & Gil-Degado, J. A. (1996). Prey preparation by adult Great Tits *Parus major* feeding nestlings. *Ibis* **138**: 532–538.

Barratt, D. G. (1997). Home range size, habitat utilisation and movement patterns of suburban and farm cats *Felis catus*. *Ecography* **20**: 271–280.

Barratt, D. G. (1998). Predation by house cats, *Felis catus* (L.), in Canberra, Australia. II. Factors affecting the amount of prey caught and estimates of the impact on wildlife. *Wildlife Research* **25**: 475–487.

Batten, L. A. (1973). Population dynamics of suburban Blackbirds. *Bird Study* **20**: 251–258.

Batten, L. A. (1978). The seasonal distribution of recoveries and causes of Blackbird mortality. *Bird Study* **25**: 23–32.

von Bayern, A. M. & Emery, N. J. (2009). Jackdaws respond to human attentional states and communicative cues in different contexts. *Current Biology* **19**: 602–606.

Bearhop, S., Fiedler, W., Furness, R. W., Votier, S. C., Waldron, S., Newton, J., Bowen, G. J., Berthold, P. & Farnsworth, K. (2005). Assortative mating as a mechanism for rapid evolution of a migratory divide. *Science* **310**: 502–504.

Beckermann, A. P., Boots, M. & Gaston, K. J. (2007). Urban bird declines and the fear of cats. *Animal Conservation* **10**: 320–325.

Beckmann, K. M., Borel, N., Pocknell, A. M., Dagleish, M. P., Sachse, K., John, S. K., Pospischil, A., Cunningham, A. A. & Lawson, B. (2014). Chlamydiosis in British garden birds (2005–2011): retrospective diagnosis and *Chlamydia psittaci* genotype determination. *EcoHealth* **11**: 544–563.

Belaire, J. A., Westphal, L. M., Whelan, C. J. & Minor, E. S. (2015) Urban residents' perceptions of birds in the neighbourhood: biodiversity, cultural ecosystem services, and disservices. *Condor* **117**: 192–202.

Belda, E. J., Barba, E. & Monros, J. S. (2007). Resident and transient dynamics, site fidelity and survival in wintering Blackcaps *Sylvia atricapilla*: evidence from capture–recapture analyses. *Ibis* **149**: 396–404.

Bell, C. P., Baker, S. W., Parkes, N. G., Brooke, M. D. L. & Chamberlain, D. E. (2010). The role of the Eurasian Sparrowhawk (*Accipiter nisus*) in the decline of the House Sparrow (*Passer domesticus*) in Britain. *The Auk* **127**: 411–420.

Berthold, P., Helbig, A., Mohr, G. & Querner, U. (1992). Rapid microevolution of migratory behaviour in a wild bird species. *Nature* **360**: 668–670.

Berthold, P. & Terrill, S. B. (1988). Migratory behaviour and population growth of Blackcaps wintering in Britain and Ireland: some hypotheses. *Ringing and Migration* **9**: 153–159.

Beven, G. (1965). The food of Tawny Owls in London. *London Bird Report* **29**: 56–62.

Beyer, W. N., Spann, J. W., Sileo, L. & Franson, J. C. (1988). Lead poisoning in six captive avian species. *Archives of Environmental Contamination and Toxicology* **17**: 121–130.

Bhatti, M. & Church, A. (2001). Cultivating natures: homes and gardens in late modernity. *Sociology* **35**: 365–383.

Bhatti, M. & Church, A. (2004). Home, the culture of nature and measnings of gardens in late modernity. *Housing Studies* **19**: 37–51.

Biard, C., Brischoux, F., Meillere, A., Michaud, B., Nivière, M., Ruault, S., Vaugoyeau, M. & Angelier, F. (2017). Growing in cities: an urban penalty for wild birds? A study of phenotypic differences between urban and rural Great Tit chicks (*Parus major*). *Frontiers in Ecology and Evolution* 5. doi: 10. 3389/fevo. 2017. 00079.

Biddle, L., Broughton, R., Goodman, A. & Deeming, C. (2018). Composition of bird nests is a species-specific characteristic. *Avian Biology Research* **11**: 132–153.

Biddle, L. E., Deeming, D. C. & Goodman, A. M. (2015). Morphology and biomechanics of the nests of Common Blackbird *Turdus merula*. *Bird Study* **61**: 87–95.

Bignal, K., Ashmore, M. & Power, S. (2004). The ecological effects of diffuse air pollution from road traffic. *English Nature Research Report* 580, Peterborough.

Bishton, G. (1985). The diet of nestling Dunnocks *Prunella modularis*. *Bird Study* **32**: 113–115.

Blackmore, D. K. & Keymer, I. F. (1969). Cutaneous diseases of wild birds in Britain. *British Birds* **62**: 316–331.

Blair, R. B. (1996). Land use and avian species diversity along an urban gradient. *Ecological Applications* **6**: 506–519.

Blakey, J. K. (1994). Genetic evidence for extra-pair fertilizations in a monogamous passerine, the Great Tit *Parus major*. *Ibis* **136**: 457–462.

Bland, R. L., Tully, J. & Greenwood, J. J. (2004). Birds breeding in British gardens: an underestimated population? *Bird Study* **51**: 97–106.

Boev, Z. (1997). Wild galliform and gruiform birds (Aves, Galliformes and Gruiformes) in the Archaeological Record of Bulgaria. *International Journal of Osteoarchaeology* **7**: 430–439.

Bohner, J. and Veit, F. (1993). Song structure and patterns of wing movement in the European Starling (*Sturnus vulgaris*). *Journal für Ornithologie* **134**: 309–315.

Bojarinova, J., Babushkina, O., Shokhrin, V. & Valchuk, O. (2016). Autumn migration of the Long-tailed Tit (*Aegithalos c.*

caudatus) at the opposite sides of the Eurasian continent. *Ornis Fennica* 93 235–245.

Bojarinova, J., Lives, A., Chemetsov, N. & Leivits, A. (2008). Body mass, moult and migration speed of the Goldcrest *Regulus regulus* in relation to the timing of migration at different sites of the migration route. *Ornis Fennica* **85**: 55–65.

Bonier, F., Martin, P. R. & Wingfield, J. C. (2007). Urban birds have broader environmental tolerance. *Biology Letters* **3**: 670–673.

Bonnington, C., Gaston, K. J. & Evans, K. L. (2013). Fearing the feline: domestic cats reduce avian fecundity through trait-mediated indirect effects that increase nest predation by other species. *Journal of Applied Ecology* **50**: 15–24.

Bonnington, C., Gaston, K. J. & Evans, K. L. (2015). Ecological traps and behavioural adjustments of urban songbirds to fine-scale spatial variation in predator activity. *Animal Conservation* **18**: 529–538.

Bonter, D. N. & Cooper, C. B. (2012). Data validation in citizen science: a case study from project FeederWatch. *Frontiers in Ecology* **10**: 305–307.

Borgmann, K. l. & Rodewald, A. D. (2004). Nest predation in an urbanizing landscape: the role of exotic shrubs. *Ecological Applications* **14**: 1757–1765.

Boyce, M. S. & Perrins, C. M. (1987). Optimizing Great Tit clutch size in a fluctuating environment. *Ecology* **68**: 142–153.

Bracey, A. (2011). Window related mortality at a migration corridor. MSc Thesis, University of Minnesota, Minneapolis, MN.

Bradbury, K. (2017). *The Wildlife Gardening Handbook*. White Owl, Barnsley.

Bradbury, R. & Stoate, C. (2000). 'The
ecology of Yellowhammers *Emberiza
citrinella* on lowland farmland':
165–172, in Aebischer, N. J., Evans,
A. D., Grice, P. V. & Vickery, J. A., *Ecology
and Conservation of Lowland Farmland
Birds*. British Ornithologists' Union,
Tring.

Bradbury, R. B., Wilson, J. D., Moorcroft,
D., Morris, A. J. & Perkins, A. J. (2003).
Habitat and weather are weak correlates
of nestling condition and growth rates
of four UK farmland passerines. *Ibis* **145**:
295–306.

Brahmia, Z., Scheifler, R., Crini, N., Maas,
S., Giraudoux, P. & Benyacoub, S.
(2013). Breeding performance of Blue
Tits (*Cyanistes caeruleus ultramarinus*)
in relation to lead pollution and nest
failure rates in rural, intermediate, and
urban sites in Algeria. *Environmental
Pollution* **174**: 171–178.

Britt, J. & Deeming, D. C. (2011). First
egg date and air temperature affect
nest construction in Blue tits *Cyanistes
caeruleus* but not in Great tits *Parus
major*. *Bird Study* **58**: 78–89.

Brittingham, M. C. & Temple, S. A. (1986).
A survey of avian mortality at winter
feeders. *Wildlife Society Bulletin* **14**:
445–450.

Brittingham, M. C. & Temple, S. A. (1988a).
Impacts of supplemental feeding
on survival rates of Black-capped
Chickadees. *Ecology* **69**: 581–589.

Brittingham, M. C. & Temple, S. A. (1988b).
Avian disease and winter bird feeding.
The Passenger Pigeon **50**: 195–203.

Brittingham, M. C. & Temple, S. A. (1992a).
Use of winter bird feeders by Black-
capped Chickadees. *Journal of Wildlife
Management* **56**: 103–110.

Brittingham, M. C. & Temple, S. A. (1992b).
Does winter bird feeding promote
dependency? *Journal of Field Ornithology*
63: 190–194.

Brittingham, M. C., Temple, S. A. & Duncan,
R. M. (1988). A survey of the prevalence of
selected bacteria in wild birds. *Journal of
Wildlife Diseases* **24**: 299–307.

Brock, M., Perino, G. & Sugden, R. (2015).
The warden attitude: an investigation of
the value of interaction with everyday
wildlife. *Environmental and Resource
Economics* **67**: 1–29.

Broggi, J. & Senar, J. C. (2009). Brighter
Great Tit parents build bigger nests. *Ibis*
151: 588–591.

Brömssen, A. van. & Jansson, C. (1980).
Effects of food addition to Willow Tit
Passer montanus and Crested Tit *Passer
cristatus* at the timing of breeding. *Ornis
Scandinavica* **11**: 173–178.

Bryant, D. M. (1975). Breeding biology of
House Martins *Delichon urbica* in relation
to aerial insect abundance. *Ibis* **117**:
180–216.

Buer, F. & Regner, M. (2002). With the
'spider's web effect' and UV-absorbing
material against bird-death on
transparent and reflecting surfaces. *Vogel
und Umwelt* **13**: 31–41.

Bugnyar, T. & Kotrschal, K. (2004) Leading
a conspecific away from food in Ravens
(*Corvus corax*)? *Animal Cognition* **7**: 69–76.

Burghardt, K. T., Tallamy, D. W. & Shriver,
W. G. (2008). Impact of native plants
on bird and butterfly biodiversity in
suburban landscapes. *Conservation
Biology* **23**: 219–224.

Burgin, S. & Saunders, T. (2007). Parrots of
the Sydney region: population changes
over 100 years: 185–194, in Lunney, D.,
Eby, P., Hutchings, P. & Burgin, S., *Pest*

or Guest: *The Zoology of Overabundance*. Royal Zoological Society of New South Wales, Mosman, Australia.

Búrquez, A. (1989). Blue Tits, *Parus caeruleus*, as pollinators of the Crown Imperial, *Fritillaria imperialis*, in Britain. *Oikos* **55**: 335–340.

Burton, D. & Doblar, K. (2004). Morbidity and mortality of urban wildlife in the Midwestern United States. *Proceedings of the 4th International Urban Wildlife Symposium*: 171–181.

Butler, C. J. (2003). Population biology of the introduced Rose-ringed Parakeet *Psittacula krameri* in the UK. PhD Thesis, University of Oxford.

Butler, C. J., Cresswell, W., Gosler, A. & Perrins, C. (2013). The breeding biology of Rose-ringed Parakeets *Psittacula krameri* in England during a period of rapid population expansion. *Bird Study* **60**: 527–532.

Butterfield, J., Coulson, J. C., Kearsey, S. V., Monaghan, P., McCoy, J. H. & Spain, G. E. (1983). The Herring Gull *Larus argentatus* as a carrier of salmonella. *Epidemiology & Infection* **91**: 429–436.

Buyantuyev, A. & Wu, J. (2010). Urban heat islands and landscape heterogeneity: linking spatiotemporal patterns in surface temperatures to land-cover and socioeconomic patterns. *Landscape Ecology* **25**: 17–33.

Byle, P. A. (1990). Brood division and parental care in the period between fledging and independence in the Dunnock (*Prunella modularis*). *Behaviour* **113**: 1–19.

Calhoon, R. E. & Haspel, C. (1989). Urban cat populations compared by season, subhabitat and supplemental feeding. *Journal of Animal Ecology* **58**: 321–328.

Calladine, J., Robertson, D. & Wernham, C. (2006). The ranging behaviour of some granivorous passerines on farmland in winter determined by mark–recapture ringing and by radiotelemetry. *Ibis* **148**: 169–173.

Callahan, D. (2014). *A History of Birdwatching in 100 Objects*. Bloomsbury Publishing, London.

Calver, M., Thomas, S., Bradley, S. & McCutcheon, H. (2007). Reducing the rate of predation on wildlife by pet cats: the efficacy and practicability of collar-mounted pounce protectors. *Biological Conservation* **137**: 341–348.

Cannon, A. (1999). The significance of private gardens for bird conservation. *Bird Conservation International* **9**: 287–297.

Cannon, A. R., Chamberlain, D. E., Toms, M. P., Hatchwell, B. J. & Gaston, K. J. (2005). Trends in the use of private gardens by wild birds in Great Britain 1995–2002. *Journal of Applied Ecology* **42**: 659–671.

Cantarero, A., López-Arrabé, J. & Moreno, J. (2015). Selection of nest site and nesting material in the Eurasian Nuthatch *Sitta europaea*. *Ardea* **103**: 91–94.

Carrete, M. & Tella, J. L. (2017) Behavioural correlations associated with fear of humans differ between rural and urban Burrowing Owls. *Frontiers in Ecology and Evolution* 5. doi: 10. 3389/fevo. 2017. 00054.

Cecere, J. G., Spina, F., Jenni-Eiermann, S. & Boitani, L. (2011). Nectar: an energy drink used by European songbirds during spring migration. *Journal of Ornithology*, **152**: 923–931.

Chamberlain, D. E., Cannon, A. R. & Toms, M. P. (2004a). Associations of garden birds with gradients in garden habitat and local habitat. *Ecography* **27**: 589–600.

Chamberlain, D. E., Cannon, A. R., Toms, M. P., Leech, D. I., Hatchwell, B. J. & Gaston, K. J. (2009a). Avian productivity in urban landscapes: a review and meta-analysis. *Ibis* **151**: 1–18.

Chamberlain, D., Glue, D. & Toms, M. P. (2009b). Sparrowhawk *Accipiter nisus* presence and winter bird abundance. *Journal of Ornithology* **150**: 247–254.

Chamberlain, D., Gosler, A. G. & Glue, D. E. (2007a). Effects of the winter beechmast crop on bird occurrence in British gardens. *Bird Study* **54**: 120–126.

Chamberlain, D. E., Gough, S., Vaughan, H., Vickery, J. A. & Appleton, G. F. (2007b). Determinants of bird species richness in public green space. *Bird Study* **54**: 87–97.

Chamberlain, D., Gough, S., Vaughan, H., Appleton, G., Freeman, S., Toms, M., Vickery, J. & Noble, D. (2004b). The London Bird Project. *BTO Research Report* **384**, British Trust for Ornithology, Thetford.

Chamberlain, D. E., Hatchwell, B. J. & Perrins, C. M. (1999). Importance of feeding ecology to the reproductive success of Blackbirds *Turdus merula* nesting in rural habitats. *Ibis* **141**: 415–427.

Chamberlain, D. E., Toms, M. P., Cleary-McHarg, R. & Banks, A. N. (2007c). House sparrow *Passer domesticus* habitat use in urbanized landscapes. *Journal of Ornithology* **148**: 453–462.

Chamberlain, D. E., Vickery, J. A., Glue, D. E. & Conway, G. (2003). Gardens as a winter feeding refuge for declining farmland birds. *BTO Research Report* **342**, British Trust for Ornithology, Thetford.

Chamberlain, D., Vickery, J., Glue, D., Robinson, R., Conway, G., Woodburn, R. & Cannon, A. (2005). Annual and seasonal trends in the use of garden feeders by birds in winter. *Ibis* **147**: 563–575.

Chandler, R. B., Strong, A. M. & Jaufman, C. C. (2004). Elevated lead levels in urban House Sparrows: a threat to Sharp-shined Hawks and Merlins? *Journal of Raptor Research* **38**: 62–68.

Charmantier, A., Demeyrier, V., Lambrechts, M., Perret, S. & Grégoire, A. (2017). Urbanisation is associated with divergence in pace of life in Great Tits. *Frontiers in Ecology and Evolution* **5**: 53. doi: 10. 3389/fevo. 2017. 00053.

Chi, J. F-C., Lawson, B., Durrant, C., Beckmann, K., John, S., Alrefaei, A. F., Kirkbride, K., Bell, D., Cunningham, A. A. & Tyler, K. (2013). The finch epidemic strain of *Trichomonas gallinae* is predominant in British non-passerines. *Parasitology* **140**: 1234–1245.

Chiron, F., Alexandre, L. & Julliard, R. (2008). Effects of landscape urbanization on Magpie occupancy dynamics in France. *Landscape Ecology* **23**: 527–538.

Chiron, F. & Julliard, R. (2007). Responses of songbirds to Magpie reduction in an urban habitat. *Journal of Wildlife Management* **71**: 2624–2631.

Christe, P., Oppliger, A. & Richner, H. (1994). Ectoparasites affect choice and use of roost sites in the Great Tit, *Parus major*. *Animal Behaviour* **47**: 895–898.

Churcher, P. B. & Lawton, J. H. (1987). Predation by domestic cats in an English village. *Journal of Zoology* **212**: 439–455.

Chvala, S., Bakonyi, T., Bukovsky, C., Meister, T., Brugger, K., Rubel, F., Nowotny, N. & Weissenbock, H. (2007). Monitoring of Usutu virus activity and spread by using dead bird surveillance in Austria, 2003–2005. *Veterinary Microbiology* **122**: 237–245.

Ciach, M. (2012). The winter bird community of rural areas in the proximity of cities: low density and rapid decrease in diversity. *Polish Journal of Ecology* **60**: 193–199.

Cicho , M., Dubiec, A. & Stoczko, M. (2003). Laying order and offspring sex in Blue Tits *Parus caeruleus. Journal of Avian Biology* **34**: 355–359.

Clark, L. (1990). Starlings as herbalists: countering parasites and pathogens. *Parasitology Today* **6**: 358–360.

Clark, L. (1991). 'The nest protection hypothesis: the adaptive use of plant secondary compounds by European Starlings': 205–221, in Loye, J. E. & Zuk, M. (eds). *Bird-Parasite Interactions: Ecology, Evolution, and Behaviour.* Oxford University Press, Oxford.

Clark, L. & Mason, J. R. (1988). Effect of biologically active plants used as nest material and the derived benefit to Starling nestlings. *Oecologia* **77**: 174–180.

Clark, N. (1999). Progress report on the effectiveness of the Mark ll CatAlert™ collar at reducing predation by domestic cats. *British Trust for Ornithology Research Report* **235**, British Trust for Ornithology, Thetford.

Clark, N. & Burton, N. H. K. (1998). A pilot field trail into the effectiveness of the CatAlert™ collar at reducing predation by domestic cats. *British Trust for Ornithology Research Report* **213**, British Trust for Ornithology, Thetford.

Clergeau, P., Croci, S., Jokimäki, J., Kaisanlahti-Jokimäki, M. L. & Dinetti, M. (2006). Avifauna homogenisation by urbanisation: analysis at different European latitudes. *Biological Conservation* **127**: 336–344.

Clergeau P., Mennechez G., Sauvage A. & Lemoine A. (2001). 'Human perception and appreciation of birds: A motivation for wildlife conservation in urban environments of France': 69–88, in Marzluff J. M., Bowman R. & Donnelly R. (2001). *Avian Ecology and Conservation in an Urbanizing World.* Springer, Boston.

Clergeau, P. & Simonnet, E. (1996). Microclimate in communal roost sites of Starlings *Sturnus vulgaris. Journal für Ornithologie* **137**: 358–361.

Clewley, G. D., Plummer, K. E., Robinson, R. A., Simm, C. H. & Toms, M. P. (2015). The effect of artificial lighting on the arrival time of birds using garden feeding stations in winter: A missed opportunity? *Urban Ecosystems* **19**: 535–546.

Colino-Rabanal, V. J., Mendes, S., Peris, S. J. & Pescador, M. (2016). Does the song of the Wren *Troglodytes troglodytes* change with different environmental sounds? *Acta Ornithologica* **51**: 13–22.

Colville, K. M., Lawson, B., Pocknell, A. M., Dagleish, M. P., John, S. K. & Cunningham, A. A. (2012). Chlamydiosis in British songbirds. *Veterinary Record* **171**: 177.

Cooke, A. S. (1980). Observations on how close certain passerine species will tolerate an approaching human in rural and suburban areas. *Biological Conservation* **18**: 85–88.

Cornelius, L. W. (1969). Field notes on salmonella infection in Greenfinches and House Sparrows. *Bulletin of the Wildlife Disease Association* **5**: 142–143.

Cornish, T. E. & Nettles, V. F. Jnr. (1999). Aflatoxicosis in Louisiana Geese. *Southeastern Co-operative Wildlife Diseases Study Briefs* **15**: 1–2.

Cotgreave, P. & Clayton, D. H. (1995). Comparative analysis of time spent grooming by birds in relation to parasite load and other factors. *Behaviour* **131**: 171–187.

Coulson, J. C. & Coulson, B. A. (2008). Lesser Black-backed Gulls *Larus fuscus* nesting in an inland urban colony: the importance of earthworms (Lumbricidae) in their diet. *Bird Study* **55**: 297–303.

Courvoisier, H., Camacho-Schlenker, S. & Aubin, T. (2014). When neighbours are not 'dear enemies': a study in the Winter Wren, *Troglodytes troglodytes*. *Animal Behaviour* **90**: 229–235.

Cowie, R. J. & Hinsley, S. A. (1987). Breeding success of Blue Tit and Great Tit in suburban gardens. *Ardea* **75**: 81–90.

Cowie, R. J. & Hinsley, S. A. (1988a). The provision of food and the use of bird feeders in suburban gardens. Bird Study **35**: 163–168.

Cowie, R. J. & Hinsley, S. A. (1988b). Feeding ecology of Great Tits (*Parus major*) and Blue tits (*Parus caeruleus*), breeding in suburban gardens. *Journal of Animal Ecology* **57**: 611–626.

Cowie, R. J. & Simons, J. R. (1991). Factors affecting the use of feeders by garden birds: I. The positioning of feeders with respect to cover and housing. *Bird Study* **38**: 145–150.

Cox, D. T. C. & Gaston, K. J. (2016). Urban bird feeding: Connecting people with nature. *PLoS One* 11 doi: 10. 1371/journal. pone. 0158717.

Cox, D. T. C., Hudson, H. L., Plummer, K. E., Siriwardena, G. M., Anderson, K., Hancock, S., Devine-Wright, P. & Gaston, K. J. (2018). Covariation in urban birds providing cultural services or disservices and people. *Journal of Applied Ecology* DOI: 10. 1111/1365–2664. 13146.

Cox, D. T., Inger, R., Hancock, S., Anderson, K. & Gaston, K. J. (2016). Movement of feeder-using songbirds: the influence of urban features. *Scientific Reports* **6**: 37669.

Crates, R. A., Firth, J. A., Farine, D. R., Garroway, C. J., Kidd, L. R., Aplin, L. M., Radersma, R., Milligan, N. D., Voelkl, B., Culina, A. & Verhelst, B. L. (2016). Individual variation in winter supplementary food consumption and its consequences for reproduction in wild birds. *Journal of Avian Biology* **47**: 678–689.

Creighton, E. (2001). Mate acquisition in the European Blackbird and its implications for sexual strategies. *Ethology, Ecology and Evolution* **13**: 247–260.

Cresswell, W. (1997). Nest predation rates and nest detectability in different stages of breeding in Blackbirds *Turdus merula*. *Journal of Avian Biology* **28**: 296–302.

Crick, H. Q. P., Dudley, C., Glue, D. E. & Thomson, D. L. (1997). UK birds are laying eggs earlier. *Nature* **388**: 526.

Crick, H. Q. P., Robinson, R. A., Appleton, G. F., Clark, N. A. & Rickard, A. D. (2002). Investigation into the causes of the decline of Starlings and House Sparrows in Great Britain. *BTO Research Report* 290, British Trust for Ornithology, Thetford.

Crick, H. Q. P. & Siriwardena, G. M. (2002). National trends in the breeding performance of House Sparrows: 163–212, in Crick, H. Q. P., Robinson, R. A., Appleton, G. F., Clark, N. A. & Rickard, A. D. (2002). Investigation into the causes of the decline of Starlings and House

Sparrows in Great Britain. *BTO Research Report* 290, British Trust for Ornithology, Thetford.

Croci, S., Butet, A. & Clergeau, P. (2008). Does urbanization filter birds on the basis of their biological traits. *Condor* **110**: 223–240.

Cromack, D. (2018). *Nestboxes: Your Complete Guide.* BTO/Jacobi Jayne & Co Ltd.

Croxton, P. J. & Sparks, T. H. (2004). Timing of berry depletion rates of three common hedgerow shrubs. *Agriculture, Ecosystems and Environment* **104**: 663–666.

Cruz, J. C., Ramos, J. A., Da Silva, L. P., Tenreiro, P. Q. & Heleno, R. H. (2013). Seed dispersal networks in an urban novel ecosystem. *European Journal of Forest Research.* **132**: 887–897.

Cuadrado, M., Senar, J. C. & Copete, J. L. (1995). Do all blackcaps *Sylvia atricapilla* show winter site fidelity? *Ibis* **137**: 70–75.

Curtis, P. D., Rowland, E. D., & Curtis, G. B. (2000). Capsaicin-treated seed as a squirrel deterrent at birdfeeders: 86–102, in Brittingham, M. C., Kays, J. & McPeake, R. (2000). *The Ninth Wildlife Damage Management Conference Proceedings.* State College, PA.

Cuthill, I. C. & MacDonald, W. A. (1990). Experimental manipulation of the dawn and dusk chorus in the Blackbird *Turdus merula. Behavioral Ecology and Sociobiology* **26**: 209–216.

Dallimer, M., Irvine, K. N., Skinner, A. M. J., Davies, Z. G., Rouquette, J. R., Maltby, L. L., Warren, P. H., Armsworth, P. R. & Gaston, K. J. (2012). Biodiversity and the feel-good factor. Understanding associations between self-reported human well-being and species richness. *BioScience* **62**: 47–55.

Daniels, G. D. & Kirkpatrick, J. B. (2006). Does variation in garden characteristics

influence the conservation of birds in suburbia? *Biological Conservation* **133**: 326–335.

Dards, J. L. (1979). The population ecology of feral cats (*Felis catus* L.) in Portsmouth Dockyard. Unpublished PhD. Thesis, University of Bradford, UK.

Davey, C. M., Chamberlain, D. E., Newson, S. E., Noble, D. G. & Johnston, A. (2012). Rise of the generalists: evidence for climate driven homogenization in avian communities. *Global Ecology and Biogeography* **21**: 568–578.

Davies, N. B. (1976a). Parental care and the transition to independent feeding in the young Spotted Flycatcher (*Muscicapa striata*). *Behaviour* **59**: 280–294.

Davies, N. B. (1976b). Food, flocking and territorial behaviour of the Pied Wagtail (*Motacilla alba yarrellii* Gould) in winter. *Journal of Animal Ecology* **45**: 235–253.

Davies, N. B. (1977). Prey selection and the search strategy of the Spotted Flycatcher (*Muscicapa striata*): a field study on optimal foraging. *Animal Behaviour* 25 1016–1033.

Davies, N. B. & Brooke, M. de L. (1989). An experimental-study of co-evolution between the Cuckoo, *Cuculus canorus*, and its hosts. 1. Host egg discrimination. *Journal of Animal Ecology* **58**: 207–224.

Davies, N. B. & Lundberg, A. (1984). Food distribution and a variable mating system in the Dunnock, *Prunella modularis. Journal of Animal Ecology* **53**: 895–912.

Davies, Z. G., Fuller, R. A., Dallimer, M., Loram, A. & Gaston, K. J. (2012). Household factors influencing participation in bird feeding activity: a national scale analysis. *PLoS One*, 7, e39692.

Davies, Z. G., Fuller, R. A., Loram, A., Irvine, K. N., Sims, V. & Gaston, K. J. (2009). A national scale inventory of resource provision for biodiversity within domestic gardens. *Biological Conservation* **142**: 761–771.

Davis, P. G. (1977). Changed feeding habits of Siskins and Lesser Redpolls. *Bird Study* **24**: 127–129.

Dawson, A., King, V. M., Bentley, G. E. & Ball, G. F. (2001). Photoperiodic control of seasonality in birds. *Journal of Biological Rhythms* **16**: 365–380.

Deeming, D. C. & Du Feu, C. R. (2011). Long-term patterns in egg mortality during incubation and chick mortality during rearing in three species of tits in an English woodland. *Bird Study* **58**: 278–290.

Deeming, D. C., Mainwaring, M. C., Hartley, I. R. & Reynolds, S. J. (2012). Local temperature and not latitude determines the design of Blue Tit and Great Tit nests. *Avian Biology Research* **5**: 203–208.

De Kort, S. R., Emery, N. J. & Clayton, N. S. (2003). Food offering in Jackdaws (*Corvus monedula*). *Naturwissenschaften* **90**: 238–240.

De Kort, S. R., Emery, N. J. & Clayton, N. S. (2006). Food sharing in Jackdaws, *Corvus monedula*: what, why and with whom? *Animal Behaviour* **72**: 297–304.

De Laet, J. F. (1985). Dominance and anti-predator behaviour of Great Tits *Parus major*: a field study. *Ibis* **127**: 372–377.

de Roode, J. C., Lefèvre, T. & Hunter, M. D. (2013). Self-medication in animals. *Science* **340**: 150–151.

del Rio, C. M. (1993). Do British tits drink milk or just skim the cream? *British Birds* **86**: 321–322.

Dhondt, A. A. (1989). The effect of old age on the reproduction of Great Tits *Parus major* and Blue Tits *P. caeruleus*. *Ibis* **131**: 268–280.

Dhondt, A. A., Altizer, S., Cooch, E. G., Davis, A. K., Dobson, A., Driscoll, M. L. J., Hartup, B. K., Hawley, D. M., Hochachka, W. M., Hosseini, P. R., Jennelle, C. S., Kollias, G. V., Ley, D. H., Swarthout, E. C. H. & Sydenstricker, K. V. (2005). Dynamics of a novel pathogen in an avian host: mycoplasmal conjunctivitis in House Finches. *Acta Tropica* **94**: 77–93.

Dhondt, A. A., Dhondt, K. V., Hawley, D. M. & Jennelle, C. S. (2007). Experimental evidence for transmission of *Mycoplasma gallisepticum* in House Finches by fomites. *Avian Pathology* **36**: 205–208.

Dhondt, A. A. & Eyckerman, R. (1979). Temperature and date of laying by tits *Parus* spp. *Ibis* **121**: 329–331.

Dhondt, A. A. & Huble, L. (1968). Fledging date and sex in relation to dispersal in young tits. *Bird Study* **15**: 127–134.

Diamond, J. M. (1999). Evolutionary biology: dirty eating for healthy living. *Nature* **400**: 120–121.

Dijkstra, E., Komdeur, J. & Dijkstra, C. (1997). Adoption of young in the Blackbird *Turdus merula*. *Ibis* **139**: 174–175.

Dingemanse, N. J., Both, C., Drent, P. J. & Tinbergen, J. M. (2004). Fitness consequences of avian personalities in a fluctuating environment. *Proceedings of the Royal Society (B)* **271**: 847–852.

Dingemanse, N. J., Both, C., Van Noordwijk, A. J., Rutten, A. L. & Drent, P. J. (2003). Natal dispersal and personalities in Great Tits (*Parus major*). *Proceedings of the Royal Society, London (B)* **270**: 741–747.

Dominoni, D., Quetting, M. & Partecke, J. (2013). Artificial light at night advances avian reproductive physiology. *Proceedings of the Royal Society, London (B)* **280**: 20123017.

Dominoni, D. M., Carmona-Wagner, E. O., Hofmann, M., Kranstauber, B. & Partecke, J. (2014). Individual-based measurements of light intensity provide new insights into the effects of artificial light at night on daily rhythms of urban-dwelling songbirds. *Journal of Animal Ecology*, **83**: 681–692.

Draycott, R. A. H., Hoodless, A. N., Ludiman, M. N. and Robertson, P. A. (1998). Effects of spring feeding on body condition of captive-reared ring-necked Pheasants in Great Britain. *Journal of Wildlife Management* **62**: 557–563.

Draycott, R. A. H., Parish, D. M. B., Woodburn, M. I. A. and Carroll, J. P. (2002). Spring body condition of hen Pheasants *Phasianus colchicus* in Great Britain. *Wildlife Biology* **8**: 261–266.

Drent, P. J. & Woldendorp, J. W. (1989). Acid rain and eggshells. *Nature* **339**: 431.

Drewitt, A. & Langston, R. (2008). Collision effects of wind-power generators and other obstacles on birds. *Annals of the New York Academy of Sciences* 1134: 233–266.

Ducatez, S., Audet, J. N., Rodriguez, J. R., Kayello, L. & Lefebvre, L. (2017). Innovativeness and the effects of urbanization on risk-taking behaviors in wild Barbados birds. *Animal Cognition* **20**: 33–42.

Duckworth, R. A., Hallinger, K. K., Hall, N. & Potticary, A. L. (2017). Switch to a novel breeding resource influences coexistence of two passerine birds. *Frontiers in Ecology and Evolution* 5 doi: 10.3389/fevo. 2017. 00072.

Dufva, R. & Allander, K. (1996). Variable effects of the Hen Flea *Ceratophyllus gallinae* on the breeding success of the Great Tit *Parus major* in relation to weather conditions. *Ibis* **138**: 772–777.

Duff, J. P., Holmes, J. P. & Streete, P. (2012). Suspected ethanol toxicity in juvenile Blackbirds and Redwings. *Veterinary Record* doi:10. 1136/vr. e7322.

Dunn, E. (1977). Predation by weasels (*Mustela nivalis*) on breeding tits (*Parus* spp.) in relation to the density of tits and rodents. *Journal of Animal Ecology* 46:633–652.

Dunn, E. H. (1993). Bird mortality from striking residential windows in winter. *Journal of Field Ornithology* **64**: 302–309.

Dunn, E. H. & Tessaglia, D. L. (1994). Predation of birds at feeders in winter. *Journal of Field Ornithology* **65**: 8–16.

East, M. (1981). Aspects of courtship and parental care of the European Robin *Erithacus rubecula*. *Ornis Scandinavica* **12**: 230–239.

Eaton, M., Aebischer, N., Brown, A., Hearn, R., Lock, L., Musgrove, A., Noble, D., Stroud, D. & Gregory, R. (2015). Birds of Conservation Concern **4**: the population status of birds in the UK, Channel Islands and Isle of Man. *British Birds* **108**: 708–746.

Ebenman, B. & Karlsson, J. (1984). Urban Blackbirds (*Turdus merula*): from egg to independence. *Annales Zoologici Fennici* **21**: 249–251.

Eden, S. F. (1985). The comparative breeding biology of Magpies *Pica pica* in an urban and rural habitat (Aves: Corvidae). *Journal of Zoology, London.* **205**: 305–334.

Edwards, P. J. (1985). Brood division and transition to independence in Blackbirds, *Turdus merula*. *Ibis* **127**: 42–59

Eeva, T. & Lehikoinen, E. (1995). Egg shell quality, clutch size and hatching success of the Great Tit (*Parus major*) and the Pied Flycatcher (*Ficedula hypoleuca*) in an air pollution gradient. *Oecologia* **102**: 312–323.

Eeva, T. & Lehikoinen, E. (1996). Growth and mortality of nestling Great Tits (*Parus major*) and Pied Flycatchers (*Ficedule hypoleuca*) in a heavy metal pollution gradient. *Oecologia* **108**: 631–639.

Eeva, T., Ryömä, M. & Riihimäki, J. (2005). Pollution-related changes in diets of two insectivorous passerines. *Oecologia* **145**: 629–639.

Eisner, T. & Aneshansley, D. (2008). 'Anting' in Blue Jays. *Chemoecology* **18**: 197–203.

Ekman, J. (1986). Tree use and predator vulnerability of wintering passerines. *Ornis Scandinavica* **17**: 261–267.

Elmqvist, T., Fragkias, M., Goodness, J., Güneralp, B., Marcotullio, P. J., McDonald, R. I., Parnell, S., Schewenius, M., Sendstad, M., Seto, K. C. & Wilkinson, C. (2013). *Urbanization, Biodiversity and Ecosystem Services: Challenges and Opportunities: A Global Assessment*. Springer, New York.

Enemar, A. & Nilsson, J. Å. (2008). Early onset of reduced reproductive performance with age in the Treecreeper (*Certhia familiaris*). *Journal of Ornithology* **149**: 117–121.

Evans, B. S., Kilpatrick, A. M., Hurlbert, A. H. & Marra, P. P. (2017). Dispersal in the urban matrix: assessing the influence of landscape permeability on the settlement patterns of breeding songbirds. *Frontiers in Ecology and Evolution* **5**: doi: 10. 3389/fevo. 2017. 00063.

Evans, C., Abrams, E., Reitsma, R., Roux, K., Salmonsen, L. & Marra, P. P. (2005). The Neighborhood Nestwatch Program: participant outcomes of a citizen-science ecological research project. *Conservation Biology* **19**: 589–594.

Evans, I. M., Summers, R. W., O'Toole, L., Orr-Ewing, D. C., Evans, R., Snell, N. & Smith, J. (1999). Evaluating the success of translocating Red Kites *Milvus milvus* to the UK. *Bird Study* **46**: 129–144.

Evans, K. L., Newson, S. E. & Gaston, K. J. (2009a). Habitat influences on urban avian assemblages. *Ibis* **151**: 19–39.

Evans, K. L., Gaston, K. J., Sharp, S. P., McGowan, A., Simeoni, M. & Hatchwell, B. J. (2009b). Effects of urbanisation on disease prevalence and age structure in Blackbird *Turdus merula* populations. *Oikos* **118**: pp 774–782.

Evans, K. L., Chamberlain, D. E., Hatchwell, B. J., Gregory, R. D. & Gaston, K. J. (2011). What makes an urban bird? *Global Change Biology* **17**: 32–44.

Evans, K. L., Newton, J., Mallord, J. W. & Markman S. (2012). Stable isotope analysis provides new information on winter habitat use of declining avian migrants that is relevant to their conservation. *PLoS One* **7** (4): e34542.

Evans, M. R. (1997). Nest building signals male condition rather than age in Wrens. *Animal Behaviour* **53**: 749–755.

Evans, M. R. & Burn, J. L. (1996). An experimental analysis of mate choice in the Wren: a monomorphic, polygynous passerine. *Behavioral Ecology* **7**: 101–108.

Evans Ogden, L. J. (1996). Collision course: the hazards of lighted structures and windows to migrating birds. *Fatal Light Awareness Program (FLAP)* 3. World Wildlife Fund Canada/FLAP.

Farrel, J. M., Litovitz, T. L. & Penafiel, M. (1997). The effect of pulsed and sinusoidal magnetic fields on the morphology of developing chick embryos. *Bioelectromagnetics* **18**: 431–438.

Feare, C. J., Gill, E. L., McKay, H. V. & Bishop, J. D. (1995). Is the distribution of Starlings *Sturnus vulgaris* within roosts determined by competition? *Ibis* **137**: 379–382.

Feliciano, L. M., Underwood, T. J. & Aruscavage, D. F. (2018). The effectiveness of bird feeder cleaning methods with and without debris. *Wilson Journal of Ornithology* **130**: 313–320.

Fennessy, G. J. & Kelly, T. C. (2006). Breeding densities of Robin *Erithacus rubecula* in different habitats: the importance of hedgerow structure. *Bird Study* **53**: 97–104.

Fernández-Juricic, E. (2000). Avifaunal use of wooded streets in an urban landscape. *Conservation Biology* **14**: 513–521.

Fernie, K. J. & Reynolds, S. J. (2005). The effects of electromagnetic fields from power lines on avian reproductive biology and physiology: a review. *Journal of Toxicology and Environmental Health – Part B* **8**: 127–140.

Fey, K., Vuorisalo, T., Lehikoinen, A. & Selonen, V. (2015). Urbanisation of the wood pigeon (*Columba palumbus*) in Finland. Landscape and *Urban Planning* **134**: 188–194.

Field, R. H. & Anderson, G. Q. A. (2004). Habitat use by breeding Tree Sparrows *Passer montanus*. *Ibis* **146**: 60–68.

Finch, T., Pearce-Higgins, J. W., Leech, D. I. and Evans, K. L. (2014). Carry-over effects from passage regions are more important than breeding climate in determining the breeding phenology and performance of three avian migrants of conservation concern. *Biodiversity and Conservation*, **23**: 2427–2444.

Finkler, H., Hatna, E. & Terkel, J. (2011). The impact of anthropogenic factors on the behaviour, reproduction, management and welfare of urban, free-roaming cat populations. *Anthrozoös* **24**: 31–39.

Fisher, J. (1953). The Collared Turtle Dove in Europe. *British Birds* **46**: 153–181.

Fisher, J. & Hinde, R. A. (1949). The opening of milk bottle tops by birds. *British Birds* **42**: 347–357.

Fischer, J. D. & Miller, J. R. (2015). Direct and indirect effects of anthropogenic bird food on population dynamics of a songbird. *Acta Oecologia* **69**: 46–51.

Fitzgerald, B. M. & Turner, D. C. (2000). Hunting behaviour of domestic cats and their impact on prey populations: 148–171, in Turner, D. C. & Bateson, P., *The Domestic Cat: The Biology of Its Behaviour*. 2nd Edition. Cambridge University Press, Cambridge.

Fitzgerald, C. S., Curtis, P. D., Richmond, M. E. & Dunn, J. A. (1995). Effectiveness of capsaicin as a repellent to birdseed consumption by Gray Squirrels: 169–183, in Mason, R., *Proceedings Repellents in Wildlife Management*. US Department of Agriculture, Animal and Plant Health Inspection Service, Animal Damage Control program, National Wildlife Research Centre. Fort Collins, Colorado.

Fitzgerald, S. D., Sullivan, J. M. & Everson, R. J. (1990). Suspected ethanol toxicity in two wild Cedar Waxwings. *Avian Diseases* **34**: 488–490.

Fitzpatrick, S. (1994). Nectar-feeding by suburban Blue Tits: contribution to the diet in spring. *Bird Study* **41**: 136–145.

Fitzpatrick, S. (1995). Utilisation of provisioned peanuts by suburban tits in Belfast. *Irish Birds* **5**: 299–304.

Fitzpatrick, S. (1996a). The foraging of wintering Blackcaps in Belfast. *Irish Birds* **5**: 391–398.

Fitzpatrick, S. (1996b). Male and female incubation in Pied Wagtails *Motacilla alba*: shared costs or increased parental care? *Ornis Fennica* **73**: 88–96.

Fitzpatrick, S. (1997). Temporal patterns in feeder use by garden birds in Belfast. *Irish Birds* **6**: 35–44.

Fleischer Jr, A. L., Bowman, R. & Woolfenden, G. E. (2003). Variation in foraging behaviour, diet, and time of breeding of Florida scrub-jays in suburban and wildland habitats. *The Condor* **105**: 515–527.

Flux, J. E. C. (2007). Seventeen years of predation by one suburban cat in New Zealand. *New Zealand Journal of Zoology* **34**: 289–296.

Fogell, D. J., Martin, R. O. & Groombridge, J. J. (2016). Beak and feather disease virus in wild and captive parrots: an analysis of geographic and taxonomic distribution and methodological trends. *Archives of Virology* **161**: 2059–2074.

Fokidis, B. H., Greiner, E. C. & Deviche, P. (2008). Interspecific variation in avian blood parasites and haematology associated with urbanization in a desert habitat. *Journal of Avian Biology* **39**: 300–310.

Foote, J. R., Fitzsimmons, L. P., Mennill, D. J. & Ratcliffe, L. M. (2010). Black-capped Chickadee dawn choruses are interactive communication networks. *Behaviour* **147**: 1219–1248.

Ford, H. A. (1985). Nectarivory and pollination by birds in southern Australia and Europe. *Oikos* **44**;127–131.

Forslund, P., & Pärt, T. (1995). Age and reproduction in birds – hypotheses and tests. *Trends in Ecology and Evolution* **10**: 374–378.

Forzán, M. J., Vanderstichel, R., Melekhovets, Y. F. & McBurney, S. (2010). Trichomoniasis in finches from the Canadian maritime provinces: an emerging disease. *Canadian Veterinary Journal* **51**: 391–396.

Foster, G., Malnick, H., Lawson, P. A., Kirkwood, J., Macgregor, S. K. & Collins, M. D. (2005). *Suttonella ornithocola* sp. nov., from birds of the tits families and emended description of the genus *Suttonella*. *International Journal of Systematic and Evolutionary Microbiology* **55**: 2269–2272.

Fox, A. D., Kobro, S., Lehikoinen, A., Lyngs, P. & Väisänen, R. A. (2009). Northern Bullfinch *Pyrrhula p. pyrrhula* irruptive behaviour linked to rowanberry *Sorbus aucuparia* abundance. *Ornis Fennica* **86**: 51–60.

Francis, M. & Hestor, R. T. (1990). *The Meaning of Gardens*. MIT Press, Cambridge, MA.

Freeman, S. N. & Crick, H. Q. P. (2003). The decline of the Spotted Flycatcher *Muscicapa striata* in the UK: an integrated population model. *Ibis* **145**: 400–412.

Freeman, S. N., Robinson, R. A., Clark, J. A., Griffin, B. M. & Adams, S. Y. (2007). Changing demography and population decline in the Common Starling *Sturnus vulgaris*: a multisite approach to Integrated Population Monitoring. *Ibis* **149**: 587–596.

French, K., Major, R. & Hely, K. (2005). Use of native and exotic garden plants by suburban nectarivorous birds. *Biological Conservation* **121**: 545–559.

Friend, M., McLean, R. G. & Dein, F. J. (2001). Disease emergence in birds: challenges for the twenty-first century. *Auk* **118**: 290–303.

Fuller, R. A., Irvine, K. N., Davies, Z. G., Armsworth, P. R. & Gaston, K. J. (2012). Interactions between people and birds in urban landscapes: 249–266, in Lepczyk, C. A. & Warren, P. S., *Urban Bird Ecology and Conservation. Studies in Avian Biology 44*. University of California Press, Berkeley.

Fuller, R. A., Irvine, K. N., Devine-Wright, P., Warren, P. H. & Gaston, K. J. (2007b). Psychological benefits of greenspace increase with biodiversity. *Biology Letters* **3**: 390–394.

Fuller, R. A., Warren, P. H., Armsworth, P. R., Barbosa, O. & Gaston, K. J. (2008). Garden bird feeding predicts the structure of urban avian assemblages. *Diversity and Distributions* **14**: 131–137.

Fuller, R. A., Warren, P. H. & Gaston, K. J. (2007a). Daytime noise predicts nocturnal singing in urban Robins. *Biology Letters* **3**: 368–370.

Fuller, R. J. & Gough, S. J. (1999). Changes in sheep numbers in Britain: implications for bird populations. *Biological Conservation* **91**: 73–89.

Fuller, R. J., Noble, D. G., Smith, K. W. & Vanhinsbergh, D. (2005). Recent declines in populations of woodland birds in Britain: a review of possible causes. *British Birds* **98**: 116–143.

Gaedecker, N. & Winkel, W. (2005). Are tits *Parus* spp. and other hole nesting passerines preferring at the choice of their breeding holes the weather-opposing side? *Vogelwarte* **43**: 15–18.

Galbraith, J. A., Beggs, J. R., Jones, D. N., McNaughton, E. J., Krull, C. R. &
Stanley, M. C. (2014). Risks and drivers of wild bird feeding in urban areas of New Zealand. *Biological Conservation* **180**: 64–74.

Galbraith, J. A., Beggs, J. R., Jones, D. N. & Stanley, M. C. (2015). Supplementary feeding restructures urban bird communities. *Proceedings of the National Academy of Sciences*, 112 (20) E2648–2657.

Galbraith, J. A., Jones, D. N., Beggs, J. R., Parry, K. & Stanley, M. C. (2017b). Urban bird feeders dominated by a few species and individuals. *Frontiers in Ecology and Evolution* 5:81. doi: 10. 3389/fevo. 2017. 00081.

Galbraith, J. A., Stanley, M. C., Jones, D. N. & Beggs, J. R. (2017a). Experimental feeding regime influences urban bird disease dynamics. *Journal of Avian Biology* **48**: 700–713.

Galligan, T. H. & Kleindorfer, S. (2009). Naris and beak malformation caused by the parasitic fly, *Philornis downsi* (Diptera: Muscidae), in Darwin's small ground finch, *Geospiza fuliginosa* (Passeriformes: Emberizidae). *Biological Journal of the Linnean Society* **98**: 577–585.

Galluzzi, G., Eyzaguirre, P. & Negri, V. (2010). Home gardens: neglected hotspots of agro-biodiversity and cultural diversity. *Biodiversity and Conservation* **19**: 3635–3654.

Garamszegi, L. Z. (2011). Climate change increases the risk of malaria in birds. *Global Change Biology* **17**: 1751–1759.

Garthwaite, D. G. & Thomas, M. R. (1996). The usage of molluscicides in agriculture and horticulture in Great Britain over the last 30 years. Slug and snail pests in agriculture. *British Crop Protection Council Symposium* **66**: 39–46.

Gaston, A. J. (1973). The ecology and behaviour of the Long-tailed Tit. *Ibis* **115**: 330–351.

Gaston, K. J., Beanie, J., Davies, T. W. & Hopkins, J. (2013). The ecological impacts of night-time light pollution: a mechanistic appraisal. *Biological Reviews* **88**: 912–927.

Gaston, K. J., Fuller, R. A., Loram, A., MacDonald, C., Power, S. & Dempsey, N. (2007). Urban domestic gardens (XI): variation in urban wildlife gardening in the United Kingdom. *Biodiversity and Conservation* **16**: 3227–3238.

Gaston, K. J., Smith, R. M., Thompson, K. & Warren, P. H. (2004). Gardens and wildlife – the BUGS project. *British Wildlife* **16**: 1–9.

Gaston, K. J., Smith, R. M., Thompson, K. & Warren, P. H. (2005b). Urban domestic gardens (II): experimental tests of methods for increasing biodiversity. *Biodiversity and Conservation* **14**: 395–413.

Gaston, K. J., Warren, P. H., Thompson, K. & Smith, R. M. (2005a). Urban domestic gardens (IV): the extent of the resource and its associated features. *Biodiversity and Conservation* **14**: 3327–3349.

Gavier-Widén, D., Duff, J. P. & Meredith, A. (2012). *Infectious Diseases of Wild Mammals and Birds in Europe*. Wiley-Blackwell, Oxford.

Geis, A. D. (1980). Relative attractiveness of different foods at wild bird feeders. US Fish and Wildlife Servce, *Special Scientific Report – Wildlife Number 233*.

Gelb, Y. & Delacretaz, N. (2006). Avian window strike mortality at an urban office building. *The Kingbird* **56**: 190–198.

Gelb, Y. & Delacretaz, N. (2009). Windows and vegetation: primary factors in Manhattan bird collisions. *Northeastern Naturalist* **16**: 455–470.

Gibb, J. A. & Betts, M. M. (1963). Food and food supply of nestling tits in Breckland pine. *Journal of Animal Ecology* **32**: 489–533.

Gibbons, D. W., Reid, J. B., & Chapman, R. A. (1993). *The New Atlas of Breeding Birds in Britain & Ireland: 1988–1991*. T. & A. D. Poyser, London.

Gilbert, N. I., Correia, R. A., Silva, J. P., Pacheco, C., Catry, I., Atkinson, P. W., Gill, J. A. & Franco, A. M. (2016). Are white storks addicted to junk food? Impacts of landfill use on the movement and behaviour of resident White Storks (*Ciconia ciconia*) from a partially migratory population. *Movement Ecology*, 4. doi: 10. 1186/s40462-016–0070-0.

Gil-Delgado, J. A. & Guijarro, D. (2008). An evaluation of the use of a spooned spatula to assess the diet of cardueline nestlings. *Ardeola* **55**: 49–57.

Gill, R. M. A. & Beardall, V. (2001). The impact of deer on woodlands: the effects of browsing and seed dispersal on vegetation structure and composition. *Forestry* **74**: 209–218.

Gill, R. M. A. & Fuller, R. J. (2007). The effects of deer browsing on woodland structure and songbirds in lowland Britain. *Ibis* 149: 119–127.

Gillies, C. & Clout, M. (2003). The prey of domestic cats (*Felis catus*) in two suburbs of Auckland City, New Zealand. *Journal of Zoology, London* **259**: 309–315.

Gillings, S. & Beaven, P. (2004). Wintering farmland birds. *British Birds* **97**: 118–129.

Gillings, S., Newson, S. E., Noble, D. G. & Vickery, J. A. (2005). Winter availability of cereal stubbles attracts declining farmland birds and positively influences breeding population trends. *Proceedings of the Royal Society B* **272**: 733–739.

Gillings, S., Wilson, A. M., Conway, G. J., Vickery, J. A. & Fuller, R. J. (2008). Distribution and abundance of birds and their habitats within the lowland farmland of Britain in winter. *Bird Study* **55**: 8–22.

Gionfriddo, J. P. & Best, L. B. (1996). Grit-use patterns in North American birds: the influence of diet, body size, and gender. *Wilson Bulletin* **108**: 685–696.

Giraudeau, M., Mousel, M., Earl, S. & McGraw, K. (2014). Parasites in the city: degree of urbanization predicts poxvirus and coccidian infections in House Finches (*Haemorhous mexicanus*). *PLoS One* **9**: p. e86747.

Glue, D. E. (1996). Goldfinches feeding in gardens. *British Birds* **89**: 459–460.

Goddard, M. A., Dougill, A. J. & Benton, T. G. (2013). Why garden for wildlife? Social and ecological drivers, motivations and barriers for biodiversity management in residential landscapes. *Ecological Economics* **86**: 258–273.

Gooch, S., Baillie, S. R. & Birkhead, T. R. (1991). Magpie *Pica pica* and songbird populations. Retrospective investigation of trends in population density and breeding success. *Journal of Applied Ecology* **28**: 1068–1086.

Goodburn, S. F. (1991). Territory quality or bird quality? Factors determining breeding success in the Magpie *Pica pica*. *Ibis* **133**: 85–90.

Gosler, A. G., Higham, J. P. & Reynolds, S. J. (2005). Why are birds' eggs speckled? *Ecology Letters* **8**: 1105–1113.

Gosler, A. G. & Wilkin, T. A. (2017). Eggshell speckling in a passerine bird reveals chronic long-term decline in soil calcium. *Bird Study* **64**: 195–204.

Götmark, F. & Post, P. (1996). Prey selection by Sparrowhawks, *Accipiter nisus*: relative predation risk for breeding passerine birds in relation to their size, ecology and behaviour. *Philosophical Transactions of the Royal Society, London B* **351**: 1559–1577.

Goulding, K. W. T. & Blake, L. (1993). Testing the PROFILE model on long-term data, in Hornung, M. & Skeffington, R. A., *Critical Loads: Concept and Applications*. ITE Symposium 28. HMSO, London.

Gourama, H. & Bullerman, L. B. (1995). *Aspergillus flavus* and *Aspergillus parasiticus*: aflatoxigenic fungi of concern in foods and feeds: a review. *Journal of Food Protection* **58**: 1395–1404.

Grau, T., Vilcinskas, A. and Joop, G. (2017). Sustainable farming of the mealworm *Tenebrio molitor* for the production of food and feed. *Zeitschrift für Naturforschung C* **72**: 337–349.

Graveland, J. & Berends, J. E. (1997). Timing of the calcium uptake and effect of calcium deficiency on behaviour and egg-laying in captive Great Tits, *Parus major*. *Physiological Zoology* **70**: 74–84.

Graveland, J. & Drent, R. H. (1997). Calcium availability limits breeding success of passerines on poor soils. *Journal of Animal Ecology* **66**: 279–288.

Gray, A., Eadsforth, C. V., Dutton, A. J. & Vaughan, J. A. (1994). The toxicity of three second-generation rodenticides to Barn Owls. *Pest Management Science* 42(3): 179–184.

Green, R. (1998). Long-term decline in the thickness of eggshells of thrushes, *Turdus* spp., in Britain. *Proceedings of the Royal Society B* **265**: 679–684.

Greenberg, C. H. & Walter, S. T. (2010). Fleshy fruit removal and nutritional composition of winter-fruiting plants: a comparison of non-native invasive and native species. *Natural Areas Journal* **30**: 312–321.

Greenwood, J. J. D. & Clarke, N. (1991). A preliminary experiment on preferences for sunflowers and peanuts for garden birds. *BTO Research Report 72*, British Trust for Ornithology, Tring.

Grégoire, A., Faivre, B., Heeb, P. & Cézilly, F. (2002). A comparison of infestation patterns by *Ixodes* ticks in urban and rural populations of the Common Blackbird *Turdus merula*. *Ibis* **144**: 640–645.

Greig, E. I., Wood, E. M. & Bonter, D. N. (2017). Winter range expansion of a hummingbird associated with urbanization and supplementary feeding. *Proceedings of the Royal Society B* 284: 20170256.

Grieco, F. (2002). How different provisioning strategies result in equal rates of food delivery: an experimental study of Blue Tits *Parus caeruleus*. *Journal of Avian Biology* **33**: 331–341.

Griffith, S. C., Owens, I. P. & Thuman, K. A. (2002). Extra pair paternity in birds: a review of interspecific variation and adaptive function. *Molecular Ecology* **11**: 2195–2212.

Groom, D. W. (1993). Magpie Pica pica predation on Blackbird *Turdus merula* nests in urban areas. *Bird Study* **40**: 55–62.

Grubb, T. C. (1987). Changes in the flocking behaviour of wintering English titmice with time, weather and supplementary food. *Animal Behaviour* **35**: 794–806.

Grubb, T. C. & Cimprich, D. A. (1990). Supplementary food improves the nutritional condition of wintering woodland birds: evidence from ptilochronology. *Ornis Scandinavica* **21**: 277–281.

Grzędzicka, E. Krzysztof, K. U. S. & Nabielec, J. (2013). The effect of urbanization on the diet composition of the Tawny Owl (*Strix aluco* L.). *Polish Journal of Ecology* **61**: 391–400.

Guarino, L. & Hoogendijk, M. (2004). Microenvironments: 31–40, in Eyzaguirre, P. & Linares, O., *Home Gardens and Agrobiodiversity*. Smithsonian Books, Washington.

Haftorn, S. (1986). Clutch size, intraclutch egg-size variation, and breeding strategy in the Goldcrest *Regulus regulus*. *Journal of Ornithology* **127**: 291–301.

Hager, S., Consentino, B., McKay, K., Monson, C., Zuurdeeg, W. & Blevins, B. (2013). Window area and development drive spatial variation in bird-window collisions in an urban landscape. *PLoS One* **8**: 1–10.

Hake, M. (1996). Fattening strategies in dominance-structured Greenfinch (*Carduelis chloris*) flocks in winter. *Behavioural Ecology and Sociobiology* **39**: 71–76.

Halfwerk, W., Holleman, L. J., Lessells, C. K. & Slabbekoorn, H. (2011). Negative impact of traffic noise on avian reproductive success. *Journal of Applied Ecology* **48**: 210–219.

Hall, A. J. & Saito, E. K. (2008). Avian wildlife mortality events due to salmonellosis in the United States, 1985–2004. *Journal of Wildlife Diseases* **44**: 585–593.

Hancock, M. H. & Wilson, J. D. (2003). Winter habitat associations of seed-eating passerines on Scottish farmland. *Bird Study* **50**: 116–130.

Handel, C. M., Pajot, L. M., Matsuoka, S. M., van Hemert, C., Terenzi, J., Talbot, S. L., Mulcahy, D. M., Meteyer, C. U. & Trust, K. A. (2010). Epizootic of beak deformities among wild birds in Alaska: an emerging disease in North America. *The Auk* **127**: 882–898.

Hanmer, H. J., Thomas, R. L., Beswick, G. J., Collins, B. P. & Fellowes, M. D. (2017a). Use of anthropogenic material affects bird nest arthropod community structure: influence of urbanisation, and consequences for ectoparasites and fledging success. *Journal of Ornithology* **158**: 1045–1059.

Hanmer, H. J., Thomas, R. L. & Fellowes, M. D. (2017b). Provision of supplementary food for wild birds may increase the risk of local nest predation. *Ibis* **159**: 158–167.

Hanmer, H. J., Thomas, R. L. & Fellowes, M. D. (2018). Introduced Grey Squirrels subvert supplementary feeding of suburban wild birds. *Landscape and Urban Planning* **177**: 10–18.

Hansell, M. H. (2000). *Bird Nests and Construction Behaviour.* Cambridge University Press, Cambridge.

Hardman, S. I. & Dalesman, S. (2018). Repeatability and degree of territorial aggression differs among urban and rural Great Tits (*Parus major*). *Scientific Reports* **8**: 5042.

Hardy, E. (1978). Winter foods of Blackcaps in Britain. *Bird Study* **25**: 60–61.

Harper, D. G. C. (1985b). Pairing strategies and mate choice in female Robins (*Erithacus rubecula*). *Animal Behaviour* **33**: 865–875.

Harper, D. G. C. (1985a). Brood division in Robins. *Animal Behaviour* **33**: 466–480.

Harper, D. G. C. (1986). Individual territories in the Robin: 2355–2363, in Ouellet, H. *Acta XIX Congressus Internationalis Ornithologici.* University of Ottawa Press, Ottawa.

Harpum, J. R. (1985). *Gloucestershire Naturalists Journal* **36**: 115–117.

Harris, A. S. (1969). Ripening and dispersal of a bumper western hemlock-Sitka spruce seed crop in southeast Alaska (Vol. 105). Pacific Northwest Forest and Range Experiment Station.

Harrison, T. J. E., Smith, J. A., Martin, G. R., Chamberlain, D. E, Bearhop, S., Robb, G. N. & Reynolds, S. J. (2010). Does food supplementation really enhance productivity of breeding birds? *Oecologia* **164**: 311–320.

Harrup, B. (1998). Wintering blackcaps taking nectar from, and probably pollinating, *Mahonia. British Birds* **91**: 201.

Hartig, T., Mang, M. & Evans, G. W. (1991). Restorative effects of natural environment experiences. *Environment and Behaviour* **23**: 3–26.

Hartup, B. K., Mohammed, H. O., Kollias, G. V. & Dhondt, A. A. (1998). Risk factors associated with mycoplasmal conjunctivitis in House Finches. *Journal of Wildlife Diseases* 34 (2): 281–288.

Hatchwell, B. J., Chamberlain, D. E. & Perrins, C. M. (1996a). The demography of Blackbirds *Turdus merula* in rural habitats: is farmland a sub-optimal habitat? *Journal of Applied Ecology* **33**: 1114–1124.

Hatchwell, B. J., Chamberlain, D. E. & Perrins, C. M. (1996b). The reproductive success of Blackbirds *Turdus merula* in relation to habitat structure and choice of nest site. *Ibis* **138**: 256–262.

Hatchwell, B. J., Fowlie, M. K., Ross, D. J. & Russell, A. F. (1999a). Incubation behaviour of Long-tailed Tits: why do males provision incubating females? *Condor* **101**: 681–686.

Hatchwell, B. J. & Russell, A. F. (1996). Provisioning rules in cooperatively breeding Long-tailed Tits *Aegithalos caudatus*: an experimental study. *Proceedings of the Royal Society, London (B)* **263**: 83–88.

Hatchwell, B. J., Russell, A. F., MacColl, A. D. C., Ross, D. J., Fowlie, M. K. & McGowan, A. (2004). Helpers increase long-term but not short-term productivity in cooperatively breeding Long-tailed Tits. *Behavioral Ecology* **15**: 1–10.

Hatchwell, B. J., Sharp, S. P., Simeoni, M. & McGowan, A. (2009). Factors influencing overnight loss of body mass in the communal roosts of social birds. *Functional Ecology* **23**: 367–372.

Haywood, S. & Perrins, C. M. (1992). Is clutch size in birds affected by environmental conditions during growth? *Proceedings of the Royal Society, London (B)* **249**: 195–197.

van Heezik, Y., Smyth, A., Adams, A. & Gordon, J. (2010). Do domestic cats impose an unsustainable harvest on urban bird populations. *Biological Conservation* **143**: 121–130.

Hegner, E. (1985). Dominance and anti-predator behaviour in Blue Tits (*Parus caeruleus*). *Animal Behaviour* **33**: 762–768.

Helbig, A., Berthold, P., Mohr, G. & Querner, U. (1994). Inheritance of a novel migratory direction in central European Blackcaps. *Naturwissenschaften* **81**: 184–186.

Henke, S. E., Gallardo, V. C., Martinez, B. & Bailey, R. (2001). Survey of aflatoxin concentrations in wild bird seed purchased in Texas. *Journal of Wildlife Diseases* **37**: 831–835.

Herrera-Dueñas, A., Pineda, J., Antonio, M. T. & Aguirre, J. I. (2014). Oxidative stress of House Sparrows as bioindicator of urban pollution. *Ecological Indicators* **42**: 6–9.

Hill, D. A. & Robertson, P. A. (1988). A population model as an aid to Pheasant management: 149–163, in Hallett, D. L., Edwards, W. R. & Burger, G. V., *Pheasants: Symptoms of Wildlife Problems on Agricultural Lands.* North Central Section of the Wildlife Society, Bloomington, IN.

Hindmarsh, A. M. (1984). Vocal mimicry in Starlings. *Behaviour* **90**: 302–324.

Hinsley, S., Bellamy, P. & Moss, D. (1995). Sparrowhawk *Accipiter nisus* predation and feeding site selection by tits. *Ibis* **137**: 418–420.

Hinsley, S., Rothery, P. & Bellamy, P. E. (1999). Influence of woodland area on breeding success in Great Tits *Parus major* and Blue Tits *Parus caeruleus*. *Journal of Avian Biology* **30**: 271–281.

Hochachka, W. M. & Dhondt, A. A. (2000). Density-dependent decline of host abundance resulting from a new infectious disease. *Proceedings of the National Academy of Science* **97** (10): 5303–5306.

Hogstad, O. (1988). Social rank and antipredator behaviour of Willow Tits *Parus montanus* in winter flocks. *Ibis* **130**: 45–56.

Högstedt, G. (1980). Evolution of clutch size in birds: adaptive variation in relation to territory quality. *Science* **210**: 1148–1150.

Hole, D. G. (2001). The population ecology and ecological genetics of the House Sparrow *Passer domesticus* on farmland in Oxfordshire. DPhil thesis, University of Oxford.

Holford, K. C. & Roby, D. D. (1993). Factors limiting fecundity of captive Brown-headed Cowbirds. *Condor* **95**: 536–545.

Hölker, F., Moss, T., Griefahn, B., Kloas, W., Voight, C. C., Henckel, D., Hänel, A., Kappeler, P. M., Völker, S., Schwope, A., Franke, S., Uhrlandt, D., Fischer, J., Klenke, R., Wolter, C. & Tockner, K. (2010). The dark side of light: a transdisciplinary research agenda for light pollution policy. *Ecology and Society* **15** (4): 13.

Hollom, P. A. D. (1966). Nocturnal singing and feeding by Robins in winter. *British Birds* **59**: 502.

Honkavaara, J., Siitari, H. & Viitala, J. (2004). Fruit colour preferences of

Redwings (*Turdus iliacus*): experiments with hand-raised juveniles and wild-caught adults. *Ethology* **110**: 445–457.

Hooten, M. B. & Wikle, C. K. (2008). A hierarchical Bayesian non-linear spatio-temporal model for the spread of invasive species with application to the Eurasian Collared-Dove. *Environmental and Ecological Statistics* **15**: 59–70.

Hope, D., Gries, C., Zhu, W. X., Fagan, W. F., Redman, C. L., Grimm, N. B., Nelson, A. L., Martin, C. & Kinzig, A. (2003). Socioeconomics drive urban plant diversity. *Proceedings of the National Academy of Sciences of the United States of America* **100**: 8788–8792.

Horn, D. J., Johansen, S. M. & Wilcoxen, T. E. (2014). Seed and feeder use by birds in the United States and Canada. *Wildlife Society Bulletin* **38**: 18–25.

Horton, D. L., Lawson, B., Egbetade, A., Jeffries, C., Johnson, N., Cunningham, A. A. & Frooks, A. R. (2012). Targeted surveillance for Usutu virus in British birds (2005–2011). *Veterinary Record* doi: 10. 1136/vr. 101275

Hughes, L. A., Shopland, S., Wigley, P., Bradon, H., Leatherbarrow, A. H., Williams, N. J., Bennett, M., de Pinna, E., Lawson, B., Cunningham, A. A. & Chantrey, J. (2008). Characterisation of *Salmonella enterica* serotype Typhimurium isolates from wild birds in northern England from 2005–2006. *BMC Veterinary Research 2008* 4: 4.

Huhta, E., Rytkonen, S. & Solonen, T. (2003). Plumage brightness of prey increases predation risk: an among-species comparison. *Ecology* **84**: 1793–1799.

Humphreys, E., Kirkland, P. & Chamberlain, D. E. (2013). The Biodiversity in Glasgow (BIG) Project.

BTO Research Report **603**: British Trust for Ornithology, Thetford.

Hurvell, B., Borg, K., Gunnarsson, A. & Jevring, J. (1974). Studies on *Salmonella typhimurium* infections in passerine birds in Sweden. *International Congress of Game Biologists* **11**: 493–497.

Hutchinson, D. K. & Kellam, J. S. (2015). A test of the self-medication hypothesis for anting behaviour in Blue Jays. *Bios* **86**: 144–151.

Ibáñez-Álamo, J. D., Pineda-Pampliega, J., Thomson, R. L., Aguirre, J. I., Díez-Fernández, A., Faivre, B., Figuerola, J. & Verhulst, S. (2018). Urban blackbirds have shorter telomeres. *Biology Letters*, **14**: 20180083.

Ibáñez-Álamo, J. D., Rubio, E. & Bitrus, Z. K. (2017). The degree of urbanization of a species affects how intensively it is studied: a global perspective. *Frontiers in Ecology and Evolution* 5. DOI=10. 3389/ fevo. 2017. 00041.

Ibáñez-Álamo, J. D. & Soler, M. (2010). Does urbanization affect selective pressures and life-history strategies in the Common Blackbird (*Turdus merula* L.)? *Biological Journal of the Linnean Society* **101**: 759–766.

Ibáñez-Álamo, J. D. & Soler, M. (2017). Male and female Blackbirds (*Turdus merula*) respond similarly to the risk of nest predation. *Journal of Ornithology* **158**: 533–539.

Inger, R., Cox, D. T., Per, E., Norton, B. A. & Gaston, K. J. (2016). Ecological role of vertebrate scavengers in urban ecosystems in the UK. *Ecology and Evolution* **6**: 7015–7023.

Inglis, I. R., Isaacson, A. J., Smith, G. C., Haynes, P. J. & Thearle, R. J. P. (1997). The effect on the Woodpigeon (*Columba palumbus*) of the introduction of oilseed rape into Britain. *Agriculture, Ecosystems and Environment* **61**: 113–121.

IPCC. (2013). *Climate Change 2013: The Physical Science Basis. Contribution of Working Group I to the Fifth Assessment Report of the Intergovernmental Panel on Climate Change.* Cambridge University Press, Cambridge, UK, and New York.

Isaksson, C. (2010). Pollution and its impact on wild animals: a meta-analysis on oxidative stress. *EcoHealth* **7**: 342–350.

Isaksson, C., Rodewald, A. & Gil., D. (2018). Behavioural and ecological consequences of urban life in birds. *Frontiers in Ecology and Evolution* 6. DOI=10. 3389/fevo. 2018. 00050

Ishigame, G. & Baxter, G. S. (2007). Practice and attitudes of suburban and rural dwellers to feeding wild birds in Southeast Queensland, Australia. *Ornithological Science* **6**: 11–19.

Ishigame, G., Baxter, G. S. & Lisle, A. T. (2006). Effects of artificial foods on the blood chemistry of the Australian Magpie. *Austral Ecology* **31**: 199–207.

Jack, S. L. (2016). The Use of Supplementary Food Sources by Bird Communities and Individuals. MSc Thesis, University of Exeter.

Jackson, R. D. (1954). Territory and pair-formation in the Blackbird. *British Birds* **47**: 123–131.

Jacob, J. & Zisweiler, V. (1982). The uropygial gland: 199–314, in Farner, D. S., King, J. R. & Parkes, K. C. (eds) *Avian Biology VI.* Academic Press, New York.

Jadczyk, P. & Drzeniecka-Osiadacz, A. (2013). Feeding strategy of wintering Rooks *Corvus frugilegus* L. in urban habitats. *Polish Journal of Ecology* **61**: 587–596.

James, M. C., Furness, R. W., Bowman, A. S., Forbes, K. J. & Gilbert, L. (2011). The importance of passerine birds as tick hosts and the transmission of *Borrelia burgdorferi*, the agent of Lyme disease:

a case study from Scotland. *Ibis* **153**: 293–302.

Jankowiak, Ł., Zyskowski, D. & Wysocki, D. (2018). Age-specific reproduction and disposable soma in an urban population of Common Blackbirds *Turdus merula*. *Ibis* **160**: 130–144.

Jansson, C., Ekman, J. & von Brömssen, A. (1981). Winter mortality and food supply in tits *Parus* spp. *Oikos* **37**: 313–322.

Järvi, T. & Bakken, M. (1984). The function of the variation in the breast stripe of the Great Tit *Parus major*. *Animal Behaviour* **32**: 590–596.

Jarvis, P. (1990). Urban cats as pests and pets. *Environmental Conservation* **17**: 169–171.

Jenni, L. (1993). Structure of a Brambling *Fringilla montifringilla* roost according to sex, age and body-mass. *Ibis* **135**: 85–90.

Jerzak, L. (2001). Synurbaization of the Magpie in the Palearctic: 403–425, in Marzluff, J. M., Bowman, R. & Donelly, R., *Avian Ecology and Conservation in an Urbanizing World.* Kluwer, New York.

Johnsgard, P. A. (1999). *The Pheasants of the World.* Smithsonian Institution Press, Washington.

Jokimäki, J. (1999). Occurrence of breeding bird species in urban parks: effects of park structure and broad-scale variables. *Urban Ecosystems* **3**: 21–34.

Jokimäki, J. & Kaisanlahti-Jokimäki, M. L. (2003). Spatial similarity of urban bird communities: a multi-scale approach. *Journal of Biogeography* **30**: 1183–1193.

Jokimäki, J., Suhonen, J., Vuorisalo, T., Kövér, L. & Kaisanlahti-Jokimäki, M. L. (2017). Urbanization and nest-site selection of the Black-billed Magpie (*Pica pica*) populations in two Finnish cities: from a persecuted species to an urban exploiter. *Landscape and Urban Planning* **157**: 577–585.

Jones, D. N. (2018). *The Birds at My Table*. Comstock Publishing Associates, Ithaca, NY.

Jones, D. N. & Reynolds, S. J. (2008). Feeding birds in our towns and cities: a global research opportunity. *Journal of Avian Biology* **39**: 265–271.

Jordano, P. & Herrera, C. M. (1981). The frugivorous diet of Blackcap populations *Sylvia atricapilla* wintering in southern Spain. *Ibis* **123**: 502–507.

Jourdain, F. C. R. (1936). On the winter habits of the Green Woodpecker (*Picus viridis virescens*). *Proceedings of the Zoological Society, London* **106**: 251–256.

Jovani, R. & Blanco, G. (2000). Resemblance within flocks and individual differences in feather mite abundance on Long-tailed Tits, *Aegithalos caudatus* (L.). *Ecoscience* **7**: 428–432.

Jovani, R., Avilés, J. M. & Rodriguez-Sánchez, F. (2012). Age-related sexual plumage dimorphism and badge framing in the European Robin *Erithacus rubecula*. *Ibis* **154**: 147–154.

Judson, O. P. & Bennett, A. T. D. (1992). 'Anting' as food preparation: formic acid is worse on an empty stomach. *Behavioural Ecology and Sociobiology* **31**: 437–439.

Junker-Bornholdt, R. & Schmidt, K. H. (1999). Comparative study of cavity-nesting passerines in urban and rural habitats. *Vogelwelt* **121**: 129–153.

Kacelnik, A. & Krebs, J. R. (1983). The dawn chorus in the Great Tit (*Parus major*): proximate and ultimate causes. *Behaviour* **3**: 287–308.

Källander, H. (1981). The effects of provision of food in winter on a population of the Great Tit *Parus major* and the Blue Tit *Parus caeruleus*. *Ornis Scandinavica* **12**: 244–248.

Kang, W., Lee, D. & Park, C. R. (2012). Nest distribution of Magpies *Pica pica sericea* as related to habitat connectivity in an urban environment. *Landscape and Urban Planning* **104**: 212–219.

Kaplan, R. & Kaplan, S. (1989). *The Experience of Nature: A Psychological Perspective*. Cambridge University Press, Cambridge.

Kapperud, G. & Rosef, O. (1983). Avian wildlife reservoir of *Campylobacter fetus* subsp *jejuni*, *Yersinia* spp and *Salmonella* spp in Norway. *Applied and Environmental Microbiology* **45**: 375–380.

Karasov, W. H., Brittingham, M. C. & Temple, S. A. (1992). Daily energy and expenditure by Black-capped Chickadees (*Parus atricapillus*) in winter. *Auk* **109**: 393–395.

Kašová, M., Nado, L. & Kaňuch, P. (2014). Structure of tree vegetation may reduce costs of territory defence in Eurasian Nuthatch *Sitta europaea*. *Bird Study* **61**: 413–420.

Kekkonen, J., Hanksi, I. K., Väisänen, R. A. & Brommer, J. E. (2012). Levels of heavy metals in House Sparrows (*Passer domesticus*) from urban and rural habitats in southern Finland. *Ornis Fennica* **89**: 91–98.

Kelleher, K. M. & O'Halloran, J. (2007). Influence of nesting habitat on breeding Song Thrushes *Turdus philomelos*. *Bird Study* **54**: 221–229.

Keller, L. F. & van Noordwijk, A. J. (1994). Effects of local environmental conditions on nestling growth in the Great Tit *Parus major* L. *Ardea* **82**: 349–362.

Kempenaers, B., Borgström, P., Löes, P., Schlicht, E. & Valcu, M. (2010). Artificial night lighting affects dawn song, extra-pair siring success, and lay date in songbirds. *Current Biology* **19**: 1735–1739.

Kempenaers, B., Verheyen, G. R. & Dhondi, A. A. (1997). Extrapair paternity in the Blue Tit (*Parus caeruleus*): female choice, male characteristics, and offspring quality. *Behavioural Ecology* **8**: 481–492.

Kennedy, R. J. (1969). Sunbathing behaviour of birds. *British Birds* **62**: 45–47.

Keymer, I. F. & Blackmore, D. K. (1964). Diseases of the skin and softs parts of wild birds. *British Birds* **57**: 175–179.

Killick, R. S., Lawson, B., MacDonald, S. J., Chan, D. & Cunningham, A. A. (unpublished). The presence of mycotoxins in wild bird food exposed to UK climatic conditions.

Killick, T. (2006). Is public feeding of the Red Kite (*Milvus milvus*) in the Chilterns AONB helping, or hindering their reintroduction? Unpublished Advanced Diploma Thesis, University of Oxford Department for Continuing Education, Oxford

Kinzig, A. P., Warren, P., Martin, C., Hope, D. & Katti, M. (2005). The effects of human socioeconomic status and cultural characteristics on urban patterns of biodiversity. *Ecology and Society* 10. www. jstor. org/stable/26267712.

Kirby, W., Black, K., Pratt, S. and Bradbury, R. (2005). Territory and nest-site habitat associations of Spotted Flycatchers *Muscicapa striata* breeding in central England. *Ibis* **147**: 420–424.

Kirkwood, J. K. (1998). Population density and infectious disease at bird tables. *Veterinary Record* **142**: 468.

Kirkwood, J. K., Holmes, J. P. & Macgregor, S. (1995). Garden bird mortalities. *Veterinary Record* **136**: 372.

Kirkwood, J. K., Macgregor, S., Malnick, H. & Foster, G. (2006). Unusual mortality

incidents in tit species (family Paridae) associated with novel bacterium *Suttonella ornithocola*. *Veterinary Record* **158**: 203–205.

Klem, D. (1989). Bird-window collisions. *Wilson Bulletin* **101**: 606–620.

Klem, D. (1990b). Bird injuries, cause of death, and recuperation from collisions with windows. *Journal of Field Ornithology* **61**: 115–119.

Klem, D. (1990a). Collisions between birds and windows: mortality and prevention. *Journal of Field Ornithology* **61**: 120–128.

Klem, D. (1991). Glass and bird kills: an overview and suggested planning and design methods of preventing a fatal hazard: 99–103, in Adams, L. W. & Leedy, D. L., *Wildlife Conservation in Metropolitan Environments*, National Symposium on Urban Wildlife, Series 2.

Klem, D. & Saenger, P. (2013). Evaluating the effectiveness of select visual signals to prevent bird-window collisions. *Wilson Journal of Ornithology* **125**: 406–411.

Kluijver, H. N. (1951). The population ecology of the Great Tit *Parus m. major* L. *Ardea* **391**: 1–135.

Krebs, J. R. (1970). The efficiency of courtship feeding in the Blue Tit, *Parus caeruleus*. *Ibis* **112**: 108–110.

Krebs, J. R. (1980). Optimal foraging, predation risk, and territory defence. *Ardea* **68**: 83–90.

Kubitza, R. J., Bugnyar, T. & Schwab, C. (2015). Pair bond characteristics and maintenance in free-flying Jackdaws *Corvus monedula*: effects of social context and season. *Journal of Avian Biology* **46**: 206–215.

Kubota, H. & Nakamura, M. (2000). Effects of supplemental food on intra-and inter-specific behaviour of the Varied Tit *Parus varius*. *Ibis* **142**: 312–319.

Kuitunen, M., Jäntti, A., Suhonen, J. & Aho, T. (1996) Food availability and the male's role in parental care in the double-brooded Common Treecreeper *Certhia familiaris*. *Ibis* **138**: 638–643.

Kunca, T., Smejkalová, P. & Cepicka, I. (2015). Trichomonosis in Eurasian Sparrowhawks in the Czech Republic. *Folia Parasitologica* **62**. doi: 10. 14411/fp. 2015. 035

Kunca, T. & Yosef, R. (2016). Differential nest-defence to perceived danger in urban and rural areas by female Eurasian Sparrowhawk (*Accipiter nisus*). *PeerJ* **4**: p. e2070.

Kurucz, K., Bertalan, L. & Purger, J. J. (2012). Survival of Blackbird (*Turdus merula*) clutches in an urban environment: experiment with real and artificial nests. *North-Western Journal of Zoology* **8**: 362–364.

Kurucz, K., Kallenberger, H., Szigeti, C. & Purger, J. J. (2010). Survival probabilities of first and second clutches of Blackbird (*Turdus merula*) in an urban environment. *Archives of Biological Sciences* **62**: 489–493.

Kyrkos, A., Wilson, J. & Fuller, R. (1998). Farmland habitat change and abundance of Yellowhammers *Emberiza citrinella*: an analysis of Common Birds Census data. *Bird Study* **45**: 232–246.

Labere, M. P., Butkus, M. A., Riegner, D., Schommer, N. & Atkinson, J. (2004). Evaluation of lead movement from the abiotic to biotic at a small-arms firing range. *Environmental Geology* **46**: 750–754.

Lachish, S., Bonsall, M. B., Lawson, B., Cunningham, A. A. & Sheldon, B. C. (2012a). Individual and population-level impacts of an emerging poxvirus disease in a wild population of Great Tits. *PLoS One* 7 (11): e48545.

Lachish, S., Lawson, B., Cunningham, A. A. & Sheldon, B. C. (2012b). Epidemiology of the emergent disease paridae pox in an intensively studied wild bird population. *PLoS One* 7 (11): e38316.

Lack, D. & Lack, E. (1951). The breeding biology of the Swift *Apus apus*. *Ibis* **93**: 501–546.

LaDeau, S. L., Kilpatrick, A. M. & Marra, P. P. (2007). West Nile virus emergence and large-scale declines of North American bird populations. *Nature*: nature05829. 3d.

Lamb, S. D., Taylor, H. R., Holtmann, B., Santos, E. S., Tamayo, J. H., Johnson, S. L., Nakagawa, S. and Lara, C. E. (2017). Coprophagy in Dunnocks (*Prunella modularis*): a frequent behaviour in females, infrequent in males, and very unusual in nestlings. *Wilson Journal of Ornithology* **129**: 615–620.

Lambrechts, M. & Dhondt, A. A. (1986). Male quality, reproduction, and survival in the Great Tit (*Parus major*). *Behavioral Ecology and Sociobiology*, **19**: 57–63.

Lambrechts, M. M., Haurez, J., Bodineau, G., Gagliardi, G., Maistre, M., Perret, P., Pihan, P., Wilhelm, B., Wilhelm, J., Bernard, C. & Blondel, J. (2016). Coal Tits *Periparus ater* build larger nests than Blue Tits *Cyanistes caeruleus* and Great Tits *Parus major* living in the same Mediterranean coniferous woodland habitat. *Acta Ornithologica* **51**: 123–129.

Landsberg, H. E. (1981). *The Urban Climate*. Academic Press, New York.

Laucht, S., Kempenaers, B. & Dale, J. (2010). Bill colour, not badge size, indicates testosterone-related information in House Sparrows. *Behavioural Ecology and Sociobiology* 64, 1461–1471.

Lawson, B., Cunningham, A. A., Chantrey, J., Hughes, L. A., John, S. K., Bunbury, N., Bell, D. J. & Tyler, K. M. (2011a). A clonal strain of *Trichomonas gallinae* is the aetiologic agent of an emerging avian epidemic disease. *Infection, Genetics and Evolution* **11**: 1638–1645.

Lawson, B., de Pinna, E., Horton, R. A., Macgregor, S. K., John, S. K., Chantrey, J., Duff, J. P., Kirkwood, J. K., Simpson, V. R., Robinson, R. A., Wain, J. & Cunningham, A. A. (2014). Epidemiological evidence that garden birds are a source of human salmonellosis in England and Wales. *PLoS One* 9 (2): e88968.

Lawson, B., Duff, J. P., Beckmann, K. M., Chantrey, J., Peck, K. M., Irvine, R. M., Robinson, R. A. & Cunningham, A. A. (2015b). Drowning is an apparent and unexpected recurrent cause of mass mortality of Common Starling (*Sturnus vulgaris*). *Scientific Reports* **5**: 17020. DOI: 10. 1038/srep17020.

Lawson, B., Howard, T., Kirkwood, J. K., Macgregor, S. K., Perkins, M., Robinson, R. A., Ward, L. R. & Cunningham, A. A. (2010) Epidemiology of salmonellosis in garden birds in England and Wales, 1993 to 2003. *EcoHealth* **7**: 294–306.

Lawson, B., Lachish, S., Colville, K. M., Durrant, C., Peck, K. M., Toms, M. P., Sheldon, B. C. & Cunningham, A. A. (2012b). Emergence of a novel avian pox disease in British tit species. *PLoS One* 7 (11): e40176.

Lawson, B., MacDonald, S., Howard, T., Macgregor, S. K. & Cunningham, A. A. (2006). Exposure of garden birds to aflatoxins in Britain. *Science of the Total Environment* **361**: 124–131.

Lawson, B., Malnick, H., Pennycott, T. W., Macgregor, S. K., John, S. K., Duncan, G., Hughes, L. A., Chantrey, J. & Cunningham, A. A. (2011b). Acute necrotising pneumonitis associated with *Suttonella ornithocola* infection in tits (Paridae). *The Veterinary Journal* **188**: 96–100.

Lawson, B., Petrovan, S. O. & Cunningham, A. A. (2015a). Citizen science and wildlife disease surveillance. *EcoHealth* **12**: 693–702.

Lawson, B., Robinson, R. A., Colville, K. M., Peck, K. M., Chantrey, J., Pennycott, T. W., Simpson, V. R., Toms, M. P. & Cunningham, A. A. (2012a). The emergence and spread of finch trichomonosis in the British Isles. *Philosophical Transactions of the Royal Society (B)* **367**: 2852–2863.

Lawson, B., Robinson, R. A., Neimanis, A., Handeland, K., Isomursu, M., Agren, E. O., Hamnes, I. S., Tyler, K. M., Chantrey, J., Hughes, L. A., Pennycott, T. W., Simpson, V. R., John, S. K., Peck, K. M., Toms, M. P., Bennett, M., Kirkwood, J. K. & Cunningham, A. A. (2011a). Evidence of spread of the emerging infectious disease finch trichomonosis, by migrating birds. *EcoHealth* **8**: 143–153.

Lawson, B., Robinson, R. A., Toms, M. P., Risley, K., MacDonald, S. & Cunningham, A. A. (2018). Health hazards to wild birds and risk factors associated with anthropogenic provisioning. *Philosophical Transactions of the Royal Society (B)*. doi: 10. 1098/rstb. 2017. 0091.

Leach, I. H. (1981). Wintering Blackcaps in Britain and Ireland. *Bird Study* **28**: 5–14.

Lee, S. I., Lee, H., Jablonski, P. G., Choe, J. C. & Husby, M. (2017). Microbial abundance on the eggs of a passerine bird and related fitness consequences between urban and rural habitats. *PLoS One* 12 (9): e0185411. Doi. org/10. 1371/ journal. pone. 0185411

Legg, E. W. & Clayton, N. S. (2014). Eurasian Jays (*Garrulus glandarius*) conceal caches from onlookers. *Animal Cognition* **17**: 1223–1226.

Legg, E. W., Ostoji , L. & Clayton, N. S. (2016). Caching at a distance: a cache protection strategy in Eurasian Jays. *Animal Cognition* **19**: 753–758.

Lehikoinen, A., Lehikoinen, E., Valkama, J., Väisänen, R. A. & Isomursu, M. (2013). Impacts of trichomonosis epidemics on Greenfinch *Chloris chloris* and Chaffinch *Fringilla coelebs* populations in Finland. *Ibis* **155**: 357–366.

Lehikoinen, E. (1986). Dependence of winter survival on size in the Great Tit *Parus major. Ornis Fennica* **63**: 10–16.

Lehikoinen, E. (1987). Seasonality of the daily weight cycle in wintering passerines and its consequences. *Ornis Scandinavica* **18**: 216–226.

Lepczyk, C. A., Mertig, A. G. & Liu, J. G. (2004a). Assessing landowner activities related to birds across rural-to-urban landscapes. *Environmental Management* **33**: 110–125.

Lepczyk, C. A., Mertig, A. G. & Liu, J. G. (2004b). Landowners and cat predation across rural-to-urban landscapes. *Biological Conservation* **115**: 191–201.

Lepczyk, C. A., Warren, P. S., Machabée, L., Kinzig, A. P. & Mertig, A. G. (2012). Who feeds the birds? A comparison across regions: 267–284, in Lepczyk, C. A. & Warren, P. S., *Urban Bird Ecology and Conservation. Studies in Avian Biology (No. 45).* University of California Press, Berkeley, CA.

Leveau, L. M. (2013). Bird traits in urban-rural gradients: how many functional groups are there? *Journal of Ornithology* **154**: 655–662.

Leaveau, L. M. & Leveau, C. M. (2012). The role of urbanisation and seasonality on the temporal variability of bird communities. *Landscape and Urban Planning* **106**: 271–276.

Liberg, O. (1980). Spacing patterns in a population of rural free roaming domestic cats. *Oikos* **35**: 336–349.

Liker, A. & Bókony, V. (2009). Larger groups are more successful in innovative problem solving in House Sparrows. *Proceedings of the National Academy of Sciences* **106**: 7893–7898.

Liker, A., Papp, Z., Bókony, V. & Lendvai, A. Z. (2008). Lean birds in the city: body size and condition of House Sparrows along an urbanization gradient. *Journal of Animal Ecology* **77**: 789–795.

Lilith, M. (2007). Do pet cats (*Felis catus*) have an impact on species richness and abundance of native mammals in in low-density Western Australian suburbia? PhD Thesis, Murdoch University, Perth.

Lima, S. L. & Dill, L. M. (1990). Behavioural decision made under the risk of predation: a review and prospectus. *Canadian Journal of Zoology* **68**: 619–640.

Lin, E. (2005). *Production and Processing of Small Seeds for Birds.* UN Food & Agriculture Organisation, Rome.

Lind, H. (1955). A study of behaviour of the Blackbird (*Turdus m. merula* L.). Dansk Orn. Foren. *Tidsskr* **49**: 76–113.

Lindén, A., Lehikoinen, A., Hokkanen, T. & Väisänen, R. A. (2011). Modelling irruptions and population dynamics of the Great Spotted Woodpecker – joint effects of density and cone crops. *Oikos* **120**: 1065–1075.

Literák, I., Šmid, B. & Vaíček, L. (2003). Papillomatosis in Chaffinches (*Fringilla coelebs*) in the Czech Republic and Germany. *Veterinarni Medicina* **48**: 169–173.

Liu, J., Daily, G. C., Ehrlich, P. R. & Luck, G. W. (2003). Effects of household dynamics on resource consumption and biodiversity. *Nature* **421**: 530–533.

Löhrl, H. (1977). Zur nahrungssuche von Grau und Grünspecht (*Picus canus, P. viridis*) im winterhalbjahr. *Die Vogelwelt* **98**: 15–22.

López-Calderón, C., Hobson, K. A., Marzal, A., Balbontín, J., Reviriego, M., Magallanes, S., García-Longoria, L., Lope, F. & Møller, A. P. (2017). Environmental conditions during winter predict age-and sex-specific differences in reproductive success of a trans-Saharan migratory bird. *Scientific Reports* **7**: p. 18082.

Loram, A., Tratalos, J., Warren, P. H. & Gaston, K. J. (2007). Urban domestic gardens (X): the extent and structure of the resource in five major cities. *Landscape Ecology* **22**: 601–615.

Loss, S. R., Will, T. & Marra, P. P. (2012). The impact of free-ranging domestic cats on wildlife of the United States. *Nature Communications* **4**: 1396.

Lowry, H., Lill, A. & Wong, B. B. (2011). Tolerance of auditory disturbance by an avian urban adapter, the Noisy Miner. *Ethology* **117**: 490–497.

Lubjuhn, T., Strohbach, S., Brun, J., Gerken, T. & Epplen, J. T. (1999). Extra-pair paternity in Great Tits (*Parus major*) – a long term study. *Behaviour* **136**: 1157–1172.

Luck, G. W. & Smallbone, L. T. (2010). The impact of urbanisation on taxonomic and functional similarity among bird communities. *Journal of Biogeography* **38**: 894–906.

Ludvig, E., Torok, J., Vanicsek, J. & Csorgo, T. (1994). Territoriality and population regulation in urban Blackbirds (*Turdus merula* L.). *Ornis Hungarica* **4**: 1–8.

Ludvig, E., Vanicsek, L., Torok, J. & Csorgo, T. (1995). Seasonal variation of clutch size in the European Blackbird *Turdus merula*: a new ultimate explanation. *Journal of Animal Ecology* **64**: 85–94.

Luna, Á., Romero-Vidal, P., Hiraldo, F. & Tella, J. L. (2018). Cities favour the recent establishment and current spread of the Eurasian Collared Dove *Streptopelia decaocto* (Frivaldszky, 1838). *Dominican Republic. BioInvasions Record* **7** (1). doi: 10. 3391/bir. 2018. 7. 1. 15.

Lundberg, K. & Brodin, A. (2003). The effect of dominance rank on fat deposition and food hoarding in the Willow Tit *Parus montanus* – an experimental test. *Ibis* **145**: 78–82.

Maas, J., Verheij, R. A., de Vries, S., Spreeuwenberg, P., Schellevis, F. G. & Groenewegen, P. P. (2009). Morbidity is related to a green living environment. *Journal of Epidemiology and Community Health* **63**: 967–973.

MacDonald, D. W. & Loveridge, A. J. (2010). *Biology and Conservation of Wild Felids*. Oxford University Press, Oxford.

MacDonald, J. W. (1965). Mortality in wild birds. *Bird Study* **12**: 181–188.

MacDonald, J. W. & Brown, D. D. (1983). Salmonella infection in wild birds in Britain. *Veterinary Record* **94**: 321–322.

MacDonald, J. W. & Cornelius, L. W. (1969). Salmonellosis in wild birds. *British Birds* **62**: 28–30.

MacDonald, J. W. & Gush, G. H. (1975). Knemidokoptic mange in Chaffinches. *British Birds* **68**: 103–107.

Mace, R. (1987). The dawn chorus in the Great Tit *Parus major* is directly related to female fertility. *Nature* **330**: 745–746.

Machovsky-Capuska, G. E., Senior, A. M., Zantis, S. P., Barna, K., Cowieson, A. J., Pandya, S., Pavard, C., Shiels, M. & Raubenheimer, D. (2016). Dietary protein selection in a free-ranging urban population of Common Myna birds. *Behavioural Ecology* **27**: 219–227.

Maciusik, B., Lenda, M. & Skórka, P. (2010). Corridors, local food resources, and climatic conditions affect the utilization of the urban environment by the Black-headed Gull *Larus ridibundus*; in winter. *Ecological Research* **25**: 263–272.

Madden, C. F., Arroyo, B. & Amar, A. (2015). A review of the impacts of corvids on bird productivity and abundance. *Ibis* **157**: 1–16.

Maddock, E. (1988). Garden feeding Goldfinches. *BTO News* **155**: 7.

Magrath, R. D. (1990). Hatching asynchrony in altricial birds. *Biological Reviews* **65**: 587–622.

Magrath, R. D. (1992). Roles of egg mass and incubation pattern in establishment of hatching hierarchies in the Blackbird (*Turdus merula*). *Auk* **82**: 474–487.

Main, I. G. (1999). Overseas movements to and from Britain by Greenfinches *Carduelis chloris*. *Ringing and Migration* **19**: 191–199.

Male, L. H. & Smulders, T. V. (2007). Memory decay and cache site preferences in hoarding Coal Tits: a laboratory study. *Behaviour* **144**: 693–710.

Malpass, J. S., Rodewald, A. D. & Matthews, S. N. (2017). Species-dependent effects of bird feeders on nest predators and nest survival of urban American Robins and Northern Cardinals. *The Condor* **119**: 1–16.

Marchant, J. H. & Gregory, R. D. (1999). Numbers of nesting Rooks *Corvus frugilegus* in the United Kingdom in 1996. *Bird Study* **46**: 258–273.

Marchetti, C. & Drent, P. J. (2000). Individual differences in the use of social information in foraging by captive Great Tits. *Animal Behaviour* **60**: 131–140.

Marquiss, M. (2007). Seasonal pattern in hawk predation on Common Bullfinches *Pyrrhula pyrrhula*: evidence of an interaction with habitat affecting food availability. *Bird Study* **54**: 1–11.

Marquiss, M. & Newton, I. (1982). A radio-tracking study of the ranging behaviour and dispersion of European Sparrowhawks *Accipiter nisus*. *Journal of Animal Ecology* **51**: 111–133.

Martin, G. R. (2011). Understanding bird collisions with man-made objects: a sensory ecology approach. *Ibis* **153**: 239–254.

Martin, G. R. & Osorio, D. (2008). Vision in birds: 25–52, in Basbaum, A. I., Kaneko, A., Shepherd, G. M. & Westheimer, G., *The Sense: A Comprehensive Review. Volume 1. Vision.* Elsevier, Amsterdam.

Martin, T. E. (1993). Nest predation and nest sites: new perspectives on old patterns. *BioScience* **43**: 523–532.

Martinson, T. J. & Flaspohler, D. J. (2003). Winter bird-feeding and localized predation on simulated bark-dwelling arthropods. *Wildlife Society Bulletin* **31**: 510–516.

Mason, C. F. (2000). Thrushes now largely restricted to the built environment in eastern England. *Diversity and Distributions* **6**: 189–194.

Massimino, D., Woodward, I. D., Hammond, M. J., Harris, S. J., Leech, D. I., Noble, D. G., Walker, R. H., Barimore, C., Dadam, D., Eglington, S. M., Marchant, J. H., Sullivan, M. J. P., Baillie, S. R. & Robinson, R. A. (2017). BirdTrends 2017: trends in numbers, breeding success and survival for UK breeding birds. *Research Report 704*, BTO, Thetford. www.bto. org/birdtrends.

Máthé, O. & Batáry, P. (2015). Insectivorous and open-cup nester bird species suffer the most from urbanization. *Bird Study* **62**: 78–86.

Matheson, C. (1944). The domestic cat as a factor in urban ecology. *Journal of Animal Ecology* **13**: 130–133.

Matsui, S., Kasahara, S., Kato, T., Izumi, H., Morimoto, G., Ueda, K. & Mikami, O. K. (2017). Badge size of male Eurasian Tree Sparrows *Passer montanus* correlates with hematocrit during the breeding season. *Ornithological Science* **16**: 87–91.

Maynard Smith, J. & Harper, D. G. C. (1988). The evolution of aggression: can selection generate variability? *Philosophical Transactions of the Royal Society (B)* **319**: 557–570.

Mazgajski T. D., Kędra A. H., Beal K. G. (2004). The pattern of nest-site cleaning by European Starling *Sturnus vulgaris*. *Ibis* **146**: 175–177.

McBurney, S., Kelly-Clark, W. K., Forzán, M. J., Vanderstichel, R., Teather, K. & Greenwood, S. J. (2017). Persistence of *Trichomonas gallinae* in birdseed. *Avian Diseases* **61**: 311–315.

McDevitt, A. D., Kajtoch, Ł., Mazgajski, T. D., Carden, R. F., Coscia, I., Osthoff, C., Coombes, R. H. & Wilson, F. (2011). The origins of Great Spotted Woodpeckers *Dendrocopos major* colonizing Ireland revealed by mitochondrial DNA. *Bird Study* **58**: 361–364.

McGowan, A., Hatchwell, B. J. & Woodburn, R. J. W. (2003). The effect of helping behaviour on the survival of juvenile and adult Long-tailed Tits. *Journal of Animal Ecology* **72**: 491–499.

McGowan, A., Sharp, S. P. & Hatchwell, B. J. (2004). The structure and function of nests of Long-tailed Tits *Aegithalos caudatus*. *Functional Ecology* **18**: 578–583.

McGowan, R. Y., Clugston, D. L. & Forrester, R. W. (2003). Scotland's endemic subspecies. *Scottish Birds* **24**: 18–35.

McGraw, K. J., Adkins-Regan, E. & Parker, R. S. (2005). Maternally derived carotenoid pigments affect offspring survival, sex ratio, and sexual attractiveness in a colourful songbird. *Naturwissenschaften* **92**: 375–380.

McGraw, K. J., Mackillop, E. A., Dale, J. & Hauber, M. E. (2002). Different colours reveal different information: how nutritional stress affects the expression of melanin- and structurally based ornamental plumage. *Journal of Experimental Biology* **205**: 3747–3755.

McHugh, N. M., Prior, M., Grice, P. V., Leather, S. R. & Holland, J. M. (2017). Agri-environmental measures and the breeding ecology of a declining farmland bird. *Biological Conservation* **212**: 230–239.

McIntyre, N. (2000). Ecology of urban arthropods: a review and a call to action. *Annals of the Entomological Society of America* **93**: 825–835.

McKenzie, A. J., Petty, S. J., Toms, M. P. & Furness, R. W. (2007). Importance of Sitka Spruce (*Picea sitchensis*) seed and garden bird-feeders for Siskin *Carduelis spinus* and Coal Tit *Periparus ater*. *Bird Study* **54**: 236–247.

McKinney, M. L. (2006). Urbanization as a major cause of biotic homogenization. *Biological Conservation* **127**: 247–260.

McKinney, M. L. & Lockwood, J. (1999). Biotic homogenization: a few winners replacing many losers in the next mass extinction. *Trends in Ecology and Evolution* **14**: 450–453.

Meilvang, D., Moksnes, A. & Røskaft, E. (1997). Nest predation, nesting characteristics and nest defence behaviour of Fieldfares and Redwings. *Journal of Avian Biology* **28**: 331–337.

Mennechez, G. & Clergeau, P. (2001). Settlement of breeding European Starlings in urban areas: importance of lawns vs anthropogenic wastes: 257–287, in Marzluff, J. M., Bowman, R. & Donelly, R., *Avian Ecology and Conservation in an Urbanizing World*. Kluwer, New York.

Mennechez, G. & Clergeau, P. (2006). Effect of urbanisation on habitat generalists: Starlings not so flexible? *Acta Oecologia* **30**: 182–191.

Merilä, J. & Allander, K. (1995). Do Great Tits (*Parus major*) prefer ectoparasite-free roost sites? An experiment. *Ethology* **99**: 53–60.

Metzger, B. & Bairlein, F. (2011). Fat stores in a migratory bird: a reservoir of carotenoid pigments for times of need? *Journal of Comparative Physiology (B): Biochemical, Systemic and Environmental Physiology* **181**: 269–275.

Miller, J. R. (2005). Biodiversity conservation and the extinction of experience. *Trends in Ecology and Evolution* **20**: 430–434.

Miller, M. W., Leech, D. I., Pearce-Higgins, J. W. & Robinson, R. A. (2017). Multi-state, multi-stage modelling of nest-success suggests interaction between weather and land-use. *Ecology* **98**: 175–186

Miller, R. S. & Miller, R. E. (1971). Feeding activity and colour preference of Ruby-throated Hummingbirds. *The Condor* **73**: 309–313.

Mitchell, K. D. G. (1967). Nocturnal activities of city Blackbird. *British Birds* **60**: 373–374.

Mizera, T. (1988). An ecological study of the synanthropic avifauna of the Solacz District of Poznan in 1975–1984. *Acta Zoologica Cracoviensia* **31**: 3–64.

Mock, D. W., Schwagmeyer, P. L. & Dugas, M. B. (2009). Parental provisioning and nestling mortality in House Sparrows. *Animal Behaviour* **78**: 677–684.

Moeed, A. & Dawson, D. G. (1979). Breeding of Starlings (*Sturnus vulgaris*) in nest boxes of various types. *New Zealand Journal of Zoology* **6**: 613–618.

Møller, A. P. (1987). Variation in badge size in male House Sparrows *Passer domesticus*: evidence for status signalling. *Animal Behaviour* **35**: 1637–1644.

Møller, A. P. (1988). Nest predation and nest site choice in passerine birds in habitat patches of different sizes: a study of Magpies and Blackbirds. *Oikos* **53**: 215–221.

Møller, A. P. (2009). Successful city dwellers: a comparative study of the ecological characteristics of urban birds in the Western Palearctic. *Oecologia* **159**: 849–858.

Møller, A. P. (2014). Behavioural and ecological predictors of urbanization: 54–68, in Gil, D. & Brumm, H., *Avian Urban Ecology*. Oxford University Press, Oxford.

Møller, A. P., Karadas, F. & Mousseau, T. A. (2008). Antioxidants in eggs of Great Tits *Parus major* from Chernobyl and hatching success. *Journal of Comparative Physiology (B): Biochemical, Systemic and Environmental Physiology* **178**: 735–743.

Møller, A. P., Tryjanowski, P., Díaz, M., Kwiecinski, Z., Indykiewicz, P., Mitrus, C., Goławski, A. & Polakowski, M. (2015). Urban habitats and feeders both contribute to flight initiation distance reduction in birds. *Behavioral Ecology* **26**: 861–865.

Mónus, F., Liker, A., Pénzes, Z. & Barta, Z. (2017). Status signalling in male but not in female Eurasian Tree Sparrows *Passer montanus*. *Ibis* **159**: 180–192.

Moreno, J., Osorno, J. L., Morales, J., Merino, S. & Tomás, G. (2004). Egg colouration and male parental effort in the Pied Flycatcher *Ficedula hypoleuca*. *Journal of Avian Biology* **35**: 300–304.

Moreno-Rueda, G. (2010). Uropygial gland size correlates with feather holes, body condition, and wingbar size in the House Sparrow. *Journal of Avian Biology* **41**: 229–236.

Moreno-Rueda, G. (2011). House Sparrows *Passer domesticus* with larger uropygial glands show reduced feather wear. *Ibis* **153**: 195–198.

Morozov, N. S. (2015). Why do birds practice anting? *Biology Bulletin Reviews* **5**: 353–365.

Morrison, C. A., Robinson, R. A., Leech, D. I., Dadam, D. & Toms. M. P. (2014). Using citizen science to investigate the role of productivity in House Sparrow *Passer domesticus* population trends. *Bird Study* **61**: 91–100.

Muirhead, L. B. (1990). Final report of the BTO/BASF Garden Bird Survey. *British Trust for Ornithology Research Report 68*. British Trust for Ornithology, Tring.

Murgui, E. (2009). Seasonal patterns of habitat selection of the House Sparrow *Passer domesticus* in the urban landscape of Valencia (Spain). *Journal of Ornithology* 150. Doi. org/10. 1007/s10336-008–0320-z

Murgui, E. & Hedblom, M. (2017). *Ecology and Conservation of Birds in Urban Environments*. Springer International Publishing, Switzerland.

Murphy, M. T., Sexton, K., Dolan, A. C. & Redmond, L. J. (2008). Dawn song of the Eastern Kingbird: an honest signal of male quality? *Animal Behaviour* **75**: 1075–1084.

Murray, K. A. (2004). Factors affecting foraging by breeding farmland birds. PhD Thesis, Harper Adams University College, Newport, Shropshire.

Musgrove, A., Aebischer, N., Eaton, M., Hearn, R., Newson, S., Noble, D., Parsons, M., Risely, K. & Stroud, D. (2013). Population estimates of birds in Great Britain and the United Kingdom. *British Birds* **106**: 64–100.

Myczko, Ł., Rosin, Z. M., Skórka, P. & Tryjanowski, P. (2014). Urbanization level and woodland size are major drivers of woodpecker species richness and abundance. *PLoS One* **9**: e94218. doi: 10. 1371/journal. pone. 0094218.

Nado, L., Kašová, M., Krištín, A. & Kaňuch, P. (2018). Cooperative nest-defence behaviour and territory quality in a resident and socially monogamous passerine. *Ethology* **124**: 514–526.

Nager, R. G., Ruegger, C. & van Noordwijk, A. J. (1997). Nutrient or energy limitation on egg formation: a feeding experiment in Great Tits. *Journal of Animal Ecology* **66**: 495–507.

Nam, K. B., Simeoni, M., Sharp, S. P. & Hatchwell, B. J. (2010). Kinship affects investment by helpers in a cooperatively breeding bird. *Proceedings of the Royal Society (B)* **277**: 3299–3306.

Napper, C. J. & Hatchwell, B. J. (2016). Social dynamics in nonbreeding flocks of a cooperatively breeding bird: causes and consequences of kin associations. *Animal Behaviour* **122**: 23–35.

Napper, C. J., Sharp, S. P., McGowan, A., Simeoni, M. and Hatchwell, B. J. (2013). Dominance, not kinship, determines individual position within the communal roosts of a cooperatively breeding bird. *Behavioral Ecology and Sociobiology* **67**: 2029–2039.

Narango, D. L., Tallamy, D. W. & Marra, P. P. (2017). Native plants improve breeding and foraging habitat for an insectivorous bird. *Biological Conservation* **213**: 42–50.

Nelson, S. H., Evans, A. D. & Bradbury, R. B. (2006). The efficacy of an ultrasonic cat deterrent. *Applied Animal Behaviour Science* **96**: 83–91.

Newson, S. E., Johnston, A., Parrott, D. & Leech, D. I. (2011). Evaluating the population-level impact of an invasive species, Ring-necked Parakeet *Psittacula krameri*, on native avifauna. *Ibis* **153**: 509–516.

Newson, S. E., Moran, N. J., Musgrove, A. J., Pearce-Higgins, J. W., Gillings, S., Atkinson, P. W., Miller, R., Grantham, M. J. & Baillie, S. R. (2016). Long-term changes in the migration phenology of UK breeding birds detected by large-scale citizen science recording schemes. *Ibis* **158**: 481–495.

Newson, S. E., Rexstad, E. A., Baillie, S. R., Buckland, S. T. & Aebischer, N. J. (2010). Population change of avian predators and Grey Squirrels in England: is there evidence for an impact on avian prey populations? *Journal of Applied Ecology* **47**: 244–252.

Newson, S. E., Woodburn, R. J. W., Noble, D. G., Baillie, S. R. & Gregory, R. D. (2005). Evaluating the Breeding Bird Survey for producing national population size and density estimates. *Bird Study* **52**: 42–54.

Newton, I. (1964). Bud-eating by Bullfinches in relation to the natural food-supply. *Journal of Applied Ecology* **1**: 265–279.

Newton, I. (1972). *Finches* (The New Naturalist Library). Collins, London.

Newton I. (1978). Feeding and development of Sparrowhawk *Accipiter nisus* nestlings. *Journal of Zoology, London* **184**: 465–487.

Newton, I. (1986). *The Sparrowhawk*. T. & A. D. Poyser, London.

Newton, I. (2000). Movements of Bullfinches *Pyrrhula pyrrhula* within the breeding season. *Bird Study* **47**: 372–376.

Newton, I. (2004). The recent declines of farmland bird populations in Britain: an appraisal of causal factors and conservation actions. *Ibis* **146**: 579–600.

Newton, I., Rothery, P. & Dale, L. C. (1998). Density dependence in the bird populations of an oakwood over 22 years. *Ibis* **140**: 131–136.

Newton, I. & Wyllie, I. (1992). Recovery of a Sparrowhawk population in relation to declining pesticide contamination. *Journal of Applied Ecology* **29**: 476–484.

Newton, I., Wyllie, I. & Freestone, P. (1990). Rodenticides in British barn owls. *Environmental Pollution* **68**: 101–117.

Niemelä, J. (2011). *Urban Ecology: Patterns, Processes, and Applicatons*. Oxford University Press, Oxford.

Nilsson, J. Å. (2000). Time-dependent reproductive decisions in the Blue Tit. *Oikos* **88**: 351–361.

Nilsson, J. Å. & Smith, H. G. (1988). Incubation feeding as a male tactic for early hatching. *Animal Behaviour* **36**: 641–647.

Nordt, A. & Klenke, R. (2013). Sleepless in town – drivers of the temporal shift in dawn song in urban European Blackbirds. *PLoS One* **8**: e71476.

Norris, K. (1993). Seasonal variation in the reproductive success of Blue Tits: an experimental study. *Journal of Animal Ecology* **62**: 287–294.

Nour, N., Matthysen, E. & Dhondt, A. A. (1993). Artificial nest predation and habitat fragmentation: different trends in bird and mammal predators. *Ecography* **16**: 111–116.

Nur, N. (1984a). The consequences of brood size for breeding Blue Tits I. Adult survival, weight change and the cost of reproduction. *Journal of Animal Ecology* **53**: 479–496.

Nur, N. (1984b). The consequences of brood size for breeding Blue Tits II. Nestling weight, offspring survival and optimal brood size. *Journal of Animal Ecology* **53**: 497–517.

Ockendon, N., Davis, S. E., Miyar, T. & Toms, M. P. (2009b). Urbanisation and time of arrival of common birds at garden feeding stations. *Bird Study* **56**: 405–410.

Ockendon, N., Davis, S. E., Toms, M. P. & Mukherjee, S. (2009a). Eye size and the time of arrival of birds at garden feeding stations in winter. *Journal of Ornithology* **150**: 903–908.

O'Connor, R. J., & Mead, C. J. (1984). The Stock Dove in Britain, 1930–80. *British Birds* **77**: 181–201.

O'Connor, R. J. and Morgan, R. A. (1982). Some effects of weather conditions on the breeding of the Spotted Flycatcher *Muscicapa striata* in Britain. *Bird Study* **29**: 41–48.

O'Connor, R. J. & Shrubb, M. (1986) *Farming and Birds*. Cambridge University Press, Cambridge.

O'Connor, T. P. (2000). Human refuse as a major ecological factor in Medieval urban vertebrate communities: 15–20, in Bailey, G., Charles, R. & Winder, N., *Human Ecodynamics. Symposia of the Association for Environmental Archaeology* 19. Oxbow Books, Oxford.

Ogden, L. J. E. (2002). Summary report on the bird friendly building program: effect of light reduction on collision of migratory birds. *Fatal Light Awareness Program*, Toronto.

O'Leary, R. & Jones, D. N. (2006). The use of supplementary foods by Australian Magpies *Gymnorhina tibicen*: implications for wildlife feeding in suburban environments. *Austral Ecology* **31**: 208–216.

Olesen, J., Gustavsson, A., Svensson, M., Wittchen, H. U. & Jonsson, B. (2012). The economic cost of brain disorders in Europe. *European Journal of Neurology* **19**: 155–162.

Olsen, G. H. (2003). Oral biology and beak disorders of birds. Veterinary Clinics of North America. *Exotic Animal Practice* **6**: 505–521.

van Oort, H. & Dawson, R. D. (2005). Carotenoid ornamentation of adult male Common Redpolls predicts probability of dying in a salmonellosis outbreak. *Functional Ecology* **19**: 1365–2435.

Oppenheimer, E. (1980). Felis catus population densities in urban areas. *Carnivore Genetic Newsletter* **4**: 72–80.

Oppliger, A., Richner, H. & Christe, P. (1994). Effect of an ectoparasite on lay date, nest-site choice, desertion, and hatching success in the Great Tit (*Parus major*). *Behavioral Ecology* **5**: 130–134.

Orłowski, G., Kasprzykowski, Z., Dobicki, W., Pokorny, P. & Polechoński, R. (2009). Geographical and habitat differences in concentrations of copper, zinc and arsenic in eggshells of the Rook in Poland. *Journal of Ornithology* **151**: 279–286.

Orros, M. E. & Fellowes, M. D. E. (2012). Supplementary feeding of wild birds indirectly affects the local abundance of arthropod prey. *Basic and Applied Ecology* **13**: 286–293.

Orros, M. E. & Fellowes, M. D. E. (2014). Supplementary feeding of the reintroduced Red Kite *Milvus milvus* in UK gardens. *Bird Study* **61**: 260–263.

Orros, M. E. & Fellowes, M. D. E. (2015b). Wild bird feeding in an urban area: intensity, economics and numbers of individuals supported. *Acta Ornithologica* **50**: 43–58.

Orros, M. E. & Fellowes, M. D. E. (2015c). Widespread supplementary feeding in domestic gardens explains the return of reintroduced Red Kites *Milvus milvus* to an urban area. *Ibis* **157**: 230–238.

Orros M. E., Thomas R. L., Holloway G. J. & Fellowes M. D. E. (2015a). Supplementary feeding of wild birds indirectly affects ground beetle populations in suburban gardens. *Urban Ecosystems* **18**: 465–475.

Ortega-Olivencia, A., Rodríguez-Riaño, T., Valtueña, F. J., López, J. & Devesa, J. A. (2005). First confirmation of a native bird-pollinated plant in Europe. *Oikos* **110**: 578–590.

Osborne, P. & Osborne, L. (1980). The contribution of nest-site characteristics to breeding-success among Blackbirds *Turdus merula*. *Ibis* **122**: 512–517.

Owen, D. F. (1956). The food of nestling jays and magpies. *Bird Study* **3**: 257–265.

Palomino, D. & Carrascal, L. M. (2006). Urban influence on birds at a regional scale: a case study with the avifauna of northern Madrid province. *Landscape and Urban Planning* **77**: 276–290.

Paradis, E., Baillie, S. R., Sutherland, W. J., Dudley, C., Crick, H. Q. & Gregory, R. D. (2000). Large-scale spatial variation in the breeding performance of Song Thrushes *Turdus philomelos* and Blackbirds *T. merula* in Britain. *Journal of Applied Ecology* **37**: 73–87.

Partecke, J., Hof, T. V. & Gwinner, E. (2004). Differences in the timing of reproduction between urban and forest European Blackbirds (*Turdus merula*): result of phenotypic flexibility or genetic differences? *Proceedings of the Royal Society, London (B)* **271**: 1995–2001.

Pazderka, C. & Emmott, A. (2010). *Chatham House Procurement for Development Forum: Groundnuts Case Study.* Chatham House, London.

Peach, W. J., du Feu, C. & McMeeking, J. (1995). Site tenacity and survival rates of Wrens *Troglodytes troglodytes* and Treecreepers *Certhia familiaris* in a Nottinghamshire wood. *Ibis* **137**: 497–507.

Peach, W. J. & Fowler, J. A. (1989). Movements of wing-tagged Starlings *Sturnus vulgaris* from an urban communal roost in winter. *Bird Study* **36**: 16–22.

Peach, W. J., Robinson, R. A. & Murray, K. A. (2004). Demographic and environmental causes of the decline of rural Song Thrushes *Turdus philomelos* in lowland Britain. *Ibis* **146**: 50–59.

Peach, W. J., Siriwardena, G. M. & Gregory, R. D. (1999). Long-term changes in over-winter survival rates explain the decline of Reed Buntings *Emberiza schoeniclus* in Britain. *Journal of Applied Ecology* **36**: 798–811.

Peach, W. J., Vincent, K. E., Fowler, J. A. & Grice, P. V. (2008). Reproductive success of House Sparrows along an urban gradient. *Animal Conservation* **11**: 493–503.

Pellissier, V., Cohen, M., Boulay, A. & Clergeau, P. (2012). Birds are also sensitive to landscape composition and configuration within the city centre. *Landscape and Urban Planning* **104**: 181–188.

Pence, D. B., Cole, R. A., Brugger, K. E. & Fischer, J. R. (1999). Epizootic podoknemidokoptiasis in American Robins. *Journal of Wildlife Diseases* **35**: 1–7.

Pendlebury, C. J. & Bryant, D. M. (2005). Night-time behaviour of egg-laying tits. *Ibis* **147**: 342–345.

Peneaux, C., Machovsky-Capuska, G. E., Raubenheimer, D., Lermite, F., Rousseau, C., Ruhan, T., Rodger, J. C. & Griffin, A. S. (2017). Tasting novel foods and selecting nutrient content in a highly successful ecological invader, the Common Myna. *Journal of Avian Biology* **48**: 1432–1440.

Pennycott, T. W. (2003). Scaly leg, papillomas and pox in wild birds. *Veterinary Record* **152**: 444.

Pennycott, T. W., Cinderey, R. N., Park, A., Mather, H. A. & Foster, G. (2002). *Salmonella enterica* subspecies *enterica* serotype Typhimurium and *Escherichia coli* O86 in wild birds at two garden sites in south-west Scotland. *Veterinary Record* **151**: 563–567.

Pennycott, T. W., Cinderey, R. N., Park, A., Mather, H. A., Foster, G. & Grant, D. (2005a). Further monitoring for *Salmonella* species and *Escherichia coli* O86 at a bird table in south-west Scotland. *Veterinary Record* **157**: 477–480.

Pennycott, T. W., Lawson, B., Cunningham, A. A., Simpson, V. & Chantrey, J. (2005b). Necrotic ingluvitis in wild finches. *Veterinary Record* **157**: 360.

Pennycott, T. W., Mather, H. A., Bennett, G. & Foster, G. (2010). Salmonellosis in garden birds in Scotland, 1995 to 2008: geographic region, *Salmonella enterica* phage type and bird species. *Veterinary Record* **166**: 419–421.

Pennycott, T. W., Ross, H. M., Mclaren, I. M., Park, A., Hopkins, G. F. & Foster, G. (1998). Causes of death of wild birds of the family Fringillidae in Britain. *Veterinary Record* **143**: 155–158.

Perec-Matysiak, A., Wesołowska, M., Leśniańska, K., Buńkowska-Gawlik, K., Hildebrand, J. & Kicia, M. (2017). Survey for zoonotic microsporidian pathogens in wild living urban rooks (*Corvus frugilegus*). *Journal of Eukaryotic Microbiology* **64**: 721–724.

Perrins, C. M. (1964). Survival of young Swifts in relation to brood size. *Nature* **201**: 1147–1148.

Perrins, C. M. (1965). Population fluctuations and clutch-size in the Great tit *Parus major*. L. *Journal of Animal Ecology* **34**: 601–647.

Perrins, C. M. (1996). Eggs, egg formation and the timing of breeding. *Ibis* **138**: 2–15.

Perrins, C. M. (1979). *British Tits* (The New Naturalist Library). Collins, London.

Perrins, C. M. & Geer, T. A. (1980). The effect of Sparrowhawks on tit populations. *Ardea* **68**: 133–142.

Perrins, C. M. & McCleery, R. H. (1989). Laying dates and clutch size in the Great Tit. *Wilson Bulletin* **101**: 236–253.

Petrak, M. L. (1982). *Diseases of Cage and Aviary Birds*. Lea and Febiger, Philadelphia.

Petrelli, A. R., Levenhagen, M. J., Wardle, R., Barber, J. R. & Francis, C. D. (2017). First to flush: the effects of ambient noise on songbird flight initiation distances and implications for human experiences of nature. *Frontiers in Ecology and Evolution* 5. doi: 10.3389/fevo.2017.00067.

Philbey, A. W., Mather, H. A., Taylor, D. J. & Coia, J. E. (2008). Isolation of avian strains of *Salmonella enterica* serovar Typhimurium from cats with enteric disease in the United Kingdom. *Veterinary Record* **162**: 120–122.

Phipps, L. P., Duff, J. P., Holmes, P. H., Gough, R. E., McCracken, F., McElhinney, L. M., Johnson, N., Hughes, L., Chantrey, J., Pennycott, T., Murray, K. O., Brown, I. B. & Fooks, A. R. (2008). Surveillance for West Nile virus in British birds (2001–06). *Veterinary Record* **162**: 413–415.

Pier, A. C. (1992). Major biological consequences of aflatoxicosis in animal production. *Journal of Animal Science* **70**: 3964–3967.

Pierret, P. & Jiguet, F. (2018). The potential virtue of garden bird feeders: more birds in citizen backyards close to intensive agricultural landscapes. *Biological Conservation* **222**: 14–20.

Piersma, T. (2013). Timing, nest site selection and multiple breeding in House Martins: age-related variation and the preference for self-built mud nests. *Ardea* **101**: 23–32.

Pikula, J. (1978). Thermostatic capacity of nests, body temperature, and thermoregulation in the young of hemisyanthropic populations of *Turdus merula*, *Turdus philomelos* and *Sylvia curruca*. *Folia Zoologica* **27**: 337–348.

Pimental, D. (1994). Insect population responses to environmental stress and pollutants. *Environmental Reviews* **2**: 1–15.

Pinowska, B. (1975). Food of female House Sparrows (*Passer domesticus* L.) in relation to stages of the breeding cycle. *Polish Ecological Studies* **1**: 211–225.

Pinowski, J., Barkowska, M., Kruszewiez, A. H. & Kruszewicz, A. G. (1994). The causes of mortality of eggs and nestlings of *Passer* species. *Journal of Bioscience* **19**: 441–451.

Pinowski, J., Pinowska, B., Zduniak, P., Tryjanowski, P., Jerzak, L. & Romanowski, J. (2009). Autumn sexual display in Tree Sparrows (*Passer montanus* L.) as a component of the winter survival strategy. *Polish Journal of Ecology* **57**: 159–169.

Pinxten, R. & Eens, M. (1997). Copulation and mate-guarding patterns in polygynous European Starlings. *Animal Behaviour* **54**: 45–58.

Pithon, J. A. & Dytham, C. (1999a). Census of the British Ring-necked Parakeet *Psittacula krameri* population by simultaneous counts of roosts. *Bird Study* **46**: 112–115.

Pithon, J. A. & Dytham, C. (1999b). Breeding performance of Ring-necked Parakeets *Psittacula krameri* in small introduced populations in southeast England. *Bird Study* **46**: 342–347.

Pithon, J. A. & Dytham, C. (2001). Determination of the origin of British feral Rose-ringed Parakeets. *British Birds* **94**: 74–79.

Pithon, J. A. & Dytham, C. (2002). Distribution and population development of introduced Ring-necked Parakeets *Psittacula krameri* in Britain between 1983 and 1998. *Bird Study* **49**: 110–117.

Plummer, K. E., Bearhop, S., Leech, D. I., Chamberlain, D. E. & Blount, J. D. (2013). Fat provisioning in winter impairs egg production during the following spring: a landscape-scale study of Blue Tits. *Journal of Animal Ecology* **82**: 673–682.

Plummer, K. E., Bearhop, S., Leech, D. I., Chamberlain, D. E. & Blount, J. D. (2018). Effects of winter food provisioning on the phenotypes of breeding Blue Tits. *Ecology and Evolution*. doi: 10.1002/ece3.4048.

Plummer, K. E., Siriwardena, G. M., Conway, G. J., Risely, K. & Toms, M. (2015). Is supplementary feeding in gardens a driver of evolutionary change in a migratory bird species? *Global Change Biology* **21**: 4353–4363.

Pollock, C. J., Capilla-Lasheras, P., McGill, R. A., Helm, B. & Dominoni, D. M. (2017). Integrated behavioural and stable isotope data reveal altered diet linked to low breeding success in urban-dwelling blue tits (*Cyanistes caeruleus*). *Scientific Reports* **7** (1): 5014.

Polo, V., Carrascal, L. M. & Metcalfe, N. B. (2007). The effects of latitude and day length on fattening strategies of wintering Coal Tits *Periparus ater* (L.): a field study and aviary experiment. *Journal of Animal Ecology* **76**: 866–872.

Pomeroy, D. E. (1962). Birds with abnormal bills. *British Birds* **55**: 49–71.

Ponz, A., Gil-Delgado, J. A. & Barba, E. (1999). Factors affecting prey preparation by adult Magpies feeding nestlings. *Condor* **101**: 818–823.

Post, P. and Götmark, F. (2006). Seasonal changes in Sparrowhawk *Accipiter nisus* predation: prey vulnerability in relation to visibility in hunting habitats and prey behaviour. *Ardea* **94**: 77–86.

Poulsen, H. (1951). Inheritance and learning in the song of the Chaffinch (*Fringilla coelebs* L.). *Behaviour* **3**: 216–242.

Prescott, J. F., Hunter, D. B. & Campbell, C. D. (2000). Hygiene at winter bird feeders in a southwestern Ontario city. *Canadian Veterinary Journal* **41**: 695–698.

Proctor, M., Yeo, P. & Lack, A. (1996). *The Natural History of Pollination.* HarperCollins, London.

Proffitt, F. M., Newton, I., Wilson, J. D. & Siriwardena, G. M. (2004). Bullfinch *Pyrrhula pyrrhula* breeding ecology in lowland farmland and woodland: comparisons across time and habitat. *Ibis* **146**: 78–86.

Prosperi, A., Chiari, M., Zanoni, M., Gallina, L., Casà, C., Scagliarini, A. & Lavazza, A. (2016). Identification and characterization of *Fringilla coelebs* papillomavirus 1 (FcPV1) in free-living and captive birds in Italy. *Journal of Wildlife Diseases* **52**: 756–758.

Rastogi, A. D., Zanette, L. & Clinchy, M. (2006). Food availability affects diurnal nest predation and adult antipredator behaviour in Song Sparrows, *Melospiza melodia*. *Animal Behaviour* **72**: 933–940.

Ratcliffe, D. A. (1967). Decrease in eggshell weight in certain birds of prey. *Nature* **215**: 208.

Ratcliffe, E., Gatersleben, B. & Sowden, P. T. (2013). Bird sounds and their contributions to perceived attention restoration and stress recovery. *Journal of Environmental Psychology* **36**: 221–228.

Reche, M. P., Jiménez, P. A., Alvarez, F., García De Los Rios, J. E., Rojas, A. M. & De Pedro, P. (2003). Incidence of salmonellae in captive and wild free-living raptorial birds in central Spain. *Zoonoses and Public Health* **50**: 42–44.

Reichholf, J. H. (2003). Warum macht die Singdrossel *Turdus philomelos* einen glatten Nestnapf. *Ornithologischer Anzeiger* **42**: 235–242.

Reid, J. M., Monaghan, P. & Ruxton, G. D. (2000). The consequences of clutch size for incubation conditions and hatching success in Starlings. *Functional Ecology* **14**: 560–565.

Reijnen, R. & Foppen, R. (1994). The effects of car traffic on breeding bird populations in woodland. I. Evidence of reduced habitat quality for Willow Warblers (*Phylloscopus trochilus*) breeding close to a highway. *Journal of Applied Ecology* **31**: 85–94.

Reinertsen, R. E., Haftorn, S. & Thaler, E. (1988). Is hypothermia necessary for the winter survival of the Goldcrest *Regulus regulus? Journal für Ornithologie* **129**: 433–437.

Reyer, H. U., Fischer, W., Steck, P., Nabulon, T. & Kessler, P. (1998). Sex-specific nest defence in House Sparrows (*Passer domesticus*) varies with badge size of males. *Behavioural Ecology and Sociobiology* **42**: 93–99.

Reynolds, S. J., Schoech, S. J. & Bowman, R. (2003). Nutritional quality of prebreeding diet influences breeding performance of the Florida Scrub-jay. *Oecologia* **134**: 308–316.

Rheindt, F. E. (2003). The impact of roads on birds: does song frequency play a role in determining susceptibility to noise pollution? *Journal of Ornithology* **144**: 295–306.

Rhymer, C. M., Devereux, C. L., Denny, M. J. H. & Whittingham, M. J. (2012). Diet of Starling *Sturnus vulgaris* nestlings on farmland: the importance of Tipulidae larvae. *Bird Study* **59**: 426–436.

Richardson, R. A., Seago, M. J. & Church, A. C. (1957). Collared Doves in Norfolk: a bird new to the British list. *British Birds* **50**: 239–246.

Richner, H. (1990). Helpers-at-the-nest in Carrion Crows *Corvus corone corone*. *Ibis* **132**: 105–108.

Richner, H. (1992). The effect of extra food on fitness in breeding Carrion Crows. *Ecology* **73**: 330–335.

Richner, H., Oppliger, A. & Christe, P. (1993). Effect of an ectoparasite on reproduction in Great Tits. *Journal of Animal Ecology* **62**: 703–710.

Richner, H. & Tripet, F. (1999). Ectoparasitism and the trade-off between current and future reproduction. *Oikos* **86**: 535–538.

Riddington, R. & Gosler, A. G. (1995). Differences in reproductive success and parental qualities between habitats in the Great Tit *Parus major*. *Ibis* **137**: 371–378.

Rijks, J. M., Kik, M. L., Slaterus, R., Foppen, R. P. B., Stroo, A., Ijzer, J., Stahl, J., Gröne, A., Koopmans, M. G. P., van der Jeugd, H. P. & Reusken, C. B. E. M. (2016). Widespread Usutu virus outbreak in birds in the Netherlands, 2016. *Eurosurveillance* **21**. Doi. org/10. 2807/1560–7917. ES. 2016. 21. 45. 30391.

Robb, G. N., McDonald, R. A., Chamberlain, D. E. & Bearhop, S. (2008b). Food for thought: supplementary feeding as a driver of ecological change in avian populations. *Frontiers in Ecology* **6**: 476–484.

Robb, G. N., McDonald, R. A., Chamberlain, D. E., Reynolds, S. J., Harrison, T. J. E. & Bearhop, S. (2008a). Winter feeding of birds increases productivity in the subsequent breeding season. *Biology Letters* **4**: 220–223.

Robertson, B. C., Elliott, G. P., Eason, D. K., Clout, M. N. & Gemmell, N. J. (2006). Sex allocation theory aids species conservation. *Biology Letters* **2**: 229–231.

Robertson, P. A. (1991). Estimating the nesting success and productivity of British Pheasants *Phasianus colchicus* from nest-record schemes. *Bird Study* **38**: 73–79.

Robinson, R. A., Baillie, S. R. & King, R. (2012). Population processes in European Blackbirds *Turdus merula*: a state–space approach. *Journal of Ornithology* **152**: 419–433.

Robinson, R. A., Green, R. E., Baillie, S. R., Peach, W. J. & Thomson, D. L. (2004). Demographic mechanisms of the population decline of the Song Thrush *Turdus philomelos* in Britain. *Journal of Animal Ecology* **73**: 670–682.

Robinson, R. A., Lawson, B., Toms, M. P., Peck, K. M., Kirkwood, J. K., Chantrey, J., Clatworthy, I. R., Evans, A. D., Hughes, L. A., Hutchinson, O. C., John, S. K., Pennycott, T. W., Perkins, M. W., Rowley, P. S., Simpson, V. R., Tyler, K. M. & Cunningham, A. A. (2010). Emerging infectious disease leads to rapid population declines of common British birds. *PLoS One* **5**: doi: 10. 1371/ journal. pone. 0012215

Robinson, R. A., Morrison, C. A. & Baillie, S. R. (2014). Integrating demographic data: towards a framework for monitoring wildlife populations at large spatial scales. *Methods in Ecology and Evolution* **5**: 1361–1372.

Robinson, R. M., Ray, A. C., Reagor, J. C. & Holland, L. A. (1982). Waterfowl mortality caused by aflatoxicosis in Texas. *Journal of Wildlife Diseases* **18**: 311–313.

Rodewald, A. D. & Arcese, P. (2017). Reproductive contributions of cardinals are consistent with a hypothesis of relaxed selection in urban landscapes. *Frontiers in Ecology and Evolution* 5. doi: 10. 3389/fevo. 2017. 00077.

Roe, J. & Aspinall, P. (2011). The restorative benefits of walking in urban and rural settings in adults with good and poor mental health. *Health and Place* **17**: 103–113.

Rollinson, D. J. & Jones, D. N. (2002). Variation in breeding parameters of the Australian Magpie *Gymnorhina tibicen* in suburban and rural environments. *Urban Ecosystems* **6**: 257–269.

Rolshausen, G., Segelbacher, G., Hobson, K. A. & Schaefer, H. M. (2009). Contemporary evolution of reproductive isolation and phenotypic divergence in sympatry along a migratory divide. *Current Biology* **19**: 2097–2101.

Rolstad, J., Løken, B. & Rolstad, E. (2000). Habitat selection as a hierarchical spatial process: the Green Woodpecker at the northern edge of its distribution range. *Oecologia* **124**: 116–129.

Ross-Smith, V. H., Robinson, R. A., Banks, A. N., Frayling, T. D., Gibson, C. C. & Clark, J. A. (2014). The Lesser Black-backed Gull *Larus fuscus* in England: how to resolve a conservation conundrum. *Seabird* **27**: 41–61.

Roux, K. E. & Marra, P. P. (2007). The presence and impact of environmental lead in passerine birds along an urban to rural land use gradient. *Archives of Environmental Contamination and Toxicology* **53**: 261–268.

Rowan W. (1938). London Starlings and seasonal reproduction in birds. *Proceedings of the Zoological Society, London (A)* **108**: 51–78.

Royle, N. J., Hall, M. E., Blount, J. D. & Forbes, S. (2011). Patterns of egg yolk antioxidant co-variation in an avian brood parasite–host system. *Behavioural Ecology and Sociobiology* **65**: 313–323.

Ruiz-Rodríguez, M., Valdivia, E., Soler, J. J., Martin-Vivaldi, M., Martin-Platero, A. M. & Martinez-Bueno, M. (2009). Symbiotic bacteria living in Hoopoes uropygial gland prevent feather degeneration. *Journal of Experimental Biology* **212**: 3621–3626.

Russell, A. F. & Hatchwell, B. J. (2001). Experimental evidence for kin-based helping in a cooperative vertebrate. *Proceedings of the Royal Society, London (B)* **268**: 2169–2174.

Rutz, C. & Deans, S. (2018). Nuthatch uses tool in London park. *Ethology* **124**: 135–138.

Ruxton, G. D., Thomas, S. & Wright, J. W. (2002). Bells reduce predation of wildlife by domestic cats (*Felis catus*). *Journal of Zoology, London* **256**: 81–83.

Ryder, T. B., Reitsma, R., Evans, B. & Marra, P. P. (2010). Quantifying avian nest survival along an urbanization gradient using citizen- and scientist-generated data. *Ecological Applications* **20**: 419–426.

Sa, R. C. C., Cunningham, A. A., Dagliesh, M. P., Wheelhouse, N., Pocknell, A., Borel, N., Peck, H. L. & Lawson, B. (2014). Psittacine beak and feather disease in a free-living ring-necked parakeet (*Psittacula krameri*) in Great Britain. *European Journal of Wildlife Research* **60**: 395.

SAC Veterinary Services (2008). Spread
of trichomonosis in garden birds in
Scotland. *Veterinary Record* **163**: 231–234.

Saether, B. E. (1990). Age-specific variation
in reproductive performance of birds.
Current Ornithology **7**: 251–283.

Sage, J. (1994). The occurrence of melanism
in the Surrey Great Tit population. *Surrey
Bird Report 1993*: 82–85.

Saggese, K., Korner-Nievergelt, F., Slagsvold,
T. & Amrhein, V. (2011). Wild bird feeding
delays start of dawn singing in the Great
Tit. *Animal Behaviour* **81**: 361–365.

Šálek, M., Riegert, J. & Grill, S. (2015).
House Sparrows *Passer domesticus* and
Tree Sparrows *Passer montanus*: fine-scale
distribution, population densities, and
habitat selection in a Central European
city. *Acta Ornithologica* **50**: 221–232.

Salmón, P., Nilsson, J., Nord, A., Bensch,
S. & Isaksson, C. (2016). Urban
environment shortens telomere length
in nestling Great Tits, *Parus major*.
Biology Letters **12**: 254–260.

Salmón, P., Nilsson, J. F., Watson, H.,
Bensch, S. & Isaksson, C. (2017).
Selective disappearance of Great Tits
with short telomeres in urban areas.
Proceedings of the Royal Society (B) **284**. doi:
10. 1098/rspb. 2017. 1349.

Samia, D. S. M., Blumstein, D. T., Díaz, M.,
Grim, T., Ibáñez-Álamo, J. D., Jokimäki,
J., Tätte, K. Markó, G., Tryjanowski,
P. & Møller, A. P. (2017). Rural–urban
differences in escape behaviour of
European birds across a latitudinal
gradient. *Frontiers in Ecology and Evolution*
5. doi: 10. 3389/fevo. 2017. 00066.

Sarker, S., Lloyd, C., Forwood, J. & Raidal,
S. R. (2016). Forensic genetic evidence of
beak and feather disease virus infection
in a Powerful Owl, *Ninox strenua*. *Emu*
116: 71–74.

Sarker, S., Moylan, K. G., Ghorashi, S. A.,
Forwood, J. K., Peters, A. & Raidal, S.
R. (2015). Evidence of a deep viral host
switch event with beak and feather
disease virus infection in rainbow bee-
eaters (*Merops ornatus*). *Scientific Reports*
5: e14511.

Schaefer, H. M., McGraw, K. & Catoni, C.
(2007). Bird use fruit colour as honest
signal of dietary antioxidant rewards.
Functional Ecology **22**: 303–310.

Schaefer, T. (2004). Video monitoring of
shrub-nests reveals nest predators. *Bird
Study* **51**: 170–177.

Scheidt, S. N. & Hurlbert, A. H. (2014).
Range expansion and population
dynamics of an invasive species: the
Eurasian Collared-dove (*Streptopelia
decaocto*). *PLoS One* **9** (10): e111510. doi:10.
1371/journal. pone. 0111510.

Schifferli, L. (1977). Bruchstücke
von Schneckenhäuschen als
Calciumquelle für die Bildung der
Eischale beim Haussperling Passer
domesticus. *Ornithologische Beobachter*
74: 71–74.

Schifferli, L. (1979). Warum legen Singvögel
(Passeres) ihre Eier am frühen Morgen.
Ornithologische Beobachter **76**: 33–36.

Schifferli, L. (1980). Changes in the fat
reserves of female House Sparrows
Passer domesticus during egg laying.
*Proceedings of the International
Ornithological Congress* **17**: 1129–1135.

Schoech, S. & Bowman, R. (2001).
Variation in the timing of breeding
between suburban and wildlife Florida
Scrub-jays: do physiologic measures
reflect different environments?, in
Marzluff, J. M., Bowman, R. & Donelly,
R. (eds), *Avian Conservation in an
Urbanizing World*. Kluwer Academic,
New York.

Schoech, S. & Bowman, R. (2003). Does differential access to protein influence differences in timing of breeding of Florida Scrub-jays (*Aphelocoma coerulescens*) in suburban and wildland habitats? *The Auk* **120**: 1114–1127.

Schoech, S. J., Bowman, R. & Reynolds, S. J. (2004). Food supplementation and possible mechanisms underlying early breeding in the Florida Scrub-jay (*Aphelocoma coerulescens*). *Hormones and Behaviour* **46**: 565–573.

Schreiber, L. A. (2010). Why we feed wild birds: a case study of BTO members' motivations for feeding birds in their gardens. MSc Thesis, UCL, London.

Schroeder, J., Nakagawa, S., Cleasby, I. R. & Burke, T. (2012). Passerine birds breeding under chronic noise experience reduced fitness. *PLoS One* 7 (6): e39200.

Schwartz, A., Turbé, A., Simon, L. & Julliard, R. (2014). Enhancing urban biodiversity and its influence on city-dwellers: an experiment. *Biological Conservation* **171**: 82–90.

Schwilch, R., Mantovani, R., Spina, F. & Jenni, L. (2001). Nectar consumption of warblers after long-distance flights during spring migration. *Ibis* **143**: 24–32.

Scott, P., Duncan, P. & Green, J. A. (2015). Food preference of the Black-headed Gull *Chroicocephalus ridibundus* differs along a rural–urban gradient. *Bird Study* **62**: 56–63.

Scudamore, K. A., Hetmanski, M. T., Nawaz, S., Naylor, J. & Rainbird, S. (1997). Determination of mycotoxins in pet foods sold for domestic pets and wild birds using a linked-column immunoassay clean-up and HPLC. *Food Additives and Contaminants* **14**: 175–186.

Seed, A. M., Clayton, N. S. & Emery, N. J. (2008). Cooperative problem solving in Rooks (*Corvus frugilegus*). *Proceedings of the Royal Society, London (B)* **275**: 1421–1429.

Selås, V. (2017). Autumn irruptions of Eurasian Jay (*Garrulus glandarius*) in Norway in relation to acorn production and weather. *Ornis Fennica* **94**: 92–100.

Selman, C., Blount, J. D., Nussey, D. H. & Speakman, J. R. (2012). Oxidative damage, ageing, and life-history evolution: where now? *Trends in Ecology and Evolution* **27**: 570–577.

Senar, J. C., Burton. P. J K. & Metcalfe, N. B. (1992). Variation in the nomadic tendency of a wintering finch *Carduelis spinus* and its relationship with body condition. *Ornis Scandinavica* **23**: 63–72.

Senar, J. C. & Camerino, M. (1998). Status signalling and the ability to recognize dominants: an experiment with Siskins (*Carduelis spinus*). *Proceedings of the Royal Society (B)* **265**: 1515–1520.

Senar, J. C., Garamszegi, L. Z., Tilgar, V., Biard, C., Moreno-Rueda, G., Salmón, P., Rivas, J. M., Sprau, P., Dingemanse, N. J., Charmantier, A. & Demeyrier, V. (2017a). Urban great tits (*Parus major*) show higher distress calling and pecking rates than rural birds across Europe. *Frontiers in Ecology and Evolution* **5**: 163. doi: 10. 3389/fevo. 2017. 00163.

Senar, J. C., Montalvo, T., Pascual, J. & Peracho, V. (2017). Reducing the availability of food to control feral pigeons: changes in population size and composition. *Pest Management Science* **73**: 313–317.

Seto, K. C., Guneralp, B. & Hutyra, L. R. (2012). Global forecasts of urban expansion to 2030 and direct impacts on biodiversity and carbon pools.

Proceedings of the National Academy of Science, US **109**: 16083–16088.

Shanahan, D. F., Strohbach, M. W., Warren, P. S. & Fuller, R. A. (2014). The challenge of city living: 3–20, in Gil, D. & Brumm, H., *Avian Urban Ecology*. Oxford University Press, Oxford.

Shannon, T. J., McGowan, R. Y., Zonfrillo, B., Piertney, S. & Collinson, J. M. (2014). A genetic screen of the island races of Wren *Troglodytes troglodytes* in the North-east Atlantic. *Bird Study* **61**: 135–142.

Sharples, E. & Baines, S. J. (2009). Prevalence of *Chlamydophila psittaci*-positive cloacal PCR tests in wild avian casualties in the UK. *Veterinary Record* **164**: 16–17.

Shaw, L. M., Chamberlain, D., Conway, G. J. & Toms, M. P. (2011). Spatial distribution and habitat preferences of the House Sparrow, *Passer domesticus*, in urbanised landscapes. *BTO Research Report 599*, British Trust for Ornithology, Thetford.

Shaw, L. M., Chamberlain, D. & Evans, M. (2008). The House Sparrow, *Passer domesticus*, in urban areas: reviewing a possible link between post-decline distribution and human socioeconomic status. *Journal of Ornithology* **149**: 293–299.

Shawkey, M. D., Pillai, S. R. & Hill, G. E. (2003). Chemical warfare? Effects of uropygial oil on feather-degrading bacteria. *Journal of Avian Biology* **34**: 345–349.

Sheldon, B. C. (1994). Timing and use of paternity guards by male Chaffinches. *Behaviour* **129**: 79–97.

Sheldon, B. C., Andersson, S., Griffith, S. C., Örnborg, J. & Sendecka, J. (1999). Ultraviolet colour variation influences Blue tit sex ratios. *Nature* **402**: 874–877.

Shochat, E. (2004). Credit or debit? Resource input changes population dynamics of city-slicker birds. *Oikos* **106**: 622–626.

Shochat, E., Lerman, S. B., Anderies, J. M., Warren, P. S., Faethm S. H. & Nilon, C. H. (2010). Invasion, competition, and biodiversity loss in urban ecosystems. *BioScience* **60**: 199–208.

Shutler, D. & Campbell, A. A. (2007). Experimental addition of greenery reduces flea loads in nests of a non-greenery using species, the Tree Swallow *Tachycineta bicolor*. *Journal of Avian Biology* **38**: 7–12.

Sicurella, B., Caffi, M., Caprioli, M., Rubolini, D., Saino, N. & Ambrosini, R. (2015). Weather conditions, brood size and hatching order affect Common Swift *Apus apus* nestlings' survival and growth. *Bird Study* **62**: 64–77.

Sierro, J., Schloesing, E., Pavón, I. & Gil, D. (2017). European Blackbirds exposed to aircraft noise advance their chorus, modify their song and spend more time singing. *Frontiers in Ecology and Evolution* 5. doi: 10. 3389/fevo. 2017. 00068.

Silva, A. Da., Diez-Méndez, D. & Kempenaers, B. (2017). Effects of experimental night lighting on the daily timing of winter foraging in common European songbirds. *Journal of Avian Biology* **48**: 862–871.

Silver, R., Andrews, H. & Ball, G. F. (1985). Parental care in an ecological perspective: a quantitative analysis of avian subfamilies. *American Zoologist* **25**: 823–840.

Simpson, V. R. & Bevan, B. (1989). *Chlamydia psittaci* infection in Robins. *Veterinary Record* **125**: 536.

Simms, E. (1965). A study of suburban bird-life at Dollis Hill. *British Birds* **55**: 1–36.

Simms, E. (1975) *Birds of Town and Suburb*. Collins, London.

Sims, V., Evans, K. L., Newson, S. E., Tratalos, J. & Gaston, K. J. (2008). Avian assemblage structure and domestic cat densities in urban environments. *Diversity and Distributions* **14**: 387–399.

Siriwardena, G. M., Baillie, S. R., Buckland, S. T., Fewster, R. M., Marchant, J. H. & Wilson, J. D. (1998a). Trends in the abundance of farmland birds: a quantitative comparison of smoothed Common Birds Census indices. *Journal of Applied Ecology* **35**: 24–43.

Siriwardena, G. M., Baillie, S. R. & Wilson, J. D. (1998b). Variation in the survival rates of British passerines with respect to their population trends on farmland. *Bird Study* **45**: 276–292.

Siriwardena, G. M., Calbrade, N. A. & Vickery, J. A. (2008). Farmland birds and late winter food: does seed supply fail to meet demand? *Ibis* **150**: 585–595.

Siriwardena, G. M. & Crick, H. Q. P. (2002). National trends in the breeding performance of Starlings *Sturnus vulgaris*: 91–120, in Crick, H. Q. P., Robinson, R. A., Appleton, G. F., Clark, N. A. & Rickard, A. D., *Investigation into the Causes of the Decline of Starlings and House Sparrows in Great Britain. BTO Research Report* 290, British Trust for Ornithology, Thetford.

Siriwardena, G. M. & Stevens, D. K. (2004). Effects of habitat on the use of supplementary food by farmland birds in winter. *Ibis* **146**: 144–154.

Sitko, J. & Zaleśny, G. (2014). The effect of urbanization on helminth communities in the Eurasian Blackbird (*Turdus merula* L.) from the eastern part of the Czech Republic. *Journal of Helminthology* **88**: 97–104.

Skórka, P., Babiarz, T., Skórka, J. & Wójcik, J. D. (2006). Winter territoriality and fruit defence by the Fieldfare (*Turdus pilaris*). *Journal of Ornithology* **147**: 371–375.

Slater, P. (2001). Breeding ecology of a suburban population of Woodpigeons *Columba palumbus* in northwest England. *Bird Study* **48**: 361–366.

Smith, H. G., Kallander, H. & Nilsson, J. A. (1989). The trade-off between offspring number and quality in the Great Tit *Parus major*. *Journal of Animal Ecology* **58**: 383–401.

Smith, J. E. & Ross, K. (1991). The toxic Aspergilli: 101–118, in Smith, J. E. & Henderson, R. S., *Mycotoxins and Animal Foods*. CRC Press, Inc., Boca Raton.

Smith, K. W. (2005). Has the reduction in nest-site competition from Starlings *Sturnus vulgaris* been a factor in the recent increase of Great Spotted Woodpecker *Dendrocopos major* numbers in Britain? *Bird Study* **52**: 307–313.

Smith, K. W. (2007). The utilization of dead wood resources by woodpeckers in Britain. *Ibis* **149**: 183–192.

Smith, K. W. & Smith, L. (2013). The effect of supplementary feeding in early spring on the breeding performance of the Great Spotted Woodpecker *Dendrocopos major*. *Bird Study* **60**: 169–175.

Smith, R. M., Gaston, K. J., Warren, P. H. & Thompson, K. (2006a). Urban domestic gardens (VIII): environmental correlates of invertebrate abundance. *Biodiversity and Conservation* **15**: 2515–2545.

Smith, R. M., Thompson, K., Hodgson, J. C., Warren, P. H. & Gaston, K. J. (2006b). Urban domestic gardens (IX): composition and richness of the vascular plant flora, and implications for native biodiversity. *Biological Conservation* **129**: 312–322.

Snow, B. K. & Snow, D. W. (1988). *Birds and Berries*. T. & A. D. Poyser, Berkhamstead.

Snow, D. W. (1958). *A Study of Blackbirds*. British Museum, London.

Soler, J. J., Peralta-Sánchez, J. M., Martín-Vivaldi, M., Martín-Platero, A. M., Flensted-Jensen, E. & Møller, A. P. (2012). Cognitive skills and bacterial load: comparative evidence of costs of cognitive proficiency in birds. *Naturwissenschaften* **99**: 111–122.

Soler, M. & Soler, J. J. (1996). Effects of experimental food provisioning on reproduction in the Jackdaw *Corvus monedula*, a semi-colonial species. *Ibis* **138**: 377–383.

Solonen, T. (1997). Effect of Sparrowhawk *Accipiter nisus* predation on forest birds in southern Finland. *Ornis Fennica* **74**: 1–14.

Solonen, T. (2000). Predation by Sparrowhawks *Accipiter nisus* and vulnerability of prey. *Ornis Fennica* **77**: 27–37.

Solonen, T. (2001). Breeding of the Great Tit and Blue Tit in urban and rural habitats in southern Finland. *Ornis Fennica* **78**: 49–60.

Solonen, T. (2014). Timing of breeding in rural and urban Tawny Owls *Strix aluco* in southern Finland: effects of vole abundance and winter weather. *Journal of Ornithology* **155**: 27–36.

Soper, E. A. & Hosking, E. (1961). Fungus disease affecting Robins and other species. *British Birds* **54**: 289–290.

Sorace, A. & Gustin, M. (2009). Distribution of generalist and specialist predators along urban gradients. *Landscape and Urban Planning* **90**: 111–118.

Southern, H. N. (1954). Tawny Owls and their prey. *Ibis* **96**: 384–410.

Spencer, R. & Gush, G. H. (1973). Siskins feeding in gardens. *British Birds* **66**: 91–99.

Sprau, P. & Dingemanse, N. J. (2017). Plasticity and non-random distributions of behavioural types along urban gradients in a wild passerine species. *Frontiers in Ecology and Evolution* **5**. doi: 10. 3389/fevo. 2017. 00092.

Stafford, J. (1956). The wintering of Blackcaps in the British Isles. *Bird Study* **3**: 251–257.

Stanyon, P. (2014). Birds feeling the pane: an investigation into avian window collisions. BSc Hons thesis, Nottingham Trent University.

Stevens, D. K., Anderson, G. Q. A., Grice, P. V. & Norris, K. (2007). Breeding success of Spotted Flycatchers *Muscicapa striata* in southern England – is woodland a good habitat for this species? *Ibis* **149**: 214–223.

Stevens, D. K., Anderson, G. Q. A., Grice, P. V., Norris, K. & Butcher, N. (2008). Predators of Spotted Flycatcher *Muscicapa striata* nests in southern England as determined by digital nest-cameras. *Bird Study* **55**: 179–187.

Stoate, C. & Szczur, J. (2006). Potential influence of habitat and predation on local breeding success and population in Spotted Flycatchers *Muscicapa striata*. *Bird Study* **53**: 328–330.

Stock, B. & Haag-Wackernagel, D. (2016) Food shortage affects reproduction of Feral Pigeons *Columba livia* at rearing of nestlings. *Ibis* **158**: 776–783.

Strubbe, D. & Matthysen, E. (2009). Experimental evidence for nest-site competition between invasive ring-necked parakeets (*Psittacula krameri*) and native nuthatches (*Sitta europaea*). *Biological Conservation* **142**: 1588–1594.

Suárez-Rodríguez, M., López-Rull, I. & Garcia, C. M. (2012). Incorporation of cigarette butts into nests reduces nest ectoparasite load in urban birds: new ingredients for an old recipe? *Biology Letters* **9**. Doi 10/1098/rsbl. 2012. 0931.

Suárez-Rodríguez, M., Montero-Montoya, R. D. & Garcia, C. M. (2017). Anthropogenic nest materials may increase breeding costs for urban birds. *Frontiers in Ecology and Evolution*: doi: 10. 3389/fevo. 2017. 00004.

Suhonen, J. (1993). Risk of predation and foraging sites of individuals in mixed-species tit flocks. *Animal Behaviour* **45**: 1193–1198.

Suhonen, J. & Jokimäki, J. (1988). A biogeographical comparison of the breeding bird species assemblages in twenty Finnish urban parks. *Ornis Fennica* **65**: 76–83.

Suhonen, J. & Jokimäki, J. (2015). Fruit removal from rowanberry (*Sorbus aucuparia*) trees at urban and rural areas in Finland: a multi-scale study. *Landscape and Urban Planning* **137**: 13–19.

Suhonen, J., Jokimäki, J., Kaisanlahti-Jokimäki, M. L., Hakkarainen, H., Huhta, E. & Suorsa, P. (2009). Urbanisation and stability of a bird community in winter. *Ecoscience* **16**: 502–507.

Suhonen, J., Halonen, M. & Mappes, T. (1993). Predation risk and organisation of the *Parus* guild. *Oikos* **66**: 94–100.

Summers-Smith, D. (1959). The House Sparrow *Passer domesticus*: population problems. *Ibis* **101**: 449–455.

Suorsa, P., Helle, H., Koivunen, V., Huhta, E., Nikula, A. & Hakkarainen, H. (2004). Effects of forest patch size on physiological stress and immunocompetence in an area-sensitive passerine, the Eurasian Treecreeper (*Certhia familiaris*): an experiment. *Proceedings of the Royal Society, London (B)* **271**: 435–440.

Surgey, J. du Feu, C. R. & Deeming, D. C. (2012). Opportunistic use of a wool-like artificial nest material as lining of tit (Paridae) nests. *The Condor* **114**: 385–392.

Svensson, E. & Nilsson, J. Å. (1995). Food supply, territory quality and reproductive timing in the Blue Tit (*Parus caeruleus*). *Ecology* **76**: 1804–1812.

Swallow, B., Buckland, S. T., King, R. & Toms, M. P. (2016a). Bayesian hierarchical modelling of continuous non-negative longitudinal data with a spike at zero: an application to a study of birds visiting gardens in winter. *Biometrical Journal* **58**: 357–371.

Swallow, B., King, R., Buckland, S. T. & Toms, M. P. (2016b). Identifying multispecies synchrony in response to environmental covariates. *Ecology and Evolution* **6**: 8515–8525.

Symonds, M. R. E., Weston, M. A., van Dongen, W. F. D., Lill, A., Robinson, R. W. & Guay, P. J. (2016). Time since urbanization but not encephalisation is associated with increased tolerance of human proximity in birds. *Frontiers in Ecology and Evolution* 5. doi: 10. 3389/fevo. 2016. 00117.

Tang, Q., Low, G. W., Lim, J. Y., Gwee, C. Y. & Rheindt, F. E. (2018). Human activities and landscape features interact to closely define the distribution and dispersal of an urban commensal. *Evolutionary Applications*. Doi. org/10. 1111/eva. 12650.

Tangredi, B. P. (2007). Environmental factors associated with nutritional secondary hyperparathyroidism in wild birds. *Avian and Poultry Biology Reviews* **18**: 47–56.

Tanner, J. A. (1966). Effect of microwave radiation on birds. *Nature* **210**: 636.

Tapper, S. C. (1999). *A Question of Balance: Game Animals and Their Role in the British*

Countryside. The Game Conservancy Trust, Fordingbridge.

Tatner, P. (1982a). Factors influencing the distribution of Magpies *Pica pica* in an urban environment. *Bird Study* **29**: 227–234.

Tatner, P. (1982b). The breeding biology of Magpies *Pica pica* in an urban environment. *Journal of Zoology, London* **197**: 559–581.

Tatner, P. (1983). The diet of urban Magpies *Pica pica*. *Ibis* **125**: 90–107.

Taylor, D. J. & Philbey, A. W. (2010). *Salmonella* infections in garden birds and cats in a domestic environment. *Veterinary Record* **167**: 26–28.

Taylor, M. (1984). The patterns of migration and partial migration at a north Norfolk bird-ringing site. *Ringing & Migration* **5**: 65–78.

Tellería J. L., Blázquez, M., De La Hera, I. & Pérez-Tris, J. (2013). Migratory and resident Blackcaps *Sylvia atricapilla* wintering in southern Spain show no resource partitioning. *Ibis* **155**: 750–761.

Thalau, P., Ritz, T., Stapput, K., Wiltschko, R. & Wiltschko, W. (2005). Magnetic compass orientation of migratory birds in the presence of a 1. 315 MHz oscillating field. *Naturwissenschaften* **92**: 86–90.

Thomas, A. (2017). *RSPB Gardening for Wildlife*. Bloomsbury Natural History, London.

Thomas, L. (2000). Wildlife and humans in a suburban setting: understanding wildlife – human interactions in south-east Queensland. PhD Thesis, Griffith University, Brisbane.

Thomas, N. J., Hunter, D. B. & Atkinson, C. T. (2007). *Infectious Diseases of Wild Birds*. Wiley-Blackwell Publishing, Oxford.

Thomas, R. J. & Cuthill, I. C. (2002). Body mass regulation and the daily singing routines of European Robins. *Animal Behaviour* **63**: 285–295.

Thompson, C. & Henke, S. E. (2000). Effect of climate and type of storage container on aflatoxin production in corn and its associated risks to wildlife species. *Journal of Wildlife Diseases* **36**: 172–179.

Thompson, C. F., Ray, G. F. & Preston, R. L. (1996). Nectar robbing in Blue tits *Parus caeruleus*: failure of a novel feeding technique to spread. *Ibis* **138**: 552–553.

Thompson, P. S. (1987). The seasonal use of gardens by birds with special reference to supplementary feeding. *BTO Research Report* 27, British Trust for Ornithology, Tring.

Thompson, P. S. (1989). The effect of interrupting regular food provision in gardens on garden bird feeding behaviour and numbers. *BTO Research Report* 46, British Trust for Ornithology, Tring.

Thomson, D. L., Douglas-Home, H., Furness, R. W. & Monaghan, P. (1996). Breeding success and survival in the Common Swift *Apus apus*: a long-term study on the effect of weather. *Journal of Zoology, London.* **239**: 29–38.

Thomson, D. L., Green, R. E., Gregory, R. D. & Baillie, S. R. (1998). The widespread declines of songbirds in rural Britain do not correlate with the spread of their avian predators. *Proceedings of the Royal Society, London (B)* **265**: 2057–2062.

Thorington, K. K. & Bowman, R. (2003). Predation rate on artificial nests increases with human housing density in suburban habitats. *Ecography* **26**: 188–196.

Thornley, C. N., Simmons, G. C., Callaghan, M. L., Nicol, C. M., Baker, M. G., Gilmore, K. S. & Garrett, N. K. G. (2003). First incursion of *Salmonella enterica* Serotype Typhimurium DT160 into New Zealand. *Emerging Infectious Diseases* 9 (4): 493–495.

Thornton, M., Todd, I. & Roos, S. (2017). Breeding success and productivity of urban and rural Eurasian Sparrowhawks *Accipiter nisus* in Scotland. *Ecoscience* 24: 115–126.

Thorpe, W. H. (1958). The learning of song patterns by birds, with especial reference to the song of the Chaffinch *Fringilla coelebs*. *Ibis* 100: 535–570.

Tiainen, J., Hanski, I. K., Pakkala, T., Piiroinen, J. & Yrjölä, R. (1989). Clutch size, nestling growth and nestling mortality of the Starling *Sturnus vulgaris* in south Finnish agroenvironments. *Ornis Fennica* 66: 41–48.

Tietze, D. T. & Martens, J. (2009). Morphometric characterisation of treecreepers (genus *Certhia*). *Journal of Ornithology* 150: 431–457.

Tilgar, V., Mänd, R. & Mägi, M. (2002). Calcium shortage as a constraint on reproduction in Great Tits *Parus major*: a field experiment. *Journal of Avian Biology* 33: 407–413.

Tinbergen, J. M. & Boerlijst, M. C. (1990). Nestling weight and survival in individual Great Tits (*Parus major*). *Journal of Animal Ecology* 59: 1113–1127.

Tizard, I. R. (2004). Salmonellosis in wild birds. *Seminars in Avian and Pet Medicine* 13: 50–66.

Tizard, I. R., Fish, N. A. & Harmeson, J. (1979). Free-flying sparrows as carriers of salmonellosis. *Canadian Veterinary Journal* 20: 143–144.

Tomiałojć L. (1992). Breeding ecology of the Blackbird *Turdus merula* studied in the primaeval forest of Białowieża (Poland). Part I. Breeding numbers, distribution and nest sites. *Acta Ornithologica* 27: 131–157.

Toms, M. P. & Newson, S. E. (2006). Volunteer surveys as a means of inferring trends in garden mammal populations. *Mammal Review* 36: 309–317.

Toms, M., Wilson, I. & Wilson, B. (2008). *Gardening for Birdwatchers*. BTO, Thetford.

Townsend, A. K. & Barker, C. M. (2014). Plastic and the nest entanglement of urban and agricultural Crows. *PLoS One* 9: e88006.

Tratalos, J., Fuller, R. A., Evans, K. L., Davies, R. G., Newson, S. N., Greenwood, J. J. D. & Gaston, K. J. (2007). Bird densities are associated with household densities. *Global Change Biology* 13: 1685–1695.

Tripet, F., Glaser, M. & Richner, H. (2002). Behavioural responses to ectoparasites: time-budget adjustments and what matters to Blue Tits *Parus caeruleus* infested by fleas. *Ibis* 144: 461–469.

Tryjanowski, P., Møller, A. P., Morelli, F., Biaduń, W., Brauze, T., Ciach, M., Czechowski, P., Czyż, S., Dulisz, B., Goławski, A. & Hetmański, T. (2016). Urbanization affects neophilia and risk-taking at bird-feeders. *Scientific Reports*, 6: 28575.

Tryjanowski, P., Skórka, P., Sparks, T. H., Biaduń, W., Brauze, T., Hetmański, T., Martyka, R., Indykiewicz, P., Myczko, Ł., Kunysz, P. & Kawa, P. (2015). Urban and rural habitats differ in number and type of bird feeders and in bird species consuming supplementary food. *Environmental Science and Pollution Research* 22: 15097–15103.

Tschanz, B., Hegglin, D., Gloor, S. & Bontadina, F. (2011). Hunters and non-hunters: skewed predation rate by domestic cats in a rural village. *European Journal of Wildlife Research* **57**: 597–602.

Tuan, Y.-F. (1990). *Topophilia: A Study of Environmental Perception, Attitudes and Values.* Columbia University Press, New York.

Tully, J. (1993). Population and distribution of winter feeding flocks of Feral pigeons in the city of Britsol. *Bristol Ornithology* **22**: 16–30.

Tully, J. (2000). House Sparrow nesting survey, Southmead 2000. *Avon Bird Report*: 181–182.

Tully, J. (2001). House sparrow nesting survey, Southmead, Bristol 2001. *Avon Bird Report*: 153.

Tuomenpuro, J. (1991). Effect of nest site on nest survival in the Dunnock *Prunella modularis. Ornis Fennica* **68**: 49–56.

Turzańska-Pietras, K. (2017). Blue Tits *Cyanistes caeruleus* breeding in a House Martin *Delichon urbicum* nest. *Bird Study* **64**: 562–564.

Ulrich, R. S. (1984). View through a window may influence recovery from surgery. *Science* **224**: 420–421.

United Nations. (2014). *World Urbanization Prospects: The 2014 Revision.* United Nations, Department of Economic and Social Affairs, Population Division, New York.

US Fish and Wildlife Service (1991). *1991 National Survey of Fishing, Hunting, and Wildlife-Associated Recreation.* United States Government Printing Office, Washington, DC.

US Fish and Wildlife Service. (2011). *2011 National Survey of Fishing, Hunting, and Wildlife-Associated Recreation.* United States Government Printing Office, Washington, DC.

Vazquez, A., Jimenez-Clavero, M., Franco, L., Donoso-Mantke, O., Sambri, V., Niedrig, M., Zeller, H. & Tenorio, A. (2011). Usutu virus: potential risk of human disease in Europe. *Euro Surveillance: European Communicable Disease Bulletin* **16**: e19935.

Veiga, J. P. (1990). A comparative study of reproductive adaptations in House and Tree Sparrows. *Auk* **107**: 45–59.

Verbeek, M. E. M., Drent, P. J. & Wiepkema, P. R. (1994). Consistent individual differences in early exploratory behaviour of male Great Tits. *Animal Behaviour* **48**: 1113–1121.

Verbeek, M. E. M., Boon, A. & Drent, P. J. (1996). Exploration, aggressive behaviour and dominance in pairwise confrontations of juvenile male Great Tits. *Behaviour* **133**: 945–963.

Verbeek, M. E. M., de Goede, P., Drent, P. J. & Wiepkema, P. R. (1999) Individual behavioural characteristics and dominance in aviary groups of Great Tits. *Behaviour* **136**: 23–48.

Verhulst, S., Geerdink, M., Salomons, H. M., Boonekamp, J. J. (2014). Social life histories: Jackdaw dominance increases with age, terminally declines and shortens lifespan. *Proceedings of the Royal Society, London (B)* **281**: 20141045. doi: 10. 1098/ rspb. 2014. 1045.

Vernon, J. D. R. (1993). Magpies and milk bottles. *British Birds* **86**: 315.

Vickery, J. A., Tallowin, J. T., Feber, R. E., Asteraki, E. A., Atkinson, P. W., Fuller, R. J. & Brown, V. K. (2001). The management of lowland neutral grasslands in Britain: effects of agricultural practices on birds and their food resources. *Journal of Applied Ecology* **38**: 647–664.

Villanúa, D., Höfle, U., Pérez-Rodríguez, L. & Gortázar, C. (2006). Trichomonas gallinae in wintering Common Wood Pigeons Columba palumbus in Spain. Ibis 146: 641–648.

Vincze, E., Seress, G., Lagisz, M., Nakagawa, S., Dingemanse, N. J. & Sprau, P. (2017). Does urbanization affect predation of bird nests? A meta-analysis. Frontiers in Ecology and Evolution 5. doi: 10.3389/fevo.2017.00029.

Voltura, K. M., Schwagmeyer, P. L. & Mock, D. W. (2002). Parental feeding rates in the House Sparrow, Passer domesticus: are larger-badged males better fathers? Ethology 108: 1011–1022.

Warren, P., Tripler, C., Bolger, D., Faeth, S., Huntly, N., Lepczyk, C., Meyer, J., Parker, T., Shochat, E. & Walker, J. (2006). Urban food webs: predators, prey, and the people who feed them. Bulletin of the Ecological Society of America 87: 387–393.

Watts, P. S. & Wall, M. (1952). The 1951 Salmonella typhimurium epidemic in sheep in South Australia. Australian Veterinary Journal 28: 165–168.

Wells, J. V., Rosenberg, K. V., Dunn, E. H., Tessaglia-Hymes, D. L. & Dhondt, A. A. (1998). Feeder counts as indicators of spatial and temporal variation in winter abundance of resident birds. Journal of Field Ornithology 69: 577–586.

Wernham, C. V., Toms, M. P., Marchant, J. H., Clark, J. A., Siriwardena, G. M. & Baillie, S. R. (2002). The Migration Atlas: Movements of the Birds of Britain and Ireland. T. & A. D. Poyser, London

Wesołowski, T. & Stawarczyk, T. (1991). Survival and population dynamics of Nuthatches Sitta europaea breeding in natural cavities in a primeval temperate forest. Ornis Scandinavica 22: 143–154.

Weyers, B., Gluck, E. & Stoeppler, M. (1985). Environmental monitoring of heavy metals with birds as pollution integrating biomonitors III. Fate and content of trace metals in Blackbird food, organs and feathers for a highly polluted and a control area. International Conference. 'Heavy metals in the environment.' Athens, V. 1: 718–720.

White, M. P., Alcock, I., Wheeler, B. W. & Depledge, M. H. (2013). Would you be happier living in a greener urban area? A fixed-effects analysis of panel data. Psychological Science 24: 920–928.

Wilcoxen, T. E., Horn, D. J., Hogan, B. M., Hubble, C. N., Huber, S. J., Flamm, J., Knott, M., Lundstrom, L., Salik, F., Wassenhove, S. J. & Wrobel, E. R. (2015). Effects of bird-feeding activities on the health of wild birds. Conservation Physiology 3(1): Doi. 10:1093/conphys/cov058.

Wilkinson, N. (2006). Factors influencing the small-scale distribution of House Sparrows Passer domesticus in a suburban environment. Bird Study 53: 39–46.

Williams, B. M., Richards, D. W. & Lewis, J. (1976). Salmonella infection in the Herring Gull (Larus argentatus). Veterinary Record 98: 51.

Wilson, J. D. (1992). A re-assessment of the significance of status signalling in populations of wild Great Tits, Parus major. Animal Behaviour 43: 999–1009.

Wilson, J. E. & MacDonald, J. W. (1967). Salmonella infection in wild birds. British Veterinary Journal 123: 212–219.

Wilson, W. E. (2001). The effects of supplemental feeding on wintering black-capped chickadees (Poecile atricapilla) in central Maine: population and individual responses. The Wilson Bulletin 113: 65–72.

Witt, K. (1989). Do Magpies (*Pica pica*) control the population of passerines in a city? *Die Wogelwelt* **110**: 142–150.

Wobeser, G. A. & Finlayson, M. (1969). Salmonella typhimurium infection in House Sparrows. *Archives of Environmental Health* **19**: 882–884.

Woods, M., McDonald, R. A. & Harris, S. (2003). Predation of wildlife by domestic cats (*Felis catus*) in Great Britain. *Mammal Review* **33**: 174–188.

Yapp, W. B. (1983). Gamebirds in medieval England. *Ibis* **125**: 218–221.

Yom-Tov, Y. (1974). The effect of food and predation on breeding density and success, clutch size and laying date of the crow (*Corvus corone* L.). *Journal of Animal Ecology* **43**: 479–498.

Zalewski, A. (1994). Diet of urban and suburban Tawny Owls. *Journal of Raptor Research* **28**: 246–252.

Index

GENERAL INDEX

Page numbers in **bold** indicate detailed coverage.

Nest Box Challenge **258–9**
nest boxes 9, 113, 119, 121–2,
155, 207, 297, 298, 325, 342,
357, 359, 365, 369
nest boxes, designs 122, 342
nest construction **116–21**,
182–3, 273, 288, 293, 326, 334,
379, 381, 385
nest materials *see* nest
construction
nest predation 82–4, 113–14,
131–2, 143–4, 198–200, 205,
270, 298, 351, 358
nest sites 113–15, 228, 285, 291,
293, 301, 304, 351, 357, 360,
363, 378, 381, 384
nesting opportunities 6, 21,
301, 310, 325, 326
nestling, body mass 101–2, 105,
141, 145–6, 182, 320–1, 351
nestling, diet 75, 101, 303, 307,
318, 345, 351, 376
nestling, survival 101–2, 105,
136, 141–4, 308, 312, 332,
351, 357
New Zealand Garden Bird
Survey 261
Niger seed 41, **46–7**, 58
nitrogen dioxide 102, 112, 210
nocturnal singing 152
noise pollution 5, 88, **112–13**,
152, 214, 340

O
omnivores 6
oxidative stress 22

P
pair bond 124, 308
parasite load 24, 134
parasites 24, 134, **180–3**, 221,
329–30
patch size 20
peanuts 30, 35, **43–4**, 189–91
personality 214–15, 321
pesticides 274, 282, 311, 342
photoperiod 152
plants *see* gardens, flora
plumage 107, 156, 183–5

plumage abnormalities 183–5,
280, 322
plumage maintenance **220–5**
plumage ornamentation 107,
280
pollution 22, 53, 102, 133,
208–10
polyandry 231
polygyny 231
population size 80
pox *see* avian pox virus
predation 60, 82–4, 113–14,
131–2, 142, **194–208**, 234, 270,
298, 345, 348, 350
predation, by cat 142, 195,
200–6, 362, 363
predation, by Magpie **198–200**,
303
predation, by
Sparrowhawk 60–1, **195–8**,
275–7
preen gland 221
preening 182–3, 188, 221–2
productivity 8, 12, 34–5, 99,
102–4, 111–12, 114, 148, 277,
281, 283, 303, 318, 346, 366,
369, 376
Project Feeder Watch 51,
259–60
provisioning rates 140–1
psittacine beak and feather
disease 184–5

R
radiation 133
recruitment 79
resources 21, 36–7, 103, 106, 134
rodenticides **208–10**
roosting behaviour 155, **232–4**,
329, 339, 343, 370, 371, 374
RSPB Big Garden
Birdwatch **250–1**

S
salmonellosis **160–6**, 387
scraps 30, 271, 273, 278
second broods 146–8
seed mixes 37, 45
seed producing plants 56

seeds 54–7, 64–5, 282, 299, 330,
334–5, 371, 383, 386
senescence 148–9
sex ratio 76, 130
sexual dimorphism 227, 337
Shortest Day Survey *see* BTO
Shortest Day Survey
song 88, 107, **110–13**, 152,
339–40, 342–3, 355, 377
songbird fever *see*
salmonellosis
source-sink dynamics 23, 202
species richness 17
stable isotope analysis 319, 327
starvation 100, 141
status 226–7, 366–7
suet 30, 47–8
sugar solution 50
sunbathing 221
sunflower hearts 30, 31, **41–3**,
332, 375, 379, 388, 391
sunflower seed, black 30,
41–3
sunflower seed, striped 58
supplementary food **28–94**,
103, 105, 129, 144, 207, 216
survival 12, 69–70, 79, 99,
105, 174, 336, 342, 357, 366,
378, 389
sutonella 177–8

T
tadpoles, predation by
Blackbirds 91
Tamodine-E 188
tassel foot *see* Chaffinch
papillomavirus
telomere 22–3
territory 86, **106–11**, 227, 231,
291, 299, 314, 334, 339, 355,
360, 371
territory quality 107
territory size 107
ticks 180–1
torpor 294
traits, ecological 6, 7, 9, **10–11**,
tree cover 19
trichomonosis 166–71, 274–5,
286, 288, 376, 381

The New Naturalist Library